"The police are there to look after us. But someone has to look closely at the police – and Tom Harper has done just that in this comprehensive overview. Some of it makes for difficult reading, for much has gone wrong in policing over recent years. But the book is also constructive and never loses sight of the importance of the role the police have in any well-functioning democracy."

Alan Rusbridger

"This magnificent book should be required reading for everyone involved in policing, in any way."

Peter Bleksley, former Scotland Yard detective and author of *The Gangbuster*

"Harper chronicles in coruscating detail 'the scandal after scandal' that has buffeted the force since the 1990s and left the Met a demoralized 'shadow of its former self'. His central message is this: the Metropolitan Police has morphed into an organization whose main purpose is to defend the Metropolitan Police."

Ian Loader, *TLS*

Broken Yard

The Fall of the Metropolitan Police

Tom Harper

Biteback Publishing

This paperback edition published in Great Britain in 2023 by
Biteback Publishing Ltd, London
Copyright © Tom Harper 2022, 2023

ISBN 978-1-78590-807-1

10 9 8 7 6 5 4 3 2 1

A CIP catalogue record for this book is available from the British Library.

Set in Baskerville

Printed and bound in Great Britain by
CPI Group (UK) Ltd, Croydon CR0 4YY

For Anna, Rachel and Maggie

Contents

'For man, when perfected, is the best of animals, but, when separated from law and justice, he is the worst of all.'
– ARISTOTLE (350 BC)

'The only thing necessary for the triumph of evil is for good men to do nothing.'
– EDMUND BURKE (1770)

Introduction

As former Metropolitan Police officers, Bethany and Paul Eaton are well aware of the disaster that has enveloped Scotland Yard: violent crime is soaring across London and thousands of officers have left the force.

Yet even they were shocked by the way police responded when their home in Chislehurst, south-east London, was burgled in 2019. The couple were on their way back from a family holiday in Dubai when their childminder called to say the back door had been smashed in. The Eatons, who now run a vegan yoghurt business, asked a neighbour – a Met civilian employee – for help and she immediately called the police. It was at this point that the first signs of institutional inertia emerged, when the operator who answered the call replied: 'I'm sorry but you don't have an appointment, so officers will not be attending the scene today.'

To this day, Paul, who worked as a Met response officer for almost twenty years, does not understand how he was supposed to book an appointment for a burglary that had not yet taken place. His friend was also confused. 'My neighbour was flabbergasted and somewhat scared, not knowing if anyone was still in the house,' Paul said. 'She was told police would attend within twenty-four hours.' The neighbour tried to persuade the operator that the Met should come, not least as she had seen three police cars dawdling outside the local café around the corner. The person on the end of the line replied that was 'just not police procedure these days'.

In the end, the only person willing to help the neighbour secure the crime scene was a passing Ocado delivery driver, who checked to see whether the burglars had fled. When Londoners' emergency service of last resort is an online grocer, we can probably agree there is a problem. Fortunately, the house was empty, although Bethany's jewellery had been stolen.

The Eatons, who have two children, followed the advice they'd been given and waited for their former colleagues to attend. When no one arrived after forty-eight hours, they tried again and Paul placed a call to his former employer. The response was shocking: 'Oh yes, the lady who took the call has closed the case.' A civilian operator had decided to record the incident as 'no crime', a move that improperly boosted overall police statistics at the expense of the victim. By this stage, the Eatons were furious. They had clear CCTV footage identifying the offender, but when they persuaded a scenes-of-crime officer to call around, he refused to take it.

The Eatons' experience is sadly all too familiar for London's 8 million residents, and millions of others across the country. They have seen the capabilities of local forces undermined by a combination of budget cuts and a dangerous passivity that has been allowed to evolve among the boys and girls in blue. In 2015, Leicestershire Police even briefly launched a policy of refusing to attend attempted burglaries at houses with odd numbers, apparently in a bizarre attempt to cut costs.

We are living through an unprecedented crisis in British policing, with a devastating direct effect on the victims of almost 6 million crimes that occur in England and Wales each year.[1] The latest figures from the Office for National Statistics make grim reading. Before the unprecedented Covid lockdowns skewed crime rates, a national rise in murders and manslaughters in 2020[2] was mainly driven by a 28 per cent rise in offences in London (67 to 86).[3] The number of knife crimes in England and Wales also rose to a record high, partly driven by a 7 per cent rise in London. This was 51 per cent higher than when data of this kind was first collected in 2011 and was the highest number on record.

By contrast, the proportion of crimes in England and Wales that are solved has fallen to a record low. In the twelve months to the end of March 2020, just 7 per cent of offences led to a suspect being charged or ordered to appear in court. That compares with 8 per cent the previous year and 16 per cent in 2014/15.[4]

These damning statistics are partly fuelled by a decision taken by the Met in 2017 – a decision that would have been laughed out of the police canteen thirty years ago. The 'crime assessment policy', drawn up by senior officers, ordered police to shelve investigations into hundreds of thousands of crimes each year, including burglaries, thefts and some assaults. The move has amazed former leaders of the force. 'The violence and the knife crime and the death rate is deeply concerning,' Sir Paul Stephenson, a former Met commissioner, told me. 'The downscaling of the seriousness of household burglary means it's almost seen as some sort of social misdemeanour. I think invading people's homes should be treated as a heinous crime.'

The measures were a response to historic government curbs on police spending that have been implemented since 2010. Scotland Yard was attempting to save £400 million by 2020, in addition to the £600 million the force had already lost from its £3.7 billion annual budget. But the flaws in the strategy were criticised on the day they were announced. Mick Neville, a former Met detective chief inspector, said:

> This is justice dreamed up by bean counters in shiny suit land. No consideration is being given to victims. The new principles will focus police attention on easy crimes where there is a known suspect. Few professional criminals target people who know them, so the worst villains will evade justice. Not investigating high volume crimes like shoplifting with a loss of under £50 will give junkies a green light to thieve.[5]

Stephenson, who led Scotland Yard between 2009 and 2011, agrees. He told me: 'It is entirely legitimate to ask the Met to try and do more with less. However, the scale of the cuts to policing was simply foolhardy, and you didn't need hindsight to come to that judgement. We can see the consequences of it now.'

The crisis deepened in March 2020 when London was hit by the coronavirus pandemic. As the Met 'war-gamed' for potential mass sickness or a breakdown in law and order, I was passed documents that detailed its contingency plans. In the event that Scotland Yard's threadbare resources were overwhelmed, senior officers were considering pulling traditional bobbies off their beats and suspending all 'proactive' police operations, where officers investigate to prevent crimes and conspiracies before they take place. The worst-case scenario outlined in the documents was to respond only to incidents involving the potential loss of life. The once-mighty Met, the first modern police force and a model for much of the world's policing, would reduce its priorities to 'major, critical and emergency incidents, serious crime, firearms incidents, protecting vulnerable people, serious public order and fatal and serious road traffic collisions'.[6]

Scotland Yard was further embarrassed in July 2021 when thousands of intruders without tickets managed to break into Wembley Stadium during the final of the European men's football championships. With the world watching on, crowds of troublemakers, including known hooligans and gang members, forced their way into the stadium as England played its first major men's final since 1966. One yob was filmed putting a lit flare up his bottom outside Wembley and even managed to enter the stadium without a ticket.[7] The father of England defender Harry Maguire was one of dozens of innocent spectators who were injured in the chaos. Ministers, London mayor Sadiq Khan, Wembley staff and the Football Association later blamed the Met for allowing public disorder and drunken and violent behaviour to develop outside the stadium in the hours before the high-profile game kicked off.[8]

Just before Mark Rowley was announced as the new commissioner in July 2022, Scotland Yard suffered the ignominy of being placed into special measures, a status applied by regulators of public services in the UK to providers who fall short of acceptable standards. The Met will now be subjected to increased monitoring and scrutiny. It is a measure commonly applied to failing schools and hospitals, not one of the world's most famous police forces.

Step by step, the Met has strayed from the nine principles laid down by its founder, Sir Robert Peel, and issued to every new police officer since 1829. The ninth of these is 'to recognise always that the test of police efficiency is the absence of crime and disorder, and not the visible evidence of police action in dealing with them'. The new contingency plans meant that they would potentially have to ignore hundreds of thousands of serious offences such as robbery and fraud. Peel's promise would not have been kept.

The force is not only suffering from chronic under-funding. Barely a week goes by without the Met finding itself at the centre of a new crisis, lambasted by MPs and criticised in once-friendly newspapers. Scandal after scandal has buffeted the force. Many are linked to the abuse of power. Two of the most recent examples include Ben Hannam, a PC who was jailed for belonging to a neo-Nazi terrorist group, and Benjamin Kemp, sacked for hitting a vulnerable teenage girl at least thirty times with a baton. The early departure of several recent commissioners has added to the sense of misery. Demoralised and depleted in numbers, the Met is a shadow of its former self.

This is a tragedy that harms each and every one of us, not least because so many of the 32,000 police officers inside Scotland Yard perform heroic acts on behalf of the public every day. Former detective superintendent John Sutherland was forced to retire early with crippling depression and has become a powerful advocate for the good that police officers do. But even he accepts that the current malaise is partially self-inflicted. 'There are times as a police officer when I just want to bury my head in my hands,' Sutherland writes in his memoir, *Blue*:

Stephen Lawrence, Plebgate, Hillsborough – the list goes on. The sins of the past and the sins of the present, conspiring and causing even good people to doubt us. There can be no escaping the fact that we have, to a very significant extent, brought it on ourselves. Society has every right to expect higher standards of police officers than they do of anyone else. That is because of the promise each of us made and the powers each of us has been given. Where we betray that promise or abuse those powers, it is absolutely right that we are held to account ... Some of our failings have been catastrophic and some of the consequences unthinkable. Sometimes it's an individual officer at fault, sometimes it's the whole institution. And, either way, the responsibility for putting things right is ours and ours alone.[9]

It should never be forgotten that police officers work in a uniquely challenging context, operating at the margins of society in the face of hostility and conflict. In recent times, no one has epitomised the Metropolitan Police at its finest more than PC Keith Palmer. In May 2017, the officer was stabbed to death by Islamist terrorist Khalid Masood while defending the Houses of Parliament. Masood had mown down dozens of pedestrians on Westminster Bridge before he was shot dead by armed police officers. Palmer's heroism should remind us of the individual acts of courage that police officers undertake on our behalf. After his death a permanent memorial was placed at the spot by the Carriage Gates where he lost his life. At the unveiling ceremony, Met commissioner Cressida Dick spoke of the pride all police officers felt for their dead comrade. 'PC Palmer was an outstanding police officer,' she said, adding:

He acted that day with no thought for his own safety, intent simply on doing his job and protecting members of the public and Parliament. He paid the ultimate price for his selfless actions and this memorial is a fitting and lasting tribute to the tremendous bravery he showed on that terrible day.[10]

Yet PC Palmer's death, which had so touched the nation, soon blew up in the Met's face in familiar circumstances, the inability to admit to mistakes. The descent into acrimony began when the dead officer's sisters, Angela Clark and Michelle Palmer, made their own enquiries into the case. They could not understand why – in an apparent breach of police procedures – their brother had been left alone and unarmed. After hearing that the over-stretched force had ordered firearms officers to conduct roving patrols to cover a wider area, rather than stay permanently on duty at the gates, the sisters began asking questions ahead of the official inquest. It was then that the shutters came down. Their requests for information were ignored and the relationship between the Met and the family broke down. The two sisters accused Scotland Yard of blocking their pursuit of the truth. They also expressed concern that the Met was 'scapegoating' junior officers over apparent security failures during Masood's attack. In an interview with *The Times*, Angela Clark said the family had 'put our faith in this system' and had been left 'utterly demoralised', adding: 'There are certain people at command level who are perhaps finding it easier to blame the people that were on the ground.' Michelle Palmer said, in the same interview:

> Keith gave his life and we are left with no answers. Eighteen months on we were hoping for some closure, but we're not going to have that. We feel like we come below Khalid Masood. We are not valued, not wanted, we feel like we are on trial. We feel like we are being battered.[11]

I have covered Scotland Yard as a journalist for sixteen years. Investigative reporters are often drawn to examine people or institutions who wield significant power over ordinary people, particularly unaccountable power. It seems to be an inexplicable part of our DNA, and almost impossible to resist. While most police officers perform incredible feats on behalf of the public, the potential for terrible behaviour is rife simply due to the power they are afforded over others, granted by statutory legislation. But when those powers are abused, it can result in innocent people suffering mental trauma, physical injury and worse.

Most investigative journalists take a good look at the police at some stage of their career. I began not long after the shooting of Jean Charles de Menezes, an innocent Brazilian killed by Met Police officers after being mistaken for a terror suspect in 2005. The Yard rightly took a lot of flak over that case, which is discussed in more detail in Chapter 10. But despite the shambles of that operation, the Met at that time still seemed immensely powerful, was largely trusted, and was not to be trifled with. Since then, reporting on Scotland Yard – and British policing in general – has been akin to witnessing a slow-motion car crash.

This book is an attempt to explain how London's world-famous police force got itself into this sorry mess – and how it might get itself out of it. During my research I interviewed Home Secretaries, Cabinet ministers, Downing Street advisers, Metropolitan Police commissioners, detectives, victims and villains to explore the most calamitous chapter in Scotland Yard's near two centuries of exist-ence. Reporting accurately on any force is a tricky task, and the Met is no different. The police are obsessed with controlling what information leaks from their stations, canteens and databases and into journalists' notebooks. They can also be dangerous. As we shall see, police officers who publicly embarrass or shame the Yard are, at best, placed under extreme pressure. The force has its own moral code of behaviour, a version of the Mafia's omertà. Speak out, and you're no longer 'one of us'; you're 'one of them'. Given the risks, it has sometimes been difficult to ask people to put their heads above the parapet. To provide a truly authentic account, therefore, I have consulted thousands of intelligence files, witness statements and court transcripts provided by police sources, and have masked the identities of those who helped me most.

* * *

Not that long ago Scotland Yard was riding high: the crime rate was low, newspapers were full of glowing stories about the police, and ministers were falling over themselves to give the force whatever it wanted. Throughout the 1980s, the government led by Margaret Thatcher relied on the Met and other forces to maintain public order in the face of wide-ranging and controversial economic reforms. The result was bumper pay packets, lucrative overtime and an establishment tendency to turn a blind eye to anything murky.

The apex of the relationship came during the miners' strike of 1984–85, a major piece of industrial action that had shut down the British coal industry. Violent confrontations between pickets and police characterised the strike, which ended in a decisive victory for the Conservative government and allowed Thatcher's successor, John Major, to close most of Britain's collieries. Mike Bennett, a leading member of the Police Federation, a union which represents more than 100,000 rank-and-file officers, said members who took on the miners 'had so much money thrown at them it was embarrassing', adding: 'People had caravans and boats named after the Home Secretary.'[12]

Ron Evans, a Special Branch protection officer, joined 'the job' in Thatcher's era and rose through the ranks to end up guarding the Prime Minister. He is effusive about his charge. 'I was one of Thatcher's boys, to whom she had given a 40 per cent pay rise as soon as she came into power in 1979,' he said. 'Most of us in the police thought she was simply magnificent ... my heroine. One of the best people I worked with – tough and fair, which is all you can ask.'[13]

Norman Tebbit, a Cabinet minister during the Thatcher era, was also very fond of his protection officers: 'They are all marvellous characters and there is a fund of family jokes that includes them,' he once said. 'I value them all tremendously and not just for the security.'[14]

It was not only the UK government that was in thrall to the Met during the 1980s. Across the globe, the words 'Scotland Yard' meant something. The Met has been immortalised since Victorian times in books and television programmes, including works by Charles Dickens, Arthur Conan Doyle and P. D. James, and shows such as *Dixon of Dock Green* and *Prime Suspect*. In 1981, when the then Met commissioner, Sir David McNee, visited the United States to brief American law enforcement on his latest strategies, the trip was covered in glowing terms by the *Washington Post*. McNee was described as a 'big, bluff, hearty man with an air of authority' who led a force renowned for cracking 'puzzling cases' in a 'most civilised manner'.[15] McNee was guest of honour at a dinner in Washington attended by representatives from the FBI, the Justice Department and the Secret Service, all of whom marvelled at Scotland Yard's low murder rate.[16]

Such was its prestige that London's finest also used to field requests from overseas governments keen to tap into their expertise. In 1991, Scotland Yard started to nurture fledgling South African law enforcement officials in preparation for the imminent collapse of apartheid. The courses were held at the Civil Service College, a vast, white mock-Palladian building in Sunningdale, Berkshire. This came following a personal request from Nelson Mandela, then leader of the African National Congress, to Prime Minister John Major. One of the attendees, Zelda Holtzman, said it was 'remarkable to see the police moving in the streets, unarmed, talking to people, playing with children – we only see our police in armoured vans … carrying heavy guns'.[17]

Scotland Yard, and policing in general, rode so high during the Thatcher years that it seemed any scandal that might have caused embarrassment was merely swept under the carpet. Those inside the Met certainly felt more protected than in the days of Robert Mark, the commissioner from 1972 to 1977, who famously remarked that a 'good police force is one that catches more crooks than it employs'. During his five years in charge, Mark – a steely Normandy veteran who brought a missionary zeal to his work – launched the most far-reaching anti-corruption drive in Scotland Yard's history, prosecuting, sacking or forcing out more than 450 officers.[18]

In his autobiography, *In the Office of Constable*, Mark said: 'I had never experienced institutionalised wrongdoing, blindness, arrogance and prejudice on anything like the scale accepted as routine at the Met.' He was particularly concerned about the influence of the detective class, the Criminal Investigation Department (CID), which had been exposed in a series of scandals linked to organised crime. After becoming commissioner, Mark assembled representatives of the CID and gave them an almighty dressing down.

> I told them that they represented what had long been the most routinely corrupt organisation in London, that nothing and no one would prevent me from putting an end to it and that, if necessary, I would put the whole of the CID back into uniform and make a fresh start.

To dilute their power, he pushed through reforms that saw them placed under the control of a uniformed commander.

But when Mark retired in 1977, more traditional forces reasserted themselves. It seemed many in positions of power believed that taking on Scotland Yard – or the police in general – would trigger a loss of confidence in the overall 'system'. Any official recognition that corrupt behaviour existed would be more damaging than the consequences of the corruption itself.

In 1980, an outrageous judicial ruling offered an insight into the mindset of the time. During an appeal by the six Irishmen who had been wrongly convicted for the 1975 IRA bombings in Birmingham, Lord Denning, the Master of the Rolls, decided that the men should lose. In his view, the strength of the evidence against the bombers, known as the Birmingham Six, was irrelevant. In the judgment Denning said:

> If they [the appellants] won, it would mean that the police were guilty of perjury; that they were guilty of violence and threats; that the confessions were involuntary and improperly admitted in evidence; and that the convictions were erroneous ... That was such an appalling vista that every sensible person would say, 'It cannot be right that these actions should go any further.'

The innocent men would spend a further eleven years in jail until a more objective judge heard another appeal and freed them without further delay. Denning believed that although police officers might be criminals, any official acknowledgement of this would be too destabilising for the nation to deal with. In effect, society should turn a blind eye.

Nowhere was Scotland Yard's shift from Robert Mark's fearless tenure through to the loose oversight of the Thatcher years more apparent than in Operation Countryman, one of the most acrimonious and ill-fated police corruption investigations in modern history. The probe, which started off by examining three City of London robberies in 1978, eventually mushroomed into a massive inquiry into eighty-four Metropolitan Police officers variously accused of taking bribes, planting evidence, conspiring with bank robbers and improperly facilitating bail. The operation resulted in just two successful prosecutions, to the frustration and anger of the independent investigators who had been recruited from Dorset Constabulary. There were two key figures at the heart of the investigation: Alf Sheppard, a bank robber who was prepared to be wired up to get evidence against corrupt officers, and DCI Phil Cuthbert, a City of London officer and leading Freemason who was one of the two men later jailed.[19]

Countryman soon found that the files they requested from Scotland Yard would disappear, or it would take weeks of pressure to get them handed over. Senior Met officers were also suspected of tipping off subordinates when they were under investigation.[20] Bizarrely, the rogue officers seemed to have some support from Sir Thomas Hetherington, then the director of public prosecutions. When he learnt that Cuthbert had been remanded in custody, Britain's top prosecutor promptly dropped the charge, informing the detective's solicitor before the investigating officers on Countryman. Arthur Hambleton, Dorset's chief constable and a decorated war hero, was furious. 'That indicated to me that we were not going to get the help and support that we expected,' he later said. 'My chaps had worked very hard cultivating the informants and at a stroke that confidence in us was lost.'[21] Countryman was eventually handed back to the Met to investigate itself. The inquiry then withered and died. John Alderson, a former chief constable of Devon and Cornwall involved in Countryman, said that he believed 'political reasons were behind the winding down of the exercise'.

'The Home Office ... were finding that the whole inquiry was reaching such dimensions that it had become embarrassing,' he later recalled. 'The Home Secretary [William Whitelaw] said that Countryman was getting into channels that it was never intended to do, deep into the Metropolitan Police, and that it was unlikely that there would never be another exercise like that.' Alderson added that Whitelaw seemed concerned that Countryman 'was getting so much more serious than anyone had contemplated in the first place'.[22]

'Countryman was there to inquire into two crimes, but within weeks the flood of information was of such a proportion ... and it was becoming something of a scandal,' he said. The cover-up was so brazen that it divided opinion across the policing community. Frank Williamson, then the inspector of constabulary, was disgusted at the turn of events. 'If the morale of the police service depends on failing to reveal things that ought to be revealed in connection with misbehaviour and malpractice, then I want no part of it,' he said, adding:

> No one needs to remind me of the gallantry, integrity and efficiency of a high proportion of the police service, but that cannot be used to offset and damage the reputation of the service done by people who misbehave. It is not the people who draw attention to misbehaviour who are being disloyal and undermining the morale, it is the people who are misbehaving themselves.[23]

Certainly, any impact that Mark's 1970s anti-corruption drive had had on the Met seemed to have been completely lost by 1983, when Edwin 'Laurie' Cork, a Flying Squad officer, was accused of involvement in a mass cocaine importation syndicate. He was acquitted but still dismissed by the Met. When later talking about corruption in the Met, he discussed officers planting evidence but seemed mystified as to why this was wrong, complaining: 'Everyone does it. I'm not a rotten apple in danger of rotting the barrel. It's a fucking rotten orchard, that's what it is.'[24]

The strange way that Scotland Yard dealt with alleged criminality in its ranks would be further exposed during the notorious case of Tony Lundy. In the 1980s, the detective superintendent became one of the Met's top thief takers when he recruited a leading London gangster as an informant. Roy Garner was an armed robber, a fraudster and a fence from north London who earned massive taxpayer-funded rewards for his information.[25] But serious questions about the relationship between the two men began to emerge, leading many to wonder whether Lundy was actually working for Garner, who was also a Freemason.

In March 1980, a trusted supergrass previously used by the Metropolitan Police alleged that Lundy was involved in the hijack of a lorry at Tilbury Docks in Essex. The supergrass allegations against Lundy were investigated for more than two years by deputy assistant commissioner Ron Steventon. His 4,000-page internal report on whether to bring criminal charges against Lundy was submitted to the director of public prosecutions. Steventon concluded: 'I feel bound to express a personal opinion and regrettably there is a dearth of evidence to support it, but it is my belief that Lundy is a corrupt officer who has long exploited his association with Garner.'[26] Lundy has always denied allegations of corruption and claims he has been the subject of a smear campaign by criminals and the media.

In July 1986, his relationship with Garner exploded into the public domain during an investigation by HM Customs and Excise (HMCE) into the largest-ever cocaine importation into the UK. The deal was arranged by Garner, who had teamed up with Nikolaus Chrastny, an international bank robber and gemstone smuggler who was on first-name terms with the Colombian cocaine king Pablo Escobar. Garner and Chrastny tried to import 392 kilograms, worth more than £100 million at street prices and far more than all British seizures for the previous year.[27]

The shipment arrived in the UK, but Customs officers were closing in on the gang when Lundy suddenly turned up in Florida, allegedly trying to intercept evidence that implicated Garner in the affair. Soon afterwards, the gang found out they were under investigation. Secret recordings of two American conspirators plotting in Florida revealed the source of the compromise: 'They heard from this fucking guy at Scotland Yard … they've got the guy paid off.'[28]

Chrastny was arrested at gunpoint in Harley Street, central London, by Customs officers who found £9 million of cocaine in his nearby flat. Chrastny agreed to turn informant in a bid for leniency, telling HMCE that Garner had assured him that he was 'getting information about necessary intelligence directly from the Yard' and 'whatever will be going on, we will know exactly about it'. The Czech-born criminal said he had pressed Garner, who eventually 'gave me the name of Mr Lundy'. Chrastny said he then made enquiries of his own and discovered 'there was actually such a man very high up in Scotland Yard'.

Two BBC investigative journalists, the late Andrew Jennings and Vyv Simson, tried to make a documentary about the affair.

The Met responded by placing Jennings under surveillance for two months and wielded its considerable power to lobby the BBC behind closed doors. An assistant commissioner wrote privately to BBC assistant director general Alan Protheroe urging restraint, and the programme was later pulled, with the Corporation citing 'insoluble legal difficulties'.[29] The journalists resigned on a point of principle and took their work to ITV's *World in Action*, where the grisly detail was laid bare for millions of viewers.

Garner was jailed for twenty-two years over the cocaine importation in 1989. Lundy was never charged with any offences but retired sick in December 1988 soon after he had been interviewed by the Met's anti-corruption squad. Not long afterwards, Jennings, the intrepid *World in Action* journalist, tracked down Lundy on a 10-mile run near his home in Hertfordshire. He tried to ask Lundy about Garner and allegations that he was corrupt, but the super-fit former detective managed to outrun the film crew.[30] A video of the wonderful encounter is still available on YouTube.[31]

There is little doubt that ministers, the director of public prosecutions and even the judiciary were much more willing to close ranks and protect Scotland Yard in the 1980s. Today, that kind of unquestioning support for the police has drained away.

But what has brought the Metropolitan Police to its knees, and is there anything we can do about it? Perhaps the best place to start is with the horrific murder of an innocent schoolboy in south-east London, not long after Margaret Thatcher left office. The case of Stephen Lawrence would open up Scotland Yard – and British policing – to independent scrutiny like no other.

Chapter 1

The Snowball

Seventeen-year-old Stephen Lawrence and his best friend Duwayne Brooks stumbled out into the cool night air, chatting and laughing as they zipped up their coats in preparation for the journey home across south-east London. It was just after 10 p.m. on an April evening in 1993 and the boys, who had become friends on their first day at Blackheath Bluecoats Church of England School,[1] had been visiting Stephen's uncle to play a popular computer game, Street Fighter II.

As they headed off to catch a bus at Well Hall roundabout in Eltham, a sprawling suburb on the borders of London and Kent, Stephen and Duwayne were engrossed in a conversation about Arsenal Football Club.[2] Days earlier, their favourite team had triumphed in a League Cup final against Sheffield Wednesday. The quality of the football had been forgettable, but the game would be remembered for its post-match celebrations, when Arsenal's captain Tony Adams accidentally broke the arm of his match-winning goal scorer, Steve Morrow.

Stephen was keen to get home, but no buses were in sight. The friends split up to monitor different bus stops on the several roads exiting the roundabout. When Duwayne called out to Stephen to ask if he'd seen a bus, a gang of five or six white youths suddenly appeared from the other side of Well Hall Road. One of them yelled at Duwayne: 'What, what, n****r?'

Duwayne, more streetwise than Stephen, instinctively sensed danger. 'I said to Steve "run" and then I just turned and ran,' Brooks later recalled in his autobiography. No one will ever know why Stephen did not follow his friend's advice. Duwayne sprinted a few hundred yards away before a 'bad feeling' struck him and he realised he had left Stephen behind.

> Everything flashed in my head. Why hasn't he run? What's he still doing there? Maybe he has run. I hope he has run. All these things were flashing in my head in that split second before I turned round to make sure he was behind me … I was sure he was running but couldn't bring myself to turn around. I was too scared. I started to cry … then my legs went to jelly.[3]

Members of the gang had cornered Stephen, stabbing him repeatedly.[4] The assault lasted seconds before the gang melted away.

By the time Duwayne looked back, his friend was somehow lurching towards him, mortally wounded, looking confused and scared.[5] Stephen collapsed 130 yards from the spot where he was attacked, bleeding copiously. Some of his wounds were 5 inches deep. A pathologist would later pay tribute to Stephen's physical fitness, saying it was remarkable that he managed to get so far.[6]

As the teenager's life ebbed away, a passing couple who saw him fall rushed to his aid. The woman placed her hand on his head and whispered in his ear: 'You are loved, you are loved.'[7] Duwayne ran off to call an ambulance. An off-duty policeman stopped his car and covered Stephen with a blanket. By the time he reached hospital shortly after 11 p.m., Stephen Lawrence was dead. One of the longest, most painful and furthest-reaching murder investigations in the history of British policing was about to begin.

*   *   *

A few months after Stephen Lawrence's death, Britain's police forces gathered to confront a very different challenge. Coaches from all over the country converged on London for an unprecedented mass protest by the men and women charged with protecting the public and maintaining law and order. More than 23,000 officers – around half of all those off duty that day – headed for Wembley Arena in north-west London. It was a warm midsummer day, but the police were in no mood for frivolities.

In July 1993, Britain's police force faced its biggest shake-up in more than 150 years. A government-sponsored report written by Sir Patrick Sheehy, chairman of British American Tobacco, had recommended the most far-reaching reforms to police pay, rank structure and working practices since the founding of Scotland Yard. The report, which was commissioned by then Home Secretary Ken Clarke, had taken a truncheon to decades of police tradition. Its 270 recommendations included the abolition of three ranks, the end of lucrative overtime payments and the replacement of automatic annual pay increases with a performance-related model.

Behind Clarke's outwardly genial demeanour and laid-back personal style lurked considerable reformist zeal. The veteran Conservative Cabinet minister felt the police were the 'last great unreformed Victorian public service', a relic of a previous age that had somehow been 'left untouched'. He told me in an interview twenty-eight years later: 'It was based on a Victorian army with multiple layers. The Sheehy reforms were an attempt to tackle this extraordinary rank structure.'

Clarke was concerned that vast swathes of the force were not crime fighters or protectors of the public but pen-pushing plodders 'whose main job was to hold the person below them to account for their performance', and whose 'main obligation was to account for their own performance to the people above them, without doing very much else'.[8] Yet such was the force's aura of public rectitude that a clear-headed, critical assessment of its flaws had seemed almost inconceivable until Clarke took on the challenge.

'The idea that a Tory Home Secretary would reform the police – would change them – was unthinkable to them,' he said.[9] A Labour government attempting to dismantle the establishment might be something to worry about, but the Conservatives were supposed to be the party of law and order. Why would the Tories go to war with the police? Scotland Yard, by far the most influential of Britain's forces, rallied its troops for a counter-offensive. Their pleas for protection from interfering politicians were to prove a potent riposte.

Sir Paul Condon, the Met commissioner, had initially impressed Clarke with reforms he had introduced as chief constable of the Kent force. Newly arrived at Scotland Yard in 1993, his credentials proved short-lived. Condon swiftly threatened to resign if the Sheehy reforms were implemented. At the same time, stories critical of the proposed shake-up began to appear in national newspapers sympathetic to the Met. The anti-reform campaign culminated in the rally at Wembley Arena, a 12,500-seat indoor facility which normally hosts sports events and rock concerts, not protests by furious police officers.

The arena was full more than an hour before the protest began;

6,000 officers were put in two overflow halls and an estimated 3,000 more were locked out.[10] There was rapturous applause as the audience listened to a succession of speakers condemn the Sheehy report. Alan Eastwood, chairman of the Police Federation, which then represented 127,000 officers up to the rank of chief inspector, said it was a 'monumental blunder' which had led the service to the edge of a cliff.

Eastwood warned that the police's role as guardians of the public was becoming vulnerable to manipulation and exploitation by unscrupulous governments:

> A force stripped of its identity. A force without shape or expectations … cynically hired and learning to cynically serve, semi-casualised, a force whose members expect to be used and turned-over … Policemen under Sheehy will not be policemen, they will be units of manpower. Will units of manpower take the same risks?[11]

As for Clarke, portrayed as the agent of pending police ruin, there was little but contempt. In one reference to the man who had moved on from the Home Office and was now Chancellor of the Exchequer, Eastwood described the proposed reforms as the work of a 'vainglorious politician who decided that the police were fair game for a shake-up'.

Mike Bennett, another senior official at the Police Federation at the time, said that 'putting Kenneth Clarke in charge of the police was like putting King Herod in charge of Mothercare. He didn't have a clue what he was doing.'[12] Bennett declared that the scale of the police protest had surprised everyone. 'It looked very impressive. We didn't frogmarch people there … It was a genuine show of support against the Sheehy recommendations.' In an aside that inadvertently hinted at some of the murkier concerns about modern police practices, he added: 'They weren't getting a backhander [for attending the protest], they weren't getting paid for it.'

All this proved quite a headache for Michael Howard, who had recently taken over from Clarke as Home Secretary. The two men had been political rivals ever since their time together at the Cambridge University Conservative Association in the 1960s. Ron Evans, the Special Branch protection officer who guarded both Clarke and Howard when they were Home Secretary, believes that Howard 'inherited a spectacular mess ... He didn't agree with the Sheehy inquiry but couldn't ditch a policy from his predecessor and had to go along with it.'[13]

Howard asked Evans about the Wembley protest during a trip in the car on the morning of the rally. 'I told him I was going to go,' the officer said. 'He was surprised and asked if he should go too. I said not to, because he would only come out of it looking bad from a policy that had been thrust upon him.'

Howard saw very quickly that fighting the police would bring him little but grief. A shrewd but largely anonymous figure with leadership ambitions, he was once memorably described by a Cabinet colleague as having 'something of the night about him'. Howard soon shelved most of Sheehy's proposals, distancing himself from his predecessor by showering the police with praise. He later recalled: 'One of the things you learn in politics is you can't fight too many battles at the same time. I looked at those reforms and some of them I did put into effect and some of them I didn't ... I wanted to avoid all-out war with the police.'[14]

It was a resounding victory. For a while it seemed that 1993 would be the year in which the police fought off the hostile scrutiny of those who had come to question its role as the frontline enforcers of state power – most notably through the long period of public protests that greeted Margaret Thatcher's economic reforms of the 1980s.

But that was not how 1993 would ultimately be remembered by police forces across the country. The murder of Stephen Lawrence, and the subsequent police investigation, would strike deep into British life, confronting every level of society with uncomfortable questions about racism, justice and the conduct of the Metropolitan Police. The death of a black teenager on the streets of Eltham would shake the foundations of Scotland Yard, reverberate for years through the committee rooms of Whitehall and Westminster, and change the way many Britons viewed the police for ever.

* * *

Cressida Dick, the Met commissioner from 2017 until 2022, has admitted that Stephen's murder 'defined my generation of policing' and said she could not 'think of any other case that has come close to the same impact',[15] while the BBC home affairs editor Mark Easton described it as a 'watershed in British cultural life'.[16] Yet no one in the immediate aftermath of the Eltham attack could possibly have seen it coming. Stephen's murder may have borne some of the hallmarks of the lynchings once inflicted by white racists on black youths in America's Deep South, but it was scarcely the first such attack in Britain. It wasn't even the first such attack in Eltham, a notorious hotbed of far-right activity.

The London suburb had long been home to large numbers of white working-class families from east London who were moved as slum housing was cleared along the river Thames from Tower Bridge to Deptford. Families who might have previously earned a living at the docks, in haulage, in the wholesale markets or in the print industry found themselves decanted into the politer surrounds of Thamesmead and new council estates in Welling, Bexleyheath and Eltham.

Some of the new arrivals were members of criminal gangs, typically organised around individual families and their relatives. They made their money from armed robbery, hijacking lorries and protection rackets. The more successful crime families – known locally as 'firms' – would plough their proceeds into legitimate businesses such as garages, scrap yards, pubs and nightclubs. These budding entrepreneurs still imposed their criminal will the old-fashioned way – through beatings, stabbings and shootings. Their gangland culture often incorporated hardened racist ideas derived from Oswald Mosley's British Union of Fascists in the 1930s and, later, the right-wing bully boys of the National Front.

By the early 1990s, Eltham was a dangerous place not to be white. One month before Stephen Lawrence's murder, Gurdeep Bhangal was attacked with a kitchen knife outside his father's branch of the Wimpy franchise after confronting a group of abusive white youths. The knife punctured his stomach and bowel, missing his spine by half an inch.[17] Police investigated the attack, but no charges were brought.

In February 1991, Rolan Adams, a fifteen-year-old black boy, was stabbed in the throat with a folding butterfly knife during a confrontation with a gang of fifteen, some shouting 'n****rs'. The following year Rohit Duggal was murdered by a white youth outside a kebab shop.[18] The families of the victims later claimed that the failure of Scotland Yard to pursue the killers had created a culture of impunity.

In Stephen Lawrence's case, the Met's response to yet another unprovoked murder would be slowly unpicked and then pored over in microscopic detail for decades to come. Like a snowball rolling down a mountain, it would continue to gather speed and mass. In the final reckoning, there would be no escape for Scotland Yard from a devastating account of incompetence, racism and corruption.

*   *   *

Most detectives agree that the first sixty minutes after any murder represent the 'golden hour' when opportunities for forensic discovery are at their greatest and the chances of solving the crime – or at least identifying principal suspects – are at their highest. Unfortunately for the distraught Lawrence family, the investigation into Stephen's death got off to the worst possible start when one of the first police officers to arrive on the scene decided to leave almost immediately. He headed for the Welcome Inn public house, in the opposite direction to the route taken by Stephen's attackers.[19]

None of the fifty-plus officers who were initially assigned to the case recorded Duwayne Brooks's claim that the attackers had said 'What, what, n****r?' No house-to-house enquiries were conducted and there was no search of the surrounding area,[20] in contravention of police protocols. The most charitable interpretation of the initial police response is that officers treated the murder as some sort of falling out among hooligans, a gangland reprisal unworthy of serious investigation. That is certainly Duwayne Brooks's view: 'I don't think they [the police] believed – well, they didn't believe – that we were just two black boys waiting to get on a bus.'[21]

At one point, Scotland Yard suggested that investigating officers had struggled to break down a 'wall of silence' in the local community, which was said to be terrified of marauding gangs. This would later prove to be entirely untrue. Within hours of the murder, local police were inundated with anonymous tip-offs. Letters left in local telephone boxes and stuffed onto the windscreen of an empty police car claimed that the murder had been committed by a gang of violent white racists. Some tipsters even offered names. In the next two weeks, five white men – Gary Dobson, brothers Neil and Jamie Acourt, Luke Knight and David Norris – were identified to detectives by no fewer than twenty-six different local sources.[22] All five would remain central to the Lawrence case as it unfolded over the next two decades.

Any outsider might have concluded that handcuffs would swiftly be applied to the leading suspects. Yet the senior investigating officer in the case, Detective Superintendent Ian Crampton, made a 'strategical' decision not to arrest anyone after the murder. Another Met detective with detailed knowledge of the Lawrence case says he has always been surprised at the failure to do so. 'The early '90s were a different time,' he said, adding:

> In 1993, if I'm honest, we arrested almost for fun – we didn't give it a great deal of thought. We certainly didn't, as happens today, almost prepare the whole bloody court case before you go out and make an arrest. Back then, if you thought someone was guilty, you'd go out and arrest them and work out the details afterwards. At the very least you would search them or their property, especially within the first hours after a crime.[23]

One of the few things that the police did do in the early days of the investigation involved surveillance of the suspects, but even this simple act of police work proved bewilderingly inept from start to finish. Inexplicably, the surveillance did not begin until three days after the murder, allowing plenty of time for any incriminating evidence – such as a bloody knife or clothes – to be dumped. Then, when surveillance teams photographed suspects removing material from their homes in black bin liners, the information was not passed on to the investigating officers, who might have been able to seize whatever the bags contained. Someone then decided to divert one of the surveillance teams away from the home of a murder suspect in order to observe a black youth who was believed to have been involved in a minor theft.[24] For Stephen's friend Duwayne, the police interest in a potential black thief rather than a suspected white murderer 'summed it all up'. He added: 'If it hadn't been in such tragic circumstances, the surveillance would have been hilarious.'[25]

Complaints about the police investigation quickly multiplied. Stephen's father Neville and his mother Doreen, members of the 'Windrush' generation, having both immigrated to Britain in the 1960s,[26] constantly pressed the police for information, to no avail. Two days after the murder, Neville found himself being questioned about a pair of gloves Stephen had been wearing. Furious, he retorted: 'What are you implying, are you implying my son was a cat burglar?'[27] Doreen said: 'We got the impression that if you are black, you must be a thief. If you are black, you must be into drugs. You are a criminal.'[28] And in an interview she gave to *gal-dem* magazine in 2018 she went further: 'We were being treated as if we were criminals ourselves, and the ones who murdered Stephen were being protected by the police.'[29]

The Lawrences still believe that no arrests for Stephen's murder would ever have occurred had it not been for an intervention from

Nelson Mandela. Then the president of the African National Congress, Mandela had recently been released from a 27-year jail sentence for opposing South Africa's apartheid regime and made time in his schedule to meet Stephen's bereaved parents during a visit to the UK.

The Lawrence family spent twenty minutes alone with Mandela, who then emerged to declare to the waiting crowd that the Lawrences' tragedy was 'our tragedy'. He went on: 'I know what it means to parents to lose a child under such tragic circumstances,' adding that public brutality was all too commonplace in his native South Africa, 'where black lives are cheap'.[30]

Mandela's involvement offered the first indication that the Lawrence case was no ordinary murder, and that the police investigation would not escape scrutiny. All five suspects in the Lawrence case were arrested the day after Mandela's speech.

The gang was questioned before being released without charge. During their brief spell in custody, the police committed another error which hampered the inquiry. Some of the suspects appeared in identification parades at Eltham police station. Among the witnesses who might have recognised the attackers were Duwayne and another black youth, Joey Shepherd, who had also been waiting at the bus stop on Well Hall roundabout that night. Minutes after the murder, Shepherd fled to the Lawrence house to tell the family Stephen had been attacked.

Joey bravely agreed to take part in the line-up, which at that point involved Gary Dobson and the brothers Neil and Jamie Acourt. He was already nervous of possible reprisals should white extremists learn he was helping the police in the case. Despite the obvious danger, police officers mentioned his name in front of a line-up that included the prime suspects. Joey became terrified and refused to help the investigation further.[31] Yet another cardinal policing rule – protect your witnesses – appeared to have been blithely disregarded.

Duwayne, meanwhile, picked out Neil Acourt as one of the attackers – potentially a huge breakthrough in the case. But his evidence was fatally undermined by subsequent statements from DS Christopher Crowley, who accompanied him home following the parade. Crowley claimed that Duwayne had privately confided to him a number of things: that he had been 'prompted' by friends prior to the ID parade and hadn't actually seen Acourt's face at the time. Crowley also claimed Duwayne had told him he had picked out the suspect wearing 'tracksuit bottoms'[32] because he looked as though he had come from a jail cell.

While Duwayne disputed a lot of what Crowley said and was furious about it, he accepted he had said things that the court felt justified excluding his evidence without going into the disputed claims. This demolished any chance of Duwayne's evidence being relied upon in a future prosecution. Duwayne remains furious to this day and disputes the detective's complete version of events:

> The police said Crowley couldn't have made it all up. I said he hadn't, told them which bits were true, and suggested that he was lying about other things he claimed I had said. The police wouldn't let me say 'lie'. They refused to put it down in the statement. They insisted I be more tactful and say that he had 'misunderstood' me.[33]

Crowley has always stood by his version of events despite Duwayne's anger.* Whatever the truth, the Lawrence investigation, it was clear, was getting nowhere fast.

---

* An independent public inquiry chaired by Sir William Macpherson later cleared Crowley of any wrongdoing.

Despite the public complaints from the family and their growing band of supporters, there had been little criticism of Scotland Yard from Westminster or the media. The Conservative government's law and order strategy once Michael Howard was installed as Home Secretary was still very much to court Scotland Yard in an attempt to cut rising crime rates. 'I did see the police as allies in the fight against crime,' Howard later recalled. 'Home Secretaries can't do these things single-handed.'

Ministers were also relying on the Met's counter-terrorism command to deal with an escalating threat from the IRA. During the Conservative Party conference in Blackpool that October, Special Branch officers received intelligence that Irish terrorists were planning to kill a senior minister in an attempt to recreate the infamous bombing of the 1984 Brighton conference, in which five people died.[34]

The warnings arrived in mid-conference, requiring a fast response. Howard's bodyguard Ron Evans said the police 'had no idea or way of knowing' exactly when the attack might be launched. So each protection officer sped their minister away from Blackpool at different times, using different routes.[35] Ministers seemed in no mood to pick fights with police officers who were trying to save their lives.

In time, however, the diffident handling of a seemingly routine murder case in Eltham would become a national scandal. And as the years passed, the Met's moral and practical authority was fatally undermined by its handling of that case. The early mistakes in the investigation into Stephen Lawrence's murder would prove to be a far more sinister indication of decay at the heart of the force.

* * *

The footage was grainy, but the pictures and audio were clear enough. A smiling David Norris reclined on a sofa at the Eltham flat of his friend Gary Dobson, his casual demeanour entirely at odds with what he was saying:

> If I was going to kill myself do you know what I'd do? I'd go and kill every black cunt, every P**i, every copper, every mug that I know. I'd go down to Catford … with two submachine guns and … I'd take one of them, skin the black cunt alive, mate, torture him, set him alight.

Warming to his theme, Norris laughed as he declared he would 'blow their two legs and arms off' and say "Go on, you can swim home now"'.[36]

The comments were recorded on a concealed listening device that police had installed in Dobson's flat. After the failure of the early arrests, the Lawrence case had gone stale. But in 1994 it was picked up by Detective Superintendent Bill Mellish, who was perplexed by the absence of progress.

Mellish, an experienced detective, could not understand why officers on the night of the attack had wrongly concluded Stephen's murder was 'drug-related'.[37] He applied for authorisation to install hidden cameras and probes in Dobson's living room, which captured conversations between the gang members over a two-week period.

Norris was not the only one to air repellent views. Neil Acourt was recorded saying 'every n****r should be chopped up'[38] while Luke Knight ranted barely coherently about the right-wing politician Enoch Powell, who in his infamous 'Rivers of Blood' speech in April 1968 had warned that mass immigration from Commonwealth countries was turning Britain into 'a nation busily engaged in heaping up its own funeral pyre'.

Knight said of Powell:

> That geezer, he knew straight away, he went over to Africa and all that. He knew it was a slum, he knew it was a shithole and he came back here saying they're uncivilised and all that, and then they started coming over here and he knew, he knew straight away, he was saying, no, I don't want them here, no fucking n****rs, they'll ruin the gaff and he was right, they fucking have ruined it.

The hidden camera also showed them brandishing a variety of long-bladed knives. Most chillingly, Neil Acourt could be seen acting out the same 'over-arm bowling' stabbing movement thought to have been used to inflict one of Stephen Lawrence's fatal wounds.

Mellish said the surveillance proved the gang were 'rabid racists with a propensity to violence on a regular basis'. He added: 'Every night they would go out and take the machete off the window sill by the front door and one of them would stick it down his belt. We were getting it on video on a nightly basis.'

Yet conclusive evidence of the gang's connection to Stephen's murder proved elusive. One problem was their use of a telephone box in the street outside to make calls, rather than the phone in the flat. Mellish thinks they might have been tipped off about the surveillance: 'They had to be briefed by somebody.'[39]

The detective decided instead to focus on Clifford Norris, David Norris's father. Clifford, then thirty-five, had become a significant figure in local crime circles. There was local chatter about the exact nature of his police connections, and rumours that he used a network of corrupt Met officers to protect himself and his close relations. One of Clifford's relatives later claimed he controlled the drugs trade from 'Bermondsey to Greenwich', and had 'the Old Bill in his pocket in every nick'. Could Clifford's influence on the Metropolitan Police explain the inexplicable failures of the Lawrence murder inquiry?

At the time of Stephen Lawrence's murder, Clifford was known as a 'thoroughbred gangster'[40] who was on the run from police for importing a massive quantity of cannabis. Mellish believed that if he could remove Clifford from the streets of south London, witnesses would feel more confidence in co-operating with police. In August 1994, Mellish's team finally got their hands on Clifford after they tracked his wife Teresa to an isolated cottage in East Sussex. Inside, next to a set of golf clubs, officers found a sawn-off shotgun and a submachine gun fitted with a silencer. After five years in hiding, Clifford Norris was eventually sentenced to nine and a half years in jail for drugs and firearm offences. A dangerous gangster had been removed from the Lawrence equation. But the development failed to generate any new leads. Mellish could make no further progress and the suspected killers of Stephen Lawrence remained at large.

Less than a year later, the grieving family's patience with the investigation finally ran out. The Lawrences took matters into their own hands. Doreen and Neville instructed Michael Mansfield, one of Britain's leading QCs, to try to bring a private criminal prosecution against the five suspects. The move would allow them to sidestep the Met hierarchy and gain access to the material acquired during the previous investigations. It was hoped that an independent assessment of the evidence might yield a breakthrough.

In April 1995, their hopes were raised when magistrates approved the private prosecution and Doreen Lawrence gave an emotional and damning speech on the steps of the Old Bailey: 'No family should ever have to experience the last two years of our lives. This is the worst kind of fame. We have been brought into the public spotlight, not by our acts, but by the failure of others who were under the public duty to act.'

Much hinged on the evidence of Duwayne Brooks. Stephen's friend remained a key eye-witness, despite his problematic conversations with Crowley, but by now he was struggling. The horror of the murder had been compounded by the rough treatment he had received at the hands of the police. Ordinarily in a case with links to dangerous criminal gangs, he would have qualified for police protection. But no such offer was forthcoming. Duwayne had left home after the attack, suffering from post-traumatic stress disorder. He cut himself off from his friends and family and moved by night from one hostel to another.

When the private criminal prosecution finally reached the Old Bailey in 1996, Bill Mellish was adamant that his star witness should be protected. In an application to the witness protection unit, the senior detective said the defendants were 'proven violent racists' who were 'fully aware of the subject's identity and appearance, his associates and his haunts'. 'It is viewed as essential that this subject be re-housed in order that his personal safety be secured ... Priority relocation is a vital prerequisite to enable this subject to resume some semblance of order in his life.'[41]

But the witness protection unit opposed the application and Duwayne was left 'frightened for his life'.[42] Eventually, on the eve of the Old Bailey trial, Scotland Yard relented and Duwayne was awarded the protection Mellish had sought. But the consequences were disastrous.

When he finally reached the witness stand, the scared young man was cross-examined for several days. During that time, police officers transported Duwayne back and forth to court from an anonymous hotel in Bayswater, central London. On the fourth day, however, a different officer took over, one whose role in the case would raise questions for years to come.

David Coles had had a controversial career at the Metropolitan Police. In 1988, undercover officers from HM Customs and Excise reported Coles to his bosses after they found him fraternising with a major drug trafficker. The villain was – Clifford Norris.

When superiors confronted him with the Customs allegations, Coles denied any wrongdoing and claimed that he had been trying to cultivate Norris as an informant – even though no such approach had been sanctioned by senior officers and he had no authority to do so.[43] Coles escaped censure but was given 'words of advice' over the incident. He was later formally disciplined for falsifying his duty statements by claiming to be at court, when he was in fact having sex with a girlfriend.[44] These matters and Coles's connection with Norris do not seem to have been common knowledge among those who worked with him, however, which perhaps explains why he had been provided with a glowing character reference by the senior investigating officer in the botched investigation into Stephen Lawrence's murder.[45]

Duwayne had no idea of any of this when Coles picked him up at the Old Bailey after he finished giving his evidence. Instead of heading back to the Bayswater hotel, the detective drove the anxious witness to Eltham, back to where he was most at risk. Duwayne was forced to spend the night in a hostel in the area where the suspects' gang was based. It was just a few hundred yards from the bus stop where he had witnessed the murder of his best friend three years earlier. That night, he lay awake in a panic. 'I must be being set up here, I said to myself,' he wrote later. 'Nobody wants to protect me. Nobody wants to ensure my safety.'[46] On another occasion he recalled: 'It was the worst area of London they could have chosen. It felt like they took me to Eltham to break my spirit.'[47]

The private prosecution finally collapsed after the doubts raised by Crowley caused the judge to rule Duwayne's evidence inadmissible. Michael Howard refused calls for a public inquiry. It would be another eighteen years before two of the accused – Gary Dobson and David Norris – stood trial again.

In 2016, a whistleblower named Frank Matthews, who worked in the Met's witness protection unit at the time of the private prosecution, contacted me. Matthews claimed that Duwayne Brooks was a prime candidate for full-blown protection from the moment he witnessed Stephen's stabbing. He said he was 'quite frankly astounded' that the Met did not enter Duwayne into the programme at a 'crucial and vulnerable stage for a witness in a very violent, racially motivated murder'.

In Matthews's opinion, the treatment meted out to Duwayne had 'seriously undermined' him and he contacted him to relay his concerns, which made Duwayne not only angrier about how he had been treated but even more determined to find out exactly what was behind it. He felt he had been 'betrayed' by Scotland Yard, adding: 'The suspects did have friends in the police and the Met knew my life was in danger. They have always insisted that corruption did not play a part. I think it's time that the Met faces up to the truth.' He told me: 'People said it was all paranoia, it was all in my head. Over the years it has been proved the fears were well founded.'[48]

Matthews, who claims the practice of undermining crucial witnesses also happened in other cases which the police did not want to succeed, helped Duwayne apply to the Met for documents relating to his treatment. When he received them, and showed them to Matthews, another disturbing anomaly was revealed.

Another of the officers minding Duwayne during the private prosecution was then under investigation for alleged racism and corruption and later left the Met under a cloud. But Matthews had overheard this same officer walking with a colleague down the corridor on the fifth floor of Scotland Yard: 'One of them put on this mocking accent and went, "Duwayne ... Doo-Wayne ... only a n****r would have a name like Doo-Wayne." They both laughed out loud, but it was bloody disgusting.'[49]

When I put all this to Scotland Yard and asked for comment, their response was that they 'do not discuss the identity or specific details of witnesses'.

David Coles was never convicted of any offence. In 2016, allegations about his relationship with Clifford Norris were put to him by the *Daily Mail*, to which his response was: 'I was young and naive and I probably did things which I would have done differently had I been older.' He still insisted his contact with Norris was 'legitimate'.

* * *

In February 1997, David Norris was back in court. He and other members of his gang were at Southwark crown court for the long-awaited inquest into Stephen's murder. Michael Mansfield QC, who was acting for Doreen and Neville Lawrence, looked up at Norris in the witness stand and frowned slightly. He repeated his question. 'Are you called David Norris?'

The witness shifted uncomfortably and glanced at his lawyer before replying: 'I claim privilege.' Laughter rippled through the courtroom – the witness wouldn't even confirm his own name. Mansfield accused Norris of abusing the court. Sir Montague Levine, the coroner, also warned the witness that he was in danger of making a mockery of the proceedings.[50]

Norris and the other four suspects cross-examined that day had decided in advance to deflect all questions using the common-law right of privilege against self-incrimination. After several attempts, an exasperated Mansfield gave up and told the court that their presence was 'completely pointless'. He went on: 'There has been a wall of silence about this case. There is somebody who knows much more than they are prepared to admit and therefore I must be entitled to ask questions which perhaps touch the conscience of those who know.'

As the five men – all dressed in three-piece suits and ties – rose to leave, the coroner issued an unusual warning: 'I wish to make this very clear, there must be no attacks on witnesses,' he said. 'That won't serve justice at all in any way.'[51]

The proceedings did little to ease Doreen Lawrence's pain; she had previously told the inquest that her son's sole crime was that he was 'walking down the road looking for a bus that would take him home'. 'Our crime is living in a country where the justice system supports racist murders against innocent people,' she added.[52] After the inquest, she said she was 'not sure whether I was in a courtroom listening to evidence of how my son was killed or at a circus watching a performance'.

The suspects' brazen display of contempt triggered a slew of negative headlines. *The Times* published a withering article under the headline 'Fury as witnesses obstruct inquest on black student'.

Norris and the others had seemed to enjoy the occasion. What they could not know, of course, is that their cockiness would ultimately be their undoing. Paul Dacre, the influential editor of the *Daily Mail*, was enraged by their behaviour. That he was following developments in a case largely championed by left-wing and ethnic minority campaigners was perhaps surprising. The *Daily Mail* under his guidance had carved out a niche as the voice of 'Middle England' and was better known for stirring frenzies of popular indignation at the supposed excesses of the liberal elite. Yet unknown to many at the time, Dacre had once employed Neville Lawrence, a skilled plasterer, to do some renovation work for him. The *Mail's* editor had warmed to the 'quietly spoken, very sensitive man'[53] and had followed the case closely since the murder.

On the last day of the inquest, Dacre happened to be having lunch with the Met commissioner, Sir Paul Condon, who privately told him that he 'bet his life the five suspects were as guilty as sin'. Condon also said it was a 'tragedy' that the police 'couldn't get the evidence necessary' but he was 'absolutely certain they were guilty'.[54] Armed with this information, Dacre returned to the *Daily Mail* newsroom in Kensington to learn that the inquest jury had returned a verdict of unlawful killing in an unprovoked, racist attack. The editor said he could sense the 'palpable frustration' and was furious at the 'arrogance' of the suspects hiding behind the 'privilege of silence'. 'These guys were taking the p*ss out of British justice,' he said.[55]

Determined to keep the case alive, Dacre made a daring last-minute decision to tear up the next day's paper. He ordered a full-blown redesign, shrugged off the warnings of his lawyers and published the most dramatic of front pages with the pictures of the five suspects displayed under the inflammatory headline 'MURDERERS'. The headline was followed by a challenge: 'The *Mail* accuses these men of killing. If we are wrong, let them sue us.'[56] They never did.

The splash had a seismic effect, and turned the Lawrence case into a cause célèbre, a pivotal moment in British cultural history. A few months later, Tony Blair's Labour Party won a landslide victory in the 1997 general election. Jack Straw, the new Home Secretary, later admitted that the 'famous headline in the *Daily Mail* helped to change the politics quite dramatically … By virtue of the fact that it was the *Mail* and not a leftish paper, it gave me space to push for an inquiry'.[57]

Scrutinising Scotland Yard was no longer a government taboo. Straw appeared willing to examine the activities of the Metropolitan Police, warts and all, saying that Margaret Thatcher had previously made it 'almost deliberately unaccountable'. 'They were judge and jury in their own courts,' he later recalled. 'Where things went wrong there was no one really who was able to hold them to account.'[58]

Straw decided to do something his Tory predecessor, Michael Howard, had refused to countenance. He ordered a public inquiry into the Lawrence case, chaired by Sir William Macpherson, a recently retired High Court judge.

The proceedings would be held in Hannibal House, a nondescript government building above the Elephant and Castle shopping centre in south London. For fifty-nine relentless days, Scotland Yard was, in effect, the accused, struggling to defend itself in the full glare of public and media scrutiny. The Macpherson inquiry attracted herds of lawyers. There were lawyers for the Lawrence family, for Duwayne Brooks, for the Met, for the police superintendents, for police officers of lower rank, for the Commission for Racial Equality, for Greenwich Borough Council and for the Crown Prosecution Service. Twelve thousand pages of transcript were amassed. Eighty-eight witnesses gave evidence under oath.[59]

That Wembley police protest, which had put paid to Ken Clarke's attempted reforms four years earlier, was now a distant memory. After Macpherson published his conclusions, Scotland Yard would never be the same again.

* * *

Ian Johnston, the assistant commissioner in charge of the Met's interaction with the Macpherson inquiry, collapsed in a chair, his face white as a sheet. Putting his head in his hands, he said: 'It's all gone horribly, horribly wrong.'[60]

Witnesses to Johnston's misery on the tenth floor of the old New Scotland Yard building on Victoria Street, central London, say this moment mid-way through the inquiry was when the Met finally accepted 'they'd cocked up'.[61] Johnston and other senior Scotland Yard officers had held a series of 'deep' conversations before returning to Elephant and Castle to offer a formal apology to the Lawrence family.

The force had been buffeted for weeks by wave after wave of damaging revelations, exposing the shortcomings of the initial investigation, the failure to follow up obvious leads, the bizarre decision to delay arrests, the botched surveillance operation, and the questionable relationship between DS David Coles and Clifford Norris, the gangster father of the prime suspect.

Delivering his opening speech to Macpherson with Doreen and Neville Lawrence at his side, Michael Mansfield argued that the investigation had been undermined by racist attitudes from the start. 'The magnitude of the failure in this case cannot be explained by mere incompetence, or a lack of direction by senior officers, or a lack of execution by junior officers, or by woeful under-resourcing.'[62]

The barrister then turned in oratorically orotund but compelling terms to the spectre of police corruption as a possible influence for the failure to secure justice: 'There is a matrix of quite exceptional coincidences and connections here which weave such a tight web around this investigation that only an ability to suspend disbelief can provide an innocent explanation.'[63]

Certainly, there was a no shortage of 'coincidences' for Mansfield to rely on. Two bloodstained tissues that police found near the crime scene on the night of the attack had mysteriously vanished from evidence.[64] Vast amounts of documentation relating to the investigation had also been lost. When Clifford Norris's house was finally searched, police officers seemed too 'overwhelmed by the magnificence' of the villain's carpets to look under the floorboards for weapons, and had decided that many of his belongings should be left undisturbed.[65]

Two days after Stephen's murder, it emerged, a skinhead given the pseudonym 'James Grant' by detectives had walked into Eltham police station and named each of the five men who attacked Stephen Lawrence (as well as tipping them off that the Acourts were in the habit of hiding their weaponry under floorboards). The same witness had also linked David Norris to a different case. One month before Stephen was murdered, another man had been stabbed in the chest with a 9-inch miniature sword as he walked down a road in Eltham. The victim, Stacey Benefield, survived, and he and another eye-witness both identified Norris as the attacker.

Shortly afterwards Benefield and the other witness were approached in the street and taken to meet a man believed to be Clifford Norris. Benefield was offered £2,000 to change his evidence against David Norris and there were allegations that the foreman of the jury had been 'nobbled'.[66] David Norris was ultimately acquitted.

Another odd episode involved Ray Adams, the Met's second-youngest commander ever and one of the most controversial police officers in Scotland Yard history. Adams has never been convicted of a criminal offence but was repeatedly investigated for corruption amid claims of links to organised criminals in south London. He was head of the Met's entire criminal intelligence division at the time of the murder. Yet in the days following Stephen's death, Adams took a break from his sensitive and senior role to effectively offer his services to the Lawrence family as a junior family liaison officer. He wrote a letter to Doreen and Neville, questioning whether they needed legal support as there should be 'no conflict of interest or purpose' between the grieving family and Scotland Yard.[67]

The Lawrence family argued that the 'incongruity' of Adams taking such a 'nominal role' in the investigation 'masked another purpose'. Their lawyers told Macpherson that a 'potential channel for such influence' was Adams's relationship with Kenneth Noye, another well-connected gangster and police informant.[68] A suspected drug trafficker, Noye once admitted stabbing to death an undercover police officer in 1985, although, remarkably, he was acquitted of murder after claiming he acted in self-defence. The Freemason was later jailed for his involvement in the 1983 Brink's-Mat robbery, where a gang stole 3 tons of gold bullion and £26 million of gold, diamonds and cash from a warehouse at Heathrow airport. At the time, it was described as the 'crime of the century'.

The Lawrence family argued that the relationship between Adams and Noye could be relevant as Noye and Clifford Norris were criminal associates.[69] Adams was in the witness box for several days, but although Macpherson noted there were 'strange features' to his evidence, he felt that it had not been established that Adams did anything other than that which he had said he had done (sign the letter) and cleared the Met commander of any impropriety.[70] This was in part due to the fact that neither the Macpherson inquiry nor the Lawrence family were made aware of questions raised over Adams's conduct before the Lawrence case which had been investigated by the Met in an operation codenamed Russell.*

The tipping point for the Met, which would so unnerve Assistant Commissioner Johnston and lead to the apology to the Lawrences on the steps of Hannibal House, was the public dismantling of the Yard's own review of the murder investigation, led by DCS John Barker, the former head of the Flying Squad. During the Macpherson inquiry, it emerged that Barker held deep misgivings about what had really happened – but omitted them from his report in order to protect the original investigating officers. This mattered a great deal to the Lawrences. For five years after Barker delivered his review exonerating every officer in sight, his findings had been used throughout Scotland Yard to deflect criticism and to sully the Lawrence family's campaign for justice. Macpherson concluded of Barker's evidence: 'Some of the answers given and assertions made ... were, in the full sense of the word, incredible.' The judge was also furious with Sir Paul Condon and his leadership team. 'The unquestioning acceptance of the Barker review by senior officers is a most serious aspect of this case,' he said. '[It] provided a convenient "shelter" to those involved. The failure of all senior officers to detect the flaws in the review is to be deplored.'[71]

---

* This observation was made by Mark Ellison QC in a later review of the case in 2014.

As the scandal slowly unravelled in the Macpherson inquiry, other stories of police corruption began to appear in the media, sending alarm throughout Scotland Yard's highest ranks. In December 1997, Condon admitted under questioning at a parliamentary select committee that up to 250 of his officers could have gone rogue. Yet the commissioner stressed to MPs that his anti-corruption command was on top of the problem.

But the damaging stories continued. A few months later, ten of the most senior police officers in the country met secretly at the headquarters of the National Criminal Intelligence Service (NCIS) in Vauxhall, south London. Roy Penrose, a former senior Met officer who had recently been appointed as head of the new National Crime Squad, was present along with the NCIS deputy director general Roger Gaspar, who had previously led the Met's anti-corruption unit. They were meeting to develop a national 'anti-corruption strategy'. The recurring leaks about the true extent of criminality inside the police meant managing the media was a prime concern. While others in the Met downplayed the issue of corruption to Macpherson, Gaspar had concluded that it was, in fact, 'pervasive' and was now on a par with the rogue police forces in 'Third World countries'.[72] His Vauxhall presentation was supposed to be confidential, but minutes from the meeting were promptly leaked to investigative journalist Geoff Seed, who splashed the story in the *Sunday Telegraph*.[73]

With its reputation under more or less daily assault, Scotland Yard changed strategy and started to be more open about its problems in an attempt to ward off criticism. Realising that Macpherson's conclusions could be devastating for the force, Condon wrote to the judge in October 1998 accepting for the first time that some of his officers were 'overtly racist' and the issue amounted to 'much more than bad apples'. 'I acknowledge the danger of institutional-isation of racism', he wrote, but noted that 'labels can cause more problems than they solve'.[74]

Two months later, Condon and his new deputy, John Stevens, held a press conference to launch their new 'Corruption and Dishonesty Prevention Strategy'. The two police chiefs pledged there would be 'no hiding place' and no 'amnesty' for rogue officers. 'No one should underestimate our determination to relentlessly pursue and prosecute corrupt and dishonest members of staff, either current or past, and those who seek to entrap our colleagues,' said Condon.[75]

In the weeks leading up to the Macpherson report's publication, there was panic on several fronts. Members of the inquiry panel began to suspect Scotland Yard had bugged and burgled their offices at Hannibal House. The secretary to the inquiry, on secondment from the Home Office, complained to the Met but was assured that his concerns were unfounded.[76] With a month to go before publication, Macpherson adviser John Sentamu, then the Bishop of Stepney and later Archbishop of York, became concerned at strange goings-on at his home, where he was writing a brief for Macpherson on institutionalised racism. He told friends that his computer had developed a fault and that his phones were bugged: 'For four days I could hear these clicks on the line when I made a call as if someone was picking up the phone and listening to us.'[77]

The Macpherson report was duly published in February 1999. The judge ruled that the original investigation into Stephen Lawrence's murder was 'marred by a combination of professional incompetence, institutional racism and a failure of leadership by senior officers'. He lambasted the police treatment of the Lawrence family and Duwayne Brooks, and the 'failure of many officers to recognise Stephen's murder as a purely "racially motivated" crime'.[78] Macpherson defined institutionalised racism as the 'collective failure of an organisation to provide a professional service ... through unwitting prejudice, ignorance, thoughtlessness and racist stereotyping which disadvantage minority ethnic people'.[79] The BBC would later describe it as 'one of the most important moments in the modern history of criminal justice in Britain'.[80]

The report made seventy recommendations and had an impact not only on policing but across society – from the criminal justice system to every public authority in Britain. Macpherson insisted that the 1976 Race Relations Act should be amended to apply not just to the police but to the whole of the public sector. In the wake of the report, the Home Secretary, Jack Straw, mandated race awareness training for Scotland Yard and every other police force in England and Wales.

On police corruption, however, Macpherson was more cautious. From the outset, the judge had said it would be more difficult to establish because the burden of proof he felt should apply was that which would stick in a criminal court. On other matters, such as institutional racism, the judge felt he could rely on the balance of probabilities, the strength of evidence one would need for a civil case. It is not clear why he distinguished in this way between racism and corruption, both of which are criminal offences. In the event, Macpherson cleared all the police officers connected to the Lawrence case of corruption, among them Adams and Coles.

After the report was published, some of those who had battled for the truth for so long felt it was time to draw a line under the matter. Stephen's father, Neville, made an extraordinarily generous statement in the circumstances, calling for everyone to 'look forward' and work together, regardless of skin colour.

'[The black community] have been here for a very long time and lot of us are not going anywhere,' he said. 'We have brought a lot of diversity, we have brought change, cultural, music, food, everything. This is a very small place, this world of ours, we have to live together and we now have to say: let us put the past behind us, join hands and go forward.'[81]

Others felt there was still unfinished business. Deep in the bowels of the Home Office, hours before the report was released to the world, Duwayne Brooks and his solicitor, Jane Deighton, had been granted an advance look at the report. He was pleased to discover that Macpherson had not only believed his evidence but concluded that the police would have treated him completely differently had he been white. He later recalled feeling 'strange' when he first read the chapter about himself, and tried to describe that strangeness: 'Elation? Relief? Vindication? Anger? Maybe a mix of them all.'[82]

Yet as he flicked through the meaty tome, Duwayne realised that no action had been recommended against any of the individual police officers responsible for what he called his nightmare. 'So that's British justice,' he said. 'It takes six years to admit that a couple of young lads had been neglected and mistreated by the police. Six years – followed by a conspiracy of silence.'

That morning in the Home Office he pushed back his chair on the verge of tears, turned to his solicitor and asked why 'nothing is changing'. Deighton, who had worked on many actions against the police, had a much more developed understanding of the opponent they faced. She smiled briefly, put a hand on her client's arm, looked him in the eye and said, 'Look, Duwayne, I'm afraid this is just the beginning.'[83]

Deighton's hunch would prove to be correct.

Chapter 2

Infiltration

In October 1995, detectives searching a bedroom above a north London nightclub were alarmed to find a statement made by one of their protected witnesses stuffed inside a training shoe. Once the document came to light they realised that any hope of solving the murder of Michael Olymbious – Greek property dealer by day, drug dealer by night – was over.

Six months previously, Olymbious had been shot dead after losing track of £1.5 million worth of ecstasy tablets. He was thought to have been minding the cache for one of London's most notorious crime families in a flat in Chelsea. But the drugs were found by a cleaner, who conscientiously called the police.[1]

Police suspected Olymbious was harbouring the ecstasy on behalf of the infamous Adams family, known as the 'A Team', who control a large slice of organised crime in north London.[2] The syndicate, run by brothers Terry, Patrick and Tommy, has been linked to drug trafficking, money laundering, armed robberies and twenty-five murders during a thirty-year reign of terror.[3] It seems Olymbious's blunder could not be forgiven. In April 1995, as the Greek business-man got into his car near the Oval cricket ground in south London, two men jumped out of a white Mercedes van and shot him dead with an antique semi-automatic German Army-issue Luger.[4]

Detectives investigating the murder made an initial breakthrough when one of Olymbious's friends gave a statement detailing the Greek's sizeable debts to the Adamses.[5] The witness also claimed that Olymbious had received a death threat not long before he was shot. As a result, Scotland Yard mounted dawn raids on the home of Terry Adams and a nightclub on the Finchley Road which was thought to be controlled by the family.

The results were dispiriting. The night before the police went in, Adams suddenly fled his house, accompanied by his wife and child. Officers believed he had been tipped off.[6] When detectives searched the nightclub, they found a photocopy of the witness statement that Olymbious's friend had made to Scotland Yard, hidden inside the trainer. 'It is obvious ... that a supposedly secret murder investigation was confidently and effectively infiltrated and compromised,' said a later Met Police report.[7] The case remains unsolved to this day.

The subversion of the Michael Olymbious murder inquiry was uncovered by Operation Othona,* the most significant anti-corruption inquiry launched by the Metropolitan Police in the past forty years. It was launched in 1994, almost exactly a year after Stephen Lawrence was stabbed to death, and continued almost until the conclusion of the Macpherson inquiry into Stephen's murder. It was an extraordinary investigation. Many say it was the last demonstrable attempt by Scotland Yard to rid its ranks of the cancer of organised crime.[8]

According to Sir Ian Blair, Met commissioner from 2005 to 2008 and at this time leader of the force's anti-corruption command, Operation Othona marked a dramatic change in strategy.

---

* The operation was named after an old Roman fort in Essex.

In a previously unpublished interview, which took place in 2013, Blair was remarkably open about the scale of criminality that he found inside the Yard in the early 1990s. 'It would be fair to say that when I took over in the summer of 1993 it felt like the watch had gone to sleep,' he said. 'The lessons that had been learned under Robert Mark [an earlier Met commissioner who led a massive anti-corruption drive in the 1970s] had disappeared – and there was a smell of corruption around.'[9]

Mark's indirect successor Paul Condon passionately believed in rooting out corruption: 'The Met I joined was fairly unsavoury around ethics. In the Met I inherited in 1993, there was a lot that needed to be done.' In another unpublished interview languishing in the archives, Condon said that he wanted to follow Mark's example and eliminate the rogue officers who permeated Scotland Yard's elite detective squad, the CID. But he felt that while Mark was commissioner, the CID had been 'almost a force within a force, and an organisation that almost lived by its own rules'.[10]

Condon also believed that by the time he became commissioner, the spectre of corruption had returned:

Because of the culture and environment of some of the specialist units, there was less monitoring day to day of what they were doing, many of them were in life-and-death situations, that buddy-buddy atmosphere meant it was more challenging for people to whistleblow or to wail against unethical ways ... There were pockets of officers, particularly in the specialist units, like the Flying Squad and one or two other squads, where there were anxieties.[11]

When Blair took over the anti-corruption command, then called CIB2, it was, he said, unable to deal with the complexity of the task as it sorely lacked skilled detectives. 'These corruption inquiries need covert methodology, which you would apply against organised crime. Bugging cars, houses, surveillance. It is top-level detective work that you needed the background to do.'[12] As a result, Scotland Yard launched Operation Othona. Every officer I have spoken to who was involved in this top-secret intelligence-gathering exercise has reacted with a mixture of pride at the scale of the operation's ambition, coupled with a nervousness that the subject was being broached at all.

At the outset, the Met set up an office in Tintagel House, an anonymous block on the Thames near the MI6 building in Vauxhall, south London. Senior officers sent out the message that it was there to receive intelligence on bent coppers. The office was a decoy, however. In reality, the corruption catchers were at a secret location, an industrial estate in Kent, using a stand-alone computer network and offshore companies to hide their existence. The squad was made up of elite detectives who had 'resigned' from their previous posts, or 'retired early' on grounds of ill health. They had to live double lives, pretending they were executives and ordinary office workers while, in effect, spying on former colleagues. The total cost of setting up and running the operation was £14 million.[13]

Roy Clark, a former Met commander who was involved in Operation Othona, says that corrupt cops are an elusive target and covert measures are vital:

If there is anybody that knows the tools of investigation, including covert and undercover [techniques], it is police officers. They know how to cover their tracks. To get a conviction you have virtually got to have 120 per cent evidence. All the methods that we had [used] so far [had] been stunningly unsuccessful, which is why I think we came up with this rather grandiose massively secret [plan], you know, people being seen to resign and people being dragged out of training school.[14]

'Dark Side of the Moon' is a 32-page summary of the task faced by Operation Othona, written in May 1994. A remarkably frank account of the criminality pervading Scotland Yard, it makes for uncomfortable reading. The document found that 'determined and ruthless criminals' were 'devoting a great deal of time, effort and re-sources' to infiltrate the Met.[15] It also noted that 'the very suggestion that a structured network of traitors operated at all levels within the Police Service had tended to bring the establishment out in an organisational "cold sweat" that had paralysed any meaningful and lasting response'.[16]

The document questioned why corruption had been allowed to metastasise inside Scotland Yard, with no one since Mark even attempting to stop it: 'It could be that there had never been a com-missioner strong enough for some serious "boat rocking".' As a po-litical strategy, the discovery of widespread corruption might have been perceived as counter-productive, particularly as the organisa-tion had – since Mark – prided itself on being free of crookedness. Perhaps they were afraid to learn the enemy's secrets.

'There appeared to be unwillingness in certain quarters of the police establishment to mount a determined and continuous cam-paign of counter-intelligence and internal security,' the document continued. 'Paranoia about what might be revealed if corruption was investigated with vigour, resourcefulness and cunning was run-ning high in some very powerful and influential circles.'[17] Examples of corruption identified police officers running unauthorised checks on the Police National Computer, leaking details of operations and copies of official documents, 'weakening' or 'losing' evidence, conspiring with 'major criminals' to commit 'very serious criminal offences' and 'offering protection from arrest and prosecution' to 'major criminals' in return for 'money and information'.[18]

But that was not all. The report also warned that rogue officers were being protected by people higher up the food chain: 'Many methods were employed to protect the core players in the danger-ous game of big-time corruption, including the reliance on well-placed senior officers who were, and remained, corrupt.'[19]

Little wonder that Commander Roy Clark had more work than he could possibly deal with when he began work on Othona. One of his colleagues would later say that the targets of the operation were 'organised criminals with police badges'.[20] One of those crim-inals was a former detective sergeant, known as 'Derek', who had retired from the Met to take up employment with the aforemen-tioned Adams family.

Terry Adams, the head of the syndicate, was the eldest of eleven children. Born in 1954 near Clerkenwell, he is said to have cut his teeth by demanding protection money from pubs and shopkeepers before making his name as an armed robber. His brother Patrick, or Patsy, was sentenced to seven years in prison for an armed robbery in the 1970s, while their younger brother Tommy would later be jailed for drug trafficking.

Terry rose to lead the gang during the 1980s as the rave scene led to high demand for amphetamines, cocaine and ecstasy. By the 1990s he had allegedly made enough money to buy both power and protection but was never convicted of drug offences. Terry is said to have managed the syndicate as if it were a corporation, acting as de facto chief executive. But beneath the gang's façade of respectability, violence was never far from the surface. Anyone who failed to pay back a debt or was suspected of being an informant was at risk of being kneecapped or 'opened up like a bag of crisps'. Terry was finally arrested for money laundering following a joint operation between Scotland Yard and MI5 and was jailed for seven years in 2007.[21]

In 2013, Patsy Adams shot motorist Paul Tiernan in the chest in Islington, north London, with a .45-calibre gun. But he was cleared of attempted murder after the victim refused to co-operate with police. Tiernan claimed that 'loyalty is everything', that being called a 'grass' hurt more than being shot, and even said that Adams didn't fire the bullet. Despite this, there was too much evidence for Adams to overcome. He admitted causing grievous bodily harm with intent and was sentenced to nine years.[22]

During the 1990s, the anti-corruption officers working for Operation Othona would also focus on the Adamses. Their employee 'Derek' was identified in 1995 when police bugged Pussy Galore, a jeweller in Hatton Garden, the heart of London's jewellery district, which also acted as an office for Solly Nahome, the Adams family's leading money launderer. The surveillance picked up on a meeting between 'Derek' and Terry Adams, whose discussion centred on the tragic case of Leah Betts, a teenage schoolgirl from Essex who had died days earlier after taking an ecstasy tablet on her eighteenth birthday. Pictures of her in hospital in a coma, released by her parents, had sparked a national outcry and triggered a huge police drugs crackdown. At the meeting at Pussy Galore, Adams was recorded discussing with 'Derek' whether to 'take out' the supplier of the ecstasy tablet.[23] The probes also picked up chatter that suggested 'Derek' was in contact with three serving Met officers who were 'assisting' the Adams family by performing 'corrupt checks' on police databases.[24]

It wasn't just the Metropolitan Police who bugged their targets. As Othona progressed, its detectives also came to rely on intelligence from a rival law enforcement agency, HM Customs and Excise (HMCE). At the time, this arm's-length branch of the Treasury had primacy over Scotland Yard in terms of investigating and prosecuting Britain's most prolific drug traffickers.[25] 'We chased people smugglers, VAT fraudsters and especially drug smugglers,' said one Customs officer in an interview in the *Financial Times* in 2010. 'We shadowed criminals by foot and by car ... I stayed up late, drove fast cars and slept in expensive hotels. It was a rock 'n' roll lifestyle. I loved it.'[26]

The leading unit in HMCE's investigative division was code-named 'Alpha Projects'. Their entire focus was on wire-tapping, the interception of phone calls in real time. 'I spent ten hours a day listening to drug smugglers talking on wire-tapped phones,' said another Customs officer. 'It gave me an insight into their obsessions, their habits – and who they were lying to.' But Customs officers became concerned when they realised the drug traffickers were talking to corrupt police officers. David Raynes was the assistant chief investigation officer at HMCE during Othona. When I met him for lunch near his home in the West Country, he admitted his team were listening in to a dozen bent cops at any one time. 'We were constantly tripping over corrupt police officers,' he told me:

The most significant source of information about bent cops was from telephone intercepts, and the range of criminality that police officers were involved in was just having a drink with a so-called informant or, in one or two cases, police officers being right at the heart of the smuggling episodes. The detectives were indistinguishable from the criminals with whom they operated. They were socially mixed up

together. We had intelligence of two criminals playing football for a
Metropolitan Police team.[27]

Another Customs officer said police officers and criminals often
grew up in the same parts of the country. He said they forged close
bonds from a young age that often strengthened when they grew
up and joined the Freemasons, the secret and ancient brotherhood
in which members swear to protect each other. 'They lived in the
milieu, mixing with these people all the time in the same Masonic
lodge,' said the Customs officer. 'The only time we would dip into
it was when we'd go and arrest somebody. If you like it was easy
for us to stay clean.'[28] Jim Jarvie, another Customs officer, said: 'We
worked with some really good Met officers. But because it is such
a big organisation, if you have 1 per cent of them corrupted that is
still a lot of people.'[29]

Just as Customs officers were raising the alarm about the Met's
penetration by organised crime in the 1990s, it emerged that their
concerns were shared by another source. Someone right at the
heart of Scotland Yard.

* * *

As head of internal audit at the Metropolitan Police, Peter Tickner
led a unit that monitored the multi-billion-pound finances of Britain's largest police force. Each year Tickner mounted up to seventy
internal investigations into contractor and staff fraud and corruption.[30] His efforts were not always welcome.

Tickner is a highly intelligent man and his restless intellect,
which once caused such difficulties for Scotland Yard's most senior
officers, has found a new outlet in retirement. When I met him,

it was in his garden in the Home Counties. He emerged from his shed, which had been converted into an observatory complete with a giant telescope. Tickner now spends his time tracking asteroids and studying collapsing stars, or supernovas, tens of millions of light years away. But it was his refusal to ignore wrongdoing inside Scotland Yard that led to a different sort of implosion, albeit one that was no less spectacular. The battles he waged against the highest echelons of the Met came at great personal cost, but it is clear that he would do it all over again if given the chance. As one deputy assistant commissioner remarked: 'The trouble with you, Peter, is you enjoy your work far too much.'[31]

In a delicious irony, the master bean counter was first brought to the Yard in the wake of a major corruption scandal. Tickner replaced Tony Williams, the Met's previous chief auditor, who had just been convicted for stealing £5 million from a covert police operation. As ever with the Metropolitan Police, the facts are stranger than fiction. Williams took advantage of the panic caused by the IRA's mainland bombing campaign that had built steadily throughout Margaret Thatcher's time in office. In response, the Met deployed an aircraft to track suspected IRA arms caches and hide-outs in southern England. The project touched on national security issues and had to be kept totally under wraps, so the Met turned to Williams, a trusted finance director, for help. 'We were bugging lots of suspected IRA stuff and the plane could track them from the air … taking detailed photographs,' said Tickner. 'They needed to keep it completely separate from the Met because they didn't want the IRA to cotton on so they had a cut-out company underneath it.'[32]

Few people in Scotland Yard knew what Williams was doing; no one looking in from the outside would have a clue either. All they would see were two firms – one apparently owning the other – that ran a small, fixed-wing aircraft. If the Cessna needed money for fuel, Williams requisitioned it. The money was paid, no questions asked. 'Williams was supposed to get the cheques out of finance and into this covert company, but he would just inflate the budget,' Tickner told me. 'So, finance would pay the budget he provided them, not the one submitted by the police officers, who never saw the other side, so they didn't know. Williams would then siphon off the money to his own accounts.'[33]

The epic swindle carried on for eight years, before Williams was finally ensnared by his greed. During the heist, he bought a Jaguar XJ6, a £500,000 Surrey mansion (now worth an estimated £2 million), a Westminster flat and a villa in Spain. The former bank clerk also bought property and land around Tomintoul, the highest village in the Scottish Highlands, and set himself up as the new lord of the manor after snapping up the title 'Lord Williams of Chirnside' for £66,000 at auction. He even used stolen Met funds to employ forty people in Tomintoul, where he built a restaurant and hotel complex that offered astonished locals the opportunity to dine on 'noisettes of lamb edged by dauphinoise potato' and 'mousseline of pigeon beside a pithivier of truffle and asparagus'.[34]

Williams was caught when the authorities finally started to examine how a £42,000-a-year civil servant with no family money had come to own a chauffeur-driven limousine and ten expensive properties. When he was sentenced at the Old Bailey in 1995, the judge, Sir Lawrence Verney, said Williams's larcenies against Scotland Yard's taxpayer-funded budget were 'so vast, so huge' that words failed him.[35]

The fallout was – unsurprisingly – damaging. Paul Condon, the commissioner, was called to an awkward session at the House of

Commons to explain how the country's leading police force could have allowed such a gigantic fraud to be perpetrated under their noses. According to Tickner, the result was that senior officers were keen on a replacement who was 'good at finding frauds – it was a match made in heaven'.[36]

When Tickner arrived at New Scotland Yard in 1995, he found 'chaos'. Almost immediately he uncovered criminals infiltrating the Met, and was exposed to the hyper-agitation of police chiefs desperate to limit who knew about it. 'I had only been there a short while and I got a phone call from the head of audit at another government department,' said Tickner. The official complained that the Met had recommended a 'dodgy works contractor'.[37] This led Tickner to take a closer look at the Yard's £70 million-a-year works department, which covers building, maintenance and repairs across the many police properties in London. It was the first of many experiences that led Tickner to feel as though he had fallen down a rabbit hole into Wonderland. The auditor identified a suspicious-looking contractor and rang up the local intelligence collator to find out what was known about him. 'He came back and said: "You don't want to go anywhere near that address. That's Bad Frank. He is a serious armed robber."'

Tickner was stunned. 'The address of this company that has a works contract with the Met is the address of a known armed robber,' he told me. 'And the police know he's an armed robber because it's one of the addresses they monitor. He's got a police works contract! "How the hell has he got that?" is the next question that crosses my mind.'[38]

Enquiries soon established that Bad Frank had been jailed for five years after holding up a post office with a shotgun. He had also been banned as a company director for involvement in a VAT fraud. Tickner saw transcripts of Bad Frank's phone calls to a well-known south London villain. 'He was reporting back what he had learned during his travels around south London police stations,' said Tickner.

> One of his jobs was Tower Bridge nick. That was where the robbery squad were based. And what was Frank? A professional robber! So, we had a professional armed robber repairing the cells of the robbery squad.
>
> Then we found out that Bad Frank had somebody on the inside in the Met. I reported that up to the [anti-corruption command]. And nothing happened. Absolutely nothing happened.

Tickner's enquiries into Met works contracts kept expanding. The more he looked, the more he found: 'We kept finding more and more dodgy contractors.' Staff at a south London police station stopped speaking to Tickner's team, which caused him to take unusual measures:

> I went there with my deputy, who was an English national power-lifting champion at two different weights. When they wouldn't open the door, I got him to open it for us and went in anyway. This went around the Met like wildfire. 'Did you hear the auditors raided the works office and broke the door down?!' You can imagine! 'He's a not a police officer, he's a civil servant. What the bloody hell is he playing at?!'[39]

Tickner's meddling came to a head when he presented his findings at a committee chaired by a very senior, and very irritable, police officer. 'He went ballistic,' Tickner told me. 'He said: "You have no right to investigate, you're not a blank, blank copper." He stood up and threw all the papers at me in front of a couple of other senior officers around the table. He was foaming at the mouth [and] ranting and raving.'[40]

By this time, Tickner had spoken to other senior government figures and had the measure of his new employer. 'Customs didn't trust them. MI6 didn't trust them. MI5 didn't trust them. Nobody trusted them.'[41]

* * *

Meanwhile, Operation Othona crept on behind the scenes. The intelligence gathered was used to mount a number of prosecutions and as the basis for Paul Condon's disclosures about 250 corrupt police officers to the Home Affairs Select Committee in December 1997, just before the Macpherson report into Stephen Lawrence's murder was published.[42] Those involved in Othona claim there were 'hidden benefits' not obvious to outsiders, but it is undeniable that the covert operation achieved few successes in court. As Roy Clark had predicted at the start of the exercise, the corrupt officers were largely wise to the police tactics deployed against them.

The Met also allowed itself to be led up the garden path by a number of notorious supergrasses, including former detective Duncan Hanrahan (of whom more later), Geoff Brennan, a southeast London businessman, and Hector Harvey, an armed robber from west London. Evidence about police corruption supplied by all three later disintegrated under cross-examination at trial. With costs mounting and very little to show for the expensive detective work, Scotland Yard moved to a different strategy.

The Met decided to go back to a technique adopted by Robert

Mark when he expelled 500 corrupt officers in the 1970s. 'People had been told that they had lost the confidence of the commissioner and they [had] got half an hour to resign or they would be arrested,' recalled Ian Blair.[43] With millions wasted on investigations that had gone nowhere, Scotland Yard tried the more informal – though less employment-law-friendly – approach.

Stephen Roberts, a deputy assistant commissioner who led the Met's anti-corruption command between 2003 and 2005, had this to say: 'There was definitely an issue in that money had to be saved. Money was tight. The heroic days of professional standards [were] over.'[44] Roberts said that the scale of the crisis meant that costly investigations simply weren't sustainable. 'It was very obvious there were so many targets … it was impossible to target that sort of number.' So the Met dusted off Mark's original strategy. 'We came up with what at first seemed like quite a silly idea,' said Roberts.

> Why don't we just call them in, tell them off, and tell them that we don't love them any more? To our surprise, everybody that we tried it on, and there were well over a dozen in the first year, signed a letter of resignation that was offered to them there and then. It was so successful that it saved us millions.

Roberts said that police chiefs christened the strategy the '23p initiative' – the cost of a second-class stamp.[45]

It may have saved money, but the strategy would ultimately prove counter-productive. Many of the rogue police officers who left the Met continued to work for organised crime groups, and simply corrupted their former colleagues from the outside. One senior officer told me it was known as the 'revolving door of corruption'.

The Met's leadership may have been pleased with the success

of the '23p initiative' but there had been very few successful prosecutions and Condon's figure of 250 corrupt Met Police officers was now part of the public consciousness. Senior officers were increasingly nervous about the extent of police misconduct being exposed. Anyone within their ranks who tried to point out that the force might have a problem was swiftly dealt with.

The unwitting figure of DS Frank Matthews[*] now stepped into the vortex. By 1998, Matthews had worked his way through the murder squads and the CID to become a member of Scotland Yard's top-secret criminal justice protection unit, responsible for the safety of judges, jurors and witnesses in Britain's most sensitive trials. Like other courageous officers in this book, Matthews was troubled by what he saw inside the Met and refused to turn a blind eye to impropriety.

The detective and his partner, DS Samir Ashar,[†] became concerned that their unit, SO10, had been compromised by organised criminals seeking to find and intimidate protected witnesses.[46] Ashar also encountered racism within the unit. The Asian officer was repeatedly called a 'P**i' by colleagues and said he was handed odd assignments, without backup, to jobs involving 'very dangerous' witnesses.[47] When Matthews defended Ashar, he too was ostracised.

Eventually, the two men blew the whistle on their colleagues' appalling behaviour, which included the abuse of police credit cards to pay for lavish meals and large quantities of alcohol. But when the pair reported their concerns up the chain of command, they found themselves under surveillance by Special Branch, a secretive unit of the Met supposedly concerned with national security. As a result, Matthews and Ashar had to be shielded in a new witness protection

---

[*]   Pseudonym given to shield Matthews from reprisals.
[†]   Pseudonym given to shield Ashar from reprisals.

programme hastily created by another force, Hertfordshire Police. More than £14,000 was spent on alarms, video cameras and other security for their homes, including infrared sensors, reinforced doors and windows and two panic alarms.[48] Their lives disintegrated, so much so they took the decision to sue the force they once loved.

During a legal battle lasting two and a half years, the two men claimed that they had their mail intercepted and their telephones tapped and were even arrested in an attempt to intimidate them into dropping their claim. The case was finally settled in 2000 after the officers' lawyers uncovered evidence that they had indeed been targeted by Special Branch. They received more than £500,000 of public money in compensation. None of the allegedly corrupt police officers they identified was ever prosecuted.[49]

I heard about this remarkable story in 2014, from Frank Matthews himself. When I visited him, he took me through the paperwork while explaining what had happened. It was not an easy process. Matthews had been diagnosed with post-traumatic stress disorder following his ordeal. (It was nothing compared to the suffering of Ashar, who had moved with his family to the other side of the world.) During our conversation, he opened up about the origins of modern-day corruption inside Scotland Yard, which he said took off in the 1990s with the explosion of the global drugs industry. When the Misuse of Drugs Act was passed in 1971, there were a little more than 1,000 known heroin addicts in Britain and almost no crime related to drug supply. Decades later, there are 350,000 addicts and more than half the prison population is inside for drug-related offences. It is a lucrative world to be in. The National Crime Agency estimates that the UK trade alone is worth more than £10 billion and costs another £7 billion of taxpayers' money in police funding.[50] Globally, the black market in drugs constitutes between one-tenth and one-eighth of all global trade, greater than the iron, steel and motor industries.[51]

In the 1990s, the criminal world benefited from a tsunami of cash, which – according to Matthews – meant that neither Scotland Yard nor any other British police force is able to cope with the potential for corruption. 'It turned the whole game upside down,' Matthews told me. 'Suddenly it's not your local copper getting corrupted – it's senior management. There's just no way to control that.'

The expansion of the trade in drugs also fuelled violence which ripped London apart and which continues to this day. In the 1990s, foreign gangs controlling the flow of illicit substances ended up playing out their battles on the streets of the capital. In the Brixton area of south London alone, there were nine murders by Jamaican gangsters, known as Yardies, between January 1993 and April 1994.[52] In that latter year, detectives told the *Sunday Times* that the murder rate in the black community had more than doubled over the previous five years, with much of the increase blamed on warfare between rival gangs struggling to control the lucrative market in crack, the cocaine derivative.[53] In 1997, the director of the National Criminal Intelligence Service attributed at least eight murders in London in a three-year spell to the Turkish-controlled heroin trade,[54] while a Crown Prosecution Service (CPS) barrister prosecuting a Turkish-linked case had a dead cat nailed to the door of his home.[55]

Matthews claims that the drugs boom also heralded a marked increase in criminal informants. The handling of such sources is something of a grey area and is often the way in which police officers are corrupted:

As the drugs thing grew and grew, so did the importance of running long-term informants. All through the early 1990s it just kept getting bigger, until I was working really serious high-level informants spread all over the world. At my peak I had eighteen active registered informants. That's slightly crazy – usually a detective would have no more than a handful at any one time. And these were all quality high-level sources as well.[56]

But, according to Matthews, becoming an 'snout' or a 'grass' is effectively just an insurance policy for gangsters:

In the old days, informants were an incredibly useful tool. The drug money has changed all that, to the point where a lot of criminals are now becoming informants specifically in order to manipulate the police. Having a corrupt officer in their pocket has become just another tool for any serious gangster. Eventually, it got to the stage with me where so many of the top echelons of any organised crime group were all registered informants that it became impossible to properly investigate anyone – because they all have their own high-level cops protecting them.

For any real detective trying to investigate organised crime, you don't know which criminal is under the protection of which of your bosses. Suddenly your investigation is getting sabotaged from above, because you're poking your nose into areas that might threaten someone else's informant. This means you can't actually solve cases.[57]

Matthews described in minute detail how the exchange between police officer and informant can become toxic:

It could start with something simple: your informant asks you a favour, to check up on a certain car. Now, this guy is giving you masses of intel on drugs, cocaine shipments, guns. Not only do you want to keep him sweet, but it's actually in your interests to advance his career in the criminal world, because then he'll get you even better intelligence. So what develops is this mutually reinforcing arrangement of interests. The cop wants the informant to rise through the criminal ranks and, on his side, the criminal also wants his handler to rise through the police, so he can offer better protection. So he keeps feeding the cop intelligence, usually on rival criminals, so that the cop gets good busts and makes a name for himself.[58]

High-level informants are particularly adept at manipulating their police handlers:

They can run rings round most coppers. And, if it's not just basic greed, everyone has vices that can make them vulnerable. These informants are people who can get you anything – officers get sucked into this world of champagne, elite clubs, women, drugs – the whole lifestyle. But, once they've crossed that line, the informant owns them. Now the informant is running the cop, not the cop running the informant.[59]

Matthews remembers tracking one informant who was in the system for decades, 'a big player in the drug world who has since been murdered'. He went through handlers in every section of the force, 'some of whom had reached senior management level'. This informant set one of his handlers up with a girl and got it on film. From then on, the cop was working for him. This officer kept climbing through the ranks, overseeing several high-level investigations. But all the time he was passing on information to this informant, including about other police informants.[60]

Matthews says the drugs busts lauded in the media are chicken feed:

> You look at what the National Crime Agency do now – they take out the odd shipload. It looks great for the headlines; there's some good pictures in it. But those jobs are easy … It's such a tiny, tiny drop in an ocean that's basically limitless. The gangsters just say: 'Let them have the headline, if it keeps them off our back.' For those guys it's a 1 per cent business loss. The whole current method is a scam. It's a sham. It doesn't really deal with the problem. And at some point – someday – someone is going to be forced to finally just be honest with the public.[61]

Matthews's story was published for the first time by the *Sunday Times* in an article I wrote in 2015. What happened to him had been hidden from public view until then. But when I mentioned the case to Peter Tickner, it was a very familiar story. When he was the Met's chief auditor, he too had investigated Matthews's colleagues in the witness protection unit due to their excessive spending on police corporate credit cards.

'Just from the records I saw, their behaviour was disturbing,' Tickner told me. 'They were abusing witnesses and writing inappropriate comments about the people they were protecting. One of them was drinking too much, one of them was womanising, and the other had a habit of some sort.'[62]

It is unsurprising, then, that Tickner was also privy to another of the Met's classified inquiries.

* * *

In the summer of 2002, the head auditor was summoned to Twickenham Cricket Club in south-west London for a meeting of Scotland Yard's corporate governance committee, which dealt with confidential and covert matters. One item on the agenda had been added by the then head of the Met's anti-corruption command, deputy assistant commissioner Andy Hayman. It sent shivers down the spines of those present. 'He was going to inform us how many corrupt gangs had infiltrated the Met,' Tickner told me. 'Andy used to bang on about this at some length: "We've got thirty gangs who have infiltrated the Met. We've got to deal with this!"'[63]

Hayman outlined the findings of Operation Tiberius, which had started a year earlier when senior officers became concerned that that operations in north and east London were 'consistently being compromised' by organised crime syndicates.[64] The senior management board at Scotland Yard sanctioned a top-secret 'strategic intelligence scoping exercise' to find out more. Operation Tiberius was compiled from intelligence sources including covert police informants, live telephone intercepts, briefings from the security services and thousands of historical files.[65]

Its conclusions were shocking. The 178-page report found that organised criminals were able to infiltrate Scotland Yard 'at will'. The findings revealed that there was 'endemic corruption' in the Met and concluded that crime syndicates – including the Adams family – had bribed scores of officers to access confidential databases, obtain intelligence on criminal investigations, provide specialist knowledge of surveillance, technical deployment and undercover techniques to help evade prosecution, and even take part in criminal acts such as drug importation and money laundering. Murder investigations had also been infiltrated, allowing the offenders to escape justice. Tiberius identified eighty corrupt individuals with links to the police, including forty-two serving officers and nineteen former detectives. Only a tiny number named as corrupt have ever been convicted. One senior investigating officer interviewed by the inquiry was moved to complain: 'I feel that … I cannot carry out an ethical murder investigation without the fear of it being compromised.'

The operation also found that other agencies had been infiltrated, including HM Revenue and Customs, the CPS, the City of London Police and the Prison Service, as well as jurors and members of the legal profession. The report concluded: 'Quite how much more damage could be done is difficult to imagine.' Tiberius also revealed that underworld syndicates used their contacts in the Freemasons to 'recruit corrupted officers' inside Scotland Yard, warning it was one of 'the most difficult aspects of organised crime corruption to proof against'.[66]

One operation described in the report targeted the Bowers family, based in Canning Town, east London. Tony, Martin and Paul Bowers owned the Peacock Gym, the iconic boxing gym. Many champion fighters have trained there, including Frank Bruno, Ricky Hatton, Amir Khan, Lennox Lewis and the Klitschko brothers from Ukraine.[67] Such was its influence that the gym attracted visits from sports ministers, retired boxing legends Sir Henry Cooper and Sugar Ray Leonard, and Hollywood actors including Sir Michael Caine and Orlando Bloom.[68] The gym's website states that the Bowers brothers had some 'close brushes with the local police' when they were growing up in the 1970s.[69] In reality, their relationship with the underworld was rather more extensive; the Peacock was a front for organised crime.

In 1999, Scotland Yard's specialist intelligence section targeted the gym in a covert operation codenamed Deenside. The Bowers brothers were suspected of involvement in money laundering, lorry hijacking, tobacco and alcohol smuggling and drug trafficking.[70] The Bowerses also employed a former Met detective inspector. It was money well spent. According to Operation Tiberius, the former detective helped to foil an attempt by the police to bug the Peacock's boardroom after detectives made a friendly request to use it as a secret observation post to tackle local car crime.[71] An analysis of the former detective's phone bills over a three-month period also revealed that he made contact with ninety-nine 'law enforcement-related' numbers, which included Scotland Yard but also the Ministry of Defence and HMCE. 'These calls, made by a former senior law enforcement officer, would not cause concern but for the fact that he is part of one of the most ruthless organised crime syndicates in the country,' noted the report.[72]

In 2001, detectives received intelligence that the Bowers family was seeking to cash in on the Docklands regeneration in Canning Town. Tony Bowers was 'considering a £6 million investment in a business venture involving the construction of a hotel and casino complex' and, taking advantage of the relaxation of gambling laws pushed through by Tony Blair's government, the brothers lobbied local Labour politicians and were invited to the House of Commons.

To raise money for the project, they decided to rob HSBC's depot at Gatwick airport. In March 2003, the three Bowerses executed the elaborate heist, using a fake Brink's-Mat van and bogus uniforms. They even convinced a hapless British Airways security guard to help them load up their haul. Unfortunately for the brothers, the plan was doomed from the start. By this stage, police had finally managed to dodge the watchful eye of the ex-detective and install a bug in the boardroom above the gym. They had listened to the whole plan unfold in real time. Detectives arrested the gang as they left the cargo terminal with a £1.2 million haul. Tony was jailed for twelve and a half years, Martin got seven years and Paul was given six. The ex-detective was never charged.[73]

In 2014, when I was a reporter at *The Independent*, the paper ran an exclusive based on the findings of Operation Tiberius. When my source handed over an encrypted memory stick, urging me to publish, he told me, chillingly: 'Nothing has changed. The Met is still every bit as corrupt as it was back then.'[74]

Chapter 3

Axe in the Head

Before Stephen Lawrence, Operation Othona and Operation Tiberius, there was another case. A murder, a mystery, a long and inconclusive police investigation, whispers of corruption, contract killings and organised crime. A Welsh private investigator named Daniel Morgan had been hacked to death in the car park of the Golden Lion pub in Sydenham, south London, in March 1987. The prime suspect was Morgan's business partner at the time of his death – another private detective, named Jonathan Rees, who was friendly with over a dozen Metropolitan Police officers.

The police investigations dragged on for three decades. Charges were brought against Rees and Sid Fillery, a former Met detective, then dropped. They later went to trial and were acquitted. There were five separate police investigations, all wrapped up in a Lawrence-like murk of menace and deception. There seemed to be a ready-made mystery waiting to be solved when I came across the case as a junior reporter. At one point I found myself interviewing a source who was so frightened of reprisals he would only discuss the case if we met in our trunks in a deserted swimming pool. He wanted to be sure that I wasn't carrying a recording device.

I had no idea what I was getting into. Step by step, I felt I was being sucked into a black hole of lies and official deceit, unsure who

I could believe or trust. Not the police, not the daunting array of south London villains claiming intimate knowledge of the case, and certainly not Rees, a former merchant seaman with a seemingly bulletproof hide.

In 1998, more than a decade after Morgan's murder, Scotland Yard launched its third major attempt to solve the crime. Code-named Operation Nigeria, the seven-month-long inquiry was led by former detective superintendent Bob Quick, who would sub-sequently become the Yard's assistant commissioner in charge of Britain's fight against terrorism. Nigeria did not solve the murder, but it would lay bare the extent of Rees's relationship with many inside Scotland Yard.

Intelligence obtained before the start of Operation Nigeria was summarised in December 1998:

Both Rees and Fillery have been subjects of interest to CIB [the anti-corruption command] for a considerable period of time. Long-term and wide-ranging intelligence shows them to be deeply involved in corruption, using a network of serving and retired police officers to access sensitive intelligence for the purpose of progressing crime and frustrating the course of justice. Both conduct criminality from the premises.[1]

In the hope of learning something new about the case, officers from Operation Nigeria broke into the dingy offices of Rees's private detective agency, Southern Investigations, in Thornton Heath, near Croydon. They installed listening devices and began to monitor Rees's calls. They learnt nothing new about the Morgan murder, but the surveillance shed light on corruption inside the Met. Rees and Fillery's contacts included DC 'Skinny' Tom Kingston, jailed for his role in stealing 2 kilos of amphetamine from a dealer; former DC Martin King, imprisoned for corruption and perverting the course of justice; and Duncan Hanrahan, a detective jailed for robbery and drugs offences. In addition, the police listening devices picked up Rees and Fillery boasting of corrupt contacts inside HM Revenue and Customs.[2] There were other surprises, too.

On one occasion Rees boasted over the phone that one of his sources had overheard the then Prime Minister, Tony Blair, call his deputy, John Prescott, a 'fucking bastard' who was 'getting on my fucking nerves'.[3] There was also a deluge of chatter about unrelated criminal matters, some of which involved serving Scotland Yard officers who had gone rogue.

It is perhaps unsurprising, then, that Rees had a reputation as a well-connected gossip-monger which made him a top source for several leading national newspapers. The names of some of his friends in Fleet Street turned up in the Met's inquiries. All this seemed to offer Rees a degree of protection from intrusive media scrutiny of his own activities. Once, when I was investigating the Morgan case, I was pulled aside by a senior colleague who told me of a briefing he had received in the early 1990s. A senior Scotland Yard officer had embarked on a tour of Fleet Street newsrooms to advise editors not to enquire too deeply into the murder of Daniel Morgan. 'He said we [police] look bad, but you [journalists] look bad as well, so it's best to just leave it,' my colleague told me.

When I spoke to John Yates, the former Met assistant commissioner who at one point took overall charge of the Morgan murder investigation, told me he thought the case was 'definitely equivalent' in scale and impact to the murder of Stephen Lawrence.[4] Unhappily for Morgan's family, Scotland Yard's efforts – at an estimated cost of more than £30 million – did not lead to a single successful prosecution. It was not until the Met's traditional alliances with Westminster and Fleet Street began to fray in more recent years that closer attention was paid to the death of a private investigator who may have got too close to a case someone did not want investigated.

* * *

Whoever attacked Daniel Morgan intended to silence him for ever. At 9.40 p.m. on 10 March 1987, his body was discovered in the Golden Lion car park lying next to his BMW, the axe that had killed him still embedded in his face, its handle covered with sticking plaster to hide any trace of fingerprints. It was immediately clear that this was no chance assault. The victim's suit trousers were ripped, but the killer or killers left £1,000 in cash untouched in Morgan's pockets. The man who found the body was Thomas Terry. He went inside the Golden Lion, called the police and then ordered a pint of Guinness to get over his shock. 'Then', as he recalled in a television documentary, 'the Keystone Cops hit the pub.'[5] Dozens of police officers trampled around the crime scene, seemingly without regard for basic precautions against the contamination of forensic evidence. It was, according to Terry, a 'charade'. 'I have never seen anything like it, they were coming from everywhere. I'm surprised they never even came down the chimney.'[6]

Former detective chief inspector Noel Cosgrove was the first CID officer on the scene. Years later, he admitted that the Morgan murder inquiry 'wasn't like other investigation I have been involved in', adding that it 'seemed to be pretty loose in the way it was run'.[7] According to Cosgrove, when the senior investigating officer, Detective Superintendent Dougie Campbell, turned up at the Golden

Lion, he slipped inside and ordered a whisky.[8] Cosgrove stated he was appalled but when he questioned the appropriateness of drinking on duty at the scene of an axe murder, he claimed Campbell told him to 'fuck off'.[9] Campbell denied this and a later review noted that Cosgrove had only raised this allegation at a later date.

Leonard Flint, a civilian scene-of-crime officer, watched plainclothes detectives open Morgan's BMW and remove his briefcase and paperwork. Flint thought this was rather unusual as nobody took notes and there was no exhibits officer present to record it.[10] A forensic photo taken by the Met photographer Michael Rhodes seemed to show fingerprints on Morgan's car door, but by the time an expert came to examine the BMW, the marks had gone.[11] When the victim's distraught brother Alastair visited the crime scene the following morning, he found no cordon in place to preserve evidence.

How could a violent death in a pub car park be treated so casually? Alastair Morgan, who led the family's tireless 35-year battle for justice, suspected from the outset that the murder was linked to Jonathan Rees and the corrupt officers he knew inside the Met.

As a co-founder of Southern Investigations with Rees, Daniel Morgan had concentrated on tracing missing or otherwise wanted persons and bailiff work for credit companies, banks and law firms. Rees liked to socialise with police officers at a nearby police station in Catford. Daniel made no secret of his concern at his partner's links to the police.

'The last time I saw my brother alive was about a month before the murder,' Alastair told the *Daily Mail* in 2014.

He was going to Malta to do a job for a client. Just before he went away, his house and office were burgled. Dan was worried about leaving his wife and kids alone while he was away, and he asked me to come and stay in a spare room and take over his desk at Southern Investigations.

On the day Daniel returned from Malta, Alastair was with him in his office when Rees stuck his head around the door and said: 'Dan, can I have a word?' Dan returned ten minutes later, Alastair recalled, 'and stood by the window chewing his lip as if he was troubled. I asked him what was the matter and he mentioned a name I had never heard of before.

'I asked: "Who's that, then?" and he replied: "He's a bent copper, Alastair. They're all over the place."'[12]

Two days before his death Morgan went to an Austin-Healey owners' event in north London and confided to two friends that he was 'dealing with serious police corruption and could not go to anyone at the Met because he could not trust them. He was thinking of going to an outside force.' After his murder, Morgan's friends decided to contact the police to share this potentially helpful information. One was interviewed but was never called as a witness at the inquest while the other was not even formally interviewed.[13]

In the early days of the investigation, suspicion fell on Rees as it emerged that his relationship with Morgan had deteriorated. Rees had hired some of his CID pals to moonlight as security guards when they were off duty. Morgan had disapproved; not only was it against police regulations but one of those security jobs had turned sour.

Southern Investigations had been hired to transport £18,000 in cash on behalf of a client, Belmont Car Auctions. Rees and some of the off-duty officers he hired claimed that they had been robbed in transit and the cash had been stolen. Belmont did not believe this story and launched a civil action against Rees's firm. According to police files, Morgan was 'extremely annoyed and upset' about the reputational damage to the firm and the £10,000 it had to pay in legal fees. On the night of the murder, Morgan, who was then thirty-seven, had met Rees at the Golden Lion to discuss the Belmont Car Auctions robbery.

Another aspect of the case that worried Alastair was the role of DS Sid Fillery, who ran the local crime squad in Catford. Fillery was a close friend of Rees. 'Sid Fillery was a friend who happened to be a policeman, rather than a friendly policeman,' Rees later said, a view echoed by Fillery himself: 'Everyone knew we were mates, and drinking buddies. We had the same blokey opinions on things. Quite chauvinistic we were, really.'[14] The night before the murder, Morgan and Rees had also met for a drink at the Golden Lion. On that occasion Fillery was there, too. There were reports of an argument between Morgan and Fillery, although the detective later character-ised their exchange as a heated discussion about arming the police.[15]

Despite his personal connection to the case, Fillery was then put in charge of the initial inquiry into Morgan's murder. The office manager at Southern Investigations would later tell police that the portly detective turned up at the agency's office the morning after the murder. The manager claims that Fillery asked for the Belmont file and filled a black bin bag with documents, which have not been seen since.[16] Two days after the murder, Fillery made a second trip to Southern Investigations, removed more papers and put them in the boot of his car. These files were also never fully accounted for. Fillery's driver would claim that sometime later he helped clear out his boss's desk and burnt some documents.[17]

It fell to Fillery, as senior investigating officer, to interview his friend Jonathan Rees, already a prime suspect in the case. It now seems barely credible that Fillery should have been anywhere near an investigation in which he plainly had a personal stake. Even at the time, the witness statement he secured from Rees angered some of his colleagues. Malcolm Davidson, another officer on the investigation, said Rees's statement to Fillery 'didn't contain anything, it didn't go into any great detail'.[18] Perhaps unsurprisingly, it also omitted the fact that Fillery himself was seen arguing with Morgan the night before he was killed.

'You trust an officer and you give him a job to do, which you think he will do to the best of his abilities,' added Davidson. 'And I'm certain, from what I've seen, Fillery didn't do that. Sid Fillery is not mentioned in the statement because Sid Fillery is taking the statement, and he does not want to put himself in the statement.'

Had Fillery's fellow officers known from the outset about their boss's connections to both Rees and Morgan, 'that would have been important to us', said Davidson, who suspected that his colleague was passing information to Rees.[19] 'We would have liked to have known the identity of everyone who was in the pub the night before.'[20]

Fillery has defended his handling of Rees's statement. 'I would never let any witness lie in a statement,' he said in a documentary about the Morgan murder, broadcast on Channel 4 in 2020. 'There are no lies in the statement. There may be omissions but not deliberate omissions, and an omission is not the same as a lie.'

Bob Quick, who investigated the case a decade later, was a sergeant at Catford at the time of the Morgan murder. He has always been concerned about Fillery's role and claims the detective 'withheld crucial information about his involvement with Southern Investigations'. 'He knew a lot more about what had been going on in the business, and he knew that Rees and Daniel Morgan had had an argument there,' said Quick. 'These are not insignificant omissions and had it been known to [senior officers] at the beginning they could have fundamentally changed the direction of the investigation.'[21]

Even with Fillery avoiding obvious questions, Rees's account of his movements after the murder unravelled. Data retrieved from his car mobile phone did not match up and he had received an untraceable twelve-minute call around the time of Morgan's death. He later told officers it was from his wife, but she declined to corroborate his statement and the Daniel Morgan review concluded that Rees had been unable to account for this call. Rees also claimed that he and Morgan had gone to the pub to meet up with a 'third party' – a celebrity bodyguard named Paul Goodridge – yet this was denied by Goodridge.[22]

Four days after the murder, Fillery withdrew from the investigation when his conflicts of interest became clear to his colleagues. He subsequently took annual leave, then sick leave. He would never return to active duty[23] – but soon found a new job. Morgan's death had created a vacancy at Southern Investigations and Fillery stepped straight into the dead man's shoes, becoming Rees's new partner. He left a murder case in tatters behind him.

* * *

The Morgan case drifted for a year until an inquest was convened in April 1988. In a grim foreshadowing of the Lawrence case, new evidence emerged that exposed the shortcomings of the original police investigation, leaving Scotland Yard with a lingering stain on its reputation.

The crucial breakthrough came from a friend of Rees's, Kevin Lennon. The Irish-born accountant, who filed and signed the paperwork for Southern Investigations, signed three separate witness statements claiming that Rees wanted Morgan dead. Lennon's role did not emerge until a retired detective chief inspector called Laurie Bucknole contacted the murder inquiry to claim that a year before the murder took place, Lennon had told him of tension between the two partners. The accountant allegedly claimed that Rees was trying to have Morgan killed.[24]

Bucknole agreed to talk to Lennon again, this time wearing a wire. When the accountant repeated his incendiary claim, the murder squad confronted him with the tape. Lennon agreed to make a sworn statement. He said that Rees had predicted that the Morgan's murder would be carried out in the Catford police station's jurisdiction so local officers could 'suppress' any information linking the murder with Jonathan Rees or themselves. Lennon further claimed that the plan would enable Rees's friend Fillery to 'take Morgan's place' as he would be a 'much greater asset' to the business. This is exactly what happened after Morgan's death.[25]

Lennon's claims were presented in public for the first time at the inquest. On the witness stand, Lennon said Rees hated Morgan and had asked him, Lennon, if he knew anyone who would kill him: 'I formed the opinion that Rees was determined either to kill Daniel Morgan or have him killed. When he spoke to me about it, Rees was calm and unemotional about planning Daniel's death.'

Lennon also said that Rees had told him 'policemen from Catford' would organise the murder for £1,000. 'When questioned by me, Rees said: "These police officers are friends of mine and will either murder Daniel or arrange for his murder."' He went on to suggest that if his police friends didn't dispose of Morgan themselves, they would find someone facing criminal charges and arrange for the charges to be dropped if they agreed to carry out Morgan's murder.[26]

Lennon's account of policemen willing to moonlight as murderers drew gasps from the public benches. Alastair Morgan described Lennon's revelations as 'absolutely astonishing', while his elderly mother, Isobel, later recalled that the jury looked 'absolutely aghast'.[27]

Rees and Fillery were quick to deny these claims, however. Fillery argued it would be farcical for someone to discuss a murder plot with their accountant, while Rees claimed that Lennon was then facing fraud charges himself and had done a deal with the police. The explanation left Alastair Morgan, among others, baffled. 'If he had been doing a deal with the police, why on earth would he have [implicated] the police in the murder?' he said. 'That would be completely counter-productive for the police, so I think that you have to attach credibility to what Kevin Lennon is saying.'[28]

More was to follow. When Detective Superintendent Douglas Campbell, the head of the Morgan murder inquiry, gave evidence at the inquest, he accused Fillery of effectively sabotaging the case. Campbell also introduced yet another layer of murkiness to the proceedings, claiming that Morgan had talked about blowing the whistle on police corruption to a national newspaper not long before he was killed.[29]

Under British law, an inquest is intended to establish the cause of death, not attribute blame – and in the Morgan case the outcome was something of a foregone conclusion. He had been killed by an axe blow to his face, and the coroner, Sir Montague Levine, duly recorded a verdict of unlawful killing. Levine noted, nonetheless, that the case left 'lots of room for disquiet'.[30]

If Daniel had indeed been about to go public with allegations of police corruption, there were many people close to Rees who might have been nervous. Fillery was not the only detective in the Southern Investigations orbit to face questions over their conduct. Jon Ross, another friend of Rees, was a former detective who had been acquitted during Operation Countryman in 1982. Ross had been accused of framing armed robbers and accepting money with menaces. He was subsequently kicked off the force by a police disciplinary board.[31]

After he left Scotland Yard, Ross bought himself a wine bar near Elephant and Castle in south London. Briefs was a drinking hole with a history. The previous owner was a lawyer who would later be convicted of laundering the proceeds of the 1983 Brink's-Mat robbery. The bar became a key meeting place for police officers and their underworld contacts. Ross was quite open about the nature of his clientele: 'The Flying Squad and the robbers used to drink together,' he boasted. 'There were no problems because they all earned money out of bank robberies.'[32]

Ross was well known to detectives across the force and his name popped up early on in the Morgan murder investigation. One of the murder inquiry detectives was shocked to discover that Ross had somehow made his way into the incident room where the evidence in the case was being gathered.[33]

It might seem that every detective in south London with a blot on their record was part of Rees's circle of friends. Duncan Hanrahan, who joined the Met in 1977 aged nineteen, was another. Hanrahan led the police investigation into the Belmont Car Auctions robbery, which got nowhere, and retired from the force in 1991. In May 1997, Hanrahan was arrested for trying to corrupt a police officer. He agreed to turn supergrass.[34] Hanrahan's debrief by anti-corruption officers suggested that more than fifty of his former colleagues inside the Met were engaged in similar activity on behalf of criminal clients. Information from the Police National Computer was being sold to criminals, police were taking bribes to destroy evidence, and there was a network of police detectives distributing cocaine.[35] For some, joining Scotland Yard had nothing to do with crime fighting; it was a short cut to a quick profit.

In March 1999, Hanrahan was jailed for eight years and four months after admitting offences including conspiring to steal 40,000 ecstasy tablets and conspiring to rob a Lebanese courier at Heathrow airport of £1 million.[36] Years later, Hanrahan would tell an interviewer:

> I don't want my kids to think that what I did was really cool. At the time I thought it was the business. We were taking the piss out of the system. We were earning a few quid here and there. But when you look back at it … we were the villains. I don't like that and I don't find it easy to live with. But that is what I was … Corrupting people was a way of life.[37]

After the inquest into Daniel Morgan's death, his mother Isobel wrote to the then Met commissioner, Sir Peter Imbert, imploring him to reinvestigate the murder. Isobel Morgan's plea and the publicity in the wake of Kevin Lennon's explosive claims at the inquest led to an independent investigation by an outside force. Detectives from Hampshire took over and the Morgan family were initially hopeful that they might make some headway in the case. However, their hopes were dashed when the Hampshire chief constable, John Hoddinott, attended a meeting at Scotland Yard in which the new investigation's terms of reference were seemingly changed to exclude the activities of police personnel (including Sid Fillery's) and focus on Paul Goodridge's and Rees's alibis.[38] Once again, the Yard's instincts looked suspect. The force seemed to be prioritising the protection of its own over the pursuit of justice.

During the independent investigation by the Hampshire force, Paul Goodridge, one of Rees's alibis on the night Morgan was killed, was arrested and charged with murder. When he was in custody, Goodridge made off-the-record allegations about Metropolitan Police involvement in the murder and told Hampshire officers that he was afraid for himself and his family: 'There is a big firm involved in this [...] that is all powerful. I can't tell anyone [...] Your lot are OK. I think I might be able to tell you,' said Goodridge. 'The Met Police are a big and powerful firm. There are about seven involved in this.'[39] Hampshire officers then made the remarkable decision to inform Scotland Yard about the disclosures. Goodridge was promptly visited in jail by Met Police officers. He never repeated his allegations again.[40]

In 1990, the Hampshire investigation privately concluded that the Met's initial inquiry had been ineffective and, in many respects, incompetent. However, in a statement to the family and the wider public, Hampshire gave Scotland Yard a clean bill of health.[41] Alastair Morgan was furious. 'My brother, I believed, had been butchered because he was about to blow the whistle on police corruption. And what did we get from the Crown? Feeble, corrupted policing, wilful blindness and sleazy denial.' He pledged to fight on. 'I said aloud: "I won't give up, Dan, I promise. I won't let them get away with this."'[42]

Alastair publicly called for Hoddinott's resignation. Soon afterwards, he began to believe he was being watched. When he told his mother, Isobel said that the day before she had found a woman taking photos in her front garden in Hay-on-Wye. Isobel then called Alastair's sister Jane, who was living in Germany. Jane, too, reported that she had just found a man taking photos of her home with a telescopic lens. Alastair was disturbed. Members of the Morgan family appeared to be under surveillance in Wales, Scotland and Germany.[43] A short time later, Alastair received a death threat and his local council arranged for him and his girlfriend to spend the night in a safe house.

Nothing much came of this and the case continued to drift. Alastair all but gave up. What he could not have known, however, was that a police constable had approached senior officers with an extraordinary story.

Derek Haslam was one of the few policemen in the Southern Investigations orbit who was not bent. He had known Daniel Morgan and claimed he knew all about Morgan's attempts to expose police corruption. Haslam's story would cost him his career, and make him fear for his life. It involved another police officer who had died in sinister circumstances four months after the murder of Daniel Morgan.

*   *   *

Leonie Holmes awoke in her bedroom on a late July morning in 1987 and went downstairs shortly before 7 a.m. to find the kitchen light and the television on. When she opened the curtains to the garden, she saw her husband, DC Alan 'Taffy' Holmes, lying on a chair, covered in blood with a shotgun at his side. It seemed as though Holmes had shot himself in the chest and the coroner would later rule his death a suicide.

The detective was a friend of both Daniel Morgan and Derek

Haslam, who does not believe for a moment that his colleague took his own life. The fingerprint officer at the scene could find no fingerprints on the shotgun.[44] Years later, I asked John Yates, a former Scotland Yard assistant commissioner, about Holmes's death, and whether it was related to Morgan's murder. His reply was interesting: 'The murder – I mean, the suicide – of Taffy Holmes was all linked of course.' Correcting himself, he continued: 'Why Taffy Holmes committed suicide, who knows, but it was a very dark episode.'[45]

Haslam claimed that Holmes and Morgan were collaborating in order to expose police corruption.[46] According to Haslam, in early 1987, Holmes told him over dinner at an Indian restaurant in Thornton Heath that he was on to a mammoth drug deal. Around £100 million worth of cocaine was due to be imported from Miami. According to Haslam, Holmes believed the deal was being overseen by corrupt Met officers and that Morgan had the evidence to support this.[47] This claim has loomed over the case of Daniel Morgan ever since, bedevilling many investigators, journalists and barristers in the process. Besides Haslam, no further evidence has emerged to support the allegation.

Before his death, Holmes had also been working with Haslam on a major corruption inquiry targeting Commander Ray Adams, head of the Met's criminal intelligence unit, which handled informants and many covert operations.[48] Operation Russell was launched on 16 April 1987, a month after Morgan's murder. The fact that the head of the Yard's criminal intelligence unit was the main subject of the inquiry prompted the lead investigator, Commander Thelma Wagstaff, to describe the case as 'the worst allegation of corruption ever levelled at the Metropolitan Police'.[49] The Russell inquiry looked at dozens of cases involving Adams stretching as far back as 1972. In total, twenty-five allegations of criminal activity by police officers were examined, including perjury, bribery, corrupt association, theft of drugs and conspiracy to pervert the course of justice.

According to Haslam, at first Holmes, who was friendly with both Haslam and Adams, tried to act as an intermediary. Haslam refused Holmes and told him to stay away from the inquiry. Haslam also suggested to the Met's anti-corruption command that he could meet Adams wearing a wire. The offer was turned down. Holmes approached Haslam again, but this time (according to Haslam) there was nothing friendly about his threat: 'Unless you start co-operating with Ray Adams, something nasty could happen to you and a member of your family.'[50]

It would be understandable if what Holmes said concerned Haslam. Adams certainly had very nasty connections indeed.

Holmes was now under intensifying pressure. Not long before his death, he had been interviewed by the Met's anti-corruption command about his attempts to influence Haslam. And when Holmes's wife discovered his body, a note by his side read: 'Under different circumstances I would never have left you and the children. But by the actions of Haslam and CIB [the anti-corruption command] I have been forced to inform on a CID police commander. I trusted Haslam completely but tell them all he is a Serpico.'[51] Was he really forced to commit suicide for fear of retribution for informing on Adams? Why would he now blame Haslam for trying to expose corruption?

Haslam laid out his version of events to Operation Russell, to little effect. The investigation, which was supervised by the Police Complaints Authority, cleared Adams of the corruption allegations, although it concluded he had behaved in a 'reprehensible' fashion and was guilty of 'highly questionable and unprofessional conduct'.[52] But it formally cleared him of corruption allegations and found no criminality in his dealings with his informant, Kenneth Noye, who had stabbed an undercover police officer to death.

The events that followed may seem wearily familiar. Haslam, the whistleblower, received a series of death threats for speaking out and was forced to move his family away from their home. In 1989 he retired from the Met on medical grounds[53] and moved out of London.

Yet Haslam had not been alone in expressing concern about the Met's handling of the Daniel Morgan investigation. Shortly after Morgan's murder, the case featured on the BBC's *Crimewatch* programme, triggering a call from a tipster who gave her name as Doreen. It was agreed that a policewoman would meet her at East Croydon railway station. At the meeting Doreen claimed that Jonathan Rees, Morgan's business partner, was heavily involved in trafficking drugs, mainly cocaine. She further claimed that Rees was involved with some 'very heavy' people, including Joey Pyle, a well-known south London gangster. Doreen told her contact that drugs were being imported from Spain and America, and that Morgan was killed because he was 'going to tell'. But after that initial meeting the police never heard from her again.[54]

The emergence of drug trafficking as a possible factor in Morgan's death was both plausible and alarming. Scotland Yard was already conducting major investigations into the import of drugs to the UK, mainly via Spain. Two of the inquiries, Operation Concorde and Operation Wimpey, had focused on the same man, Jimmy Holmes (no relation to 'Taffy' Holmes). Jimmy Holmes had faced prosecution for cannabis importation but was acquitted with the help of evidence from Jonathan Rees's brothers-in-law, Garry and Glenn Vian, who were also suspects in Morgan's murder. Glenn Vian has been accused of being the man Rees paid to kill Daniel Morgan. In November 1986, police officers carrying out surveillance for Operation Wimpey had noted vehicles registered to the Vians visiting Jimmy Holmes's house. Intelligence reports suggested that Garry Vian was trading in cocaine with Joey Pyle. There seemed to be extensive links between Rees and a drug-related network of south London gangsters.

Holmes's calls were being monitored by the Flying Squad. Officers found themselves listening in on a call between him and Vian in which the murder of Daniel Morgan was mentioned. In the call, Vian and Holmes had apparently also mentioned Pyle, who had travelled to America around the time of Morgan's murder because he believed he was wanted in Britain as a suspect.[55] The Flying Squad immediately tipped off the Morgan murder inquiry. But nothing happened.

Other witnesses, in statements to the police, recalled Morgan talking about taking a big story to a newspaper. The private investigator's former boss, Brian Madagan, told police in 1987 that he believed Morgan was hoping to 'hit the jackpot' with a media exposé on 'police officers'.[56] 'The first time he told me the story, I thought "That's so dangerous",' Madagan recalled years later. '"You must be mad" … he said he would get £40,000, and [the story] was about the drugs squad.'[57]

Another police officer, DC Kinley Davies, has also alleged that he was also told Morgan was about to blow the whistle on a case of 'major police corruption' – but internal police documents detailing his claim were removed from the murder inquiry's incident room. Davies claimed that he and two of his colleagues tried to investigate emerging allegations of Met Police malpractice but were 'suddenly removed' from the squad by senior officers.[58] A friend of Davies later told me, somewhat cryptically: 'There were a number of things from that time that Kinley and his colleagues found unsavoury. There were other things going on that seemed to overlap with the Morgan murder.'[59] It was all left to gather dust in the Met's vaults and, years later, a painstaking review of the case would find no evidence that the murdered man was trying to sell a story to the press.

But the lack of a breakthrough tormented Daniel Morgan's family. Alastair Morgan continued to write letters and lobby politicians, all to no avail.

Then, after lying dormant for several years, former PC Derek Haslam made a dramatic reappearance in the Morgan case. Once again, he would be prepared to make a stand for what he thought was right. Once again, it would come at great personal cost.

* * *

In 1996 Detective Superintendent David Wood took over the Met's anti-corruption command, having previously run the South East Regional Crime Squad (SERCS) office in Surbiton, south-west London. While there, Wood had been shocked at the criminality in its ranks and estimated that a dozen of the fifty-odd detectives at Surbiton were bent. It is widely believed that there was a similar ratio at every SERCS office in the London area.[60]

With his new, wider remit for anti-corruption across the Met, Wood wanted another crack at solving the Morgan murder. He needed someone on the inside, a source who could get close to longstanding suspects Jonathan Rees and Sid Fillery to see what they were up to. Wood tracked down Derek Haslam. During a meeting at a three-star hotel in a small market town several hours' journey from London, Wood asked him to work as an undercover agent for the Met. He told Haslam that he knew about his previous involvement in the case and agreed that he had been 'badly treated and badly let down' by the Met. He allegedly said that decisions were taken in order not to jeopardise other convictions secured by officers later suspected of corruption.[61]

Haslam was wary. He did not want to leap back into bed with the Metropolitan Police unless certain conditions were met:

> Bearing in mind the catastrophic effect that the previous corruption investigation had on my life, my family's life, and my career, I would only undertake such a role if I could be guaranteed full protection and an undertaking that, bar witnessing a murder or serious assault, I would be unwilling to give evidence in a Crown Court.[62]

Wood agreed. And so Haslam began a precarious new life as a CHIS (covert human intelligence source) for Scotland Yard, returning to south London after nearly a decade away. He approached Rees and Fillery posing as a disgruntled ex-cop, knowing that they were always keen to exploit former officers who still had friends on the force.

Haslam started his undercover work not long before the Met launched Operation Nigeria, the third investigation into Daniel Morgan's murder. The surveillance devices police had installed at the offices of Southern Investigations had already picked up a number of leads and some of the conversations on the probes deeply alarmed those involved in the Morgan investigation. A report by one senior officer in the anti-corruption command said:

Rees and Fillery are a crucial link between the criminal fraternity and serving police officers. There is nothing that they do that in any way benefits the criminal justice system … I see the ongoing intrusion as crucial to our efforts to control corruption within the Met. Should we be able to prosecute Rees and Fillery for corruption matters, it will be seen within police circles as 'untouchables' having been touched.

Yet there was a contrasting dimension to Southern Investigations' activities that would carry the Morgan case in a surprising new direction. The largest client of Southern Investigations by far, according to the probes, was the *News of the World*, then Britain's biggest-selling newspaper, always desperate for agenda-setting scoops and widely known as the 'News of the Screws' for its enthusiasm in reporting the extramarital activities of public figures. Rees's main contact at the paper was a senior journalist named Alex Marunchak, who had known Rees and Fillery since the 1980s.[63]

In one year alone – 1996/97 – the *News of the World*, owned by Rupert Murdoch's News International, paid Southern Investigations more than £166,000.[64] Rees was a happy man. 'I tell you what I loved about the *News of the World*,' he once told me. 'It was the only paper that allowed people like me to play at being a detective. To go out and dig. To spend fortunes on equipment. To get involved in things … the *News of the World* offered that.'[65]

The police officers listening in to the chatter at Southern Investigations were appalled. Bob Quick, one of the detectives assigned to the Morgan case, later outlined how Rees's agency obtained confidential information from serving police officers in order to sell stories to newspapers. 'One of the journalists suspected was Alex Marunchak,' he said. 'During the operation it became clear that officers were being paid sums of between £500 and £2,000 for stories about celebrities, politicians and the royal family, as well as police investigations.'

Rees had built up quite the network.

By this time, Derek Haslam had befriended Rees and Fillery and was gaining an insight into their activities. He was alarmed to discover that Southern Investigations had a new subject under surveillance: the Met's then deputy commissioner, John Stevens. Unlike many senior Met officers, Stevens trained as a plain-clothes detective and once headed the Yard's murder squads. In 1998, he returned to the Met following senior positions at Hampshire, Cambridgeshire and Northumbria police forces. Throughout his career, Stevens was known for his legendary temper, but also as a 'copper's copper', passionately loyal to the organisation and those within it prepared to repay his trust.

Stevens's father had been a commercial pilot and he had inherited his love of flying. Rees was hired by the *News of the World* to establish whether the police chief was using taxpayer funds to fly a Met Police plane up to Northumbria to visit his mistress. It was classic *News of the World* territory, but there was no evidence that Stevens had a mistress or was using taxpayer funds to fly anywhere, and none ever emerged to support the allegations, but Haslam suspected at the time Southern Investigations would have wanted the information to use as leverage. Haslam told his handler: 'You'd better tell him they are on to him and they are looking at anything.'[66]

Rees rejects the idea that he sought to find compromising information on Stevens. When I asked him if he had the deputy commissioner put under surveillance, he phrased his answer warily: 'We were given instructions and an allegation that he was using a Met Police plane from Biggin Hill to see his mistress in Northumbria.

We did organise a surveillance team because it's what the *News of the World* wanted, and we had a team in Northumbria and here. But he never showed, so whether the allegation is true or not, who knows…'

Regardless of Rees's interest in Stevens, Haslam had strong views on Southern Investigations. He claims he told the Yard that Southern Investigations was breaking the law – often on behalf of the *News of the World*. Given the numerous breaches he was reporting back to his handlers, Haslam was astonished when no one was arrested. He eventually concluded that the reason was 'an unhealthy association between senior police officers and News International'.

In a confidential briefing sent to investigators, Haslam claims he told the Met that Southern Investigations was 'a corrupt organisation that was corrupting police officers and illegally accessing all sorts of confidential information'. He added: 'I told my handlers that MPs, ministers and Home Secretaries were targets. They fell into two categories, one they could earn money from and the other was to use blackmail, influence, to do their own thing. Anything that put the Met in a bad light.'[67]

When I put this to Rees he insisted that Haslam's allegations were 'nonsense'. He framed his activities in a radically different light, saying that Scotland Yard had asked Haslam to infiltrate his firm to invent 'blatant lies' and smear them at a time when they were bravely uncovering police corruption on behalf of the press:

Haslam was tasked by senior officers to … come in there and find out … what we were doing against CIB3 [the Met's anti-corruption command] … they knew we were investigating CIB3 … it was a force within a force, they were given total autonomy to do whatever they liked, their own accounts, their own finances. History tells us that when you allow policemen to do that it goes wrong ... if you let these squads run themselves it leads into trouble.[68]

Haslam claims that Alex Marunchak paid Southern Investigations to obtain confidential information from corrupt serving officers on celebrities and high-profile police chiefs. Apart from John Stevens, the roster of subjects reportedly included Tony Blair, the Duchess of Cambridge, Alastair Campbell, Jack Straw, Lord Mandelson and John Yates – a claim both Southern Investigations and Marunchak deny.* When asked about these allegations Marunchak replied that he had never commissioned Southern Investigations to commit illegal acts nor to obtain any confidential information relating to celebrities, politicians, the royal family or police investigations.

Perhaps the most shocking allegation from Haslam was that Southern Investigations burgled MPs' homes and photocopied documents in a bid to obtain embarrassing material they could sell to the *News of the World*. Rees denies he was ever involved in anything illegal. He said:

---

* The Daniel Morgan independent review would later reveal that the Met held prima facie evidence of corrupt payments to police officers by Southern Investigations regarding jobs commissioned by Marunchak: 'In February 2000, Metropolitan Police data revealed 273 instances in which journalists were provided with confidential police information by [Southern Investigations]. Of this total of 273 illegal transactions, 216 (79 per cent) involved various journalists from the Mirror Group and the remaining 21 per cent involved one journalist from the *News of the World*.

'The 273 instances can be divided into two categories:

1. those in which there was evidence of an offence, although a further search – including of journalists' records – was required to retrieve additional evidence; and
2. those where there was insufficient evidence at present, and a search warrant would be required to retrieve files.

Category 1 totalled eighty-one instances (30 per cent of instances) and category 2 totalled 192.

'Of the eighty-one instances in which there was prima facie evidence of an offence, seventy-five instances involved Mirror Group journalists; the names of fifty-seven of those journalists were not recorded. The six remaining instances involved the journalist Alex Marunchak of the *News of the World*.'

The allegations in that report are not true ... They knew it's not true, and the people who were instructing him didn't care. I think he was directed to make the worst report, the worst allegations he could. [Haslam] alleges that ... [Southern Investigations] burgled an MP's garage to remove a briefcase, photographed the contents of the briefcase and put that back ... that is a lie.

Later, he added: 'If there was one iota of evidence in there, [the Met] would have liked nothing better than to kick our door in and arrest us. They never did that, because there was no evidence there. It's in Haslam's fabricated reports ... it's smoke and mirrors.'[69]

In May 1999, the Met overheard something that did prompt them to act. Their surveillance picked up a plot to frame an innocent woman. Rees and his associates were paid £18,000 by a man called Simon James who wanted to discredit his estranged wife, Kim, and help him win custody of their child. There was a discussion with a detective constable, Tom Kingston, about burgling Kim James's flat. Then Sid Fillery suggested planting drugs in her car.

Another bent detective constable, Austin Warnes, was brought in to help with the fit-up. Warnes used to steal drugs during police raids, and sold criminals information about ongoing police investigations for up to £10,000.[70] Scotland Yard finally moved in. Rees and his associates were arrested and later jailed for perverting the course of justice. For reasons that remain unclear, the bugs were then removed from Southern Investigations' premises. The murder of Daniel Morgan remained unsolved.

The Met's surveillance applications were authorised by John Stevens himself. He later wrote about the corruption identified by Operation Nigeria in his autobiography.[71] Officers involved in the operation told me that Stevens was kept well briefed of the investigation throughout, including the involvement of Alex Marunchak and the *News of the World*. Stevens told an independent review of the case that he did not know Marunchak and, as far as he knew, he had never met him. This claim appears to be contradicted by Dick Fedorcio, the Met's former head of press, who claims that he had lunch with Stevens, Marunchak and his then editor, Rebekah Brooks, months after the conclusion of Operation Nigeria in 2000. Scotland Yard was no closer to solving the Daniel Morgan murder. But all those present that day would play recurring roles in the saga for years to come.

Rees is convinced that the Yard justified the secret surveillance by claiming that Southern Investigations might 'undermine the structure and the moral wellbeing of the Metropolitan Police ... or even bring it down'. Still seething with anger years later, Rees told me:

> We've got this poxy little firm of private investigators, half a dozen men, and suddenly they are alleging that we were going to bring down the Met Police. Good arguments to get your surveillance and come in and listen to what we are saying about them. They were abusing and using the process to see what we're doing against them. So a battle started ... things got very dirty indeed.[72]

Chapter 4

Above the Law?

Ashfaq Siddique is a well-trained liar. For years, it was his job to infiltrate drug trafficking gangs and organised paedophile rings as an undercover police officer working for the Metropolitan Police's covert SO10 unit. During those high-stakes operations, Siddique's life often depended on his ability to fool violent criminals into thinking that he, too, was a bona fide villain.

But it wasn't only criminals he fooled. His bosses at Scotland Yard proved just as vulnerable to his elaborate lies.

November 2002 was a busy month for undercover detectives engaged in several ongoing operations, including Siddique. One night he was required to purchase several kilograms of heroin from a drug dealer. A few days later Siddique was due to be deployed with his covert unit on what was subsequently described as a 'sensitive inquiry' in Portugal. But the mission was thrown into disarray when he approached his boss with a personal request.

Detective Superintendent Martin Smith, who was head of SO10 at the time, still remembers their conversation. 'Siddique contacted me and informed me that his niece, whom he felt responsible for, had been involved in a serious road traffic accident near Bournemouth. She was in a critical condition.'[1] Under the circumstances Siddique, who was from a prominent and close-knit Muslim family in east London, said he did not want to leave for Portugal. 'I immediately relieved him of his operational responsibilities,' Smith recalls, 'and allowed him whatever time and support he needed.'[2]

When Smith later discovered there had been no Bournemouth crash, he was furious. Siddique had lied in order to embark on a mission of his own. Far from being in a 'critical' condition, his niece, Sadhia Ahmed, then a sixteen-year-old schoolgirl, had eloped with her Albanian boyfriend, Fatjon Precaj, who was a Roman Catholic. Sadhia's family were apoplectic with rage. It fell to her uncle Siddique, the Scotland Yard detective with years of investigative experience, to look for the missing couple.

Days later, Precaj's body was found wrapped in a tarpaulin and dumped outside an industrial estate in Stratford, east London. It quickly became clear he was the victim of a so-called 'honour' killing, punished by Sadhia's family for enticing her away. The case made headlines in the UK, the Middle East and India. Sadhia's father, Mushtaq Ahmed – Ashfaq Siddique's brother-in-law – was later convicted of Precaj's death and sentenced to life imprisonment.

There the story might have ended. But twenty years later, new questions are being asked about the death of Fatjon Precaj – questions that have caused alarm in the highest ranks of the Metropolitan Police. The original exoneration of Ashfaq Siddique by those investigating the murder of Precaj and the subsequent finding by a Thames Valley Police inquiry that he had been unlawfully discriminated against have been called into question. The issues are now being reviewed by a former High Court judge, Sir John Mitting. They may well be found to be without substance, but if they are found by the judge to be believable, this will constitute one of the most serious scandals concerning the Metropolitan Police and will inevitably raise questions as to how this could have happened.

The background to this complex story begins more than fifty years ago, in the city of Mirpur in Pakistani-administered Kashmir, where Mushtaq Ahmed was born. One of twelve children, he was never taught to read or write, and worked from a young age to support his impoverished parents. Ahmed established a small sewing business in Pakistan but watched with envy as many of his contemporaries left Mirpur for Britain, in search of regular work. But when Ahmed's parents arranged a marriage to his cousin, Shaista Siddique, who lived in Barking, the young tailor found that he, too, had an opportunity to start a new life.

Shaista was the daughter of Ahmed's uncle, Mohammed Siddique, who has lived in the UK for more than fifty years. He has risen to become one of the most prominent Muslim community leaders in London. Siddique senior is on the board of the East London Mosque, one of the largest in Europe. Besides his role in the East London Mosque, Mohammed Siddique was for many years the chairman of the Al Madina Mosque in Barking and his leadership saw him made an honorary freeman of the London Borough of Barking and Dagenham. Ashfaq Siddique, the former undercover police officer, is Mohammed's son. He became Ahmed's brother-in-law when the tailor married his sister.

Ahmed, who moved to the UK in 1983 to be with his new wife, claims that the Siddiques arranged his wedding to Shaista because they had problems with her when she was growing up, and they believed the solution was to marry her off. 'My parents felt under pressure not to refuse this proposal; they wanted me to marry my cousin and to go to the UK as I would then be able to work, build a life, and financially support my family back in Pakistan,' he said.[3] 'This was considered a good opportunity and a good thing to do.'

Ahmed threw himself into his work and his abilities as a tailor helped him to establish a clothing company. Over time, it developed into a small factory in Ilford.

The couple had a daughter, Sadhia, and although he loves her dearly, Ahmed admits that his marriage was 'unhappy'. He had particular issues with his brother-in-law, who he claims 'likes to control others and show his power'.

'I always felt intimidated by him,' he claimed, adding:

> He behaved aggressively towards me, and towards others, using his status as a police officer to intimidate me and other people as well. He was a proud and arrogant man. He would often take out his police ID card and show it to me and to other people as well and many people complained about him doing this in such a way as to make them feel pressured and threatened.[4]

Police sources who knew Siddique during his time in the Met all agree that he was an immensely capable officer. He joined Scotland Yard in 1986 and quickly advanced to the CID, the elite unit of detectives who work on the most important and complex investigations. Intelligent and quick-witted, Siddique was later promoted into the National Crime Squad where he was responsible for two of its largest heroin seizures at that time. He first trained as an undercover officer in 1992, and in June 2000 was elevated to the undercover SO10 unit, proudly claiming to be its first 'visibly ethnic' officer. By the time of the Precaj murder two years later, Siddique had been commended eighteen times by senior Met chiefs.[5]

His niece, Sadhia, was sixteen when she met Precaj in 2002. He was raised in a small village outside the city of Shkodër, near Albania's northern border with Montenegro. Posing as a Yugoslavian asylum seeker, he travelled to the UK in October 1998 and eventually found work in Barking. Unfortunately for Precaj, this would place him in the orbit of the Ahmeds and the Siddiques.

According to police files, Sadhia's family were furious to discover that she was dating a Christian. Ahmed confirms this. He said that the Siddiques felt 'disgraced' by Sadhia's choice and were concerned that the relationship would cause them to 'lose respect within the community'. They tried to persuade her that Precaj was not the young man she thought him to be. According to police files, the family told Sadhia that Precaj was seeing other girls at the same time, and was also into drugs and prostitution.

Sadhia later told police that the family had expressed concern about the relationship. None of this pressure proved successful, however, and the young couple remained together. Matters finally came to a head when Sadhia and Precaj ran away for a second time on 29 October 2002. It was at this moment when Siddique lied to his boss about his niece being involved in a car crash in order to be able to look for them. Within days, he had somehow managed to track the couple to a YMCA in Bournemouth. Siddique dealt swiftly with this display of youthful insolence and the couple found themselves transported back to east London by the evening of Friday 8 November.

Over the next week, Precaj tried to convince Sadhia's family that he was serious about the relationship. He adopted an Islamic name, Rexhap Hasani, and offered to marry Sadhia in a *nikah* ceremony that he hoped would conform to their beliefs. It seemed to have an effect. Precaj was offered work in the clothing factory and, according to Ahmed, a wedding was hastily arranged for Saturday 16 November.

The night before the wedding, however, Precaj was brutally attacked in Ahmed's clothing factory. His badly beaten body was found a couple of days later, dumped carelessly on the side of

Carpenters Road, then a nondescript thoroughfare dotted with industrial estates. Today it is the main arterial route bisecting the Queen Elizabeth Olympic Park in Stratford, built to host the 2012 games. Precaj's feet and hands were bound, and a gag had been wrapped around his mouth. The post-mortem concluded Precaj died by asphyxiation.

The evidence against Ahmed was overwhelming. The police investigation quickly identified CCTV footage that showed Ahmed's white van in the area where the body was found. When it was seized, forensic investigators discovered Precaj's blood inside. The cloth that was used to tie Precaj up was also traced back to Ahmed's factory. At his trial, the factory owner declined to give evidence and pleaded guilty to manslaughter. But the jury found him guilty of murder. Ahmed was sentenced to life imprisonment.

Outside the court, John McDonald, one of the investigating officers, said:

> Rexhap was clearly murdered because his girlfriend's father disapproved of their relationship. They wanted to marry and Ahmed couldn't face the thought of his daughter being with an Albanian asylum seeker, who in his eyes was not suitable.
>
> This result will again demonstrate that 'honour'-type killings will not be tolerated and will be investigated as thoroughly as any other murder.

Ahmed's conviction was a huge success for Scotland Yard. Investigations into 'honour killings' in the UK are notoriously difficult, with the communities affected often suspicious of the police and unwilling to co-operate.

Eighteen years after the conviction, however, the Met was

horrified to learn that Ahmed was now prepared to give a very different account of how the Albanian was killed. His version of events raises disturbing new questions about the Metropolitan Police. A long-running and ongoing judge-led public inquiry into undercover policing chaired by Sir John Mitting now has to determine where the truth lies. In a witness statement which has been handed to the inquiry, Ahmed claims that Siddique was 'fully involved' in the death of Fatjon Precaj. He says he was not directly involved himself but does admit that he was present during the fatal attack on the Albanian. Ahmed alleges that two men were guilty of the crime: Siddique and another Asian man who was also a Metropolitan Police officer. He says that he kept quiet for years as he was 'afraid' of Siddique, and feared that speaking out would have 'consequences' for his family in the UK and in Pakistan.

'I was scared. I was shocked. I did not know how to deal with things,' he says. 'I have always been worried in case I gave information to the police which would not be acted upon because it concerns a police officer.'[6]

* * *

On the day of the 'honour killing', Ahmed says he made a return trip from London to Sheffield, to deliver clothes to a customer. He claims he arrived back at his factory in the early evening to find Precaj alone with Siddique and another friend from the police. According to Ahmed, they then severely beat Precaj, kicking him while shouting 'We are going to teach you a lesson'. 'When they tied [Precaj's] hands and feet I said to them "Leave him" and Siddique said in English, "You are stupid, you don't know what's going on." Precaj's eyes were very big and his lips were swollen.'[7]

Ahmed claims the men then decided to leave Precaj in the factory overnight. Siddique's plan was apparently to force Precaj into the back of a friend's lorry the next day, ferry him across the Channel, and dump him in France. It was hoped that the Albanian's uncertain immigration status would prevent him from returning to the UK, and Sadhia.

But when Ahmed returned to the factory the next morning he discovered that the plan had backfired with fatal consequences. During the night, a clothing rail draped in plastic had fallen on Precaj. Badly injured and with his hands and feet bound tightly together, the Albanian could not remove the material from around his face, and he had suffocated.

At this point, Ahmed admits he panicked, 'I was very upset about what had happened, my brain was not working,' he says in his statement. 'I was afraid to let Ashfaq take control of Rex's body once I discovered he was dead. I did not want the body to be destroyed or dumped where he would never be found. In Islam, the body must be preserved and protected until ready for burial.'[8] Ahmed wrapped the body in a tarpaulin and left it in a place where it would be discovered by the authorities. 'I didn't know what was going to happen to Precaj,' he said. 'Because of what Ashfaq Siddique and his friend did, everything went upside down.'[9]

The new claims over the Precaj murder did not come entirely out of the blue for Scotland Yard. Days after the discovery of the body, Siddique had been identified by the investigating officers as a close family member with a possible motive.

His dishonesty did not help. According to Martin Smith, the head of the undercover unit, Siddique appeared in his office around the time of Precaj's death and confessed to lying about his whereabouts in the run-up to the crime. 'He told me that there had been no road traffic accident, and that he had been trying to locate his niece who had run away with her boyfriend,' said Smith. 'I recall showing my annoyance at being lied to … I told him that he owed the whole office an apology as they had all been very concerned, and some visibly upset.'[10]

Murder squad detectives were soon searching Siddique's desk at SO10 and, behind the scenes, his potential involvement in the 'honour killing' had reached the very highest levels of the Met. A gold group – a meeting of senior officers which is established during a crisis – was formed at New Scotland Yard because of the potential involvement of a serving police officer in a murder.[11]*

The investigating officers were initially suspicious when they discovered that Siddique had switched his phone off around the time of the killing, which meant that the police were unable to locate his whereabouts by tracking the cell site data – a key weapon in the armoury of the modern detective. Furthermore, evidence collected from seven witnesses prompted police to arrest Siddique and interview him under caution. One witness, Maznur Rahman, said that Precaj had claimed that the 'uncle who was a policeman did not like the relationship and was looking for him'. Rahman also said that he had received a phone call from the uncle, who had 'threatened to beat him up' if he did not disclose Precaj's location when he was missing.[12]

Preng Precaj, a London-based uncle of the deceased, also told police that Fatjon had once been stopped by the 'policeman uncle' in the street. 'At the same time, a car containing black males pulled up and took a photo of Precaj then handed it to the uncle,' he said. 'The uncle said: "Now I even have got your photo. If we see you

---

* Siddique has always strongly denied any such involvement and was subsequently exonerated by Thames Valley Police and received compensation.

again with our girl, we'll kill you.'" A Bournemouth resident who has never met or communicated with Preng Precaj offered some corroboration for this line of enquiry. She told murder detectives that the 'uncle' who was searching for the runaways had shown her a 'polaroid photo' of the love-struck Albanian.[13]

Preng Precaj added that he had briefly given the couple shelter on another occasion when the 'policeman uncle had been chasing them, and they were scared of him'.[14] Four other witnesses who knew Fatjon Precaj also made statements that alleged he had previously complained of threats or harassment by his girlfriend's 'uncle' or 'police officer uncle'.[15]

To top it all off, police files show that Scotland Yard received an anonymous phone call during the inquiry that alleged Siddique used to boast that 'if he wanted to kill someone he could get away with it' as he 'knows the right people'.

Precaj's father lived 1,700 miles away in Albania but had heard enough to also be suspicious of Siddique. At the conclusion of Ahmed's trial, when the officer in the case, DS Gary Staples, travelled to Shkodër to brief the victim's family, he found the father 'puzzled as to how the daughter's uncle, the policeman, remained unpunished'. 'He explained that his son had frequently phoned him upset and distressed, telling him how the girl's uncle was continually harassing and threatening him,' said Staples.[16]

* * *

The historical evidence against Siddique, coupled with Ahmed's new testimony, have led some to question whether senior officers had protected a Muslim police officer. And why, whatever the strength of the allegations about Ashfaq's involvement in these events, his overall conduct as a serving police officer had not been fully investigated. Yet this appears incongruous with the findings of the Macpherson inquiry, which labelled the Met 'institutionally racist'. In such a poisonous climate, why would a Muslim officer be afforded kid gloves treatment? And why were these allegations not fully investigated, whatever the facts of the matter? The truth is that the issue of race inside the Met is complex. Many ethnic minority officers undoubtedly suffer appalling discrimination. But, in the wake of Macpherson, some have also said that managers turn a blind eye to allegations of misconduct by black or Asian officers, for fear of being labelled racist.

Javaria Saeed, a practising Muslim who worked in Scotland Yard's counter-terrorism division, complained to her bosses after she witnessed a fellow Muslim officer saying female genital mutilation – illegal in the UK since 1985 – was a 'clean and honourable practice' and 'shouldn't be criminalised'.[17] The same officer also said that female victims of domestic violence should resolve their cases in a sharia court. Saeed, a former detective sergeant, says that another Met officer openly supported the Taliban. She says her colleagues said she was labelled a 'bad Muslim' for not wearing a hijab and told she was 'better off at home looking after your husband'.[18]

But when Saeed raised these comments with senior officers they failed to take any action because they were afraid of being accused of racism. She resigned from the Met in 2016 after becoming disheartened by 'political correctness', which she says allowed an 'us and them' culture to thrive among some Muslim officers.[19] 'Racism in the Met is not from white officers in my case, but from Muslim officers who the service refused to properly investigate because they were afraid of being called Islamophobic and racist,' she told the *Sunday Times* in 2016.[20] 'My experiences were that it was Muslim officers being racist towards my individual views; also in private, holding racist views against white officers, and sexist views against females. If such views were held and expressed by white officers, they would be fired.' Saeed's career appears to have been unaffected by her whistleblowing; she now works in the counter-extremism division of the Home Office.[21]

A Met detective chief inspector told me he received intelligence in 2007 that suggested criminal gangs were intentionally trying to corrupt ethnic minority officers inside Scotland Yard, because they were seen as above the law. 'We were told this by an informant inside a major organised crime group,' said David McKelvey, who retired in 2010. 'They were seen as untouchable as a result of the findings of the Macpherson inquiry. The Met would never investigate them as they were seen as too politically sensitive.'[22]

The most infamous police officer to take advantage of such nervousness was Ali Dizaei, nicknamed the 'Teflon Commander'. For nearly three decades, the disgraced Met officer considered himself above the law and played the race card in an attempt to silence his critics.

In 1997, while Dizaei was still at Thames Valley Police, a Scotland Yard informant alleged that he was involved in drugs, subverting court cases for money, and using prostitutes. The allegations were never substantiated and no disciplinary action was taken. In the wake of the Macpherson report in 1999, Dizaei applied to become a superintendent in the Met, which at the time was desperate to present a more ethnically diverse leadership. He was appointed even though deputy assistant commissioner Barbara Wilding described him after his interview as the most arrogant man she had ever met.[23]

In September 1999, Operation Helios, a multi-million-pound investigation into Dizaei's integrity, was launched. Intercepted communications from the inquiry demonstrated that he was no ordinary police officer. Dizaei was monitored associating with a conman and four major criminals suspected of money laundering. Surveillance also suggested that he took £800 from a man on bail, in apparent exchange for help with a drink-driving charge. Other wire-taps revealed unauthorised links with a number of embassies. Dizaei apparently stood to gain £2 million by brokering the £24 million sale of the Ethiopian embassy in London. Further diplomatic concerns touched directly on national security. Dizaei had contacts with senior staff in the Iranian embassy and sometimes drove a Liberian embassy car with diplomatic plates.[24]

Damning telephone messages that Dizaei left to an Iranian ex-lover, Mandy Darougheh, were also recovered. She had split up with the police officer after discovering he was married. Dizaei's reaction, left on her voicemail, was recorded by Helios. 'I will take such revenge from you, that like a dog, you will be sorry that you will never treat me like this again,' he warned:

Mandy, I am going to declare war on you and I have declared it as of now. See what I will do to you. From now on you are dead. I will start with your mum first. I am so emotionally disturbed now that anything is possible from me.

I give you an hour and see what I will do to you. If you think I am worried about my career, to get back at you, you must be joking. Just remember what I did to ******'s [name unknown] husband. You are not safe. I am going to come and catch you, on my mother's life. If you are at home, get out because if I see you, I am going to lose it right now.

You want war, bitch, you're going to get some war. You will see now what I can do so you will cry for years. First I will start with your family, then I come to you and your reputation. I will spread all over London that you are a prostitute.[25]

At Dizaei's eventual trial, even his barrister, Michael Mansfield QC, admitted: 'No police officer, no human being, should be talking like that. We all make mistakes, but it's unacceptable.'[26]

To the consternation of the Helios team, Dizaei was found not guilty. Other fraud charges were formally dropped by the prosecution in September 2003. But Helios had exposed appalling errors of judgement if not gross misconduct and nine serious disciplinary matters were still outstanding. Dizaei thought the best form of defence was to attack. Helios, he said, had been a 'racist witch hunt' and launched a claim for discrimination.

David Blunkett, the Home Secretary, reportedly panicked. Nearing retirement, Met commissioner John Stevens also did not want his 'legacy' tainted by a race war.[27] All disciplinary matters were dropped. Dizaei was returned to duty, given £80,000 compensation and fast-tracked for promotion. Stevens said: 'The investigation of Superintendent Dizaei highlighted some areas where his conduct fell far below the standards expected of a police officer. He has already publicly expressed his regret for these and acknowledged the lessons he has learned.' The commissioner then added, to the concern of the anti-corruption unit: 'Superintendent Dizaei is returning to the Met with his integrity demonstrably intact.'[28]

Scotland Yard may have backed down, but Dizaei continued to attack the Met for racism, even as he was promoted to commander. The counter-offensive began to unravel in 2008, however, when he got into a row in the street with a young businessman. Dizaei arrested Waad al-Baghdadi and accused him of assault. But CCTV evidence proved that the Met commander had attacked the young Iraqi first, before attempting to frame him. Dizaei was branded a 'criminal in uniform' and found guilty of perverting the course of justice in February 2010. Since his release from jail, Dizaei has maintained murky associations. In 2018, he was pictured in the back of a Rolls-Royce with a suspected money launderer with connections to Terry Adams, the head of the notorious north London crime family.[29]

Police fears about accusations of racism are far from confined to the Met. Over the past decade, investigative journalists have exposed the systematic targeting and sexual abuse of teenage girls by groups of men who were largely of south Asian origin. It has emerged that police across the country had failed for years to take any action against the criminals for fear of being labelled racist.

In 2014, an independent review concluded that 1,400 children from the Yorkshire town of Rotherham were subjected for sixteen years to 'appalling levels of crime and abuse' by organised groups of men. The identified offenders were 'almost all' of Pakistani heritage.[30] Once the media broke the story, prosecutions against similar gangs were mounted in Rochdale, Oxford, Telford, Burnley, High Wycombe, Leicester, Dewsbury, Peterborough, Halifax and Newcastle upon Tyne. Former detective Maggie Oliver, who helped expose the Rochdale grooming ring, said the country had suffered an 'epidemic of this kind of abuse' because 'protective agencies chose not to address this particular kind of sexual crime because of the ethnicity of the perpetrators'.[31]

* * *

The case of Ashfaq Siddique may prove equally controversial. The potential involvement of a detective in an 'honour killing' is one of the most serious allegations ever levelled at a police officer in the UK, and the enormity of the situation has not been lost on Scotland Yard. Even if the allegations are found to be without substance, very serious issues arise as to how the investigation was handled by the police. Cressida Dick, the Met commissioner, personally requested a full briefing on the implications of the case when she first heard of Mushtaq Ahmed's new claims in 2019. They are now being scrutinised by the long-running public inquiry into undercover policing, led by Sir John Mitting. The then Home Secretary, Theresa May, announced its formation in March 2015, and said she was 'profoundly shocked' at the revelations emerging from one of the Met's most secretive units. These included undercover police officers having sexual relationships with unwitting targets, and detectives stealing the identities of dead children. Siddique's alleged involvement in the death of Fatjon Precaj, however, is by far the most disturbing claim against an undercover police officer and, if proven, would elevate the scandal to a new level. Lawyers examining Ahmed's claims on Mitting's behalf are aware of the implications. An inquiry source said the allegations are of 'immense interest' and sound 'relevant' to the inquiry's 'terms of reference'.

It should not be forgotten, however, that Ahmed is a convicted murderer, with the sharpest of axes to grind. Criminals frequently make bogus allegations against police officers in an attempt to undermine investigations, collapse prosecutions, or simply to cause trouble. Ahmed makes no secret of his dislike of Siddique and may also harbour a personal vendetta against his brother-in-law. But what makes the Precaj case unique is that the convicted murderer has received some measure of support from the very investigating officers who led the original investigation – and who helped to put Ahmed behind bars.

In 2002, Steve Hobbs was a detective chief inspector attached to the murder command based at Edmonton police station in north

London when Precaj's bruised body was found on Carpenters Road. Hobbs, one of the Met's most experienced detectives, who led more than 200 murder inquiries during his thirty-three years in the force, became the senior investigating officer. He, DS Gary Staples, the case officer, and Martin Smith, Siddique's then boss at SO10, all now believe their former colleague may have a case to answer. They have each submitted witness statements to Ahmed's solicitors for submission to the public inquiry. Hobbs says Ahmed's allegations have 'some measure of credibility' and is calling for a fresh review of the forensic evidence that his team first seized back in 2002.[32] Staples, who worked in the Met for thirty-two years, also believes that the convicted murderer's version of events is 'credible and worthy of further investigation'.[33] In the summary of Ahmed's submission to the public inquiry, his lawyer, Stephen Kamlish QC, states: 'As far as we are aware, this is unprecedented.'[34]

Both Hobbs and Staples say they were always of the view that Ahmed, a slight and unassuming man, must have had assistance in the attack on Precaj, who was very fit, and used to box regularly at a gym. The former police officers are also taken with Ahmed's new claims about Siddique's alleged plan to forcibly remove Precaj from the UK in a friend's lorry. SO10 owned and ran its own lorry company with a fleet of large vehicles on standby for covert operations.[35] Hobbs said he is aware that his former colleague had 'extensive experience in international covert operations' and would 'probably have the knowledge and skills to arrange this type of transportation had he been minded to do so'.[36]

Back in 2002, as the police inquiry unfolded, the situation for Siddique had initially looked pretty bleak. But before Ahmed made his allegations, the police had no direct evidence that Siddique was involved in the killing. One crucial factor also weighed in his favour.

He had an alibi. Siddique claimed that he was on the other side of London on the night of Precaj's death – and his story was supported by a young female police officer who, according to Hobbs, was 'aspiring to become involved in undercover police work'.[37] The veteran detective said that the female officer had stated she had joined Siddique at a covert police flat in the Docklands area on the night of the murder, before the pair travelled to have dinner at Sarastro, a lively Turkish restaurant in Covent Garden.[38]

An independent review of the case would later criticise Siddique for the 'potential compromise of the covert flat', which could have 'jeopardised live operations' and the 'safety and welfare of the operatives' that regularly used it.[39] However, the alibi was pivotal and the Crown Prosecution Service advised the police not to charge Siddique with any involvement in the 'honour killing'. At the time, it seemed he was in the clear.

In light of Ahmed's new disclosures, Hobbs now believes that some other evidence needs to be revisited by the public inquiry. He points out that, at one point, Siddique claimed that his mobile phone was switched off at 6 p.m. while he was in the restaurant in Drury Lane. However, on another occasion, Siddique stated that he was still in the covert police flat in the Docklands at 6 p.m. 'waiting for his female friend to arrive'.

'This is a severe contradiction at a crucial time for the investigation,' said Hobbs. 'It should be remembered that Siddique has a very sound understanding of the relevance of cell site analysis and could have been capable of manipulation of his story of events to suit that material.'[40]

The reopening of the Precaj case will likely infuriate Siddique, who retired from the Metropolitan Police in 2017 and has decided to follow in his father's footsteps. He has taken a very public role at the

Al Madina Mosque, which can attract as many as 9,000 worshippers from across east London. He remains an influential member of the Muslim community and in 2015 hosted an inter-faith meeting where he was pictured with Theresa May at a London mosque. But some in the Met have always remained suspicious about Siddique's role in the Precaj 'honour killing'.

At the time, the furore around the case caused Siddique to be ejected from the undercover unit. In his report recommending the expulsion, Martin Smith said: 'Retention of the officer is clearly untenable … and his transfer within the Met will be accompanied by his removal from the National Index of Undercover Officers.'[41] But the decision promptly blew up in the Yard's face. After he was transferred, Siddique threatened to launch a claim for racial discrimination. He sent senior officers a detailed report about his alleged mistreatment at the hands of his colleagues, which was referred to an outside force, Thames Valley, to investigate.

The report may provide an explanation for the rancour against Siddique that still lingers. It includes claims that the Muslim officer twice had bananas thrown at him and suffered the indignity of a colleague mimicking an ape in front of him. Siddique claims he was repeatedly called a 'P**i', was told by one colleague that he would 'get lost in a pile of shit' because his 'skin colour would blend with it', and was once called 'Osama bin Laden', the terrorist mastermind who launched the 9/11 attacks in 2001.[42]

It is understood that shortly after Siddique lodged complaints with the Met, the force reached an out-of-court settlement with him, which included a confidentiality agreement. The final bill to the taxpayer, including the gagging clause, is reckoned to come to more than £400,000. If Siddique is ever formally implicated in the murder of Precaj, it is a payout that would embarrass the Met.

His former boss Smith is still not a fan. 'Siddique lied not only at the time in respect of the accident when there was no need to, especially given the relationship that we both had, but he further lied and manipulated facts in order to support a claim against the Metropolitan Police,' he said.[43]

Thames Valley disagreed with Smith. Its review concluded that Siddique was mistreated because he had been moved from the undercover role, which was seen as an over-reaction that could not be justified given that he had been cleared over the murder. 'Detective Sergeant Siddique was wrong to lie [to Smith] and he quite rightly received words of advice, but he also lost his job,' said the Thames Valley Police report.

Back in Pakistan, Mushtaq Ahmed's family believe he was unfairly blamed by Siddique and the incident still causes tensions within the family. In 2014, Ahmed's brother Khalid became embroiled in a dispute with Siddique's London-based father, Mohammed, over a property in Pakistan. The row became heated. In a remarkably frank and sinister letter to his troublesome relative, Mohammed Siddique warned Khalid that he seemed to have 'forgotten what I did with your brother Mushtaq', adding menacingly: 'Maybe you want that I treat you same?'

'Today I want to tell you: listen with your ears open, you may not be aware of my power,' he wrote. 'I can destroy your life like I did to your brother and he is gone to jail for life. I could get you locked up as well.'

At the time of the letter, dated 13 August 2014, Mohammed's son Ashfaq Siddique was still serving in the Metropolitan Police – a role that Mohammed seemed to believe might be of use. 'My son is in the UK police,' he warned. 'He can destroy you and your whole family.'[44]

Chapter 5

Sabotage

Detective Chief Superintendent David Cook had been out walking his dog when he returned home to find two vans parked outside his house. The gruff Scotsman thought nothing of it until the next morning when one of the vehicles followed him as he drove his two-year-old son to nursery. It reappeared on his tail when he took his five-year-old daughter to school. Cook's instincts kicked into gear. He had led numerous inquiries into murders and organised crime and was no stranger to suspicious behaviour. Keeping an eye on his rear-view mirror, the policeman took a long route back to his home in Surrey. The van followed him all the way. Cook knew he was under surveillance.

The detective alerted his superiors and a covert Met team was swiftly deployed to investigate. The unit tasked a uniformed team to stop one of the vans on the pretext of a broken tail light. When he was questioned, the driver revealed he was a photographer for the *News of the World*. The van's registration number was traced back to News International (NI), the tabloid's parent company and the UK arm of Rupert Murdoch's global media empire.[1]

It's not a crime to drive around Surrey, so the police let the van go. Soon, it was back outside Cook's house, its occupant brazenly snapping away with his camera.[2]

Why was the 'News of the Screws' suddenly interested in Cook? The only possible explanation seemed to be the policeman's appearance on national television a few days earlier. It was June 2002 and the superintendent had been introduced to millions of viewers of BBC1's *Crimewatch* as the head of yet another investigation into the Daniel Morgan axe murder. Jonathan Rees, the late man's former business partner, remained the prime suspect in the case, along with several associates. Appearing on *Crimewatch*, Cook said the identity of the murderers was 'the worst-kept secret in south London' and offered £50,000 as a reward for witnesses who came forward. He told viewers that police already knew the identity of the man who had split Morgan's skull with the axe. Cook also claimed that police knew the getaway driver, the make of the getaway car and where it had been stored overnight.[3] They knew all these things, but seemed to lack the evidence required to press charges.

Two days after his appearance on TV, Cook was summoned to a meeting with his bosses. He was told that police had intercepted a call between Sid Fillery, the former detective sergeant who had set up shop with Rees at Southern Investigations, and Alex Marunchak, the ex-*News of the World* crime reporter who was now editing the Sunday tabloid's Irish edition. Marunchak had known Fillery since the 1980s. Rees and Fillery had both been valuable sources of stories for Marunchak during his crime-reporting days.

Cook was told that police officers listening to the intercepted call heard Fillery and Marunchak 'exploring ways to discredit' him.[4] The journalist then contacted a London-based colleague, Greg Miskiw, the assistant editor of the *News of the World*. Marunchak asked Miskiw to put surveillance on Cook and a woman named Jacqui Hames, another former police officer who had started a new career as a presenter on *Crimewatch*. The reason Marunchak gave for the expensive newspaper surveillance operation was wholly in keeping with the *NotW*'s interest in the sexual arrangements of people in the public eye. Marunchak told Miskiw that Cook and Hames were having an affair. They were, of sorts. They had been married for years, with two children – a detail Marunchak failed to mention.[5]

Much later, giving evidence to the Leveson inquiry, Hames commented that the supposed purpose of the surveillance was 'utterly nonsensical', adding: 'I believe that the real reason for the *News of the World* placing us under surveillance was that suspects in the Daniel Morgan murder inquiry were using their association with a powerful and well-resourced newspaper to try to intimidate us and so attempt to subvert the investigation.'[6]

The Met witness protection team visited Cook's home and installed covert CCTV cameras around the property.[7] The experience was particularly painful for Hames. She had been a close friend of Jill Dando, a former *Crimewatch* presenter who was shot dead in 1999 on her doorstep in Fulham, west London. Dando's death prompted a massive police investigation, but the case remains unsolved more than twenty years later. A year after Dando's murder, Cook and Hames's house had been ransacked by unknown intruders, adding to the family's sense of unease. Now there were vans parked outside the house, Hames knew she was being watched and her children were being followed to school.

Rees, Fillery and their associates had reason to be nervous about the new inquiry into Morgan's murder, codenamed Operation Abelard. In 2002, Rees was still in prison, serving a sentence for perverting the course of justice. Intelligence reports from inside the prison suggested that the disgraced private detective was furious at the continuing campaign of Morgan's grief-stricken brother,

Alastair. The reports noted that Rees thought Alastair was 'causing more problems' and that he might have to 'take steps to sort him out once and for all'. When I asked Rees about this, he said that he merely planned to sue Alastair for libel.

The Abelard inquiry had been triggered by a new lead. Police heard from one of their most valuable informers – a supergrass named Steve Warner – that another man, Jimmy Cook (no relation to DCS Cook), was the getaway driver on the night of Morgan's murder.[8] At the time the new inquiry was announced on *Crimewatch*, the police had already installed bugs in the suspects' homes and cars, to see if the revival of the Morgan investigation would trigger underworld 'chatter'. The night before the broadcast, the listening devices picked up Glenn Vian, long suspected of wielding the axe on Rees's behalf, anxiously saying he would 'get life or twenty years'.[9]

Immediately after the programme, Jimmy Cook went out to his car and made a phone call, in which he discussed the reward money on offer for information. He seemed to make a reference to Sid Fillery: 'Fifty grand! One was a copper who works there now. They're going to need proper evidence.' The bug also picked up his concern that the police now had a knowledgeable new inform- ant who might give evidence in court. 'They have to fucking stand in the dock and fucking point the finger, ain't they?' the alleged getaway driver complained. 'They can't do us by just a little bit of verbal, they have to go sit in the dock.'[10]

Operation Abelard also made progress with a man called Barry Nash, who was thought to have stored the getaway vehicle for Jimmy Cook. Nash was arrested in October 2002 and told police he was visited by Cook on the night of the murder. Nash claimed that Cook admitted to standing over Daniel's body while the axe was embedded in his face.[11]

Hours after Nash's arrest, Marunchak attempted to contact Fillery on six occasions in a forty-minute period.[12] Jimmy Cook also visited some family friends, Gwen and John Sturm, who he had known for thirty-five years. Their conversation, relayed to the police by the bug in his car, appeared to indicate that they were concocting an alibi. Cook and the Sturms were later arrested for conspiracy to pervert the course of justice. Cook refused to comment in his police interview.[13]

The Abelard team also managed to 'flip' another former Met detective who worked at Southern Investigations. Richard 'Boris' Zdrojewski didn't know anything about the Morgan murder, but he was able to shed more light on the relationship between the PI agency and the Murdoch empire. In his witness statement to police, he claimed one 'particularly memorable job' was when Southern Investigations 'fitted up' a police officer for a *News of the World* story. Zdrojewski had arranged to meet a chief inspector in a McDonald's car park with some information on a bogus crime. Zdrojewski told the team that he 'shoved [the papers] into his hands. He was photographed and his photo and report appeared in the *News of the World* to look like he was taking a bribe.'[14]

'It is a ridiculous allegation … it's nonsense,' Rees told me, claiming it was yet another smear invented by police to discredit him. 'The truth is that we were serving an injunction on a senior police officer who happened to be the head of the domestic violence unit … we were serving an injunction from his wife because of domestic violence on her … that was a story.'[15]

After his encounter with the *News of the World* vans, DCS David Cook started digging into Southern Investigations' relationship with the paper. In August 2002, he obtained new statements from Bryan Madagan, a veteran private eye and Daniel Morgan's former employer. Madagan alleged what Cook already suspected: that Morgan was trying to sell a story about police corruption to Fleet Street just before he was murdered. Madagan also claimed to be able to identify the journalist Morgan had approached: the *News of the World*'s Alex Marunchak.[16] Then, from the unlikeliest of quarters, came a startling new revelation. Rees's long-term girlfriend, Margaret Harrison, had been with Daniel hours before he was murdered. It turned out that she was sexually involved with both Rees and Morgan.[17] Harrison also claimed that Daniel had told her 'he was going to sell a story to the newspaper'.[18] The claims that Morgan had been looking to sell a story on police corruption were later reviewed at a public inquiry and dismissed, mainly on the basis that no journalist had come forward to support this claim.

Harrison's relations with both the murder victim and the prime suspect provided another possible motive. Soon, the police had more evidence to suggest that it might well have been a factor in Morgan's death. When Operation Abelard was launched in 2002, Met Police chiefs discovered that Glenn Vian's nephew, Dean, had recently joined Scotland Yard. 'I remember being really pissed off that he passed the vetting,' said one officer involved. 'I know people want the police to be diverse, but villains as well? I think that strikes me as taking diversity a little too far!'[19]

Dean Vian was duly arrested and questioned about his knowledge of the Morgan murder. In a statement, he said his mother had told him that Rees had paid his uncle Glenn to kill Daniel. 'Glenn was struggling financially and he was desperate,' said Dean. 'It is hearsay but I believe it to be true.' His mother also told him 'that Jonathan Rees and Daniel Morgan had had a falling out because they were both seeing the same woman'.[20]

Rees dismisses the suggestion that he had been cuckolded by

his partner and was out for revenge. 'Some people might want to make something of that, but in the greater story, it's meaningless.' Alastair Morgan is similarly unconvinced, saying: 'Jealousy is not a motive for an axe murder.'[21] Dean Vian was never charged with any offence but his family connections were deemed too risky, and he was sacked. Meanwhile, David Cook and his team intensified their scrutiny of the Marunchak connection between the *News of the World* and Southern Investigations.

On 27 August 2002, Cook's deputy, Neil Hibberd, sent an urgent request to Andy Hayman, then head of the Met's anti-corruption command, urging him to investigate the financial relationship between Marunchak and Rees's firm. Hayman never responded to the request. The following evening, Rebekah Brooks, the editor of the *News of the World*, met Sir John Stevens, now Met commissioner, at the Ivy Club. Two weeks later, they met for a second dinner at the same location.[22]

Brooks seemed to play an increasing role in the Daniel Morgan saga thanks to her close relationship with senior officers at the Metropolitan Police. Brooks was a world-class networker, a potent cocktail of clear-eyed ruthlessness and dazzling charm. It wasn't just the management board of Scotland Yard who fell under her spell. She also enjoyed close friendships with Tony Blair and later David Cameron while Rupert Murdoch came to view Brooks as a member of his own family.

Despite Brooks's connections, David Cook was determined not to let the matter of the *News of the World* surveillance rest. He repeatedly raised his concerns with his bosses, who eventually relented and agreed to do something about it. A meeting was arranged in January 2003 between Cook, his commander Andre Baker, Rebekah Brooks and Dick Fedorcio, the Met's head of press.

In the lift up to the sixth floor, Cook recalled, he was warned by a senior officer that 'the boss' – which he took to mean Sir John Stevens – did not want trouble with the *News of the World*. (Stevens later denied giving any such indication and noted 'the boss' could have been a reference to any senior officer.)[23] He was undeterred. When the meeting began, Cook told Brooks about the surveillance of his family home. He briefed her about the material picked up by police listening devices, including Rees's boasts of possible 'backhanders' paid to Marunchak. Cook also mentioned a witness statement given by an employee of Southern Investigations, Marjorie Williams, who claimed that the agency paid private school fees for Marunchak's children and paid off his credit card debts.[24] (Marunchak has always denied the allegation.[25])

Brooks was unmoved. She defended Marunchak, saying that since he had been promoted to edit the Irish edition, sales had gone up and he was doing a fine job.[26] As for the surveillance, Brooks repeated the claim that Cook and Hames were suspected of having an affair with each other – even though they were married with two children, and a profile of them had appeared in *Hello!* magazine. Fedorcio said later that he took Brooks from the meeting with Cook straight to a drinks party at Scotland Yard, where he left her talking to the commissioner, John Stevens.[27]

Some in the Met were concerned about Stevens's apparent relationship with the *News of the World* – and with Alex Marunchak in particular. We have already seen that Stevens was kept informed of the earlier investigation into Morgan's murder linking Marunchak to Rees and Fillery, yet according to Met Police records he had lunch with Brooks and Marunchak in 2000, not long after that inquiry – Operation Nigeria – was wound up. During my conversations with Rees, he let slip a disturbing claim about his old friend Marunchak, seeking to raise further questions about Stevens's role. The garrulous private eye told me that the former Met commissioner was a 'good source for Marunchak', adding: 'They were always going out on a regular basis.' When told that Stevens was adamant he had only met Marunchak once, at the lunch with Brooks in 2000, Rees replied: 'Did he really?' Stevens has always denied knowing Marunchak and there is no independent evidence to support Rees's claim.

Marunchak certainly seemed to live a charmed life. One police intelligence report from the Morgan murder investigation noted: 'Marunchak is still highly thought of by Murdoch and can do no wrong.'[28] Rees also told me that reporter and proprietor were personally close. 'Some people [at the *News of the World*] tried to stab Alex in the back and Rupert Murdoch [stopped it],' Rees said. 'Rupert Murdoch loved Alex Marunchak because he got good stories.'[29]

Compelling though this was, it didn't seem to be getting the Abelard inquiry any closer to solving the murder of Daniel Morgan. There were so many odd threads to unravel, so many holes in witness statements and so many dark alleys to explore. At almost every turn the inquiry was sidetracked by discoveries that were sufficiently alarming to require a police response, yet seemed to have little to do with the main purpose of the investigation.

When Fillery was under surveillance, for example, police officers noticed he made frequent trips from his office to a public lavatory, where he would spend a considerable amount of time before returning to work.[30] Suspecting wrongdoing, police arrested Fillery and seized his work computers. They found that he had accessed porn sites with unambiguous names such as 'schoolboy/schoolgirl anal', 'sicko porn/sicko anal' and 'hot naked boys'. Police found graphic images on his hard drive and he was charged with fifteen counts of making indecent images of children.[31] He later pleaded guilty at Bow Street magistrates' court, but avoided jail when the judge took into account his previous 'good character' and gave him a three-year community rehabilitation order. She was told nothing of his previous history.[32] It was a long way from an axe murder in a London pub car park.

In September 2003, the Crown Prosecution Service decided that no charges could be brought for Daniel's murder, to the anguish of Alastair Morgan and the rest of the family. From a prosecutorial standpoint, the case was holed below the waterline for a number of reasons, including when Steve Warner, the supergrass whose claims had launched Operation Abelard, suddenly decided to change his story. Warner later claimed that he had been 'pressured' to sign statements naming Jimmy Cook as the getaway driver on the night of the murder. He also claimed that his police debriefers had offered him improper inducements, including the promise of conjugal visits in jail and a case of beer.[33]

Meanwhile, Stevens's relationship with the *News of the World* continued to flourish. In December 2004, just before he was due to step down as Met commissioner, he again dined with Brooks at the Ivy. A month later she hired him as a columnist for a fee most of the paper's staff couldn't have earned in a month – £7,000 per column.

* * *

A few months later, in Easter week 2005, Alastair Morgan received a letter. 'I sympathise with your family situation and all that you are going through since your brother's death,' it began, before continuing:

What is so unbelievable is the level of corruption that existed in the police force then, and the fact that it looks like it is still going on. Each time you hear of a horrific murder, you are looking to the one source that is supposed to be in the position to provide you with justice, and it is not there.

The letter was from Doreen Lawrence. She went on:

I would support your call for a public inquiry that would get to the bottom of your brother's murder and the issues that led to his death. I can see why you are having an uphill struggle with this. This is a whole can of worms that you are opening ... it is going to be a long struggle, and a lot of people will be covering their backs.[34]

By this stage, Alastair Morgan had been pressing for a judicial inquiry for some time, lobbying senior policemen, civil servants and politicians, all of whom fobbed him off. Finally, towards the end of 2005, he won support from the Metropolitan Police Authority (MPA), the body that then provided Scotland Yard with political oversight at a local level. The MPA's chairman, Len Duvall, told Alastair his family had been treated appallingly and he felt it was his duty to do something about it. The MPA called Sir Ian Blair, Stevens's replacement as commissioner, in for a meeting.

In his memoir about the case, Alastair recalled Blair telling the meeting that the first inquiry was 'compromised'. 'No commissioner had ever before admitted any failures in the original investigation,' he said. 'As he uttered the word, I knew we'd made a huge breakthrough.'[35]

David Cook, who led Operation Abelard, developed a productive working relationship with the Morgan family and won their trust in a way that no other police officer had managed since the murder in 1987. Privately, he had been even more frank than Blair when briefing the MPA. 'Dave Cook went further than ever before in admitting what had gone wrong,' said Alastair. 'Sid Fillery's role as an investigating detective in the initial police inquiry was at the heart of the "mischief".' He even conceded that, in his view, Fillery had been protected by other officers. Cook described the first investigation as 'the worst mess he had ever seen'.[36]

While the MPA was questioning Blair, there were developments elsewhere. In 2005 Garry Vian, the man allegedly hired by Rees to murder Morgan, was convicted of drug trafficking, along with a man called Jimmy Ward. Vian got fourteen years and Ward was jailed for seventeen. Concerned that he might die in jail, Ward offered to co-operate with police in return for a reduction in his sentence. He had been in prison at the time of Daniel Morgan's murder in 1987. But on his release he met up with Garry Vian, who told him that his brother Glenn had swung the axe and a man called Jimmy Cook had driven the car.[37]

Ward told the police that Garry Vian had let slip further details. Ward claimed that Vian privately confessed to the murder in conversation with his brother. He told him it had cost between £20,000 and £25,000.

With Ward's new testimony and pressure from the MPA, Operation Abelard was exhumed. Cook remained the senior investigating officer of what became known as Abelard 2. The new investigation was overseen by then deputy assistant commissioner John Yates, who was also more open with the bereaved family. During one meeting with Alastair Morgan, Yates admitted the case was 'one of the most deplorable episodes in the history of the Metropolitan

Police'. 'I can't prove some things but in my view it's deplorable and we have to face up to it as an organisation,' he added.

Daniel Morgan's elderly mother Isobel was also present, and pressed Yates about Fillery's role. He didn't mince his words. 'Fillery is and was corrupt. We know he was corrupt and he's a corruptor as well. He's a thoroughly bad lot.'[38] Fillery has always denied allegations of corruption and says he has been subjected to false allegations spanning several decades. He has never been convicted of any criminal offences linked to corruption.

Yet this novel burst of candour from Yates and Blair did little to comfort the Morgans. 'Two decades of dealing with the Metropolitan Police had changed my relationship with the world forever,' Alastair Morgan recalled. 'I trusted no one in authority.' As for Fillery, Alastair was furious. 'Jonathan Rees had betrayed us, but Fillery's betrayal was much worse: he was a cop. Worse still was the fact he'd been protected by colleagues of every rank in the police service. We'd experienced layer upon layer of betrayal.'[39]

His scepticism was justified; the dishonesty was far from over. Just as Abelard 2 kicked off, the informant at the heart of Rees and Fillery's operation, the retired detective Derek Haslam, had his cover blown in extraordinary circumstances. Soon, he too would feel betrayed by Scotland Yard.

* * *

In October 2005, Haslam was at his home three hours' drive from London when his computer stopped working. After his first encounter with the Morgan investigation, sixteen years earlier, he had fled the capital afraid for his life. It had taken considerable persuasion from the Met's anti-corruption command to persuade him to go

undercover. For nine years, Haslam passed back sensitive intelligence that suggested Southern Investigations was involved in a vast
array of criminal activities, including work for organised crime syndicates (claims that are strenuously denied by Jonathan Rees).[40] He
was surprised that the Met failed to act on the intelligence, but kept
sending it to his handlers via email.

When the computer started to run slowly, a worried Haslam informed the Met, whose experts agreed to examine the device. They
quickly found that a virus had been put on the machine.[41]

Then, Haslam took a call from Rees, who asked him if he knew
someone named Joe Poulton. The undercover asset was dumbstruck.
Joe Poulton was the cover name he had used in his clandestine communications with Scotland Yard, known only to his handlers – or
so he had thought. Haslam told the Met then packed his bags and
left hastily for Gatwick airport with his wife. The couple flew off to
monitor events from what they hoped was a safe distance: India.[42]

While he was away, the Met decided that Haslam's life could be
in 'serious danger'. When he returned to England, it was agreed
that his cover was 'irretrievably blown' and he was offered a place
in the Met's witness protection system. Given that Haslam had
watched that system being compromised by the same people he
was now hiding from, it was an offer he was quick to decline. In the
end, the police beefed up security at his house, installing an alarm
system linked to the local police station, a panic button and two
covert CCTV cameras.[43]

Throughout all this, David Cook was completely unaware that
the Met had an undercover source inside Southern Investigations,
the gang he had been investigating for four years. It was only after
Haslam's cover was blown that Abelard 2 was briefed of his existence.

Haslam was called in for a debriefing session. It did not go well. The former detective was shown two signed statements he was supposed to have made about corruption inside the Met in the 1980s, at the time of Daniel Morgan's death. They bore no resemblance to what he had actually said. When he told the interviewing officers that his statements had been falsified, they seemed 'very embarrassed'. 'I realised that when the cover-up was undertaken at the time nobody involved had ever envisaged the situation occurring in the future where I would be viewing these forged documents,' he later recalled.[44]

Who then had hacked Haslam's computer and blown his cover? Suspicion fell immediately on Rees, who was no stranger to the possibilities of digital breaking and entering. In 2002, while he was in prison, the police intercepted communications between Rees and Fillery. The inmate claimed he had made contact with someone in Germany selling seemingly magical products for invisible intrusion into private online activity. 'One is a small device you attach to your computer and link to emails,' said Rees. He continued:

> It enables you to get a copy email of the same email every time they get an email – you merely send them an email and receive all theirs – of course it's illegal – but not illegal to sell? He has other devices which are absolutely brilliant but I will talk to you face-to-face on those – absolutely out of this world devices which would have any newspaper journalist drooling over.[45]

Rees now dismisses this discovery: 'We were talking about something that was being developed ... he was looking for sponsorship to develop these things ... there is nothing like that available.'[46] And yet he had boasted to all and sundry that he was in possession of the secret intelligence reports written by the undercover agent who had spied on him for nine years.[47] One of his contacts also managed to obtain copies around the same time. Sylvia Jones, a former crime reporter at the *Daily Mirror*, has known Rees for decades. In the aftermath of the Daniel Morgan murder in 1987 she received a tip-off that Rees was going to be arrested the next day and contacted Southern Investigations. She later told police that she 'may well' have inadvertently warned Rees about the impending operation – whoever tipped off the press was guilty of a major compromise of the murder inquiry.[48] Over the years, Jones has written various newspaper articles that take a less harsh view of the private detective's role in the Daniel Morgan murder.

Previously, Haslam had reported back to his handlers on Jones's friendly relationship with Rees, and noted that she was also close to some of Britain's most senior police officers.[49] Jones makes no secret that she had access to the intelligence reports hacked from Haslam's computer. She told me that they had been posted to her anonymously. Jones even wrote to Scotland Yard to complain that the undercover agent's allegations about her were false.[50] Rees has conflicting explanations for how he got hold of the documents. On one occasion he told me they were leaked to him by a 'sympathetic source' inside the Met,[51] but on another he advanced a more compelling version of events.

In the second account, Rees claimed that Haslam was identified as an undercover police agent by another of his associates, Philip Campbell Smith. A former British Army intelligence officer who operated in Northern Ireland, Smith was a specialist in technical surveillance. Rees told me that Smith had identified Haslam using an IP address – the identifying internet protocol number associated with a specific computer or network. While it isn't hard for an experienced computer user to track an IP address to a geographical location, it is much harder to link it to a specific individual. When asked if Smith had used legal means to find Haslam, he replied: 'Well, there's ways and means, technical ways and means. I would imagine legal means … I don't know.'[52]

A document drafted by Rees's legal team shed more light on the hacking: 'In late 2006 Rees received a document that appeared to be a print of a computer file, in the format of a draft report or reports to "handlers" by "Joe Poulton". Rees was convinced from factual references that the author must be Derek Haslam.' A footnote to the document reads: 'This seems to have been "hacked" from Haslam's computer by Philip Campbell Smith.'

Rees still insists he had nothing to do with it: 'It may have come from Smith's computer, but there won't be any links to me.' When pressed further he told me: 'Thank God Smith was out there and exposed Haslam for what he was … if he did hack Haslam, good.'[53] Smith himself flatly refused to discuss it, telling me in 2012: 'That is something they [the police] will have to justify and prove.'

It would not be unreasonable to suppose that the hacking of an undercover agent's computer might trouble someone at Scotland Yard – all the more so if the hacking was linked to an organised crime gang suspected of involvement in a notorious unsolved murder. The fact that the undercover agent was a former detective who spent nine years risking his life as a police informant might further provoke some determination to investigate.

But no one was charged with hacking Haslam's computer. To this day, he still receives threats and intimidating visits to his home. The detective-turned-informer has been left to fend for himself.

*　*　*

At 9.49 a.m. on 5 July 2006, a seven-page fax arrived in the Irish offices of the *News of the World*, marked 'FAO Alex Marunchak'.[54] The fax contained extracts from the private emails of Ian Hurst, a former colleague of Philip Campbell Smith in the British Army's security services. From the covering note, Marunchak learnt that Hurst had 'first-hand information on operations that would cause serious problems at very high government levels'.[55] Smith had hacked into the retired spook's account, and was now forwarding items of interest.

Hurst served with Smith in the Intelligence Corps and the force research unit in Northern Ireland between 1980 and 1991. His main task was to recruit and work with agents within Republican terror groups. Hurst's emails were of interest to Smith because Marunchak, the *News of the World* executive, was keen to locate an agent, codenamed 'Stakeknife', who was one of the British Army's most valuable assets inside the IRA during the Troubles. The agent had his cover blown in 2003 when Hurst co-authored a book that blew the whistle on his illicit activities. Hurst claimed that Stakeknife was really Freddie Scappaticci, the former head of the IRA's feared internal security department – known as the 'nutting squad'. The unit was responsible for counter-intelligence, maintenance of discipline and administration of punishments, from kneecappings to killings. Scappaticci is currently under investigation for seventeen murders as part of a £35 million inquiry into possible collusion between Irish terrorists and the British security agencies.

The fax sent to Marunchak in June 2006 also included messages about a second informant, known as Kevin Fulton. Since both informers were regarded as high-risk targets for assassination, these hacked emails were extremely sensitive, containing information that might have led their enemies to them.[56]

What has all this got to do with Daniel Morgan? Once again, the link is Jonathan Rees. The *News of the World* wanted to get to Stakeknife. Emails and other records show that Marunchak hired Rees to find Scappaticci. Rees then subcontracted the job to Smith, who hacked Hurst's computer. The malware planted gave Smith access to the former spy's personal data including his email, hard drive, social media accounts and webcam. Hurst later said: 'He could have actually seen me or my kids at the desk.'[57]

On 2 June 2006, Marunchak wrote to a colleague telling them that Rees had managed to track 'Scap' to Manchester through a police Special Branch source, who had also revealed that Scappaticci's witness protection was surprisingly loose. In February that year, Rees had already provided the paper with the phone records of Scappaticci's wife. He made no attempt to conceal his role in the theft of private material, sending the *News of the World* an invoice marked 'Scappaticci Phone Records'.

The odd thing here is that Scotland Yard knew all this was happening yet failed to move against Rees or his associates.[58] Neither did they want to warn Hurst he had been a victim of crime, although it is understood MI5 did modify Scappaticci's arrangements.

The matter lay dormant for the next five years. But in March 2011, the Fleet Street phone hacking scandal erupted. Amid a slew of allegations involving corrupt private investigators working for the Murdoch media empire, disgruntled police sources inside the Met decided to leak information about the hacking of Hurst's computer to the BBC's *Panorama* programme. Hurst was approached by investigative journalists and concluded that Smith must have been responsible. Working with *Panorama*, Hurst contacted his old Army intelligence comrade and arranged a meeting at a hotel in Milton Keynes which was secretly recorded. The military bonds between the two men, forged in the heat of war, remained strong. Within minutes of their sitting down together Smith was happy to confirm everything, freely discussing how he had hacked into Hurst's emails. He also identified the individual who commissioned him.

'The faxes would go to Dublin,' Smith said. 'He was the editor of the *NoW* for Ireland. A Slovak-type name. I can't remember his fucking name … Alex, his name is. Marunchak.'[59]

Panorama's very public exposure of the Scappaticci hacks meant the Met had no choice but to act against Rees and his high-profile associates. Following the broadcast, the police launched Operation Kalmyk, intended to establish the truth about the hacking of Hurst's computer. Rees, Marunchak and Smith were duly arrested in October 2012.

It was around this time that I first started investigating the Daniel Morgan murder. I began speaking to Rees about the events he had been embroiled in for the last three decades. Some journalists shy away from speaking to criminals, often with good reason, but I was keen to hear from everyone involved. At the same time, I didn't want to end up like Marunchak, hunting for headlines by any means possible. By its very nature, the subject of police corruption needs to be approached carefully. It is never quite clear who is telling the truth, what agendas might be hidden, and when you might tread on a landmine. But if I could get Rees to open up, and the information could be corroborated, then it might be useful. The private eye was out on bail for computer hacking charges when I started meeting with him on various occasions in pubs across south London. Intriguingly, Rees never seemed particularly concerned that he was headed back to jail, despite prima facie evidence of his alleged crimes featuring prominently on the BBC and in national newspapers. Indeed, he mainly seemed annoyed and surprised at this point that police had failed to arrest the right man. Another of Rees's associates – a former Metropolitan Police officer – had somehow escaped scot-free over the hacking of Hurst's computer.

*　*　*

Not many people would recognise the name Alec Leighton, once a detective sergeant in the Met. Leighton had close ties to Rees, both before and after he left the force in 1996. Unlike Rees's partner Sid Fillery, however, Leighton's relationship with Southern Investigations has stayed hidden from view. The former detective has cultivated relationships with prominent journalists who investigated the Morgan murder, which might explain why he has been able to stay in the shadows, his reputation intact.

Leighton joined the Met in 1977 and fell in with a group of detectives allegedly under the control of controversial former commander Ray Adams, who figured conspicuously in the Stephen Lawrence inquiries. According to his police driver between 1983 and 1985, Adams would regularly visit CID offices in south London to be greeted like a rock star by Fillery, Leighton and Duncan Hanrahan, the corrupt police officer who would later turn supergrass.[60] They were all Freemasons.[61]

Leighton was undoubtedly a skilled detective but his career at the Yard started to disintegrate after he was implicated in a serious corruption scandal. In September 1993, another *Panorama* programme broadcast an expose of a detective constable named John Donald. The rogue officer was the handler of Kevin Cressey, a drug dealer who was also a registered police informant. The relationship turned sour and Cressey took his revenge by approaching the BBC with a sneaky plan to secretly record him paying Donald for sensitive information. Journalists from *Panorama* recorded fourteen meetings between Cressey and his handlers, catching DC Donald on camera receiving money in a carrier bag. The detective was also caught on tape offering to help burgle a police station for surveillance logs that the police held on Cressey. The price was £30,000 because, as Donald explained it, he'd also have to pay his boss – DS Alec Leighton.[62]

The *Panorama* tapes tell the story. 'I've been thinking about it,' Cressey told Donald. 'And for that one, I find it a lot of fucking money, John, to be honest with you … thirty large, you know.'

'That's what I told him yesterday,' replied Donald. 'I'll tell him that, and see what he says.'

'If he wants to come back to me with a different price, then I'll talk to him,' said Cressey.

'What if he says "Well, what do you want?"'

'Well, I see it about ten large, John. That's the way I see it.'[63]

As on so many other occasions, it was the public exposure of corruption inside its ranks that forced the Met to be seen to do something about it. A new investigation was launched into *Panorama*'s findings. It was given another enigmatic title – on this occasion, Operation Gallery – and it was led by Ian Blair, the future Met commissioner, who was then only a superintendent. Blair had Leighton and Donald arrested and thought there was enough evidence to prosecute both of them.[64] During Donald's trial, Leighton was described as the 'real governor'[65] and Donald made a statement implicating his boss. Then Donald pleaded guilty the night before he was due to give evidence in court.[66] The CPS dropped the case against Leighton, who went on to claim that Donald made a false statement against him as part of a secret deal with the Met. In a letter to his lawyers at the time, Leighton wrote: 'CIB [the anti-corruption command] refer to me as some sort of "godfather" orchestrating a cell of corruption from my exalted position as leader of the gang. This is absolute nonsense.'[67]

Donald was sentenced to eleven years. Leighton resigned from the Met shortly afterwards on 31 July 1996.[68] He soon set up a private detective agency, Mayfayre Associates, with Duncan Hanrahan, the former police officer who would later be jailed for eight years over corruption offences. Hanrahan ran the agency of out of Leighton's garage, and the pair recruited another former Met detective, a man who would later also be arrested for corruption.

When Derek Haslam infiltrated Southern Investigations between 1997 and 2006, many of the intelligence reports that he sent to his handlers featured Leighton's name. Police probes installed in the private detective agency also picked up a phone call where Rees and the former detective discussed a conspiracy to offer Kevin Lennon £2,000 in order to change his evidence.[69] Nothing happened to Leighton, who grew closer to Rees throughout the 2000s. The closeness of their relationship may explain why he was surprised that Leighton had not been arrested: 'Why hasn't Alec Leighton got knocked over?' he asked me one night. 'Leighton was the conduit between me and Philip Campbell Smith … How did I get dragged into all this?'[70] Rees claimed that Scotland Yard had invoices and bank statements showing that Leighton was paying Smith, the hacker who had installed a virus on Ian Hurst's computer. When I asked him why he thought Leighton had escaped arrest, he simply said: 'Grass.'[71]

It's a familiar enough word to anyone who has ever watched a television crime drama, but Rees was referring to a very particular type of informant. Many a villain has been recruited to the Met's cause in return for what amounts to freedom from harassment, surveillance or even prosecution. As we have seen, becoming a Scotland Yard 'tout' – as this protected class of informants is known – can be beneficial for both crooks and bent cops. They pass on enough underworld chatter to be useful to their handlers – who in turn let them get on with their own criminal careers. In theory, police are not supposed to allow an informant to carry on committing crimes unless several strict criteria have been met. In practice, of course, informant status can be a licence for criminals to operate with total impunity, as long as every now and then they help their handlers lock someone up. The only way this mutually advantageous back-scratching survives is silence; no one involved, neither the police nor the criminals, tends to speak of their cosy rackets, for fear of public and political revulsion.

As for the hacking of Hurst's computer, it isn't hard to see why Rees was upset. There is a wealth of evidence showing that Leighton played a key role in the search for Scappaticci – the IRA mole – and the subsequent targeting of Hurst. What Rees might not have known, however, is that the police had already seized computers from Leighton's home, and interviewed the former detective under caution.

Among the items recovered were emails, photographs of Hurst, a 'to do list' mentioning an 'Irish job NOTW', and a 'Phil invoice' mentioning 'Scap job', which seems to refer to Philip Campbell Smith and his surveillance of Scappaticci. One email between Leighton, Rees and Smith discussed their belated discovery of a court injunction which would have prevented the *News of the World* from revealing Scappaticci's whereabouts. Leighton replied: 'Well that about settles it, best get paid up and fuck off and get on with something else.'[72]

Another read: 'Jon [Rees] came round yesterday for an hour.

I've given him some tasters concerning what [Hurst] is up to and I understand he's spoken to the Ukrainian [Marunchak] and he is supposedly speaking to his legal people.' The email goes on to say: 'I have also told them that not a lot is going to get done until Phase One of the Italian job (Scappaticci is of Italian heritage) has been paid for.'[73]

The issue of money, or lack of it, became more urgent. In September 2006, Leighton emailed Smith, saying: 'I still haven't had my SCAPP money or the one thousand five hundred I fronted. The Ukrainian failed to turn up with the dough on Friday, how surprised was I. I think you're right when you said our mate had the dough but used it himself.'[74] The invoices clearly show that Leighton was heavily involved in the Hurst job[75] and that it was Leighton, not Rees, who had personally supervised Smith's hacking efforts. The detective had met the former intelligence officer in 1995, and when he became a private investigator he had regularly commissioned Smith for surveillance work. Yet despite clear evidence of a conspiracy to hack a personal computer on behalf of a newspaper, the Yard did not arrest Leighton and he has never been charged in connection with the Hurst case.

Nor were Rees or Smith. The prime suspect for the murder of Daniel Morgan had escaped justice once again. Rees and his friends might have thought the matter would have ended there. But Ian Hurst, the former Army intelligence officer who was the victim of their hacking plot, was not a happy man. His private emails had been stolen and read, the police had known about it, no one warned him and nothing was done about it. Unfortunately for Rees, Marunchak and Smith, they had made an enemy who was not inclined to let things drop. Scotland Yard's inaction had left a vacuum in the case – a vacuum that Hurst was only too willing to fill.

Chapter 6

The Electrician

A slim man in a denim jacket stepped out of the front door to his block of flats. It was a warm summer's morning and 27-year-old Jean Charles de Menezes was on his way to fix a fire alarm at a property in Kilburn. The Brazilian electrician was also having to deal with the ongoing disruption to the capital's public transport system caused by two recent terror attacks.

On 7 July 2005, four young suicide bombers had launched co-ordinated explosions on London's Tube and bus network, killing fifty-two people. It was Britain's deadliest terrorist incident since the 1988 bombing of Pan Am flight 103, which crashed onto the Scottish town of Lockerbie. On 21 July, the day before Jean Charles left his flat, four more Islamist terrorists tried to carry out repeat attacks using bombs made with chapati flour mixed with hydrogen peroxide and stuffed into rucksacks. Fortunately, none of the devices detonated properly and, on that occasion, no one was injured. But the four attackers had disappeared, triggering the largest manhunt in British history.

At 4.20 a.m. on 22 July, Commander John McDowall of Scotland Yard's counter-terror branch was alerted to a breakthrough. Detectives examining a rucksack bomb that failed to explode at Shepherd's Bush Tube station, west London, had found a gym membership card belonging to Hussain Osman, one of the attackers. Osman was traced to an apartment block on Scotia Road in Tulse Hill, south London – the flats where Jean Charles lived.

So began a series of events that led to the death of an innocent man, a rift at the very top of Scotland Yard, a series of excruciating court cases and a troubling loss of faith in the Metropolitan Police.

Commander McDowall gave orders for a surveillance operation on Scotia Road. The surveillance 'red team', deployed closest to the address from 6 a.m., was issued with copies of Osman's gym photograph, which was poor quality and two years out of date.[1] 'Nettletip', as Osman was codenamed, was dark-skinned, clean-shaven and had short, dark hair. The team all knew that he was not afraid to die.

More than three hours passed. The clock ticked past 9 a.m. If the terror suspect was planning a rush-hour bomb he was cutting it pretty fine. With timing which might have bordered on farce had it not been so tragic, the front door to the flats opened and Jean Charles strode out – just as the officer who was meant to definitively identify Nettletip was relieving himself into a bottle.

Officers scrambled across south London to try and rectify the mistake. Around twenty undercover and surveillance personnel attempted to get a good look at Jean Charles, variously reporting back to senior officers that the man was 'north African', a 'white male' and had 'distinctive Mongolian eyes'.[2]

De Menezes's features were similar to Osman's, but his skin was considerably lighter. Even so the surveillance team remained suspicious. Despite Commander McDowall briefing senior firearms officers about the operation at 6.40 a.m., there were still no armed personnel on site. No one had been deployed specifically to stop and question the suspect, nor had anyone earmarked a 'safe area' where he could be confronted. With gaping holes emerging all over the police operation, police officers watched as Jean Charles, a suspected suicide bomber, was allowed to board a crowded bus.

Five miles away at New Scotland Yard, the operation was being co-ordinated by Cressida Dick, the future commissioner of the Metropolitan Police. A highly intelligent woman, one of the first to graduate from Balliol College, Oxford, Dick rose rapidly through the ranks after joining the police in 1983. At the time, Scotland Yard was a male-dominated place and female officers had only just been granted the right to wear trousers instead of skirts.

Dick had impressed her superiors with a tough, uncompromising attitude that belied her diminutive height (she is only 5 feet tall). She was a close friend of Jackie Malton, one of the first women to serve on the Flying Squad, who became the real-life inspiration for Helen Mirren's character DCI Jane Tennison in the ITV drama *Prime Suspect*.[3] When Dick took part in a course for police high-flyers, she wrote a dissertation arguing that the way Margaret Thatcher had used the police to crush the miners' strike had 'undermined public support by creating the impression that the police had been reduced to the status of political tools'. The pursuit of Jean Charles de Menezes was a more demanding and urgent challenge. Dick's direction of the hunt for Jean Charles would later be described in court as a scene of 'chaos, confusion and indecision'.

Some of those tailing de Menezes believed they were in a position to arrest him safely. An undercover officer managed to get alongside him on the bus. He told the control room that the subject was not Osman.[4] Yet the confusion continued. The official Scotland Yard log illustrates the fast-changing and contradictory nature of orders from the control room. It reveals that Dick insisted that if there was a 'good IDent' of the suspect he could not be allowed to go down into the Tube. In the space of thirteen minutes, surveillance teams were told: 'I don't want your people going up to this man – that will be [the armed officers]'.[5] Next, an order went out to stop him and to let the surveillance officers tackle him. Then Dick told the surveillance teams not to intervene. Another red team member, 'James', asked at least three times for permission to intervene. But he was told to wait, even though Jean Charles had now disembarked from the bus and was about to enter Stockwell Tube station. The Brazilian walked down the escalator at 10.05 a.m. – more than half an hour after he had first strolled out into the sunshine. It was at that moment that the firearms team were handed a 'state red' – the fatal authorisation to proceed.

Jean Charles descended into the bowels of the station and boarded a Northern line train en route to Willesden in north-west London. 'Ivor', a surveillance officer, was in hot pursuit. The police officer kept his eye on Jean Charles while holding open the Tube doors for the firearms team, shouting: 'He's here.'

For other passengers the scene was first confusing, then terrifying. One witness, Mark Whitby, said: 'As the man got on the train I looked at his face. He looked like a cornered rabbit. He looked absolutely petrified.' Whitby said Jean Charles was then tripped or pushed to the floor. 'One of the police officers was holding a black automatic pistol in his left hand. They held it down and unloaded five shots into him.'[6] Another hit his neck, a seventh lodged into his shoulder. Scotland Yard had executed the wrong man.

This shocking incident swiftly became a nightmare for the new commissioner, Sir Ian Blair, who had taken over from Sir John Stevens just five months earlier. Blair was seen within the force as the antithesis of his predecessor. Stevens was tall, imposing and feared by the rank and file for his assertive demeanour. But he was also a highly successful detective. Blair, by contrast, was thoughtful and strategic. Importantly, he was well regarded by Downing Street. When he secured the top job Blair admitted, somewhat prophetically, that he knew danger would lie ahead. 'You don't come in here without a pair of copper-bottomed trousers,' he once quipped.[7] But the new commissioner was not universally popular among his senior command. One senior Met officer who worked under him recalled:

As far as Ian Blair was concerned, becoming commissioner was an end in itself rather than a means to an end. I went to congratulate him when he became commissioner and he said he had two overwhelming feelings. One was joy that he had the ultimate job and the other was, what the hell have I done?![8]

Almost immediately, damaging leaks about him started to emerge.

But worse was to follow. The stain on the Met's reputation for shooting an innocent man would be compounded almost immediately by a cack-handed attempt to smear Jean Charles. Someone high up in the Met started to brief the media that the Brazilian had been acting suspiciously. The police claimed that Jean Charles had vaulted over a ticket barrier and run down an escalator to escape the firearms officers. He was also said to have worn a bulky coat which could have concealed explosives. This would later be exposed as false. In fact, Jean Charles had walked calmly into the station, picked up a free newspaper and then strolled down the escalator. He was wearing only a light denim jacket.

Questions soon emerged over exactly when senior officers knew they had made the terrible mistake, and how long they allowed false narratives to linger. By 3 p.m., police officers on the scene in

Stockwell had recovered Jean Charles's wallet and seized bank cards
and driving permits that revealed his identity. They had also examined his mobile phone.[9] But that afternoon, just after 3.30, Blair addressed the media at the Queen Elizabeth II Centre at Westminster,
saying the shooting of the man was 'directly linked' to anti-terror
operations and telling reporters: 'As I understand the situation, the
man was challenged and refused to obey police instructions.' By
this stage, however, Blair's chief of staff and staff officer had both
been told that the dead man was a Brazilian, and could not have
been the real target of the operation – the Ethiopian-born Osman.
The two officers later said they did not pass this crucial information to Blair before the press conference.[10] Immediately afterwards,
assistant commissioner Andy Hayman – who had left the anti-corruption unit and was now head of the counter-terrorism command
– briefed the Crime Reporters' Association (CRA). He told journalists that Jean Charles was not one of the four terror suspects.
Hayman then left to go to a meeting of senior officers. Minutes
of that meeting record him as having said, in direct contradiction
to what he had told the media just minutes before: 'There is press
running that the person shot is not one of the four bombers. We
need to present that he is believed to be.'[11]

Dealing with the fallout of a botched police execution on the
streets of London would be a baptism of fire for any new commissioner. But there seems little doubt that Blair helped neither himself
nor the force he led. Within three hours of the shooting, he sent
an ill-judged letter to the Home Office asking that there should
be no inquiry into Menezes's death by the Independent Police
Complaints Commission (IPCC) – contrary to standard practice
when police kill a suspect – which immediately set the conspiracy
theorists running. At around 9.30 the following morning, he gave an

interview in which he still insisted that the Met was performing at the highest standards. It was only later that day that Blair was finally briefed that his officers might have shot dead an innocent man. Late that afternoon, Scotland Yard confirmed that Jean Charles was 'not connected' to the failed 21 July bombings. The force expressed regret over his death, describing it as a 'tragedy'.

For Sir Paul Stephenson, who had recently been appointed deputy commissioner of the Metropolitan Police, the fallout was a fiasco. 'Dreadful mistakes were made regarding what we said in the early parts of the investigation,' he told me. He continued:

> The commissioner got himself into deep trouble through insensitivity in some of the things he said. Wanting to exclude the IPCC for operational reasons was a huge mistake. I said so at that time. The row with the IPCC was completely unnecessary, astonishingly unwise. Trying to deny them access was illegal, in my opinion. But I was the new guy. I'd only been there three months, and no one was listening.

As the news filtered out, Jean Charles's cousin in Britain, Alex Alves Pereira, could barely contain his anger. He said: 'What can the police say? They will try to justify this but there's no way. My cousin's body had his head blown apart with bullets in the back of the head.' He added: 'Jean came from a tight-knit family. We are all absolutely devastated.' The matter also threatened to spiral into a diplomatic incident. The Brazilian government said it was 'shocked and perplexed' at the killing and expected a full explanation.[12]

The death of Jean Charles had a particularly damaging effect on Blair, who would later be questioned under caution. His account of the aftermath of the shooting was challenged when one of his most senior officers, deputy assistant commissioner Brian Paddick, made a statement to the IPCC that contradicted his boss's version of events. This in itself was astonishing – the men had once been close allies. Paddick had come to prominence as a commander in Lambeth, south London, pioneering a policy whereby people arrested with small amounts of cannabis were cautioned rather than charged, saving police time. Paddick had been in Blair's outer office just before the press conference about Jean Charles was due to take place, and claimed one of the commissioner's aides had groaned: 'We've shot a Brazilian tourist.'

Blair always maintained he knew nothing about the horrific mistake made by the officers on the ground until the day after Jean Charles was shot. However, new evidence raises fresh doubts about when Blair was first told. Peter Tickner, the Met's powerful former head of audit, was a key figure at the heart of Scotland Yard for fourteen years. He was also close to Catherine Crawford, who at the time of the de Menezes scandal was chief executive of the Metropolitan Police Authority (MPA). Crawford, who died in 2015, told Tickner that she and Blair were briefed by Andy Hayman on the day of the shooting over the emerging fears about Jean Charles's identity. 'Blair asked Hayman: "Are you absolutely sure about that?" And Hayman replied: "Well, no, guv, I haven't got any forensics". So [Blair said:] "You don't know you've made a mistake yet?"'

'I think he saw that in his head as his get-out,' Tickner told me. 'There was no actual concrete evidence, despite the fact that everyone on the ground was screaming "We've fucked this up big time".'[13]

It is not entirely clear why Scotland Yard delayed admitting to their mistake. Would it really have been so damaging for the public to have been told on the day that a dreadful error had been made?

Everyone knew that the Met was dealing with one of the worst terrorist crises in the nation's history. Although the police error that led to the death of an innocent man was tragic and upsetting, it was not without precedent. What did senior officers really have to gain by concealing this? When the truth quickly emerged, the apparent cover-up made the Met's handling of the incident look far more sinister.

In the days that followed, Blair continually tried to shield the Yard from scrutiny by the IPCC. At a meeting with senior Home Office officials three days after the shooting, the commissioner argued forcefully that the Met should run its own inquiry. However, Sir John Gieve, then Permanent Secretary at the Home Office, and Len Duvall, then chair of the MPA, pointed out that under the law the IPCC should have been brought in immediately. According to one officer, Blair then held his head in his hands and warned that bringing in outside investigators would lead to his firearms officers 'dropping their guns' and effectively going on strike.[14]

The suspicion that crucial information was being suppressed deepened when it emerged that Special Branch officers had altered a surveillance log detailing their movements during Jean Charles's journey to Stockwell station. The log had originally said that their unit had positively identified the man they were following as Hussain Osman, the terror suspect in the failed 21 July attacks. But the amendments changed the sense completely. From reading 'it was Osman', the record was changed to read 'and it was not Osman'. The deputy surveillance co-ordinator of the botched operation also deleted a line from the notes on his computer saying that it was Cressida Dick, the commander in charge, who had decided that Jean Charles could 'run on to Tube as [he was] not carrying anything'. The man, known only as 'Owen', later said he had removed the line because he believed it was 'wrong and gave a false impression'.[15]

A month later, the Yard was embarrassed yet further. For weeks, the narrative that Jean Charles had behaved suspiciously was allowed to crystallise. False claims, including that he had vaulted the ticket barrier, were made to the media by unnamed police sources. The smears became too much for Lana Vandenberghe, who was at the time an administration secretary at the IPCC. Initially, Vandenberghe had had little sympathy for the dead man. 'I thought, like lots of others, that if this guy was a terrorist it was a shame that he was killed but it had been warranted,' she said. Then she saw photographs and statements to the IPCC from the police officers and witnesses directly involved in the shooting. 'After seeing the pictures of him lying there and how he had looked as he had entered the station, I knew it was different.'[16]

She still vividly recalled the incident sixteen years on:

It was reported that Jean Charles was wearing the heavy jacket and the backpack and all that stuff. None of that was [corrected] as wrong and I was flabbergasted. The weeks go by and I'm like: 'Oh my God, when are the police going to come forward and tell the truth?'[17]

Vandenberghe, who now lives in Alberta, Canada, her home province, told me that the case had become political, 'it wasn't about what was right or wrong'. She was 'totally appalled' when she saw a letter from the Home Office to the IPCC ordering the supposedly independent watchdog to 'leave out certain information' from its final report.[18] Vandenberghe began to assemble copies of statements. 'I collected anything relevant to show the public the police were lying about what was going on. I came to the conclusion that I could make a difference.'[19] She then passed the documents to a friend whose partner was a producer at the television news channel ITN.

When the story broke it led the news bulletins and featured on the front pages of several national newspapers. Vandenberghe was amazed by the impact. 'I thought it would be a little story about what the police had done and how they had lied to the public,' she recalled.

Within days she was suspended. The leak had been traced to her. Vandenberghe subsequently resigned, but that was not the end of her ordeal. Leicestershire Police was appointed to lead a leak inquiry and she was arrested when ten officers raided her flat in Walthamstow, north-east London. 'I was scared to death,' she said. 'I did not know what to think or do.' As they began to search her flat, she was taken away to Bishopsgate police station in central London. 'I was upset, scared, I was crying. I had never been in any kind of trouble before and I was frightened. It had never crossed my mind that I would be treated as if I was a criminal for telling the truth.'[20]

Vandenberghe believes that she was targeted because she had embarrassed the police and they wanted to intimidate her. 'I was very frightened,' she said, continuing: 'I didn't know what to do. I was crying and felt sick – all I had done was reveal the truth. The police attitude towards me was rude and bullying. They made it very clear that I had done something wrong and that I could possibly be put in prison.'[21]

On the same day as the arrest, Ian Blair was forced to appear on television to apologise for not correcting misinformation about the case – misinformation that Vandenberghe had helped to reveal.

Devastated and exhausted, she returned home shortly before midnight. 'I was afraid and depressed,' she said. 'It really worked a toll on me. My life was on hold.'

But throughout the nine months of investigation, police questioning, fear and uncertainty, she was sustained by the belief that she had acted properly. 'I did the right thing,' she said. 'I helped the parents of Jean Charles and the public in finding out the truth and in finding out what they had been told was not the truth.'[22] Eventually, all charges against her were dropped. Vandenberghe believes she escaped partly because she built up a 'huge following' and public opinion was behind her.[23]

Sixteen years on, though, she still had contempt for the commander in charge of the operation, whose career in the Metropolitan Police was undamaged by the terrible events of July 2005. A protégée of Blair, Cressida Dick continued to rise swiftly through the ranks of Scotland Yard until, in 2017, she was appointed the force's first female commissioner. It was a memorable moment for equality campaigners in the UK. But for Vandenberghe, the decision was a disgrace. She told me:

> Out of all the people that I think should have got fired it has to be Cressida Dick. I can't believe she is in the role she is in now. To me, that is politics. She headed that whole thing and could have stopped it at any time. Jean Charles didn't have to die. He wasn't carrying anything. How could he have been a bomber when he wasn't carrying anything? He didn't have to die.[24]

A year after the shooting, the Crown Prosecution Service announced there was insufficient evidence to prosecute any individual police officers over Jean Charles's death. However, they did decide to prosecute Scotland Yard under health and safety laws. The family described the decision as 'shameful' and repeated their accusation of a 'cover-up'. At a press conference in London, Jean Charles's cousin Vivian Figueiredo said: 'I think the authorities have a strategy so that this case won't come to a conclusion. It has been nearly a year since the crime happened, the extermination happened. At the moment we only have question marks and hope and disappointment. They always find some sort of excuse.' In Brazil, Jean Charles's tearful mother Maria was 'outraged' and called for Blair to be sacked, adding: 'I thought I had cried all my tears, but I haven't. We still miss Jean Charles as much as ever. It feels as painful and as bad as the day Jean Charles died.'[25]

During the health and safety trial, the judge, Sir Richard Henriques, told the Old Bailey jury that July 2005 was a 'dark month' in the history of London. He reminded them of the deadly suicide bomb attacks on the Tube and the buses on 7 July, and the failed attacks two weeks later on 21 July. The judge told the jurors that the prosecution claimed that the Met carried out the operation 'so very badly' that the public were put at risk.[26] He stressed that no individual officers were on trial, including Dick, who had since been promoted to deputy assistant commissioner.[27] In his memoir, *From Crime to Crime*, Henriques would later comment that the indictment 'if proved amounted to a catalogue of mismanagement and incompetence. The alleged failures involved misdirection in briefings, poor incident planning, technical issues relating to communications, unclear operational objectives, inaccurate profiling, ambiguous instructions and individual errors.'[28]

The Met's traditional defensiveness was on full display during the trial. Ronald Thwaites, the QC representing Scotland Yard, was criticised by Henriques on a number of occasions, including when he tried to raise concerns about Jean Charles's immigration status. Henriques was angered when this caused 'visible distress' to the de Menezes family.

> This was but one of several ... untenable and unworthy defence assertions, or suggestions made, that Jean Charles by his own behaviour had brought about his own death. A chain of events had taken an innocent young man's life in tragic circumstances. Compassion, explanation and some degree of contrition were the order of the day. They were conspicuously absent.[29]

After a five-week trial, the jury took just four hours unanimously to convict the Met of breaching health and safety laws and putting the public at risk. The force was fined £175,000 and ordered to pay £385,000 costs.[30]

Jean Charles's family hailed the verdict but immediately accused Met lawyers of trying to 'blacken' his name in a desperate attempt to win the case. Apart from questioning Jean Charles's immigration status, Thwaites had also claimed that the Brazilian behaved suspiciously because he used cocaine. Even after the guilty verdict, Blair defended the alleged slur, saying the Met's legal team had pointed out these factors to 'explain to the jury some of the reasons why Mr de Menezes acted as he did when confronted by armed police'.[31]

Confidence in the Met and its commissioner drained away. Speaking in the House of Commons, David Davis, the shadow Home Secretary, said: 'The failures were systemic, falling within the clear responsibility of the commissioner of the Met Police. His position is now untenable, in light of these findings and the overriding need to restore public confidence.' Nick Clegg, then the Liberal Democrat home affairs spokesman, added: 'This guilty verdict makes it unavoidable that Ian Blair should take responsibility on behalf of his whole organisation and resign.'

But Blair retained the backing of the New Labour government. The Prime Minister, Gordon Brown, and Home Secretary, Jacqui Smith, swung in behind him and, on the steps of the Old Bailey, the commissioner rejected opposition calls to fall on his sword. Blair claimed that the court case had failed to reveal systemic failings in the Met, and put the whole episode down to a 'single day' of 'extraordinary circumstances'.[32]

Once the criminal case was out of the way, the long-delayed IPCC investigation was published. Although the commissioner was cleared of any suggestion that he had lied to the public about what he knew and when, the report painted a picture of a leader kept totally in the dark about the dead man's identity – despite repeated demands by him for information.[33]

'When the commissioner left New Scotland Yard mid evening on 22 July 2005 he was almost totally uninformed,' the report concluded. 'He did not know of the considerable information within the [Met] in relation to the emerging identity for Mr de Menezes and the likelihood that he was not involved in terrorism. Numerous others within the MPS [Metropolitan Police Service] did know.'[34]

But the IPCC eviscerated assistant commissioner Andy Hayman. Known as 'Asbo Andy' for his abrasive manner and wideboy Essex vocabulary, Hayman had briefly left the Met to become chief constable of Norfolk. Blair persuaded him to return in 2005 and asked Hayman to take charge of Britain's fight against terrorism, despite having no experience of such policing. The IPCC was far from happy with the way Hayman managed the aftermath of the de Menezes shooting. The watchdog slammed the police chief over the apparent inconsistencies he made in separate briefings within minutes of each other to crime journalists and senior Met officers. 'It is apparent that he deliberately withheld the information, both that he briefed the [CRA] and on the contents of that briefing, despite being asked for information by the commissioner,' the report concluded.[35] 'He therefore misled the commissioner, other senior MPS officers and representatives from the MPA [Metropolitan Police Authority] and HO [Home Office] who were present.'[36] A senior Met officer who worked with Hayman told me he was an 'absolute and abject disaster', adding: 'I can't for the life of me understand why Blair appointed him.'

The saga was not over, however. A year later, and more than three years after Jean Charles's death, the long-delayed inquest began. Owing to the huge interest, it was decided that Southwark coroner's court in south London – where such an inquest would normally be held – was too small. The event was moved to the John Major Room at the Oval cricket ground nearby.[37] Conference space was hired to accommodate the battery of lawyers and provide enough room for any member of the public to attend. The Long Room, usually the preserve of Surrey County Cricket Club members, was also set aside as an overspill area and media annexe. More than forty police officers gave evidence, including two officers from the specialist firearms unit who shot Jean Charles dead and Cressida Dick. The inquest heard that the future Met commissioner went to the wrong room, thus missing the start of an important meeting of senior police officers to discuss strategy on the morning of the shooting. The control room she ran at Scotland Yard was also described as 'very noisy and quite chaotic'.[38] When she took the stand, Dick also raised eyebrows with the declaration that Scotland Yard 'did nothing wrong' on the day, and said the electrician was the victim of a series of 'unfortunate' coincidences.

'He was extraordinarily unfortunate to live in the same block as Hussain Osman had been, he was desperately unfortunate to look very like Hussain Osman,' she told the inquest. As Dick described Jean Charles's last moments, his mother had to be escorted from the room in floods of tears.[39] The future commissioner also wept as she described her dismay when she was told an innocent man had died. 'It's a terrible thing to happen and from that day to this, I have thought about this every day, and wondered what we could have done differently,' she said. Her insistence that it was circumstances rather than human error which led to the shooting conflicted with evidence heard a week earlier from her commanding officer, John McDowall. He had admitted that the 'mistaken identification' was 'instrumental'.[40]

The de Menezes family still hoped for some sort of justice. They thought the inquest would help to bring closure and ease their pain. After more than three years, two inquiry reports and an Old Bailey trial, the twelve-week inquest was supposed to end the rumours, conspiracies and misunderstandings. It was going to be modern, open and hugely expensive. Justice would be done, and would be seen to be done.

The family would be disappointed. The coroner, Sir Michael Wright QC, banned the jury from finding that Jean Charles was illegally killed by the Metropolitan Police. Wright, a retired High Court judge, told the eleven jurors that they could only consider two outcomes: either that Jean Charles was lawfully killed or an open verdict. Referring to Jean Charles's mother Maria, he said: 'I know that your heart will go out to her. But these are emotional reactions, ladies and gentlemen, and you are charged with returning a verdict based on evidence. Put aside any emotions – put them to one side.'

When Wright did this, he was acting within the coroners' rules. But the impression given, in such a sensitive case, was that the freedom of the jury to make their own decision was being severely restricted. One de Menezes supporter asked: 'If a coroner in Oxford could rule that a British Army soldier was unlawfully killed by "friendly fire" in Iraq, why is a jury in London not allowed to consider the same finding?'[41]

The decision infuriated the de Menezes family, who declared it a 'whitewash'. Maria de Menezes walked out of the courtroom. They later released a statement saying: 'After three months of evidence, 100 witnesses and millions of pounds, the coroner, Sir Michael Wright, has presided over a complete whitewash. He has failed on every count of the purpose of an inquest investigation.'[42]

The jury deliberated for seven days and their verdict restored some of the family's faith in the proceedings. Their findings were intensely critical of the police on the day of the shooting. They rejected the accounts of the police marksmen who killed Jean Charles and sided with Tube passengers who said that the officers failed to issue a warning to the Brazilian before opening fire.[43] The jurors opted for an open verdict – the strongest available to them – but spelt out in answers to questions set by the coroner that they did not believe some of the police witnesses about what happened that fateful day on the 10.05 Tube train from Stockwell.

*   *   *

The de Menezes case was not the only scandal to hit the force under Sir Ian Blair's leadership. In March 2006, during the IPCC investigation into the case, it emerged that Blair had secretly taped a phone conversation he had with the attorney general, Lord

Goldsmith, during a call about counter-terrorism policy. Goldsmith was said to be 'cross and disappointed' when he learnt of the recording. He spoke to the Home Secretary, Charles Clarke, and the commissioner personally apologised to Goldsmith and said he had been 'very strongly rebuked' for what Whitehall sources said was 'unethical and discourteous' behaviour.[44]

In February 2008, relations between Scotland Yard and the government cooled further when it emerged that counter-terrorism officers had secretly bugged Sadiq Khan, MP for Tooting and a government whip, during a private meeting with one of his constituents. Khan, who subsequently became mayor of London with political oversight of the Metropolitan Police, was recorded by a listening device hidden in a table at Woodhill prison in Buckinghamshire. The bugging operation recorded conversations with Khan's constituent, Babar Ahmad, who faced deportation to the United States. Khan had been a friend of Ahmad's since childhood and had campaigned vigorously against his extradition.* Bugging MPs is a breach of a government edict that bars law enforcement agencies from eavesdropping on politicians, put in place following allegations that MI5 covertly recorded Prime Minister Harold Wilson in the 1970s. Khan was outraged and called the bugging an 'infringement of a citizen's right to have a private meeting with his MP'.[45] Mark Kearney, a detective from Thames Valley Police

---

* Ahmad spent eight years in prison without trial in the United Kingdom from 2004 to 2012 fighting extradition to the United States. The US accused him of providing material support to terrorism via a website that he set up in the UK in 1996 to publish stories about the conflicts in Bosnia and Chechnya, but which in 2000–01 allowed two articles to be posted offering support to the then Taliban government in Afghanistan. Ahmad was finally extradited to the US in October 2012, having become the longest-serving British prisoner to be detained without trial in the UK. He spent the next two years in solitary confinement at a US Supermax prison. In December 2013, Ahmad pleaded guilty to two of the charges against him as part of a plea bargain that would allow him to return home within the year. In July 2014, US federal judge Janet Hall sentenced Ahmad to an unexpectedly lenient sentence of twelve and a half years in prison, meaning that with credit for time served he only had another twelve months to serve. Judge Hall concluded that Ahmad was never interested in terrorism. She stated that Ahmad 'never supported or believed in or associated with Al-Qaeda or Osama bin Laden'.

involved in the operation, said it was 'never justified' and claimed he was forced to carry out the surveillance after 'significant pressure from the Metropolitan Police'.[46]

When the eavesdropping on Khan and his constituent emerged, Jack Straw, then Justice Secretary, ordered an investigation headed by Sir Christopher Rose, the chief surveillance commissioner. Rose later concluded the correct procedures had been followed as Andy Hayman, the assistant commissioner who authorised the operation, did not realise that one of those recorded would be an MP. Khan was sceptical and, in a written statement to Rose, said he would be surprised if the process of authorisation by senior officers 'did not reveal his occupation' and went on to say that his visits were 'covered by legal privilege and/or the Wilson doctrine. It beggars belief that [the police and prison authorities] did not know who I was.'[47]

Scotland Yard's illicit surveillance of Babur Ahmad was eventually ruled unlawful. In 2009, the High Court awarded him £60,000 compensation after the Met admitted that its officers subjected Ahmad to 'serious gratuitous prolonged unjustified violence' and 'religious abuse' during his arrest, which left him with seventy-three injuries. During the case, it emerged that the officers who abused Ahmad were also accused of dozens of other assaults on black and Asian men.[48]

* * *

Another unexploded bomb would eventually go off during Blair's tenure, embarrassing Scotland Yard and claiming the scalp of Andy Hayman, the third most senior police officer in the land.

It centred on the police use of corporate credit cards, which were given to thousands of Met officers to pay for on-the-job expenses.

But few if any checks were made on where the money went. The Yard's forensic chief auditor, Peter Tickner, no stranger to police misconduct, had first raised concerns about potential fraud when a bent protection officer crossed his path in 2004.

Twelve years after leaving the Met, Tickner is still amazed at the pushback he received when he asked Scotland Yard to account for the expenditure. 'The cards were given out, quite rightly, to people trying to catch criminals but nobody bothered to chase them up afterwards to account for how they spent the money. It might have been for perfectly legitimate reasons but we had no records.'[49]

The Special Branch protection officer, Ron Evans, who guarded Margaret Thatcher when she was Prime Minister, was remarkably open about the behaviour in his unit. In his memoir, Evans recalled:

By the time I joined Special Branch and first went out of town I witnessed the corruption that went on from all ranks. Buying alcohol, meals for wives and girlfriends, was the norm. I knew what all of us were doing was wrong and in those early days I knew that this shouldn't be happening and I should say something about it. But it was so endemic and, being a very junior officer, having just joined one of the most specialist departments in any police force, I kept quiet.

In my naivety, I thought that because so many other officers were swimming in the same pool as me, all that would happen was that the job would ask me to resign and go quietly.[50]

When Tickner spotted Evans submitting false receipts he ordered an audit of ninety-five other officers in the diplomatic protection squad. 'We realised quite early on that a number of them had serious problems,' he told me. 'They were clearly not following the rules.'[51] Tickner went to see Steve Roberts, then head of the Met's anti-corruption command. According to Tickner, Roberts told him that the evidence sample looked 'dodgy' and advised him to guard the evidence until his team could take possession of it. 'These things have a habit of disappearing or getting burnt, you know?' Roberts added.[52]

A couple of months later Tickner had heard nothing more, so approached Roberts again, only to be told that the investigation had been put on the backburner after 'pressure from above'. The anti-corruption chief said the timing could not have been worse; at that very moment the armed protection officers were once again threatening to down tools over another botched operation.

Harry Stanley, a father of three, was shot dead by armed police in 1999 as he left a pub in Hackney, east London. The Scottish-born painter and decorator was carrying a table leg he had just repaired but the police had mistaken it for a sawn-off shotgun. The fall-out from the case dragged on for years. In November 2004, just as Tickner began investigating the unit, two of the shooters were suspended, triggering uproar among their colleagues.[53] Around 120 firearms officers went on strike. 'There was a huge furore,' Tickner said, adding ruefully: 'My timing could have been better.'[54]

Tickner told me that his team found a significant number of firearms officers were 'not following the correct processes' with their expenses. But a decision was made to pursue just one officer in order to send a message. It was the unfortunate Ron Evans who was prosecuted and convicted on nine counts of false accounting, and he was understandably furious. 'I had been cast adrift, hung out to dry, the sacrificial lamb. Other officers that I worked with were doing the same as me.'[55]

If only the scandal had ended there. The abuse of taxpayer-funded credit cards then proliferated yet further after the terror attacks of July 2005. According to Tickner the ensuing climate of fear meant that a panicked Scotland Yard doled out more and more corporate credit cards with fewer and fewer checks on where the money went. This went unnoticed for around a year until one day an alarmed auditor burst into his office. 'Christ, Peter. They've given them to everybody doing counter-terrorism work,' said his underling. 'There are 3,500 cards, we've spent £8.5 million and we can only account for £3.5 million. What are we doing?'[56]

At a management meeting in October 2006, Tickner reported this and Ian Blair ordered that the lavish expenditure should cease. But nothing happened. Tickner continued to investigate the counter-terror command. He told me that he uncovered criminality that went way beyond Evans's unauthorised spending. 'One of them had paid off his gambling debts – about eighty grand's worth. Another had been using it to enhance his wife's breasts. £13,500 [was spent] on the surgery!' Tickner's inquiries led to Richard de Cadenet, an anti-terror detective, being jailed in September 2008 for spending more than £73,000 on his corporate credit card, including a lavish holiday in Thailand and a box at a Premiership football club. Southwark crown court heard that he withdrew £18,000 from cash machines and racked up £5,910 on supermarket bills, £3,500 on clothes and £3,000 on electrical goods. De Cadenet had made 415 transactions on the American Express card in fifteen months, but only twenty-eight were legitimate.[57] He was far from the only offender, according to Tickner. 'We found about 300 of them acted in a manner that could be fraudulent, and I would say 100 of them were definitely fraudulent,' he said. 'That was out of 1,400 officers. But we only pursued a handful. The numbers were just too big to handle.'[58]

By 2007, Tickner was so unhappy at the failure of the Met's high command to heed his warnings that he decided to take a few risks. 'We started auditing every commander and above, including the commissioner and the deputy commissioner.'[59] His rigorous approach made him powerful enemies and he was soon accused of 'interfering in operations'. The inquiries had by this point zoomed in on Andy Hayman, who was already vulnerable. Britain's leading counter-terrorism officer had been criticised over the execution of Jean Charles de Menezes. He had since been forced to issue a public apology after another innocent man was accidentally wounded during an anti-terrorism raid in Forest Gate, east London. Embarrassing details were also leaked to the press about trips that Hayman, who was married, had taken overseas with a female staff officer, although he denied any form of impropriety. But Hayman was then damaged further over his friendship with another female colleague, the IPCC official Nikki Redmond. First, newspapers published pictures of him and Redmond in pubs on two consecutive nights near Liverpool Street station. At the time Hayman was meant to be supervising a high-terror alert triggered by an alleged plot to blow up transatlantic airliners at Heathrow airport. Then details were leaked of 400 texts to Redmond during the period when the IPCC was drafting its report into the de Menezes shooting. Hayman again denied any improper contact, saying the pair had known each other professionally and as friends for several years.

Tickner sent Hayman schedules of his corporate credit card spending and asked him to account for each item. 'It all came back and the answer to every question was "I'm an assistant commissioner, it was my authority". That was the answer to every one. He was taking the piss.' Tickner's view is that Hayman 'wasn't corrupt, he was just stupid'. 'He spent about £300 on alcohol having lunch with a chief constable. I was concerned about the amount of alcohol he was consuming on operational duty.'

With Catherine Crawford's help a meeting was arranged with Sir Paul Stephenson, then the deputy commissioner. Tickner recalls:

Stephenson started having a go at me. So I said to him: 'How much do you think Andy has actually spent on his expenses, Paul?'

He said: 'How much?'

I said: 'Last year and the year before he spent £19,000 on his corporate card.'

That got Stephenson's attention. 'Nineteen fucking thousand! I haven't spent a thousand the entire time I have been in the police!'

Before the issue could be resolved, Hayman resigned, denying any misconduct. 'Recent weeks have seen a series of leaks and unfounded accusations about me, which I have and will continue to refute strongly,' he said in a statement. 'However, these events take their toll … and I feel now is the right time for me to step aside. I wish my successor and all my colleagues every success in their efforts to defend the United Kingdom.'

When asked about Hayman's departure, Stephenson said:

On a personal basis, Tickner could be quite an irritating man in the way he went about his business – but that doesn't mean to say he was wrong. Hayman and I had a number of disagreements and that would have been one of them. We didn't have the easiest of relationships. The departure of Hayman was yet another embarrassment in the Ian Blair era.

Nothing seemed to go right on Blair's watch. Perhaps he never had a chance. Former deputy assistant commissioner Brian Paddick later claimed that negative briefing against Blair had intensified before he was even chosen as Stevens's successor.[60] Blair said criticism of him as commissioner – for being too liberal and too close to the Labour government – resulted from 'political forces and the press' combining to deliver a 'monstering' that lasted throughout his entire term of office. 'I can think of no equivalent long-term treatment of a public servant in this manner.'[61] Long after he had departed Scotland Yard, Blair finally went public, blaming senior colleagues for passing information to journalists in order to 'improve their own profile'.[62]

Stephenson, then deputy commissioner, and the second most senior police officer in the UK, told me he was astonished at the 'in-fighting' when he arrived at the Met in 2005. 'It was the practice of senior people around that board table to go out and brief their favoured journalists. They were showing deplorable standards. You couldn't have a discussion with your colleagues without it being leaked to the media, and that added to pressure on the commissioner.'

Peter Tickner had a front row seat to all this. He claims that the Met was divided between those who supported Blair and those who were loyal to the previous commissioner, John Stevens. 'Everything went wrong with the Ian Blair and John Stevens fight,' Tickner told me, continuing:

Blair had a habit of giving jobs to the wrong people. It's almost like he couldn't read them. Andy Hayman was one of them. Andy was a favourite of Ian Blair's. He was as combustible as John Stevens, but not as competent. He did a hell of a lot of damage.

A lot of the stuff went wrong because the top of the office wanted to do one thing, the people on the ground wanted to do another, and the people in the middle had their own agenda. And whoever had the power at the time bludgeoned their way forward to what they wanted to achieve. It had nothing to do with what was right, it was about what that bludgeoning person wanted to achieve.

The final nail in Blair's coffin came with a row over the Met awarding multi-million-pound contracts to a technology company owned by Andrew Miller, one of the commissioner's university friends and skiing buddies.

In 2002, when he was deputy commissioner, Blair had chaired a panel that handed Miller's firm, Impact Plus, a £150,000 consultancy contract to oversee the introduction of a computer program to link London's thirty-two borough control rooms. Between 2002 and 2008 Impact Plus was awarded further contracts worth £3 million. Prior to joining the panel, Blair declared his friendship with Miller in a private letter to the Metropolitan Police Authority (MPA).[63] Years later, as Blair's authority as commissioner melted away, rumours that a newspaper was about to expose the contracts swept Scotland Yard. Tickner was called in to investigate in July 2008. He asked for the original procurement files to be retrieved from storage and sent to him. But to his fury they were intercepted en route and brought to the office of Ian Blair himself. Copies were also made for Sir Paul Stephenson, as the deputy commissioner has overall responsibility for propriety and ethics. Only then were the files passed to Tickner.[64]

As the auditor reviewed the files he became concerned about correspondence suggesting that Blair had discussed the Impact Plus decision with the Met's head of IT, despite recusing himself from the process. 'It was in Ian's own hand,' Tickner recalled. 'I'm thinking "Oh dear, you stupid man, we've got to ask the Home Office for an investigation, we've got no choice".'[65]

But the details were then leaked to the *Mail on Sunday*, triggering a media firestorm. Tickner is convinced that the story could only have come from the papers he examined.[66] He told me that to his recollection only two other people had then seen the files. 'Only Paul Stephenson and Ian Blair had ever seen that stuff,' Tickner claimed.

When asked about Tickner's recollection, Stephenson was adamant: 'I didn't leak. I don't leak. It wasn't part and parcel of my background. I certainly didn't leak anything about Impact Plus.' He calls the furore 'another deeply difficult issue' and a 'very clumsy episode'. 'Ian got himself into a number of positions that were very unfortunate, which was a shame because he had lots of great qualities,' he told me. 'It undermined his commissionership. The story of the commissionership became bigger than the story of the Met.'[67] It made no sense that Blair would leak the information, so Tickner's recollection may have been wrong.

After fourteen years of skirmishes with senior officers, Tickner left Scotland Yard at the end of 2009. Reflecting on his time there, he admitted it was an 'extremely difficult organisation to challenge' and 'hits you in ways you don't expect'.[68]

'There is a tendency to be very defensive and that is part of the problem,' he told me. Andrew Miller, Blair's old skiing partner, had certainly been hit in ways he didn't expect. The businessman was furious at the inference that he had somehow behaved improperly.

He launched a three-year legal battle against the *Daily Mail*, which published other articles about the Impact Plus contracts. In 2012, the High Court found there were no reasonable grounds to suspect that Miller was a willing beneficiary of improper conduct and cronyism because of the friendship and he was awarded £65,000 in damages.

Blair, too, was eventually cleared of misconduct following an inquiry by the MPA. But the slow erosion of credibility that he and Scotland Yard had suffered over the last three years had taken a toll. When Boris Johnson was elected as Conservative mayor of London in 2008, he told Blair that he did not have his support. The commissioner fell on his sword.

But for some Blair's fall from grace was long overdue. The commissioner's defenestration was announced just as the inquest into the death of poor old Jean Charles de Menezes was taking place. Outside the Oval cricket ground, his cousin Erionaldo da Silva expressed delight: 'Ian Blair should have resigned three years ago when he and his men killed the wrong man.'[69]

Chapter 7

Damage Limitation

In September 2011, I was sent a cache of invoices, memos and minutes from private meetings which purported to show bribery and corruption in the Metropolitan Police. They had been sent by email from an 'Elizabeth Jennings' – clearly a cover name – and contained attachments which appeared to show how James Ibori, a charismatic and wealthy Nigerian politician, had compromised a Scotland Yard investigation into his financial affairs.

Ibori had been the prime target for the Met's proceeds of corruption unit (SCD6), a squad charged with tackling the laundering of illicit foreign assets through the City of London. The unit was set up in 2006 following a G7 summit of the world's leading nations and was placed under the control of Cressida Dick, not long after she oversaw the botched operation that led to the death of Jean Charles de Menezes. Ibori had fallen under suspicion due to a spectacular change in his fortunes after entering Nigerian politics.

He had grown up in modest surroundings in the UK, once working as a cashier at a Wickes DIY store in west London. On return to Nigeria, however, he rapidly became one of Africa's richest men, as governor of the oil-rich Delta State. During his time in office, he allegedly stole £157 million from public budgets – intended to support some of the world's poorest people – and then laundered it through UK companies and the London property market. Ibori bought a £2.2 million townhouse in Hampstead, north London, and a £3.2 million mansion in Johannesburg, the largest city in South Africa, and sent his three daughters to Port Regis boarding school in Dorset, where each place cost £23,000 a year. The five-year investigation into Ibori – codenamed Operation Heimdal – was complex. It saw detectives spend tens of thousands of pounds on flights to New York, Miami and Honolulu in an attempt to follow the money flooding out of Nigeria and into opaque tax havens.

The documents sent to me claimed to show that Ibori's representatives had paid for inside information from Met detectives working on the case. The sensitive information could then, in theory, be used by Ibori to move assets, destroy evidence and intimidate witnesses. According to the documents, the alleged bribes were organised by a private investigation firm hired by Ibori. Like its client, RISC Management had a colourful history. It was set up in 2000 by Stephen Curtis, a tax and commercial lawyer, with offices in Cavendish Square in Marylebone, central London. The respectable setting belied the firm's dubious practices. Police sources say that Curtis was believed to be laundering money for a number of high-level organised crime gangs based in the UK, although he was never charged or convicted with any wrongdoing.

The firm was initially called ISC Global and provided services for a number of Russian billionaires seeking to hide their wealth in London, including Boris Berezovsky. When Vladimir Putin became Russian President in 2000, however, he grew to resent the power of the so-called 'oligarchs', accusing them of misappropriating vast chunks of Russian's sovereign wealth and squirrelling it out of the country. A number of those oligarchs who were based in London subsequently faced investigation by the Russian authorities for fraud, embezzlement and corruption. ISC Global was created to provide security and protection for them in their new country of residence.

Curtis died in a mysterious helicopter crash in 2004. The agency was taken over by Keith Hunter, a former detective superintendent who had been recruited chiefly for his nineteen years at Scotland Yard. Hunter rebranded it as RISC Management and focused on corporate intelligence, a fast-growing industry involved in most big City deals, even though few would wish to admit it. The commodity it sold was information. Hunter took to the trade like a duck to water.

Business boomed and Hunter quickly expanded into new premises in Israel and Dubai. In 2006, the agency was caught up in the international furore that erupted after the murder of the former Russian spy Alexander Litvinenko in London. The retired KGB officer had fled Russia for Britain in November 2000 after falling out with the Putin regime and became a paid employee of MI6. He also became a source for RISC. Litvinenko visited the agency's office shortly before he died of polonium poisoning administered by Russian assassins. Traces of the radioactive substance were later found at RISC's premises in Cavendish Square.

The agency did not just employ former KGB agents. Hunter's Scotland Yard career meant that RISC had close links with serving and former Metropolitan Police officers. The firm cultivated those relationships. In August 2006, a senior member of Hunter's team organised a 'boys' holiday' on the Costa del Sol for ten serving officers. On another occasion, RISC booked a table at the annual dinner for retired CID detectives at the New Connaught Rooms in Holborn, one of Britain's leading Masonic eateries.[1]

The agency also employed former Met officers – even ones

with criminal records. One of RISC's investigators was Duncan McKelvie, who used to head the west African organised crime section at the National Criminal Intelligence Service. McKelvie was convicted in 2006 over his role in a £275 million money laundering scam. The former detective sergeant had abused his position on behalf of a gang of British fraudsters who paid him to track a police investigation into their activities, and generate false intelligence reports to keep the investigators off their trail.[2] Hunter was not deterred by this and gave McKelvie a job after he was released from jail. Indeed, the former detective superintendent was remarkably open about RISC's modus operandi when later questioned by anti-corruption detectives. 'We obviously do employ former police officers because it goes with the territory,' Hunter said. 'We've got guys that have had SFO [Serious Fraud Office] experience and we've got ex-City of London Police that have worked for us, as we have with the Met Police and ex-Customs.'[3]

RISC was the perfect fit for a millionaire Nigerian politician facing serious charges and desperate to find out what Scotland Yard had on him.

Ibori hired RISC in January 2007. Hunter dispatched one of his top men – Clifford 'Cliff' Knuckey, a former Met detective inspector – to meet the runaway governor in Paris. Scotland Yard's intelligence files note suspicions that Knuckey may have been responsible for a number of compromised police operations when he worked for the force.[4] It's unsurprising, then, that when the former detective boarded the Eurostar to meet his new client, he had already called the senior investigating officer in the Ibori investigation.[5]

DC John McDonald was one of Scotland Yard's most experienced financial investigators. McDonald – known as 'Macca' to his colleagues – worked for Barclaycard for five years before joining the Met, and knew his way around the byzantine global financial system. McDonald had also known Knuckey for years, working under him on the Met's money laundering team before the latter's retirement. The two men were close. They had gone on rugby tours together. Knuckey was present at the christening of McDonald's son in 2001.[6]

The documents sent to me by Elizabeth Jennings contained notes of meetings with Ibori's legal team where Knuckey boasted of his contacts with McDonald. The paperwork appeared to lay bare his intimate knowledge of the investigation led by his former colleague. Information apparently leaked to Knuckey included bail details, the strength of the evidence against particular suspects, lines of enquiry that detectives were actively pursuing in Nigeria, and police attempts to seize Ibori's £10 million private jet, which had been grounded in Montreal.[7] Crucially, however, the documents also contained RISC invoices that Knuckey had submitted to Ibori's lawyers, Speechly Bircham. They detailed several cash payments the former detective made to 'confidential sources'. One £5,000 payment to source 'C22' was allegedly made on 10 September 2007.

The same day Knuckey made the £5,000 payment, he spoke to McDonald by phone and later met the police officer at a pub in central London. The next day a legal attendance note detailed a meeting at Speechly Bircham where Knuckey revealed new information from the Scotland Yard investigation. Knuckey openly admitted that the insight came from a meeting the day before with a 'senior officer'.[8] No one at Speechly Bircham seemed to bat an eyelid.

Seven months later, Knuckey made another payment. The RISC invoice submitted to Ibori's law firm on 8 April 2008 suggested that the payment was to 'elicit information re forthcoming interview strategy to be deployed by police'. Just days before, Knuckey had been at a leaving party for a retiring Met officer at the Freemason's Arms on Long Acre. Also present was his former comrade, DC John McDonald.[9]

The documents Elizabeth Jennings shared with me were incendiary – but who was behind them?

It would be several years before I learnt the source. Bhadresh Gohil, a lawyer working for Ibori, had come across the evidence of illicit payments while marshalling the Nigerian's estate. A commercial solicitor of Indian heritage, Gohil had represented Bollywood stars, Air India, the Taj hotel chain and the Indian government itself. But his career imploded when he took on Ibori as a client.

Police had also found evidence that Gohil was up to no good, helping Ibori to manipulate his wealth through complex offshore structures. A year before 'Elizabeth Jennings' dropped into my inbox, Gohil had been convicted of fraud and money laundering at Southwark crown court. He was jailed for seven years. Before the prosecution, Gohil had thought about exposing the alleged police corruption he was privy to, in the hope that it might collapse the case. However, he decided against blowing the whistle after a friend, a former senior officer in the Met, advised caution. 'They will kill you,' the retired police chief said. 'Trust me, they have much bigger guns than this, and they will destroy you.'

Gohil had been sufficiently frightened at the time to keep his powder dry. Given what transpired, perhaps he should have heeded the warning for longer. But during the hot summer of 2011 – punctuated by the worst rioting in London for generations – he became frustrated. He had found himself holed up in Wandsworth prison, sharing a mess hall with Julian Assange, the founder of the rogue information website WikiLeaks, who faced extradition to Sweden over allegations of rape. Gohil didn't want to stay in prison a moment longer, and arranged for an associate to set up the 'Elizabeth Jennings' email account.

I didn't know who had sent me the documents, but it was immediately obvious that they were explosive. I spent the next six weeks speaking to contacts, tracking down witnesses and trying to substantiate the allegations, which had also been sent to prominent politicians and senior officers at Scotland Yard. It soon became clear that the Met was also investigating the claims, which gave the London *Evening Standard*, for whom I then worked, enough to run a story.

We contacted the Scotland Yard press office to give them the opportunity to reply before publication. Word quickly filtered back to McDonald and, at RISC, Keith Hunter was also briefed.

The prosecution of Ibori at the Old Bailey was about to start. As a result the *Evening Standard* was prevented from publishing many details of the saga, including the Nigerian's name, amid fears it could impact unfairly on the verdict. But Gohil had also sent the documents to the trial judge, who was sufficiently concerned to make his own enquiries about the alleged corruption. The lead prosecuting counsel, Sasha Wass QC, assured His Honour Judge Pitts that there was 'no person who is currently or has recently been the subject of an investigation arising out of this complaint'. Wass also told the judge that the Crown had 'complied with their duties of disclosure' and there was nothing in the Met's files that could either help or hinder Ibori's defence.[10] This reassurance would not be the last time that Wass inadvertently found herself reassuring judges in the Ibori saga in a manner which led to allegations of her making misleading statements.

After the hearing, even the investigating police officers were worried about Wass's comments. A police notebook that was later recovered showed they were concerned the judge may have been inadvertently 'misled'.[11] But Ibori's apparent attempt to subvert Operation Heimdal had proved unsuccessful. He pleaded guilty to fraud and embezzlement charges. Wass told the court that Ibori accepted that he had been involved in 'wide-scale theft, fraud and corruption when he was governor of Delta state'[12] and he was jailed for thirteen years.

Ibori was a notable scalp for Scotland Yard. Indeed, Prime Minister David Cameron was soon citing the Ibori conviction during a speech in Singapore in which he unveiled proposals to target fraudsters who launder money through the London property market. But inside the Met, nerves about the original investigation were starting to mount. The inquiry triggered by Gohil's disclosures – Operation Tarbes – was uncovering evidence that could, if exposed, threaten the integrity of the convictions. To make matters worse, Gohil's damaging paperwork had found its way into the hands of other journalists, including Mark Easton, the home affairs editor of the BBC. Easton was appalled by the dossier. When he contacted the Yard for their comments on the documents, he was invited in for a friendly chat.

To Easton's astonishment, Commander Peter Spindler, then head of the anti-corruption command, and Detective Chief Inspector Tim Neligan admitted that a full eight months after Gohil had circulated documents suggesting that Met detectives had been corrupted, they had done absolutely nothing to establish if they were genuine. The police had contacted neither RISC nor their clients, the law firm Speechly Bircham, to whom RISC had supplied the confidential information. Despite failing to carry out even the most basic enquiries, Neligan claimed that the RISC ledgers Gohil had distributed were 'fake'.[13]

This assessment by the anti-corruption command supported the version of events offered by John McDonald, who claims that he was able to 'dismiss pretty quickly the majority of the document'. 'By way of example, at a reported meeting with RISC Management on 23 May 2007 I was being commended at New Scotland Yard following an off-duty arrest for bravery when I disarmed a violent criminal who was threatening members of the public with a firearm,' he said. 'My wife and my six-year-old son were present at the ceremony. Another example in the document stated I had attended a meeting after work in August 2007. I was in fact on holiday abroad at the time.'[14] McDonald has always denied ever receiving payment in exchange for information, or committing any criminal offences.[15]

But at the meeting with Spindler and Neligan, Easton revealed he had spoken to Speechly Bircham, who had confirmed the authenticity of the papers. Neligan swiftly changed tack. He then tried to convince Easton that they should focus on who was distributing the documents in the first place. He already suspected Gohil and said the leaks could be a conspiracy to pervert the course of justice. When Easton interrupted, saying: 'I thought you were investigating corrupt officers?' Neligan let slip what was really worrying Scotland Yard. If the corruption claims were verified, Ibori and Gohil's convictions would collapse and a 'multimillion pound fraud trial ... would have been scuppered'.[16]

Days after the BBC meeting, Neligan was briefed on a 'suspicious activity report' regarding Ibori, which had just been filed to the Met by Speechly Bircham. It seemed media interest in the case had led Ibori's former law firm to review their files. They did not like what they saw. Following established procedures, Speechly Bircham alerted Scotland Yard and Neligan immediately visited their offices in Chancery Lane to review the paperwork. The detective found copies of the documents circulated by Gohil, detailing Knuckey's claim that he had both met with a police source on 10 September 2007, and paid a confidential source £5,000 in quick succession.[17] The papers also showed the private detective boasting about his contacts with McDonald, the investigating officer, and revealing his inside knowledge of the inquiry.[18]

Police logs show officers realised that the disclosures by Speechly Bircham 'confirmed the validity' of some of the paperwork Gohil had distributed.[19] One of the Speechly Bircham lawyers even admitted to police officers that he was worried he 'may have made a payment to McDonald through Knuckey'.[20] Speechly Bircham later 'categorically denied that either Mr Timlin or this firm knew of any payments being made by RISC to police officers'.[21]

Given what police knew by the end of the summer of 2012, what followed is outrageous. Despite the mounting concerns about corruption, McDonald was not suspended from duty. Any hint that he was under suspicion might have affected Scotland Yard's reputation.[22] The Met's hand would soon be forced, however. Gohil's lawyer appeared before the Home Affairs Select Committee and revealed his evidence of corruption under the protection of parliamentary privilege. The lawyer's intervention was reported by both *The Guardian* and the BBC as soon as the allegations were aired in front of MPs. Scotland Yard creaked into action. Anti-corruption detectives arrested Hunter, McDonald and Knuckey, who had by then left the private eye agency for a job as a money laundering compliance officer at Royal Bank of Scotland.

Hunter immediately denied all allegations of wrongdoing, telling *The Guardian*: 'RISC management does not need to pay serving police officers for confidential information as we pride ourselves on our ability to provide positive solutions and accurate information legitimately.' He added that his company was 'proud to have a network of highly professional consultants, contacts and resources'. He accused Gohil's lawyer of 'grandstanding' in front of the Commons committee, instead of taking the 'correct course of reporting the matter to the police'.

Whether reporting the allegations to the police would have ensured an objective examination of the facts is open to question. When Knuckey was interviewed by the anti-corruption squad, he denied all allegations against him and complained that his friend, DC McDonald, was the victim of a stitch-up. The interviewing officers agreed with him. Betraying their true intentions a little too readily, one of them replied: 'One of the victims in this is Mr McDonald, DC McDonald, and we are doing everything we can to try to help him, if we can, prove his innocence.'[23]

Meanwhile, Sasha Wass, the QC who had accidentally misled the court during the Ibori prosecution, was on 'tenterhooks' following the arrests. She emailed Met Police contacts asking why they had arrested McDonald: 'I have been terribly upset by the developments of the past week, as I am sure you have,' she wrote. 'I have total confidence in JMD [McDonald] and hope that this matter is resolved as soon as possible.'[24]

Operation Tarbes inched forward. For two years, the anti-corruption command gathered evidence on RISC's working methods and its relationship with the Metropolitan Police. Cressida Dick, who had once led the SCD6 unit, was forced to make a statement denying that she had briefed a private detective about the Ibori case. The future commissioner clarified her position after the discovery of a Speechly Bircham legal attendance note claiming that Dick was feeding information back to the defence team. 'I have no recollection whatsoever of having any contact [with] any individual … regarding the Ibori investigation,' she said.[25]

Detectives were astonished to discover that RISC had paid out £370,000 in cash to confidential sources between 2006 and 2008. Some of the sources were identified and alleged to be living in Dubai and the United Arab Emirates. But when Met counter-terrorism officers tracked them down the addresses were found to be non-existent. One invoice seized by the police showed a RISC investigator billing the company for £2,180 regarding 'personal meetings with confidential sources, serving and retired law enforcement officers'. Another RISC investigator submitted an expenses claim for a £12 taxi ride with a 'deputy commissioner of police'. On the same day, RISC's ledgers recorded three cash payments to confidential sources totalling £8,500.[26] Operation Tarbes also uncovered a handwritten record that noted a RISC investigator had claimed for a 'quick lunch' with a detective inspector 'to keep up contact'. Another detailed 'drinks and light refreshment' with a detective sergeant from Waltham Forest, north-east London, who has 'assisted in the past'.[27]

Hunter, the enigmatic boss, had more expensive habits. Police found that he had transported $93,000 in cash from the UK to the United States during four trips between 2007 and 2010. The former detective superintendent had deposited most of it at the Mandalay Bay casino in Las Vegas, a 43-storey desert resort which boasts its own beach and three swimming pools.[28]

As Operation Tarbes dragged on, Gohil made another attempt to clear his name. In 2014, his case was heard by the Court of Appeal. Lawyers for the Indian lawyer claimed that the relationship between

Knuckey and McDonald was not properly considered during his original trial, which rendered the conviction unsafe. Sasha Wass QC led the Crown's response to the appeal, claiming that 'nothing untoward was found between John McDonald and Knuckey'. This assurance was surprising given that Operation Tarbes had revealed that Gohil's documents were genuine – a message that had also been passed to the Crown Prosecution Service. Gohil's appeal duly failed.

It seemed as though the Yard would manage to keep a lid on the affair. But then both the Met and the CPS made a ruinous error, one that would come back to haunt them. Gohil was charged with perverting the course of justice for falsely alleging that officers were corrupt, despite knowing that his allegations were false. This was despite all the evidence seized by Operation Tarbes that supported Gohil's wider allegations. Even detectives involved in Tarbes were shocked by the charging decision, with one emailing another: 'I have a feeling that a whole new can of worms is about to be opened!'[29]

Knuckey, too, was charged with false accounting after telling police that he had not actually paid the £5,000 cash to a confidential informant. He said he had pocketed it as compensation for a Spanish holiday that had been ruined when RISC made him fly to Paris at very short notice. Other documents recovered by Operation Tarbes cast doubt on this claim,* but the story suited the narrative pushed by the Met and the CPS.

The aim seemed clear. Discredit Gohil, and no one could take the allegations of corruption seriously. This may seem fantastical, but it is how some of those inside Scotland Yard behave. Brian Paddick, the former Met deputy assistant commissioner who is now in the House of Lords, told me:

---

* Knuckey had not been on holiday when he went to Paris, while he booked his flight a week in advance.

There is a culture in the Met. It doesn't matter if the enemy is inside the Met or outside the Met. If someone is perceived to be damaging the reputation of the Met, or have one over on the Met, then the Met goes into damage limitation. A decision is made, like with Duwayne Brooks, like with Jean Charles de Menezes – trying to make out he's a bad guy. They decide this guy is going to damage us. They just try to undermine the credibility of the critic: 'Let's get everything we can on him, and try and discredit him.'

The problem, in this case, was that charging Gohil afforded him new rights of disclosure. This is granted to all defendants in court cases, who can request any documents from other parties that they believe are relevant. With properly focused disclosure requests and a barrister prepared to stand up to the Crown, Gohil could target the files that Scotland Yard held on RISC Management. If he could prove that the Met (and the CPS) believed his allegations were substantially true, he hoped the case against him would fail.

Up to this moment, the Indian lawyer had suffered many losses. But his appointment of Stephen Kamlish QC was a genuine victory. A pugnacious barrister with a reputation for independence, Kamlish had a long history of fighting the police. He was a junior to Michael Mansfield QC during the Macpherson inquiry in 1998, and had risen to become a pre-eminent criminal defence silk. He is also a streetwise operator. Kamlish once convinced a judge that his client's trial was so absurd that he should be allowed to question the prosecution barrister about the deliberate suppression of vital evidence. In a highly unusual move, the lead counsel was forced to take the stand. He collapsed under cross-examination from Kamlish and was later found unconscious and curled up in the witness box.[30]

Kamlish was the perfect silk for Gohil and the QC's command of the facts would result in mayhem for the Metropolitan Police. Over the course of eighteen months, Gohil's legal team, led by the barrister and his forensic junior, Catherine Oborne, swamped prosecutors with questions about the relationship between RISC Management and Scotland Yard. They were seeking evidence that supported Gohil's allegations of police corruption. The defence team was told repeatedly – and erroneously – that there was nothing left to disclose. But they kept chipping away. At first, they encountered a wall of silence. But step by step, pulling on different threads to see where they would lead, they started to unravel the scandal.

As the trial date approached, Kamlish's increasingly refined disclosure requests had the Yard backed into a corner. The Crown had nowhere to hide. After claiming for years that there was nothing further to disclose, prosecutors finally released more than 7,000 pages of Met Police files that caused the trial judge, Peter Testar, to say he had never seen anything like it 'in all my years at the Bar'.[31]

Gohil's legal team could not believe what they had found. The documents released included a report from Operation Limonium, a secret Met investigation into RISC's activities dating back to 2007 – the year of the Ibori inquiry. It labelled the private investigations agency an 'organised crime network' that was 'attempting to penetrate high-level Met operations'.[32] It went on to say: 'Intelligence shows that RISC Management is an aggressive corruptor of serving MPS [Metropolitan Police Service] officers and staff. Members of RISC are in ongoing and corrupt relationships with police officers.'

The report's conclusion was damning:

The RISC network poses a serious strategic threat to the MPS. It has the financial means, proven corrupt intent and contacts to mount a sustained assault on the integrity of MPS assets. The commodity in question is information and their chosen method of acquisition is the focused exploitation of MPS officers and staff.[33]

Intelligence reports revealed that more than 300 phone calls were made between Met Police officers and RISC investigators over a twelve-month period.[34] Operation Limonium said the threat posed by RISC 'cannot be understated [*sic*]' and concluded: 'The longer these networks are allowed to flourish unchecked, the more profound the problem will become.'[35]

Police investigations feared to have been compromised by RISC included the 'cash for honours' probe. In 2007, the Met had launched an inquiry into claims that political parties had effectively traded the award of peerages and knighthoods in return for large donations. In 2007, the Met's anti-corruption command launched Operation Bartonia into RISC's suspected attempt to corrupt the investigation. One report said: 'Bartonia is concerned with the suspected leakage of information from the "cash for honours" enquiry to an employee of RISC Management Limited.' According to the files, RISC is said to have received details of charging decisions regarding three suspects in the honours probe before they were made public. Bartonia suspected that RISC had been hired by Sir Christopher Evans, a prominent Labour donor who was one of those arrested.[36] Evans, who led the investment fund Merlin Biosciences, said that he hired RISC but that the work had nothing to do with the inquiry. There is no suggestion that Evans was aware of RISC's activities or requested such an approach.

More pertinent to Gohil's defence, however, was the revelation that the Met's anti-corruption command knew all about the relationship between Knuckey and McDonald. Indeed, detectives were monitoring the RISC operative and his former colleague right at the moment that Gohil had alleged the bribery took place. Gohil's most serious allegation had centred on a £5,000 payment that Knuckey had paid to one of his confidential sources on 10 September 2007. It turned out that the Met's anti-corruption command were briefed on the alleged bribe when it took place. HM Revenue and Customs (HMRC) were investigating Knuckey on suspicion of VAT fraud, and were listening into his phone calls in real time. After Knuckey had left McDonald on the evening of 10 September 2007, the live intercept picked up a phone call in which he was heard 'bragging' about the payment to McDonald. The alleged bribe was even logged in the Operation Limonium report: 'Intelligence from a non-attributable source was received on 10 September 2007 that indicates that KNUCKEY is currently in contact with officers working on the IBORI investigation and has recently met with DC John McDONALD and paid McDONALD money for information.'[37] At the time of the alleged payment, Commander Peter Spindler, the head of the anti-corruption command who would later fob off the BBC's Mark Easton, was briefed on the situation.[38]

No action was taken against McDonald, who continued to work on the Ibori investigation for a further five years. Nothing happened to Knuckey, either. Sasha Wass told several judges that no information about their allegedly corrupt relationship had ever existed. But when Gohil tried to make similar allegations, he had faced criminal charges for lying.

The case is very revealing in a number of important ways. Firstly, this sort of rogue, 'black ops' treatment is often deployed against people who try to expose police corruption. But it is very rare to see it laid out in such detail. It should not be forgotten that Bhadresh Gohil was a convicted money launderer with motives that were less than pure. He had helped a fraudster secrete his wealth, was privy to Ibori's attempts to corrupt the police, and only tried to blow the whistle on it when he got caught. Even so, this was stunning evidence of police misconduct. Many in the Met claim the 'bad old days' are behind them. But Gohil's claims, which were circulated to the highest echelons of the Yard,[39] were very current. Yet rather than dealing with criminality in their ranks, the Met tried to annihilate the source of the information. It speaks to the culture of cover-up referred to by Brian Paddick, a culture that still thrives today.

Secondly, the Ibori case shows the lengths that Scotland Yard will go to deny and deflect accusations of corruption. They know it is there; they monitor it every day. But very little has been done to tackle it since the days of Operation Othona. Just as the price of liberty is eternal vigilance, the price of a clean police force must surely be a relentless and enduring fight against corruption. Yet as one Met Police source puts it: 'The Yard is like a voyeur when it comes to corruption. They just like to watch.'

In many ways, Knuckey, McDonald and Hunter are themselves victims of the Met's warped ideology. Evidence detailing their involvement in some pretty disconcerting events was now in the public realm. The decision, however, was taken that they were not to be prosecuted. Of course, this might come as a relief to them. But the decision also prevents them from being exonerated by a jury, and the reputational stain lingers.

When Stephen Kamlish secured the release of documents showing that DC McDonald had made at least nineteen unexplained cash deposits totalling thousands of pounds into his bank account while working on the Ibori case, it was the final blow for the Met's case against Gohil.[40] It goes without saying that the Met and the

CPS had insisted for months that no such evidence existed. By this stage, Kamlish was getting increasingly animated during the pre-trial hearings:

> The Crown is prosecuting Mr Gohil in the knowledge that there is clear and compelling, direct and circumstantial evidence of a corrupt relationship between Risc and MPS officers, both within the Ibori case and outside it … The Crown is prosecuting Mr Gohil for falsely alleging that this corruption existed. To do so runs contrary to the known and objective facts as served and disclosed by the Crown itself.[41]

Kamlish was particularly troubled by events during Gohil's unsuccessful appeal against his conviction, which was made two years previously. When the lawyer first tried to overturn his conviction, the police, the CPS and prosecuting counsel, including Wass, had to decide what to tell the Appeal Court judges about the corruption allegations he had made. A note was drafted. It referenced the phone call intercepted by HMRC and admitted that the Met had evidence that 'Cliff Knuckey had bragged to others that he had paid DC McDonald for information'. However, this sentence was removed from the final note presented to the judge, which simply read: 'Intelligence suggested that DC McDonald and RISC operative Cliff Knuckey were known to each other.'

When the appeal hearing commenced, Wass was forced to provide more detail. She assured the judge:

> Nothing untoward was found between John McDonald and Knuckey at all. What is more untoward is what the source of that intelligence was … It doesn't undermine the Crown case at all. It

shows that somebody made a phone call to say there was a corrupt relationship, it was taken very seriously, looked at thoroughly, and nothing untoward discovered.

Wass did not mention that the phone call was from Knuckey himself. Kamlish was incandescent two years later when these facts emerged during Gohil's prosecution and argued that the Court of Appeal had been seriously misled.

The case was threatening to spiral off in directions that the Crown could no longer control. Alison Saunders, the director of public prosecutions, stepped in and collapsed the case, seemingly before any more damage could be done. She also ordered an inquest into what had happened.

Wass and Scotland Yard blamed each other. Wass was furious that the Met's anti-corruption command 'were aware from 2007 of the matters which eventually led to the termination of the prosecution case'. She said the police made 'vague and ambiguous suggestions' to her about the intercepted phone call, with its significance only being communicated to her just before the trial was due to commence. 'Prior to that date, I had specifically been told that the material was anonymous, unsubstantiated, that it had been thoroughly investigated and had been dismissed,' she told the internal inquiry. The revelation, she continued, 'was met with universal astonishment by the CPS and counsel, none of whom had been told the source of this intelligence previously'.[42]

By contrast, anti-corruption detectives claimed that they had told the CPS and counsel the source of the intelligence on many occasions between 2012 and the collapse of Gohil's trial in 2015. It should be noted that when the *Mail on Sunday* published a critical story about Wass's handling of the Gohil prosecution in 2016, the

QC sued for libel and the *Mail on Sunday* paid Wass substantial damages. The newspaper read out a statement in court saying that Wass 'acted honestly, entirely professionally and in accordance with both her knowledge and instructions'.

> She complied fully with her duties to the Court; she has not in any way lied or deliberately misled any Court and there is no basis whatsoever for questioning her integrity. In addition, Ms Wass was in no way involved in any attempt to bury or tamper with evidence of police corruption.[43]

Wass put the Gohil case behind her and went on to forge a successful television career. She now works as a libel lawyer and hosts *Murder, Mystery and My Family*, a BBC One series which examines historic cases involving the death penalty, to see if any of them resulted in a miscarriage of justice.

And DC McDonald continued fighting crime at the Metropolitan Police until 2018, when he retired with a certificate of 'exemplary conduct'.[44] He continues to vehemently deny all allegations of wrongdoing, adding: 'The attack on my professional reputation and integrity due to these unfounded allegations has been severe, the effect on me and my family should not be understated.'[45]

Chapter 8

The Supergrass

Clive Driscoll could not believe his eyes as he rifled through the dusty papers.

The detective chief inspector had gone to a decommissioned police station in Deptford, south-east London, to give it a final check before it was sold off to a private developer. The Grade II-listed red-brick building with magnificent wrought iron gates was due to be converted into a network of artists' studios and the Met was days away from handing over the keys.[1]

It was the summer of 2006 and Driscoll wanted to make sure his colleagues had removed everything the force needed to retain before the sale went through. In the basement there was a door he had to force open. Behind it, he found an extraordinary trove of police files relating to several high-profile unsolved cases. One of them was the murder of Stephen Lawrence. The case files were grouped under the title of the original police investigation: Operation Fishpool. 'I couldn't believe it,' Driscoll told me. 'Deptford police station was like the *Mary Celeste*. The police had already gone but when I went into that room there were stacks and stacks of papers. Stephen's wasn't the only murder ... there were several in there.'[2] It was thirteen years after Stephen's death and seven since the landmark public inquiry led by Sir William Macpherson had ripped into the original police investigation, branding Scotland Yard 'institutionally racist'.

Driscoll represents the best of the Metropolitan Police. He is a tall, genial figure with a keen sense of duty and passionately devoted to his job. When he asked a Scotland Yard superintendent what he should do with the 560 crates of material on the Stephen Lawrence case, he was alarmed at the reply: 'Bin them.'[3] Driscoll could not bring himself to comply. He had been inspired to join the Met by the popular BBC series *Dixon of Dock Green*, a gentle and reassuring account of the mostly petty crimes dealt with at a fictional London police station. Driscoll was impressed by the show's central character, PC George Dixon, who he said 'struck fear into the hearts of criminals' while retaining 'a sense of community, of putting people first, of knowing what was right and wrong … he had a way with him that put you at ease'. Driscoll possessed a similar quality. He would soon use it to dramatic effect in the Lawrence case.

Driscoll ignored his superintendent and decided to approach a more senior officer he thought would be more sympathetic. Cressida Dick was already on her way to becoming Scotland Yard's first female commissioner. But in 2006 she was still a commander, steering her way through a number of other controversial cases including the killing of Jean Charles de Menezes. Driscoll made an appointment to see her and secured her agreement to take over Operation Fishpool.

He already knew something of the case. During the Macpherson inquiry in 1998, Driscoll had worked in New Scotland Yard. He had witnessed senior officers privately panicking about the public hearings. It had prompted him to take a closer look and he didn't much like what he saw.

'From the outside, the investigation team did seem to have been presented with some A1 evidence, wrapped up with a bow,' Driscoll recalled in his autobiography, *In Pursuit of the Truth*. 'Even before Macpherson published his report, it struck me that the Met had gone to extraordinary lengths to deny any wrongdoing.'

Driscoll was more independent-minded than many of his Met colleagues, more willing to pursue evidence without fear or favour and more open to the possibility that Scotland Yard might, on occasion, make mistakes. The behaviour of the Met during the Lawrence inquiry led him to privately question the decision making at the top of the force. 'Whatever the truth [about the Met's handling of the case] was, somebody knew it and thought they could suppress it. And while it's all very well looking after your own – who wouldn't want a boss to fight their corner? – this was a murder case,' he explained. 'There was a grieving family out there whose pain was exacerbated every time the police denied making mistakes. And at the heart of it all was a young, innocent boy stabbed to death for no reason at all.'[4]

Driscoll was well aware of the risks involved in taking on a case tainted by racism and hints of police corruption. One of his first actions was to move all the Operation Fishpool papers from Deptford to a secure office in Kingston. 'The way the case had gone on I didn't want someone driving by and lobbing a petrol bomb through the window,' he said. 'There was little enough strong evidence as there was – I didn't need the rest going up in a literal puff of smoke.'[5]

Any outsider might conclude that Driscoll's Met colleagues would be delighted one of the force's finest investigators had agreed to take on such a difficult case. What officer wouldn't want to right the wrongs of the past and restore the Met's reputation? Yet Scotland Yard at that time was far from the haven of honour and trust imagined by those outside.

Most of Driscoll's colleagues discouraged him from getting involved in the Lawrence case. One officer after another responded along similar lines: 'What makes you think you won't fail, too? There's no point letting it ruin your career, like it has everyone else's.'[6]

The caution and scepticism he encountered was part of a self-serving, inward-looking management culture at the Met which Driscoll now believes inhibits the talents the police have at their disposal. 'Managers seemed to be more concerned with protecting themselves than encouraging officers to perform the duties they had joined to carry out,' he said.

> I got sick of bosses asking me: 'What's your exit strategy?' I've always felt that by taking on another case there is an obligation – a moral one, perhaps for want of a better word – for me to finish it. I have to say the choruses of 'Bin it', 'Shelve it' and 'Walk away' became a regular, sometimes daily, occurrence. But I never got into the job for gold stars. All I cared about – all I still care about – was the victim. Do they or do they not get justice?

Yet the darkness that smothered the Lawrence case began to yield a few sparks of light. 'The family are a nightmare,' one of Driscoll's colleagues told him. 'They won't give you the time of day. Doreen Lawrence wouldn't even let the original investigation have access to her son's school records. So much for wanting the killers caught.'[7] As he started what became a two-year trawl through his cache of police files, Driscoll had occasion to remember that warning. It couldn't have been more wrong.

The new boss of Operation Fishpool decided to get a better feel for the case by reading the old files on a bench by Well Hall roundabout in Eltham, close to where Stephen lost his life. It was a slightly eccentric ploy, even by Driscoll's maverick standards. Yet he soon realised that the Scotland Yard gossip about Doreen and the supposedly obdurate Lawrence family was nonsense. 'The more I read the more I despaired,' he said.

> There was absolutely nothing that woman would not have done, no permission she had not given, no stone she would not have agreed to overturn in the pursuit of her son's killers. So where the hell had this other story [about Stephen's school records], this other image of her, come from? I'm not sure I ever found the answer to that. What I did discover was that no one's word was to be trusted.[8]

There was further progress when Driscoll ordered his team to stage a blow-by-blow re-enactment of the murder. It took six hours with a police officer fitting the height and build of Stephen. As the carefully choreographed re-enactment unfolded, the detective realised that everyone, from the original investigating officers through to Sir William Macpherson himself, had missed a crucial element in the assault.

'All the original police reports, all the forensic descriptions and even the Macpherson report, all said that Stephen had been the victim of a "brief" attack,' Driscoll said. Following the re-enactment, the detective concluded that it must have lasted up to sixty seconds.

> It was a massive mental breakthrough, because suddenly I realised everyone had been coming at it all wrong. If you think something was over quickly you don't anticipate finding much evidence. Whereas if you think a crime took a while to go down, you'll expect more clues

so you might spend longer looking for them. All my instincts said the crime scene and the evidence we had already held more information than it was letting on.[9]

Driscoll gathered the junior officers on his team and issued his instructions. 'Think of the number of times you can be hit in thirty or forty or fifty seconds,' he said.

Think of the amount of contact you might have with those who are trying to hurt you. Think of each of those seconds and think how much blood and fibres and who knows what could have jumped across in that time. Think of those fibres and, if at all possible, go and find them.[10]

Driscoll's new team set off on a promising new approach to the case, but within weeks old ghosts had returned to haunt it.

* * *

It started with a bent former cop who found God, went to jail and turned on his corrupt former colleagues. Neil Putnam had become a supergrass, a significant informer on criminal activity inside Scotland Yard. Now he was telling a team of investigative journalists from the BBC's *Panorama* programme everything he knew about the Stephen Lawrence murder. The interview, broadcast just a month after Driscoll took over the police investigation, would detonate yet another bomb under the case, leaving Scotland Yard reeling.

Putnam had been working for the South East Regional Crime Squad (SERCS), a unit that would later become notorious when he and five of his colleagues were jailed for selling narcotics and other goods they had seized during criminal investigations. In 1998 Putnam had undergone a crisis of conscience, turned to religion and handed himself into the Yard's anti-corruption command, confessing to sixteen criminal offences committed over a period of six years. Putnam told investigators he succumbed to temptation when his SERCS team seized 200 kilograms of cannabis resin. One of his colleagues stole some of the drugs and then handed him £300 two weeks later. 'You're caught unawares, on the hop,' said Putnam. 'You're not expecting it and then suddenly this money is just thrust into your hand, and the words are "That is for you", and it's there, it's on you, and you have a split second to make your decision. In that split second, I made the wrong decision.'[11]

Among the colleagues he implicated in illicit activities was his close friend DS John 'OJ' Davidson.[12] The detectives used to play football together and visited each other's family homes. Davidson was present at the christening of Putnam's son.[13] The allegation was all the more devastating as Davidson was one of the investigating officers on the original Stephen Lawrence murder inquiry. Davidson was never charged, and for years Putnam's allegations remained hidden from view.

By 2006, however, Putnam was out of jail and willing to talk to *Panorama* about his criminal career. This caused panic inside Scotland Yard. 'The Met was extremely jumpy about the programme,' Driscoll told me. 'Cressida Dick asked me what I was going to do with it.' But he saw it as an opportunity. 'It got people talking. I got the BBC to put our incident room number on it and we got loads of phone calls.'[14]

The broadcast may have helped Driscoll's inquiry. But the *Panorama* episode was seen as another calamity for Scotland Yard. Putnam told a television audience of millions that Stephen's killers had been protected by Davidson because his former friend had a corrupt relationship with Clifford Norris, the gangster father of David Norris, one of the prime suspects in the murder.

'Davidson told me that he was looking after Norris,' Putnam told *Panorama*. 'That to me meant he was protecting him. He was protecting his family against arrests and any conviction. Davidson told me he was making a "nice little earner" out of it. And by "nice little earner", I knew that meant he was receiving corrupt payment.'[15]*

The programme caused pandemonium – in the media and in Parliament. Neville Lawrence said it 'all fits in with what we, in the family, were worried about ... No one believed us then – but perhaps they will now.'[16] He renewed his call for a new investigation into 'corruption and collusion'.

Putnam's interview emboldened others to come forward, some from the unlikeliest of quarters. Less than twenty-four hours later, John Grieve, a deputy assistant commissioner who had led the Lawrence case in 2000 – without getting anywhere – admitted he too feared that corrupt officers might have helped to protect Stephen's killers.[17]

Putnam claimed that criminality was endemic throughout Scotland Yard, 'At least somewhere within every branch, there was at least one officer who was corrupt.'[18] He made several specific allegations against his old friend Davidson, including a claim that the two men once split the proceeds from a stolen consignment of Omega watches. Putnam also claimed that Davidson gave him £50 he described as 'Sargey's Christmas box' – part of the proceeds

---

* Years later, the Independent Office for Police Conduct and the National Crime Agency investigated corruption in the Stephen Lawrence case and found no evidence to support Putnam's allegations. They concluded there was 'no indication of corruption on the part of Davidson relating to the original Stephen Lawrence murder investigation'.

from the sale of a recovered haul of electrical goods from a hi-jacked lorry in 1994.

When a cocaine dealer was stopped at a Dulwich pub several months later, Putnam also said he saw Davidson had been passed a white carrier bag. 'I could see that there was a brick-shaped object inside ... He just turned around and walked away,' he said. The next day, Putnam says Davidson gave him £500 in an envelope, telling him it was his share of the proceeds from the unspecified package.[19]

When Putnam first came forward, John Yates's anti-corruption squad was so concerned about the sensitivity of his allegations that they moved their gabbling colleague in secret to a police station in Folkestone, a safe distance from prying ears at Scotland Yard. It proved the oddest of excursions. Putnam was taken for long walks and bought pints of beer and fish and chips on the beach by his police handlers. On one occasion, bizarrely, he was allowed to test drive an Alfa Romeo.[20] Most curious of all, however, was the way officers dealt with Putnam's claims. In a move that would once again stir controversy for the Lawrence investigation, Yates's team decided not to tape-record the initial interviews with Putnam – a breach of standard police procedure. Instead, they jotted down his allegations in A4 notebooks.[21] This might be explained by the timing of Putnam's conversion to honesty, which came at a polit-ically perilous time for the Yard. His claims about Davidson were made in 1998 – just as his old friend was called as a witness to the Macpherson inquiry to defend his decision making in the original Lawrence investigation.

Putnam would later say that when he first linked Davidson to Clif-ford Norris, the officer interviewing him declared that the allegation would 'blow the Metropolitan Police wide apart'.[22] Yet Macpherson was told nothing about Putnam's claims. His report criticised Davidson's conduct but concluded that he had not tried to thwart the investigation.[23] By now it should surprise no one that there was no trace of Putnam's claims connecting Davidson to Norris in the notes of his interviews with Scotland Yard. Putnam believes that his debrief filled at least fifteen A4 notebooks. But when the Met was later ordered to produce them, only five were presented.[24] And after the *Panorama* broadcast in 2006, the Met denied that Putnam had made any allegations about Davidson and Clifford Norris.

All this was profoundly awkward for Scotland Yard, which found itself in the position of trying to undermine Putnam's integrity despite the fact that his evidence as a supergrass had led to several corrupt police officers being jailed. Yates himself told colleagues that Putnam was a 'credible witness' whose value 'cannot be over-estimated'.[25] Years later, Putnam is still astonished by the contortions his Scotland Yard superiors went through in trying to defend their handling of the Lawrence case. 'They believed me about everything, except Stephen Lawrence,' he told a friend.[26]*

After that *Panorama* broadcast, more information emerged to support Putnam's version of events. His ex-wife Gail always supported her former husband, and emphasised the 'consternation and sense of injustice' that Putnam felt when his allegations about Davidson were not acted upon. Furthermore, a leaked memo written by David Hamilton, the former head of legal affairs at Scotland Yard, warned that 'disclosures relevant to Davidson's contact with the Norris family' could adversely affect the Met's attempts to defend a legal claim brought by Doreen and Neville Lawrence. A former

---

* Years later, an independent review of the Stephen Lawrence case found that it was impossible to conclude whether or not Putnam was telling the truth, and said it remained 'a live issue with powerful arguments on both sides'.

senior Crown Prosecution Service lawyer, Martin Polaine, who used to prosecute the Met's corruption cases in the late 1990s, has also said he recalls hearing of an 'association between Clifford Norris and John Davidson'.[27]

According to Clive Driscoll, who also interviewed Putnam, the supergrass 'never changed his story'. Driscoll also noted that Putnam's allegations were never passed on to Macpherson, which he found strange. 'But it won't seem strange to the Met,' he added enigmatically.[28] The implication is that once again the Met was trying to protect itself from allegations that that the original investigation into Lawrence's murder had been corrupt. Unfortunately for Scotland Yard, there was a lot more still to emerge about the criminal connections of DS John 'OJ' Davidson.

* * *

It was still dark when a team from the Met's anti-corruption command entered the SERCS offices in Kingston, south-west London. During the dawn raid in October 1995, officers seized diaries, work rosters, vehicle logs and paperwork all relating to a most unusual complaint.[29] The Met had been tipped off that five of its officers were secretly and illicitly doubling up as bodyguards for Reg Grundy, the Australian TV mogul. Grundy, who died in 2016, was responsible for a string of television hits including *Neighbours*, *Bruce's Price Is Right*, *Wheel of Fortune* and *Prisoner: Cell Block H*. When Grundy was staying at his Belgravia mansion, he paid for freelance police protection. One of his minders was John Davidson. As a result of the tip-off, the Met's anti-corruption command sent in a surveillance team and officers disguised as joggers watched Grundy's bodyguards in a central London park.[30]

When confronted with the evidence of improper police behaviour, Davidson and the others called in sick, claiming to be too ill to appear before a disciplinary panel. Under the rules in force at the time this meant the hearings could not take place, and they could retire with all their benefits still intact. Commander Roy Clark, head of the anti-corruption command at the time, expressed his frustration in a written note:

> Davidson is, in my opinion, attempting to avoid a Discipline Board and obtain an enhanced pension in the process. I feel we should resist at all costs such a venture as it damages the image of the police service in the eyes of the public and does nothing to reassure officers who do not involve themselves in circumstances resulting in discipline hearings and are content to retire on ordinary pension grounds.[31]

The case caused great embarrassment to the Met when details emerged in 1998 during a hearing of the Home Affairs Select Committee attended by Sir Paul Condon, then the commissioner. Within months the Home Secretary, Jack Straw, announced sweeping changes to police discipline to make it easier to weed out corrupt officers.[32]

Several of the rogue detectives who worked for Grundy were named by the media following briefings from the Met, just before the Macpherson inquiry was due to start hearing evidence from witnesses, including Davidson. His role in the Grundy affair would only emerge after the *Panorama* programme was broadcast in 2006.

The Met had separate intelligence that raised questions about Davidson's integrity, but that too was never disclosed to the Macpherson inquiry. One report, from Operation Othona, was particularly damning. While he was suspended over the Grundy affair, Davidson paid an unauthorised visit to a south London criminal 'well known as having corrupt links with MPS officers'.[33] The man in question, who was also a police informant, had been 'seriously injured' during a drugs transaction that went wrong. He was taken to Greenwich Hospital and placed under armed guard. Davidson had visited the informant in hospital, raising the suspicions of a colleague, who wondered what a suspended detective was doing anywhere near the case.

The intelligence report also said: 'As can be seen by the numerous allegations of corrupt practice against Davidson he is a thoroughly corrupt individual. Davidson has no qualms about mixing with known criminals and utilising serving MPS officers to progress both his legitimate and corrupt enquiries.' It continued: 'His many corrupt contacts within both the serving and ex-police arenas coupled with his level of expertise and knowledge of police techniques make him a viable commodity among the criminal community,' concluding that 'DS John Davidson is intrinsically corrupt. The weight of intelligence from the numerous operations levelled against him is damning.'[34]

After Davidson retired in 1996, the Met continued to receive reports of his activities. According to other intelligence files that were never disclosed to Macpherson, Davidson once sought out a former Met colleague to conduct checks on the Police National Computer,[35] to which access is strictly limited. In June 1999, just after Macpherson published his report, Davidson also approached a former colleague in the Met's extradition squad and asked him to carry out passport checks to locate the wife of a client, according to the files.[36]

Adding to all this were intelligence reports that Davidson was 'known to associate' with some of the prime suspects for the 1987 murder of private investigator Daniel Morgan, who had been found dead in a south London pub car park (see Chapter 3). This may be a reference to the job Davidson took up on retirement. He went to work for Mayfayre Associates, the private detective firm set up by Alec Leighton and Duncan Hanrahan, the Met detectives who were friendly with Jonathan Rees, the prime suspect for the Morgan murder.

John Yates, the senior officer involved in the original debrief of Neil Putnam, has never been in any doubt about Davidson's true nature. He recorded that Davidson was one of fourteen 'core nominals' – detectives whose 'criminality is extensive and, in essence, amounts to police officers operating as a professional organised crime syndicate'.[37] And in the 2006 *Panorama* programme on Davidson, Yates, who by then had been promoted to deputy assistant commissioner, did not mince his words. 'From all the evidence I've seen, the intelligence I've seen, I have no doubt he was corrupt.'[38]

Davidson has always denied any links to corruption and has never been convicted. But he had begun to loom large in Clive Driscoll's inquiry into the death of Stephen Lawrence.

* * *

On the fifteenth anniversary of Stephen's death in April 2008, politicians, police officers and interested members of the public gathered at the church of St Martin in the Fields in Trafalgar Square, to remember a young man whose murder had not yet been solved. As the lead investigator on the Stephen Lawrence inquiry, Clive Driscoll was seated close to Gordon Brown, the Prime Minister, and David Cameron, then Conservative Leader of the Opposition.

The veteran detective had only recently been allowed to start calling his work an 'investigation'. His boss, Cressida Dick, had until then insisted on describing it as a 'review'.

'If anyone asked me, I said "Yeah, I'm investigating", because we were going out and speaking to witnesses,' he told me. 'But if you spoke to Cressida or any of the senior management team, they would say it was a review, because [the case] makes people do daft things. It's bonkers.'[39]

Whatever the label, Driscoll's activities had benefited from a change in the law of double jeopardy, which for centuries had prevented people from being tried for the same crime twice. The collapse of the private prosecution of the five Lawrence suspects might have prevented them ever facing trial again – had the then Home Secretary, David Blunkett, not changed the law to allow re-trials in 2003, provided there was 'new and compelling' evidence.

Driscoll's perception of the Lawrence case had shifted dramatically after the re-enactment showed the attack might have lasted for up to a full minute. He ordered a fresh round of forensic tests on the clothes and exhibits he recovered from the dusty corner of Deptford police station. He also argued – successfully – that the job should be taken away from Forensic Science Services, a government-owned laboratory which had carried out hundreds of thousands of scans on Lawrence-related material and found nothing of value.

Driscoll had previously been impressed with a private firm, LGC Forensics, based in Oxford. He organised the transfer of the Lawrence evidence in the hope that they would spot something new. Within weeks his hunch paid off. LGC analysts found red fibres from Stephen's polo shirt on a jacket belonging to prime suspect Gary Dobson, and on jeans belonging to David Norris. The scientists summoned Driscoll to a meeting to reveal their findings with 'smiles like Cheshire Cats', he later recalled. 'This discovery was the spark the case had been crying out for for thirteen years. It was the breakthrough to rescue the Met's reputation.'[40]

The detective had done more to crack the case than any police officer had managed throughout the investigation into Stephen Lawrence's murder. But if he thought his findings would finally overcome internal resistance from malign forces inside Scotland Yard, he was in for disappointment. Senior officers reacted to the breakthrough by shutting down Driscoll's office and ordering his team to move thousands of sensitive files to another site across London. 'This was a massive disruption – not least because the loss of just one piece of paper might jeopardise our case,' he said. Driscoll wondered about the Met's true motives: 'During my six-year investigation, I had to move offices five times. It was either the worst form of stupidity, or someone somewhere was trying to cause problems.'[41] The 'top brass' also started 'plucking people out from my team to work on other jobs', causing Driscoll to write to a senior officer, saying: 'If I didn't know better, I'd think you were trying to disrupt this case.'[42]

These tensions were still very much on Driscoll's mind as he warbled away in the Prime Minister's ear at the Lawrence anniversary service. Then his mobile phone rang and he stopped singing at once. In a scene that a Hollywood scriptwriter might have dismissed as too corny, Driscoll left the church and was standing outside, looking up at a massive poster of Stephen Lawrence, when he learnt he had cracked the case.

'I was literally looking straight at [Stephen] when I was told [forensics] had found blood on Gary Dobson's jacket,' he said. Driscoll knew the discovery would strengthen the earlier breakthrough on fibres. He looked up at the poster and said quietly: 'Well, Stephen mate, it ain't going to be long now.'

Driscoll briefed Doreen and Neville Lawrence on the development in confidence. The anguish of their bereavement had proved a terrible burden and the couple had split up several years earlier. Driscoll won over both parents by simply being honest and straightforward with them. He had visited Doreen over tea and doughnuts at the memorial centre for her son in Deptford and found her character wholly at odds with the angry, uncooperative mother described by some of his colleagues. 'I take people as I find them,' Driscoll recalled. 'With Doreen Lawrence, I saw a fragile, fifty-something woman who had lost a son, who had been a victim of police incompetence and probably corruption, and who had run out of patience with the police. But she hadn't run out of patience with me.'[43]

Driscoll also made an important connection with Neville. 'Previous [investigating officers] on Stephen's case have met Neville Lawrence in Florida; they've met him in Jamaica; they've met him in Scotland,' said Driscoll. 'I met him in a noodle bar in Plumstead. And I bought the noodles.'[44] They quickly struck up a rapport. 'The person who says Neville Lawrence isn't lovely is a liar,' said Driscoll. 'Despite going through everything he has – including the breakup of his marriage – he remains the most upbeat, kindly gent you could hope to meet. He just said: "Do your best, officer. That's all we've ever asked. Do your best for Stephen."'[45]

Driscoll certainly tried. By 2010, he had persuaded the then director of public prosecutions, Keir Starmer, to authorise charges against Dobson and Norris. But as the case was being prepared for trial at the Old Bailey, Driscoll decided he needed someone to inject some emotion into the proceedings. He had been around the block often enough to know that a successful prosecutor engages a jury and keeps them interested by turning the crime into a human tragedy – in this case the story of a promising young man felled by an unprovoked attack.

Driscoll was concerned that a long and potentially dry discussion about fibres and blood samples would leave jury members looking at their watches.[46] He needed an eye-witness to the murder, someone to relive the horror of the Eltham attack in a London courtroom. Someone to talk warmly of Stephen and his life. But the only person to fit that bill was no friend of Scotland Yard. Duwayne Brooks would take a lot of persuading.

* * *

When he saw the blue lights flashing in his rear-view mirror, Duwayne Brooks pulled over. He knew the drill by now. A police officer approached, told him to get out, and promptly searched the car. It was 1999, a few months after the Macpherson report had ruled that Duwayne was also a victim of the attack, and had castigated his treatment at the hands of Scotland Yard. But Duwayne was still a black man, driving around south London. He still had a target on his back.

Duwayne was arrested several times in the years after the attack, but no charges ever stuck.[47] That day on Consort Road in Peckham, the police were looking for trouble. When they couldn't find it, they made it up. By then Duwayne had left school and was working as a photocopy engineer. Some of the tools of his trade were lying on the back seat and a police officer identified a metal rod as an 'offensive weapon'. Duwayne was carrying a credit card and chequebook, which the police promptly accused him of stealing, even though both bore his name. He was charged and only escaped prosecution after his employer confirmed to the court that the rod was indeed part of his toolkit.[48]

There were other more sinister incidents. On another occasion, an officer reached through his open car window, 'grabbed my collar and punched me in the face five times' before pulling him into a police van screaming: 'Get on the floor, you fucking n****r.'[49] He was later released on bail and faced no charges. Duwayne's car was also broken into ten times in the two years immediately following the Macpherson inquiry. He blames rogue elements inside Scotland Yard.[50]

'I was sure people wanted me out of the picture and had done for years,' he said.

Somehow, the police and the government – the establishment – felt I was a danger. I was the survivor, the one who had seen, albeit imperfectly, what had happened; the one who'd experienced the brunt of police racism at first hand … They knew I was explosive, that I wouldn't be shut up easily, that I was liable to question anything at any time.

In August 1999, Duwayne announced that he was going to sue the Metropolitan Police for negligence and racism.[51] He made the news public during an audience Q&A after a performance of a play about the Macpherson inquiry and predicted there would be a serious attempt to discredit him.[52]

Sure enough, weeks later Duwayne was arrested again. This time the charges were much more serious. Duwayne had ended a brief relationship with a young woman and, before he knew it, she had been swept up by police officers and was making allegations of attempted rape and sexual assault.

The story immediately leaked out. As he was driven from court to be held on remand, Duwayne saw *Evening Standard* billboards all over London which read 'Lawrence friend on attempted rape charge'. He later discovered that a *Sun* reporter had been tipped off by a source – presumably a police officer – minutes after midnight, the moment he was charged.[53]

Duwayne was held for seven days in Belmarsh prison, south-east London. It proved a punishing ordeal:

> I wanted to think about nothing, but pictures of Steve and me kept coming into my mind – sitting on the wall waiting for a bus, down at the kebab shop, watching kung fu movies, running back trying to beat his Mum's curfew, the attack, his blood bubbling up in his jacket.
>
> I felt sick. It was seven years since Steve had been killed, and here I was in prison charged with a sex offence. Somehow, I knew it was all connected, but I found it hard to work out exactly how. I'd been attacked, my best mate had been murdered in the attack, and for some reason the police resented me so much, perhaps resented the fact that I had lived to tell the tale of their racism and their incompetence, that they wanted to stitch me up bad.[54]

The prosecution case was a mess from the start.[55] The alleged victim had tried to withdraw her allegations almost immediately. But the police put her up in a hotel and promised her a furnished flat and financial assistance if she agreed to press charges.[56] A lay mediator, Augusta Gibrill, was appointed to assist the alleged victim, who promptly confessed that Duwayne had not assaulted her and she had made the whole thing up.[57] Her own mother claimed that she was being used by police to get at Duwayne.[58] Despite this, Duwayne was charged.

The Met knew all this by November 1999 yet Duwayne was made to endure a further four months of anguish before a judge finally ruled that the case against him was an abuse of process.[59] Several officers were disciplined following the collapse of the prosecution. Duwayne did indeed sue the Met and was eventually awarded damages. To say that he was no friend of Scotland Yard is in fact an under-statement. He had every reason to despise the police.

When Clive Driscoll first contacted Duwayne about giving evidence against Dobson and Norris, he was not surprised to find the going hard. 'On the one hand, [Duwayne] was charming, erudite, really, really supportive and desperate to help,' he said. 'But on the other, as soon as I stepped over a line that he could see and I couldn't, he'd just shut up shop and the shutters would tumble down. More than a decade of being on the rough end of Old Bill will do that for you.'

Duwayne had sworn never again to co-operate with Scotland Yard. But just as he had won over the Lawrence family, Driscoll slowly but surely put Duwayne at ease, persuading him of the good that he could do for his friend. Such was the trust that developed between them that even the death of Duwayne's father on the morning he was due to give evidence was not enough to keep him from court. Driscoll said: 'I've never had more respect for anyone than at that moment.'[60]

*   *   *

Officers at Sutton police station in south London had no idea that their premises were about to be commandeered for the Met's most infamous case. After all he had been through guiding his investigation to court, Driscoll was taking no chances. When the time came to arrest the suspects, he took unusual steps to protect the integrity of his case. The detective decided to hold Gary Dobson and David Norris at Sutton, but didn't want anyone at the station to know what was going on. Before the arrests, Driscoll booked two cells for Norris and Dobson under Sri Lankan names that he found on a Tamil baby website. Gary Dobson became Gurutither Dobaranga and David Norris was Daaresh Nattar.[61]

'The duplicity didn't end there,' said Driscoll. He had to provide Sutton police station with some kind of justification, so he invented a name for a non-existent operation. As a loyal supporter of Fulham Football Club, he hit upon 'Operation Sir Woy', in honour of the club's manager, Roy Hodgson, whose fans know he can't pronounce his 'R's.[62]

Driscoll finally felt safe enough to move on his suspects. Dobson and Norris were duly arrested and stood trial in December 2011. Duwayne overcame his suspicion of the police and the trauma of the murder and gave evidence on behalf of his friend, who by then had been dead for eighteen years.

Driscoll thought the trial was going well, so he was nonplussed to hear that the press seemed be under the impression that the prosecution was in trouble. One day, he collared a crime reporter during a lunch break and asked whether they had been sitting in the same courtroom.[63] 'I don't know where you get half your information,' said Driscoll. The reporter looked surprised: 'We get it from your press office.'[64] Driscoll said:

He wasn't the only journo I spoke to about negative coverage and they all said a similar thing: 'The Met press office told us this, that, the other.' Was it intentional? Was someone still trying to knock us off track, hoping the jury would read a negative story and change their minds? Or was it just another error? The problem with the Met is you are never far from either.[65]

In the end, though, the bad press proved irrelevant. The jury saw through Dobson and Norris's lies. On 3 January 2012, they returned guilty verdicts, triggering relief and delight in equal measure among Stephen's many supporters.

Doreen Lawrence wept as the verdicts were read out.[66] She later recalled: 'When it was announced that they were guilty, you wanted to shout out and say "Yes, at long last". But I felt like I was restricted with how I could behave. How can I celebrate when my son lies buried?' If it hadn't been for Clive Driscoll, she added, 'Stephen's killers would still be walking the streets'.[67] For Neville Lawrence, the verdicts had put a smile on his face 'for the first time in years'. He added: 'At last, there had been some kind of redress.'[68]

In 2018 Cressida Dick, by then Met commissioner, declared: 'When the verdict came through, not just in the Met, but in police stations all around the country, people were cheering. They saw it as a great moment.'[69]

The top brass at Scotland Yard were now determined to take the credit for an outcome that so many had tried to forestall. As soon as the verdicts were in, one of Driscoll's superiors at the Met was introduced to the media as the senior investigating officer in the Lawrence case,[70] which was news to most of Driscoll's team. The real hero, who'd spent six years fighting off sabotage attempts by malign forces inside the force, was in danger of being sidelined – until the trial judge intervened.

A few weeks after the guilty verdicts, Dobson and Norris returned to the Old Bailey for sentencing. The world's media gathered to hear their fate. As he was about to jail the two killers, Mr Justice Treacy asked: 'Is DCI Driscoll in court?' The detective identified himself and was led to a witness box by an usher. Treacy addressed him directly: 'DCI Driscoll, have you been working on this case since 2006?'

'Yes, I have, your honour.'

'Then I congratulate you,' the judge went on. 'This case has been dreadful for the police and a stain on the United Kingdom. However, you and your team have done an excellent job and through you I commend them all. At least a measure of justice has been achieved at last.'[71]

Treacy also told Driscoll that he expected him to bring the remaining suspects from the Norris gang to justice. The police officer assured the judge he would do all he could. Yet the very next day, senior officers at Scotland Yard told Driscoll that the case was closed. Once again, the pursuit of justice appeared secondary to the dubious priorities of a policing establishment that seemed to regard the Lawrence case not as a murder to be solved, but as a threat to its reputation. For some of the men and women who ran Scotland Yard, Driscoll's devotion to the Lawrence case was a worrying excess, not a source of pride.

It is a stance that has angered and baffled the Lawrence family ever since the first policeman on the scene turned away from Stephen's body. 'I found it amazing that some officers would put so many obstacles in the way of someone who wanted to catch criminals,' said Doreen. 'For victims, they need an officer with integrity, someone who cares about them and what they are going through, and this is what you get with Clive.'[72]

Neville concurs. 'Clive Driscoll helped my family and I to regain some of the lost confidence in the Met, due to the way he treated us,' he said.

> He understood the need for us to have a proper investigation for the murder of our son. He did not hide behind the need to save the blushes of the Met and other police forces by managing the truth.
>
> He even sometimes put his own position at risk because he felt he needed to go to where the evidence and the investigation led him.[73]

Yet that was not a policing approach that Scotland Yard seemed to favour.

Chapter 9

Tory Wars

Bob Quick, Britain's most senior counter-terrorism officer, had just arrived in his fifth-floor office at New Scotland Yard when an official handed him a letter marked 'Confidential'. The director of security at the Cabinet Office had written to say he was concerned at a series of leaks to journalists emanating from the Home Office. 'We are in no doubt that there has been considerable damage to national security already as a result of some of these leaks and we are concerned that the potential for future damage is significant,' he wrote. Would he consider launching an investigation?[1]

It was October 2008. Quick had recently replaced Andy Hayman as assistant commissioner in charge of counter-terrorism, effectively the third most senior officer in the country. He had joined the Met aged eighteen as a police constable but had displayed investigative skills and was transferred into the elite detective branch, dealing with armed robbery, drug trafficking and murders. Identified as a high-flyer, Quick won plum roles at the side of successive commissioners, Paul Condon and John Stevens. In 1999, he became head of the Met's anti-corruption command and led one of the many investigations into the Daniel Morgan murder. In 2004 he had been appointed chief constable of Surrey, but when Hayman fell on his sword three years later, Ian Blair contacted Quick to offer him the job. He had spent almost his entire career at Scotland Yard and was one of the few senior officers in the UK to have served as a detective, with experience of complex investigations into serious crimes. For the man leading Britain's fight against Al-Qaeda, a proposed Cabinet Office leak inquiry seemed like small beer.

The leaks from the Home Office were embarrassing the then Labour government led by Gordon Brown. Someone was handing journalists confidential documents detailing all manner of errors. Among the disclosures were memos showing that the Home Secretary, Jacqui Smith, had been warned that thousands of illegal immigrants had been cleared to work in sensitive Whitehall security jobs; an email that revealed Smith had appeared to accept press office advice not to disclose the number of illegal immigrants in the UK; another email to Liam Byrne, then a Home Office minister, which showed he was told about an illegal Brazilian immigrant who allegedly worked in the Houses of Parliament on a fake ID card; a list of Labour MPs likely to rebel against the government's plans to allow the detention of terror suspects for up to forty-two days without charge; and a letter from Smith to Brown privately warning that a recession would lead to a rise in crime.

But who was behind them? Were the leaks really a threat to national security? Quick asked his deputy – Cressida Dick, who was then embroiled in the Jean Charles de Menezes inquest – to find out. Two weeks later, she had prepared a briefing. 'It was apparent from this exercise that documents had been stolen from a safe in the Home Secretary's private office and letters from the Home Secretary to the Prime Minister were being intercepted and the contents leaked without authority,' Quick later told the Leveson inquiry. 'I was informed that the investigation may also involve at least one member of the opposition front bench.'[2]

A criminal investigation was launched which, according to Quick, also had the backing of the Cabinet Office and the Crown Prosecution Service. It also had the support of then deputy commissioner Paul Stephenson. He was effectively running the Yard as Ian Blair was working out his notice after recently announcing his resignation. The son of a butcher, Stephenson's career had been spent in Lancashire, Merseyside and Northern Ireland. He had never worked at the Met until Blair appointed him deputy commissioner in March 2005. 'I love the Met, but I was a newcomer,' Stephenson told me. 'It's got such a strong culture that it is very resistant to external influence. It was a very difficult place to join.'

Detectives investigating the Home Office leaks identified a potential suspect, a civil servant named Christopher Galley. He was arrested and was extremely forthcoming in his police interview. In 2006 Galley, a member of the Conservative Party, had approached the shadow Home Secretary, David Davis, with concerns about the Home Office. The civil servant said he was willing to 'help the party' by providing the opposition with confidential material. Davis immediately introduced Galley to Damian Green, the shadow immigration minister, who became his main point of contact.[3] It was a relationship that both men would come to regret.

Green was equally aware of the gifts Galley could offer. A PPE graduate, he had served as president of the Oxford Union and it was at Oxford that he became friendly with another young Conservative student, Theresa May, with whom he would forge a close political alliance. Green and May both became MPs in 1997, in the election that saw Tony Blair's Labour Party win by a landslide.

The Conservatives were forced to spend more than a decade in the political wilderness. But by the time Galley approached Davis, the wheels were starting to come off New Labour. The Tories scented blood and Green's new source inside the Home Office had the potential to cause severe damage to Gordon Brown's administration.

Galley also made an admission which led Scotland Yard and the CPS to suspect that Green's behaviour might have gone beyond traditional Westminster machinations. Galley told detectives that the shadow immigration minister had encouraged him to leak the information. Quick's team also uncovered texts and emails to suggest this was indeed the case. It was a crucial development. The Met consulted with the CPS lawyers, who said that the shadow minister might be guilty of conspiracy to commit misconduct in a public office for 'aiding and abetting' Galley's behaviour.[4]

Yet the gold group meetings of senior officers, led by Quick, also recognised the potential for controversy in arresting a MP who was arguably just doing his job. Initially the police wanted to invite Green to an interview under caution. But officers became more alarmed when Galley contacted them the day after his release on bail to say Green had told him to plead 'not guilty', and advised him not to mention him or Davis. 'This, at face value, indicated Green might wish to conceal some aspects of what had occurred and this put the police in a difficult position as it was felt his co-operation could not necessarily be relied upon,' said Quick.[5]

The police chief convened another gold group meeting, at which they continued to discuss whether or not to arrest the shadow minister. Public interest was mentioned, as was proportionality. But until the police knew exactly what had been leaked, they believed they had a duty to investigate. Chief in their minds was the warning from the Cabinet Office that 'national security' had been compromised. Galley and, potentially, Green might have been facing even more serious charges under the Official Secrets Act.[6]

'The gold group were satisfied on the advice of the CPS that there were strong and reasonable grounds to suspect Green of a serious offence and that this must be investigated in order to establish conclusively what material had been leaked and the precise role of individuals in the leaks,' said Quick. 'On balance it was agreed by the gold group unanimously that the arrest of Green was a legal, proportionate and necessary course to progress the investigation.'[7]

The decision was backed by Sir Paul Stephenson and Scotland Yard also obtained consent to search Green's office on the parliamentary estate from then speaker of the House Michael Martin and Jill Pay, the serjeant-at-arms, who is responsible for security at the Palace of Westminster.

The political sensitivities remained foremost in the minds of Quick and his officers. Boris Johnson had recently been elected as a Conservative mayor of London, pushing through reforms that put him in charge of the Metropolitan Police Authority, which oversees Scotland Yard. Given the imminent arrest of a Tory MP, Stephenson felt he should brief Johnson privately. On the day of the arrest, the deputy commissioner took the mayor to one side during an early morning meeting and told him that the operation was under way. At 1.14 p.m., Quick briefed David Cameron, then the Leader of the Opposition, as the search operation reached Green's Westminster office.[8]

The pushback was rapid. Johnson told Stephenson that he feared the decision to arrest Green would create a 'hoo-hah or a kerfuffle'. 'I think the phrase I used was that "this thing will go off like a rocket" and that we would need to have pretty good reason to think that the arrest of an MP was not a disproportionate response,' he later said.[9]

Johnson's behaviour during the incident raised a number of questions. Quick became uneasy when he learnt that the mayor had called Green after speaking with Stephenson. During questioning by the Home Affairs Select Committee, Johnson denied speaking to Cameron about the incident on the day of Green's arrest. But he was later forced to clarify that they had indeed spoken by telephone, and also 'briefly' in person at a memorial service for murdered teenager Damilola Taylor at Southwark Cathedral.[10]

Keith Vaz, the chair of the Home Affairs Select Committee, said that Johnson changing his evidence in such a way was a 'serious matter'. In its report on the affair, the committee said Johnson had been 'unwise and his motives could have been misinterpreted'. The MPs concluded: 'It would be sensible not to keep politicians informed during police operations.'

Green was arrested in his car outside his Kent home and escorted to a central London police station. It caused a political firestorm. As searches were conducted at Green's constituency office and home in Ashford, his office in the House of Commons and his London home, the Conservatives accused the Met of a 'perverse sense of priorities'. Unnamed Tory sources told the press that David Cameron was 'extremely angry' and branded the decision to arrest the shadow minister as 'Stalin-esque'.[11] A senior Met officer from the time told me that the reaction was unwarranted. 'Traditionally the police enforce the law against the working classes and were seen as servants of the middle and upper class,' he said. 'Perhaps the arrest of Damian Green was a turning point for Tory parliamentarians. Bad enough that the police were no longer deferential to the middle and upper class, but to turn on a Conservative Party politician was seen as the Met getting above their station.'[12]

Successfully controlling the narrative was uppermost in everyone's minds. In his allotted call from the police station, Green elected to phone former *News of the World* editor Andy Coulson, then Cameron's director of communications. Immediately after his release from custody, Green gave a late-night television interview to protest his innocence. 'I was astonished to have spent more than nine hours under arrest for doing my job,' he said, continuing:

> I emphatically deny that I have done anything wrong. I have many times made public information that the government wanted to keep secret, information that the public has a right to know. In a democracy, opposition politicians have a duty to hold the government to account. I was elected to the House of Commons precisely to do that and I certainly intend to continue doing so.

Green continued his counter-attack. A few days later in the Commons, he stood up and said:

> Those who have the real power in this country – ministers, senior civil servants and the police – are not beyond the law or beyond scrutiny, either. An MP endangering national security would be a disgrace; an MP exposing embarrassing facts about Home Office policy that ministers are hiding is doing a job in the public interest. The day when exposing facts that ministers would prefer to keep hidden becomes a crime will be a bad day for democracy.[13]

In the days following Green's arrest, right-wing tabloid criticism of Quick and his officers went into overdrive. Much of it was nonsense.

'Completely unfounded claims were being made that the arrest had been sanctioned at the highest levels of government and comparisons were being made to Robert Mugabe's regime in Zimbabwe,' said Quick. He continued:

> Recurring themes were that the search of Parliament was unlawful without a search warrant; that the arrest was heavy-handed and disproportionate; and that the investigation was politically motivated and authorised at the top of government. All of this was untrue.
>
> Various spokespeople portrayed an image of Green being a passive recipient of leaked material that embarrassed the government and that he was merely doing his job as an MP. The Met was not in a position to counter these claims or publicly set out the evidence it was relying on as this could prejudice the ongoing investigation and any future prosecution.[14]

Quick was particularly concerned by the criticism from Johnson and Cameron. But his team kept finding more evidence. Leaked documents from Christopher Galley were found inside a folder marked 'Animal Rights Activists' in a filing cabinet in Green's parliamentary office.[15]

The media frenzy led to frayed nerves at Scotland Yard. When Quick returned to work on the Monday following the arrest, Stephenson – who had assumed the title of acting commissioner that very morning – called him into his office.

'Stephenson looked very anxious and told me he had written out his resignation,' Quick said.

> I asked him why as he had done nothing wrong. We discussed the situation and it became very apparent that Stephenson was beginning

to position himself against an investigation he had sanctioned and an arrest and searches he had supported. I reiterated my position that we had acted lawfully after taking careful legal advice and consulting all parties, and that it was our duty to undertake this investigation regardless of whether it was unpopular with the media and some MPs.

I suggested the [Met] should not panic or be intimidated and must weather the immediate storm as it would dissipate over the course of the week.

Stephenson later said that he had not threatened to resign, and had only raised the prospect of withdrawing his application for the post on a permanent basis.[16]

Quick started to hear whispers that gave him more cause for concern. During a conversation with another senior officer, the police chief mentioned in passing that the then director of public prosecutions (DPP), Keir Starmer, wanted to see the Green investigation completed. But Quick was surprised when his colleague warned that 'Stephenson would go ballistic and would pull the inquiry anyway'.[17]

Pressure was also mounting from another senior officer. John Yates, then an assistant commissioner, told Quick to 'cut his losses' and drop the inquiry. Quick rejected the advice, believing that doing so would be 'unethical and possibly unlawful' given the CPS view that criminal offences might have been committed.[18]

Quick was starting to conclude that the behaviour at the top of Scotland Yard was improper: 'These interventions constituted persistent pressure to cut short the investigation before legitimate lines of inquiry were completed.' By this stage, however, Stephenson had concluded that the Green investigation was 'flawed'. The new commissioner thought that Scotland Yard had been 'duped' by the Cabinet Office. The leaks had nothing to do with national security.

They had merely exposed failings in the government which ministers would rather have stayed under wraps. Stephenson believed that the incident should not be troubling the Met's busy counter-terrorism command. According to one source, 'Paul wishes he had stopped it at the time. He didn't like what Green and the Tory Party were doing. So while there might have been legitimacy in the first place, he didn't think it was a matter of national security by the time Green was arrested.'[19]

False stories about the investigation continued to appear in the press for a further six weeks. Quick suspected the source was 'someone senior at Scotland Yard' attempting to sabotage the inquiry before the evidence had been collected and assessed. The pressure continued to build until just before Christmas when Quick learnt that the *Mail on Sunday* was due to publish a bizarre story revealing that his wife Judy ran a wedding car business from their house. Dick Fedorcio, the Met's head of press, told him that the article would allege that Judy employed serving police officers as drivers. The allegation was untrue, but the story refused to die.

Fedorcio told Quick that the *Mail on Sunday* had spent 'a lot of money' on its investigation, and would 'need to run some kind of story'. As a result, the article was amended pre-publication and instead suggested that the business being run from the Quicks' home amounted to a 'security risk'. It also included a threatening quote from a 'senior Yard source': 'Bob Quick needs to ask himself whether he is happy that all this is out and about. There will need to be a review, bearing in mind his position. He needs to review all of this.'

Quick was furious. He remains convinced that Scotland Yard refused to intervene on his behalf. While the fact of his wife's wedding car business did not pose a security risk, the story linking him, the head of counter-terrorism, to the business certainly might. After all, his team at the Met had only recently wrapped up Operation Gamble, a case in which extremists had plotted to kidnap and behead a British Muslim soldier. Quick was all too aware of the risk from terrorists seeking to harm public servants. 'It was clear that it was the publication of the article itself that would create a substantive risk that otherwise was a negligible risk,' he said.[20]

The Home Office agreed, raising the risk level to Quick and his family. Days before Christmas, he had to organise the temporary transfer of his family out of the house, leaving his children distressed and in tears. His wife was also very upset as she realised she would have to close the business.[21] The stress was overwhelming.

It was at this moment that Quick admits he made a monumental blunder. Judy Quick received a call on her business mobile from a journalist who had somehow tracked it down. 'She was so distressed she could not speak to him so she handed the telephone over to me,' her husband later recalled. 'The journalist asked me how I felt about the *Mail on Sunday* article and in the heat of the moment I told him of my initial thoughts.'

His exact words to the enterprising journalist from the Press Association would lead to his downfall:

> The Tory machinery and their press friends are mobilised against this investigation in a wholly corrupt way, and I feel very disappointed in the country I am living in … I think it is a very spiteful act, possibly to intimidate me away from investigating Mr Green, and I feel it has put my family at risk.

Looking back, Quick said his remarks 'reflected a pattern of events which I saw as connected'. But although he had his suspicions, he instantly regretted the statement as he knew it was impossible to prove. The Conservative Party leapt on the error with glee. Cameron demanded that Quick should withdraw the 'completely baseless' allegations. The Tory leader added that he was 'perfectly happy' to work with Quick but the investigation against Green was 'misconceived and the sooner it comes to an end the better'.[22] The shadow Home Secretary, Dominic Grieve, piled in, calling on Quick to 'reflect on whether he has maintained the necessary objectivity to continue' with the investigation.

Quick apologised and withdrew his statement. But the damage had been done, a development which upset some of his fellow Met colleagues. According to a senior counter-terrorism officer who worked alongside him at the time, 'Bob is a very considered man. I have seen him in situations of remarkable stress and he's always been calm, but that was something that was an affront to his family, and it's difficult when you're in that media spotlight.'[23]

The investigation limped on. Another article appeared in the press, this time quoting a 'well-placed Conservative' who commented on the Green arrest: 'Bob Quick is behind this. I am going to fucking get him this time.' The assistant commissioner was increasingly resigned to his fate. In April 2009, secret documents that Quick had carried into Downing Street for a meeting with Gordon Brown were photographed and published. He concluded that he should resign. 'I decided it was right and proper to offer my resignation,' he said. 'I felt very disillusioned by the attempts to stop the investigation and it seemed like the time to leave.'

His departure infuriated many within the Met. Brian Paddick told me: 'Bob was a very good man.' Another source was more forthright. 'Bob was one of the few good men. He always did the right thing. And they wanted rid of him. Because they couldn't rely on him to lie.'

Yet within a week of Quick's resignation, Keir Starmer effectively confirmed that he had been right all along. In his written opinion on the saga, the DPP said that there was indeed evidence that Green had 'aided or abetted' Galley's conduct, and material had shown an 'ongoing relationship' between the MP and the civil servant. Starmer also said that Green had indeed 'encouraged' the contact 'in the hope and expectation that Galley would continue to supply confidential information to him'. This was the basis on which Quick and his team (including Cressida Dick, who had emerged unscathed from another catastrophe) had worked. But Starmer then displayed the acute political antenna that would carry him to the Labour leadership twelve years later. The DPP concluded it would not be in the 'public interest' for either Green or Galley to face trial, despite there being enough evidence to justify their arrests. This was only a decision that the CPS could take. Prosecutors have two considerations to determine whether someone faces prosecution: evidential and public interest tests. The latter – where prosecutors ask whether it is worthwhile to bring something before a court – is a test for the CPS alone, not the police. In other words, Scotland Yard had no basis for closing down the investigation until the evidence had been fully assessed.

This was no help to Quick, whose 32-year policing career was over. Once the investigation had started the Met had a duty to pursue all available leads. That said, Sir Paul Stephenson's view that the investigation went nowhere from the start must also be partially correct. The Met had indeed been 'duped' by the Labour government and the Cabinet Office, who wrongly claimed that the leaks risked 'national security'. As the evidence emerged, this proved to be patently absurd. Galley and Green were exposing hugely embarrassing matters of public interest. The Cabinet Office did not need to gild the lily and browbeat the Yard. The leaks did not amount to a Russian intelligence operation, nor had jihadi sympathisers penetrated the Home Office. It is surely valid for opposition parties to receive confidential information about government failings from whistleblowers, even if they have complicated private agendas.

Reflecting on the fiasco years later, Quick feels the Met became embroiled in a 'vicious political and media controversy' which caused some of his colleagues to lose their heads. When policing touches on political or sensitive matters the outcomes are rarely successful. However, he still believes that due process must be followed, and claims it is central to the public interest in any democracy:

> Throughout my thirty-two years' policing experience it was crystal clear that if the thresholds for investigation are reached then a necessary, lawful, proportionate and accountable search for evidence must occur in all criminal matters. When the police stray from this doctrine, particularly in serious cases, they risk catastrophic consequences for themselves and others.

Galley was elated when Starmer announced the investigation was over. He immediately took to the airwaves, proclaiming that he had acted on behalf of 'the country'. 'My colleagues were aware of my sympathies towards the Conservative Party but I never actually let that affect my work.' Galley also felt that he had been justified in releasing the information:

> I think the public needed to know that certain aspects of the immigration system were in, what I would term as, disarray. I don't have any particular regrets about what I have actually done but the only real regret I have is not taking a solicitor into the police interview.[24]

The affair was a seminal moment in the deterioration of the alliance between the Conservative Party and Scotland Yard. When the Tories took power in 2010, Nick Timothy became chief of staff to Theresa May, first at the Home Office and then in Downing Street. He is convinced that the treatment of Damian Green was a 'factor in the souring of relations' with the police.[25] The episode was unfortunately timed for the Met. David Cameron was months away from entering Downing Street as the first Tory Prime Minister since 1997. Once in office, the coalition he led decided to slash police budgets in a way no Conservative government had ever contemplated before. Quick told me that he believes the Tories built up animosity towards policing – and the Met in particular – during their years in opposition. But it wasn't just about the arrest of Damian Green.

'There was deep antipathy and resentment because of the relationship between the police and the New Labour government through the 2000s,' Quick said.

If you understand the psychology of the Conservative Party, they saw themselves very much as the party of law and order and the one with the special relationship with the police, and yet Tony Blair very comprehensively stripped them of that, and actually forged an incredibly good working relationship with the police service and invested very heavily in neighbourhood policing.

Crime fell pretty comprehensively throughout the Blair years. The government listened to the police and took advice on a whole range of issues but once the Conservatives returned to power the whole thing turned sour pretty quickly ... They were on a mission and I think it was very apparent that they wanted to take the police down a peg or two.[26]

* * *

Green put his arrest behind him. He was appointed immigration minister in Cameron's government. He rose steadily up the greasy pole, becoming police minister, Work and Pensions Secretary and, finally, First Secretary of State under Theresa May, his old university friend, when she became Prime Minister in 2016. The role effectively gave Green the powers of a Deputy Prime Minister. He was seen as a shrewd political operator with a calm and conciliatory manner, chairing a number of important Cabinet committees and playing a vital role during May's difficult premiership.

Old ghosts would return to haunt him, however. Women began to share their experiences of sexual misconduct in Westminster at the height of the 'Me Too' scandal, triggered by claims of rape against the Hollywood film producer Harvey Weinstein. In October 2017, Kate Maltby, a journalist and Tory activist, wrote an article alleging that Green, who was a friend of her father, had offered her a job while making sexual advances towards her. Maltby also revealed a text message sent to her by Green that said he had admired her wearing a corset in a photograph published by *The Times* and felt 'impelled' to ask her for a drink.

'This is not the most terrible thing that has ever happened to a woman,' wrote Maltby.

Mr Green belongs to a different generation, and Damian, as you read this, I doubt you had any idea of how awkward, embarrassed and professionally compromised you made me feel. Perhaps you didn't realise why I was avoiding you. Perhaps you didn't feel you were doing anything wrong.

This is the problem. The ruling generation are not sensitive to the reality of Westminster's power dynamics. That's why for some of us, bracing ourselves for backlash, now feels the time to speak out.[27]

Sexual harassment was a hot topic in Westminster at the time and the matter was referred to Sue Gray, the long-standing director of propriety and ethics at the Cabinet Office. One of the most feared and respected officials in Whitehall, Gray exerted what had previously been described as 'astounding' influence. In his memoir, David Laws, the Liberal Democrat politician and former Chief Secretary to the Treasury, recounts a conversation with Oliver Letwin, then a Cabinet Office minister, who told him: 'It took me precisely two years before I realised who it is that runs Britain. Our great United Kingdom is actually entirely run by a lady called Sue Gray, the head of ethics or something in the Cabinet Office. Unless she agrees, things just don't happen.' Paul Flynn, the Labour MP, went further, describing Gray in one parliamentary hearing as 'Deputy God'.

The civil service inquiry provided an opportunity for Quick, Green's old nemesis. Hearing of the Deputy Prime Minister's predicament, he contacted Gray, whom he knew from his time in the police. Quick told her that parliamentary computers seized from Green during the 2008 operation had revealed extensive viewing of pornography – something that Commissioner Stephenson had been willing to keep quiet. Further details were revealed in an unpublished witness statement that Quick prepared for the Leveson inquiry, which was leaked to me. Scotland Yard had had an expert examine the material. It was believed that the material was of a kind that could result in 'gross misconduct proceedings and dismissal'.[28] In the leaked witness statement, Quick had said that there was a 'clear reticence' from Stephenson to notify the parliamentary authorities of the potential misconduct. A source close to Stephenson says that he still believes it was right not to have informed the parliamentary authorities about the abuse of their IT equipment:

> It was straightforward porn. There was nobody at risk, there was no paedophilia. Unless there was a matter of overwhelming public interest it should have stayed private. Should [Green] be looking at stuff like that on a workplace computer? No, he shouldn't, of course he shouldn't. But I don't think we should have the police as moral arbiters, starting to run HR departments for various occupations.[29]

The weekend after the publication of Maltby's article, the *Sunday Times* planned to run a story based on Quick's leaked witness statement. The paper contacted Green and asked for his comment ahead of publication. Green's response was a misjudged mixture of fury and venom. His lawyers, Kingsley Napley, were robust, threatening legal action. By Saturday evening, however, it was clear that the Cabinet Office was investigating Quick's claims and the paper considered there was sufficient public interest to publish the story.

At 9.59 p.m., as the presses rolled, Green broke his silence with a furious tweet that – together with a statement the following week – would incinerate his Cabinet career. The story was 'completely untrue', according to Green, who said there was a 'complete lack of evidence' and labelled Quick 'tainted and untrustworthy'. He went on: 'Police have never suggested to me that improper material was found on my parliamentary computer.'

But Downing Street aides were already concerned about inconsistent responses by Green and his team. The tweet compounded those concerns. His strong denials were widely reported. But they were lies.

In fact, Green had known for years that pornography had been found on his computers. His lawyers had been informed during the original investigation in 2008, and police had briefed him again when he was police minister in 2013. When a second *Sunday Times* article revealed that Stephenson had also been told about the pornographic material, Green lied again. He said no allegation about improper material had 'ever been put to me'.

On that Sunday, Green's fate was sealed. He had lied to the same newspaper twice in as many weeks. A senior government source said that Green might have survived one false denial by explaining that it had been an emotional response to a perceived nine-year police vendetta. But to compound the dishonesty with a second lie was fatal. A Whitehall source was blunt: 'He's toast.'[30] But the extraordinary political events of November and December 2017 were to prolong Green's career by almost six weeks. Theresa May faced a budget, crucial Brexit negotiations and the EU Withdrawal Bill going through Parliament. She had recently lost two Cabinet ministers: Sir Michael Fallon, the Defence Secretary, who quit over inappropriate behaviour, and Priti Patel, who was sacked as International Development Secretary over unofficial meetings with Israeli ministers. The last thing May wanted was to push Green overboard.

The delay became even more embarrassing for all involved when Neil Lewis, an earnest former police officer who knew that Green was lying, stepped into the vacuum. He had analysed the computers for the Met and now came forward with a painstaking account of what he had found, patently shocked by the vast quantity of pornography on two of Green's parliamentary computers. He told the BBC: 'The computer was in Mr Green's office, on his desk, logged in, his account, his name. In between browsing pornography, he was sending emails from his account, his personal account, reading documents … it was ridiculous to suggest anybody else could have done it.'

The disclosure by a police officer of yet more intimate details further enraged the Conservative Party. Andrew Mitchell, the Tory MP, appeared on the BBC Radio 4 *Today* programme accusing both Lewis and Quick of trying of blacken the minister's name:

> Mr Green has been absolutely emphatic repeatedly that he never downloaded nor viewed this material. And I think that Mr Green is entitled to be believed. You are not guilty until proven so in this country. I think the hounding of Mr Green over information which everyone is clear was entirely legal, and which he has emphatically denied either downloading or viewing, is completely wrong.[31]

The support shown to Green in the wake of the Lewis interview raised hopes among his allies that he would be spared. But in December 2017, eight weeks after she was first commissioned to investigate the matter, Sue Gray handed her report to Sir Jeremy Heywood, the Cabinet Secretary. She had concluded that Green lied twice in response to articles published in the *Sunday Times*. Britain's de facto Deputy Prime Minister had breached the ministerial code, which requires holders of public office to be truthful. The inquiry also found Maltby's claim to be 'plausible'. Just before Christmas 2017, leaks from Scotland Yard meant that Theresa May, the Prime Minister, was forced to end the Cabinet career of her closest political ally.

Chapter 10

Cover-Up

The malevolent machinations of the *News of the World*, and the murky relationship between Scotland Yard and Rupert Murdoch's media empire, might have stayed hidden for ever were it not for an intervention from the future king.

On 6 November 2005, the *News of the World*'s royal editor, Clive Goodman, reported that Prince William, eldest son of the Prince of Wales and second in line to the throne, had pulled a tendon in his knee playing football. He had gone for treatment, Goodman's story continued, to his father's doctor. Unfortunately, there was one key mistake in what otherwise seemed like a harmless tabloid report on a mundane royal development. William had certainly been injured. But he had not visited Charles's doctor. There were a number of people who might have been aware of the injury, but William couldn't understand how anyone could possibly have known which clinician he had considered approaching. The prince had mentioned his father's doctor only once – in a voicemail he left for a trusted aide who would never have tipped off the press. Buckingham Palace quickly suspected the story could only have come from some sort of phone hack. It approached Scotland Yard seeking answers.

For years, the Met had been loath to investigate potentially criminal activity inside NI. They had turned a blind eye to the activities of Jonathan Rees, prime suspect for the Daniel Morgan murder, who was repeatedly commissioned by the *News of the World* to dig out scoops by whatever means necessary. Nor was Rees alone in benefiting from such treatment. In October 2005, Mazher Mahmood, the *News of the World*'s investigations editor, was interviewed under caution by Scotland Yard detectives and freely admitted to paying policemen for stories. 'I've got bent police officers that are witnesses, that are informants,' he told his interrogators. Later he boasted: 'I've got some senior officers in Britain who are also my informants.'[1] No charges followed. No one at the Yard seemed especially bothered.*

A few months later John Ross, a former Met detective, was acquitted after being accused of paying another officer for information. He was caught during an investigation into *The Sun* – another of Murdoch's tabloids – after Lenny Henry, the actor and comedian, complained that the police had leaked details of racist threats against him. Ross told the *Press Gazette* that the police dropped their investigation into *The Sun* because 'they didn't want to open that can of worms'.[2] While Henry's complaint could be shuffled aside relatively easily, Prince William on the war path represented a more daunting challenge.

In early 2006 detectives investigating the breach of William's security raided the home of Glenn Mulcaire, a private investigator. They seized evidence showing that he worked as a prolific phone hacker for the *News of the World*. The arrest of Mulcaire, a former non-league footballer who once played for AFC Wimbledon, had repercussions that no one at the Yard nor in Fleet Street could have

---

* Mahmood would finally be convicted of perverting the course of justice after the phone hacking scandal changed the attitude of police and prosecutors towards News International.

foreseen. The phone hacking scandal would conclude years later with the closure of the *News of the World*, Britain's biggest-selling newspaper, colossal payouts to the victims of the Murdoch empire's intrusions, the resignation of a Metropolitan Police commissioner, the incarceration of a senior Downing Street aide, and a breakdown in relations between Scotland Yard and the Labour Party.

During their search of Mulcaire's south London home, police seized 11,000 pages of evidence, including documents relating to 6,349 potential hacking victims.[3] They also found audio recordings of 745 intercepted voicemail messages including some left by David Blunkett, the former Labour Home Secretary, at a time when he had overall responsibility for Scotland Yard.[4] The investigation, codenamed Operation Caryatid, also uncovered evidence that Mulcaire had penetrated the Met's top-secret witness protection programme.

When the Met found out that Blunkett's communications had been compromised by a tabloid newspaper investigator, they somehow failed to alert him. Nor did they tell dozens of other high-profile victims, including several military figures, the Met's then commissioner Sir Ian Blair, two other Labour Home Secretaries (Charles Clarke and the incumbent at the time, John Reid), and John Prescott, then the Deputy Prime Minister. When the cover-up became public, the Labour government was aghast at the Met's handling of the inquiry, with many seeing the failure to alert victims as an inexcusable dereliction of duty.

Sadiq Khan was a Labour government minister when the hacking scandal broke. He told me: 'None of the [New Labour ministers] had any idea [that they were being hacked] during the Labour government. Everyone was shocked. The vast majority of the Labour front bench were offside.'

Despite holding evidence on 6,349 potential victims of Mulcaire, the Met only contacted twenty-eight people to warn them that their phones had been compromised.[5] Among them was Rebekah Brooks, who had moved from the *News of the World* to edit *The Sun*. She had been hacked by her own underlings. Just a month after the arrests of Mulcaire and Goodman, the former *News of the World* editor received a personal, two-hour briefing from police about the investigation.[6] Brooks later said she was concerned 'from a corporate view to know where the police were'. She added: 'Journalists are curious creatures by nature. I went in hoping to discover the latest from the horse's mouth.'[7]

Brooks had not risen that high by being dim. She immediately realised the gravity of the situation and, after meeting the police, briefed fellow NI executives including Andy Coulson, her successor as *News of the World* editor, and Rupert Murdoch himself. She told them the police had details of 100 to 110 victims, but were 'not widening the case to cover other *NotW* journalists' – unless new evidence emerged. She also passed on the names of a number of other suspected victims, including Labour minister Tessa Jowell, the actor Hugh Grant, the socialite Jemima Khan, John Prescott and his mistress Tracey Temple – and David Blunkett. Only eight victims would feature in the limited charges to which Goodman and Mulcaire pleaded guilty two months later; none of them were among those named by Brooks.

She had told her colleagues following the meeting that she believed there was not too much to worry about; although police 'do have GM's [Mulcaire's] phone records which show sequences of contacts with *News of the World* before and after accesses … obviously they don't have the content of the calls so this is at best circumstantial'.[8] However, these remarks clearly show that Brooks knew the police suspected the *News of the World* of a criminal conspiracy to hack phones on an industrial scale. Yet for the next four and a half years Murdoch executives would attempt to keep a lid on the scandal by blaming it on a 'single rogue reporter'.[9]

Three years after the first hacking case, Brooks became CEO of News International, sticking throughout to the line that no one other than Clive Goodman at the *News of the World* had been involved with Mulcaire's activities. How the company reached this conclusion is a mystery. NI executives later turned out to be in possession of an email making it clear that the *News of the World*'s chief reporter, Neville Thurlbeck, was also involved in phone hacking; they had also sought legal advice from Michael Silverleaf QC, who warned the company that there was 'a powerful case that there is (or was) a culture of illegal information access' at the paper.[10]

Coulson denied any knowledge of illegal practices but resigned as *News of the World* editor when Goodman pleaded guilty in January 2007. The setback didn't seem to harm his career prospects. Six months later he became director of communications for David Cameron, then Leader of the Opposition. The former tabloid editor would follow Cameron into Downing Street after the Tory victory at the 2010 election. This soon caused problems for the Tories, and Cameron in particular.

The story exploded in July 2009 – three years after Goodman and Mulcaire pleaded guilty – when *The Guardian* published a front-page article claiming there had been hundreds of phone hacking victims and that Murdoch had paid out £1 million to settle their claims out of court, for fear of a public scandal. The newspaper accused the Met of failing to alert all of those who were targeted and named John Prescott as one of the victims.[11]

The revelations sparked a political furore. The following day,

John Yates, the Met's assistant commissioner, was asked to conduct a review of the historic Operation Caryatid material to see what evidence lurked in the Met's vaults. It didn't take him long. Within about four hours Yates had managed to conclude that Scotland Yard was innocent and *The Guardian* was guilty of getting its facts wrong. He emerged from the Yard to give a press conference. 'Where there was clear evidence that people had potentially been the subject of tapping, they were all contacted by the police,' he told waiting journalists, adding that the case had been the object of 'the most careful investigation by very experienced detectives'. He claimed the facts of the matter had been 'established' and went on to insist: 'We have been diligent, reasonable and sensible and taken all proper steps to ensure that, where we have evidence that people have been the subject of any form of phone-tapping, or that there is any suspicion that they might have been, that they have been informed.'[12] In short, the Yard was sticking to that most hackneyed of policeman's refrains: 'Move along please, ladies and gentlemen. Nothing to see here.'

Many things Yates said that day later proved to be incorrect. First, the police were very far from 'establishing the facts'. Yates had asked Phil Williams, the original lead on Operation Caryatid, to prepare a detailed memo about the case. This was not completed until three days after the press conference at which Yates had provided his cast-iron reassurances.[13] Keith Surtees, Yates's deputy, also admitted later to repeatedly raising his 'concern' with Yates that the 'criminality extended beyond Mulcaire and Goodman'. Surtees said he had recorded his view in his logbook in 2006 that an extended investigation was needed, and later emphasised that Yates had access to the logbook during the hasty review in 2009.[14]

At his farcical press conference, Yates also denied that any senior

Labour politicians had been hacked. As things turned out later, this was so wide of the mark that at best it made Yates look like a fool. Ian Blair told me that the attempt to rubbish *The Guardian*'s story 'was the stupidest decision I think I have ever heard of at a senior level. To make it in four hours was bizarre.'[15]

When Yates's assurances turned out to be false, there was fury from hacking victims, David Blunkett among them. He had been a special target for the *News of the World*. The paper hacked the voicemails of many people close to the Home Secretary, notably in 2004 when the paper was trying to gather evidence of his relationship with a married woman. Rebekah Brooks went to see Blunkett personally on a Saturday to inform him that her paper was about to break the story the following day. Seven years later, when the police raided the *News of the World* during the phone hacking scandal, detectives found a dozen tapes of Blunkett's voicemails in the safe of the newspaper's lawyer, Tom Crone. There was also a copy of the birth certificate of the Home Secretary's love child. Blunkett felt that the number of Labour Party hacking victims who were kept in the dark by the Met suggested some sort of dark politics might have been at play. 'Yates was almost doing a job on behalf of the Conservatives, it was that blatant,' he told me.[16] 'John Reid [the Home Secretary at the time of Operation Caryatid] was absolutely incandescent.'

After Yates's 2009 blunder, the reality would slowly reveal itself. Over the next two years hundreds of people who believed they were victims of phone hacking launched civil claims against the *News of the World*. Scotland Yard was forced to disclose the evidence it had been holding for up to three years. The gap between what had happened and what Scotland Yard pretended had happened was becoming too vast to ignore.

In January 2010, not long after Brooks was elevated to the top rung of Murdoch's UK news ladder, the new CEO personally negotiated the settlement of a civil action with phone hacking victim Max Clifford in order to prevent Mulcaire being forced to name the staff on the paper who had instructed him to hack phones. Brooks offered to settle with the abrasive publicist in return for a £200,000 retainer for which he would 'represent *The Sun*/do business for *The Sun*'. In a move that would later raise eyebrows, she agreed with colleagues that nothing should be put in writing because it 'would look terrible if seen to be "buying off" Max'. A note of the meeting records that she offered to 'physically turn up with cash this evening'. The deal with Clifford was eventually done for £1 million.

Brooks maintained that she did not know what names Mulcaire might implicate: 'Glenn Mulcaire, by anyone's standards, was an unreliable witness.' She later set out her reasons for wanting to shut him up anyway. 'It had the potential for financial and reputational damage to the company,' she said. 'The main reason for settling was damage limitation.'[17]

The company's official line remained that whoever else Mulcaire might have been hacking phones for, it could not have been anyone at the *News of the World*. Yet none of this prevented NI from agreeing just months later to indemnify Mulcaire 'in respect of his legal costs and disbursements for dealing with and defending proceedings in which he and [NI subsidiary] News Group Newspapers [NGN] are joint defendants'. An additional clause noted that 'the fact of NGN providing Glenn with an agreement to meet his legal costs shall not be disclosed to any third party'.[18]

The scandal simmered away until July 2011 when Brooks's efforts to shield her company from meltdown finally blew up in her face. *The Guardian* revealed that the *News of the World* had hacked the mobile phone of a murdered schoolgirl, Milly Dowler, in the time between her disappearance in 2002 and the discovery of her body some months later. It is hard to over-state the public revulsion that the hacking of Milly's phone aroused. This was no longer a case of privileged celebrities or reality TV stars angry that their privacy had been invaded by a nosy tabloid. This was a reckless intrusion into the grief of an ordinary family. When Milly's parents learnt that her voicemails had been accessed after her disappearance, it gave them hope she might still be alive. But it was not Milly who accessed her messages. It was a hacker in the pay of the *News of the World*.

The ensuing uproar spelt serious trouble for the tabloid, its editors and corporate executives. At the time of the Dowling hacking, Brooks had been editor and Andy Coulson was her deputy. Both would be arrested within days of the *Guardian* report appearing.

Scotland Yard was next in the firing line. Sir Paul Stephenson, the Met commissioner, came under pressure after his PR adviser Neil Wallis, the former *News of the World* deputy editor, was also arrested for phone hacking.* Stephenson also faced questions about his relationship with others at NI. Damian McBride, a former senior aide to Gordon Brown, claims that Brooks had successfully lobbied No. 10 for Stephenson to replace Sir Ian Blair as commissioner in 2008.[19] It then emerged that Britain's most senior policeman had accepted a £20,000 stay at Champneys, a luxury health spa in Tring, Hertfordshire, at a time when Wallis was acting as the spa's PR representative. Stephenson and his wife Linda benefited from a five-week break at Champneys while he recovered after on operation on his leg.

---

* Wallis was later cleared.

Boris Johnson, then London mayor, chose an unfortunate phrase to express himself, but there was no doubting his alarm at Stephenson's behaviour. He said he was 'very hacked off' to discover there had been 'this relationship with Neil Wallis', and added: 'I was very, very angry that I hadn't been told about this.'[20]

Wallis was paid £24,000 by the Met to work two days a month as a PR consultant. His contract was cancelled less than six months before the launch of the investigation into phone hacking, code-named Operation Weeting. It eventually emerged that Stephenson had shared eighteen dinners with NI executives – eight of them with Wallis – even as his officers were investigating the company. He also met the *News of the World*'s deputy editor for drinks on up to four occasions over a two-year period. The paper and the policeman appeared to be on the best of terms.

Shadow Home Secretary Yvette Cooper said there was now a 'cloud' over the Met. Nick Clegg, the Deputy Prime Minister, admitted he was 'incredibly worried' about the impact of recent stories on the public perception of the police. Years later, Nick Timothy, who at the time was the chief of staff to the Home Secretary, Theresa May, told me that Scotland Yard had been embroiled in so many different scandals during his time at the Home Office that the resignation of the Met commissioner seemed to be a matter of routine. 'It was a very serious moment but it wasn't even close to being the most serious of the propriety stuff because there was so much of it,' he said. 'Theresa was very disappointed when Stephenson resigned, which was a surprise because I thought it was open and shut.'[21]

In his resignation statement, Stephenson said that there had been 'no impropriety'. He said the attempt to 'represent' his visit to Champneys in a 'negative way' was both 'cynical and disappointing'. Stephenson also stressed that he played no role in the 'letting or management' of the contract between Wallis and the Met and described their relationship as 'one maintained for professional purposes'.[22]

In his first interview since his resignation in 2011, Stephenson told me there was much more to his departure. The operation on his leg was far more serious than has previously been made public. 'I had to get a tumour removed from inside my femur. I had a bone cancer. It was quite a rare one. Then my leg fractured. I came very close to losing the leg.' The trip to Champneys was therefore an attempt to recover from serious illness and had been signed off by the police authority.

> I was under medical supervision. It was to facilitate intensive phys-
> iotherapy, to learn to walk again and return to fitness. Wallis wasn't
> involved at all. It suddenly came out that he was doing PR work for
> them but he was nothing to do with it. It was all very bizarre.[23]

When the hacking scandal erupted, Stephenson had had enough. 'I returned to duty, against medical and family advice, a lot earlier than I should have done, following media reports of tensions between some of my senior team.' He had been forced to attend the royal wedding of Prince William and Kate Middleton 'on a walking stick' and

> no longer felt I was fit to be in command [of] and do justice to [the
> Met's] 50,000 people. The media maelstrom around the office of
> commissioner was becoming more important than the mission of
> the Met and I felt I was getting into the same territory as Blair. It was
> just before the Olympics and I didn't know what else I could do.[24]

A day after Stephenson's resignation, his assistant commissioner was also out the door. John Yates resigned after his dismissal of phone hacking concerns was linked repeatedly to the extensive hospitality he too had enjoyed, courtesy of the *News of the World* expense account. During a twelve-year friendship, Yates had gone drinking with Wallis on dozens of occasions, including several encounters during the period when he was reviewing the phone hacking investigation. At the time, Dee Doocey, a Liberal Democrat spokeswoman on policing, said it was 'shameful' that Yates 'found time' to lunch with *News of the World* executives 'but after just a few hours decided there was no additional evidence to justify a further investigation into phone hacking'.[25] Scotland Yard was certainly in the eye of a storm. Two of its most senior officers had been forced out within hours of each other. Yet Stephenson stresses years later that neither he nor Yates had any intention of covering anything up. He told me the main problem was that everyone at the Met was so full of respect for Peter Clarke, the police chief with oversight of Operation Caryatid, that they couldn't believe he hadn't uncovered the full extent of the wrongdoing:

> When Peter Clarke – who is one of the best of the best there has ever been, in my opinion – did that investigation, I think there was a tendency from others to think 'Job done'. Not realising that Clarke had gone in with a very focused investigation, which was right for him to do, but didn't try to solve the problems of the world. And no one really realised the extent of [it].

Clarke had not been tasked with looking at the wider issues and there is no suggestion he did not do what he was asked to. Clearly there was at best a disconnect:

When it came back [in 2009] there was complete bafflement as to why everyone was obsessed with hacking. 'What on earth is going on here?' Yates was baffled. He looked into it and said 'It has been investigated'. He and Clarke were on the counter-terrorism command and were very busy. We were never intent on covering up. We made the mistake of adopting a defensive mindset and saying 'We think this is about politics' and saying 'We've got far better things to do'.[26]

Stephenson now admits that this was a 'huge mistake'. 'We should have stepped back and challenged our own preconceptions. But I don't think we did it for any ulterior motive. I remember briefing Alan Johnson [then the Home Secretary] and saying "We just don't believe there is anything in this [the *Guardian* story]." I feel bad about that.'[27]

With Scotland Yard's management board in turmoil, the fallout then spread to the top of David Cameron's government. As Prime Minister he had hired Andy Coulson, and was a personal friend of Rebekah Brooks. Both had now been arrested. The Prime Minister had no choice but to act. His response was to order a public inquiry into the scandal, to be led by Lord Justice Leveson, a former QC who once successfully prosecuted serial murderer Rose West. Announcing the inquiry to the House of Commons, Cameron said: 'What this country has to confront is an episode that is frankly disgraceful: accusations of widespread law breaking by parts of our press; alleged corruption by some police officers; a failure of our political system over many, many years to tackle a problem that's been getting worse.' He promised: 'No one should be in any doubt of our intention to get to the bottom of the truth and learn the lessons for the future.'

As it transpired, the bottom of the truth was nowhere in sight. The law breaking, corruption and failures were way beyond anything Cameron could have imagined. The Leveson inquiry would end up having to ignore the most serious aspects of police misconduct inside the Met. In fairness, there had been no way of predicting that the phone hacking scandal would erupt just as the unsolved murder of Daniel Morgan returned to haunt Scotland Yard. Britain's foremost police force was under siege.

* * *

Jimmy Ward didn't realise it at the time, but he had lit a slow-burning fuse on a stick of dynamite. It was January 1996 and Ward, a serial offender, had just been arrested yet again for drug trafficking. In common with many a sensible villain, Ward had also secured a comfortable berth as a police informant, codenamed 'Bert Roote'. He immediately offered to trade information on others in the underworld in return for leniency. As he described to his police handlers the whereabouts of a cocaine stash hidden in a nearby cemetery, he slipped in a name that shocked his interlocutors. It was the name of one of Britain's most senior police officers.

Ward told the two officers from the South East Regional Crime Squad that he once paid a £50,000 bribe to a senior Scotland Yard officer to help him escape justice after a previous arrest.[28] This was potentially a nightmare for the Met. There is no evidence to support Ward's claims and he could have just been exacting revenge against an officer who was a thorn in his side so I will not name him.

To make matters worse, it is possible that Ward's revelation ended up helping to compromise the final attempt to prosecute Jonathan Rees and others for the murder of Daniel Morgan.

Garry Vian, the thug who was allegedly hired by Rees to murder Morgan, had been jailed with Ward for drug trafficking in 2005. In return for a reduction in his sentence, Ward approached the police to reveal that Vian had told him it was his brother, Glenn, who had killed Morgan. He said he was prepared to testify in court that Glenn had also privately confessed to the murder in a separate conversation with him.

Ward's testimony was a significant breakthrough for Scotland Yard and Abelard 2, the fifth inquiry into Daniel's murder, which was led by Detective Superintendent David Cook. After getting nowhere for decades, the Yard finally got out its handcuffs. The Vian brothers, Rees and his business partner, former detective sergeant Sid Fillery, were arrested in 2008. For the first time in over twenty years, it looked as if the murder had been solved and that justice might finally be served.

The prosecution case took another leap forward when Cook found another supergrass to give evidence. It seemed that Gary Eaton, a serial criminal from south London, was prepared to allege that the Vian brothers killed Morgan. His evidence was seen by police as being crucial to the case, but it was thrown out by the trial judge before the prosecution got started. Mr Justice Maddison was appalled to learn that the rules governing contacts between police officers and witnesses had been breached by the Abelard 2 investigation. Cook, the senior investigating officer, had repeatedly contacted Eaton after he had signed an agreement to testify. Under the so-called 'sterile corridor' guidelines designed to prevent improper pressure on witnesses, only officers independent of the prosecution were supposed to talk to Eaton.

One of the contacts that most concerned the judge had taken place on 5 September 2006, a month after Eaton was recruited as a supergrass. Cook was still trying at that point to persuade his witness to implicate the Vian brothers in the Morgan murder. The detective took Eaton, who had a history of psychiatric problems, to a 'covert location' near Reading. Eaton was known to be mentally fragile yet he was then left alone in the bedroom of a hotel, where he became distressed and broke down.

Half an hour later Cook sent Eaton a text message which the officer then deleted from his phone. Whatever the message said, it seemed to have a dramatic effect. An hour after Eaton had been put into the hotel room he changed his story and for the first time prepared a statement implicating the Vian brothers in the murder of Daniel Morgan.[29]

Cook was cross-examined for seven days over his handling of Eaton. In the end, the judge ruled that that the supergrass could not give evidence to the jury. This in turn meant charges against Fillery were also dropped. It was a brutal blow for Alastair Morgan, who had been waiting since 1987 to see some kind of justice for his brother. Daniel's sister Jane was so overwhelmed that she considered ending her life. She described her reactions later: 'It was just the rage inside me, I wanted to put it somewhere, let it out. I wanted blood to be shed, for blood. At that moment, I didn't care if it was my blood.'[30]

Nor was Cook's conduct the half of it. Scotland Yard's handling of what should have been routine disclosure of evidence turned out to have been riddled with errors. Whether this was deliberate or accidental is not easy to judge. In criminal trials, the police and prosecutors are supposed to hand over all relevant material to the defence, whether it helps their case or not. Yet Jonathan Rees, the prime target of the Morgan investigation, had been manipulating the criminal justice system for decades. He was friendly with police officers, and knew the procedural loopholes, shortcuts and pitfalls inside out. Rees embarked on what seemed like either a fishing expedition or a calculated effort to compromise the prosecution – or both. Through his lawyers he made repeated disclosure requests for material related to the case. As the pre-trial process unfolded, it emerged that eighteen crates of potential evidence inside Scotland Yard had not been disclosed to the defence, in breach of court rules. Lurking in the mass of documents and recordings was the interview with Jimmy Ward telling his police handlers that a senior police officer had taken a £50,000 bribe.[31] The fuse that Ward lit back in 1996 was about to ignite.

Rees had been working on his defence when he started getting assistance from an unexpected quarter. A source who had contacts close to the prosecution is alleged to have started tipping off the defence team about specific documents it ought to apply for under disclosure rules.[32]

The questions over another key witness in the case – first Eaton, now Ward – proved disastrous for the prosecution. The case was falling apart, prospects for a successful prosecution were doomed and Mr Justice Maddison called a halt to proceedings in March 2011. Rees and the Vians were free men; Fillery had already walked away. It was too much for the Morgan family to bear. As the judge handed down his decision, Daniel's sister Jane stood up in the public gallery, shouting: 'My brother was butchered in a car park by these men and I am sick, I am sick of listening to your offensive tone with hard-working police officers who are attempting to put them in prison. Please call security and have me evicted.'[33]

Assistant commissioner John Yates was Cook's boss and had some involvement in the prosecution case. How had so much evidence apparently been kept from the defence – eighteen crates of it? 'We just didn't know what we had,' he told me. 'We kept finding bits of paperwork everywhere, which was embarrassing. It's much more cock-up than conspiracy around disclosure. It's the chaotic aspect of the Met's record keeping rather than anything else.'

Others take a less charitable view. Ian Blair believes that the failure of Abelard 2's Morgan prosecution is linked to Scotland Yard's handling of its cache of documents and other materials relating to Southern Investigations. 'The dots join up. That connection has not been spelled out,'[34] he told me. In any event it was clear that Cook had badly mishandled his case, with disastrous consequences for his career – and his marriage. When the *News of the World* was watching his house and he was followed as he drove his children to school, in 2002, it had placed unbearable stress on him and his wife, Jacqui Hames, the BBC *Crimewatch* presenter.[35] Eventually they separated. Alastair Morgan, who became close to Cook, acknowledged that the newspaper surveillance had 'introduced a personal animus' for the detective. Who could blame him for feeling bitter that his life had become fodder for the tabloids? But that also invites a question. Why did the Yard leave Cook in charge of the case? If the Met wanted to solve the Morgan murder, should it really have been left in the hands of a detective who so clearly had an axe to grind against the suspects, a potential bias that could have wrecked a future trial? Given how hard it was for DCI Clive Driscoll to overcome hostile internal pressures to bring the killers of Stephen Lawrence to justice, it is impossible not to wonder whether Scotland Yard really wanted to solve any case that might expose corruption. There seemed to be a category of impenetrably murky murder inquiry that no amount of detective work could resolve. Any officer foolish enough to pick up the investigative baton on behalf of a grieving family risked ending up a defeated wreck. And any number of subsequent investigations would fail to establish exactly why justice had been denied.

Insult was about to be piled upon injury. Liberated from legal scrutiny by the collapse of the case against them, the suspects in the Morgan murder launched a claim for compensation for the ordeal the Met had put them through. A High Court judge later ruled that Rees and Glenn Vian should each receive £155,000, and Garry Vian should get £104,000. The award included a sum to 'highlight and condemn the egregious and shameful behaviour of a senior and experienced police officer' who oversaw the investigation that led to the aborted trial. Mrs Justice Cheema-Grum described Cook as a prosecutor who had acted maliciously, adding: 'Honest belief in guilt cannot justify prosecuting a suspect on false evidence.' An independent review of the case would also lambast Cook for 're-moving confidential and secret' material about the suspects from the Met's archives and unlawfully leaking it to journalists.[36]

Nevertheless, Alastair Morgan does not believe Cook is corrupt. Daniel's brother has said: 'I know there were injudicious contacts between [Cook and Eaton] but I think that was because [he] was such a difficult witness,' he said. '[Eaton] had mental health prob-lems, but that doesn't mean he wasn't telling the truth.'[37] Cook denies any impropriety. 'There is so much more to this. I think the Met is institutionally corrupt,' he told the *Sunday Express* in 2021. 'I absolutely refute that I ever coached Gary Eaton – this could not be further from the truth. They needed a scapegoat.'[38]

Although she is now divorced from Cook, Jacqui Hames remains sympathetic towards her ex-husband. The trauma and stress they were put through meant he saw solving the case 'as a way of getting a result for the family, and for us I suppose … He certainly took it personally, why wouldn't you?' Hames also raised the question that had occurred to many others outside Scotland Yard: 'There is a sense that David is being persecuted now for trying to solve that case, so I do wonder what else is going on.'[39]

Cook has since made what he thinks was going on perfectly clear. In a documentary on the Daniel Morgan murder, broadcast in August 2020, the former detective said that 'one of the motives' he was investigating was that 'Danny was killed because he was about to expose a drugs conspiracy which was potentially linked into police corruption going back to the late '8os'. He summed up his conclusions as follows:

> It involved a toxic combination of sophisticated criminals and corrupt police officers. I believe that Jonathan Rees organised the murder and lured Daniel Morgan to his death at the hands of Glenn Vian, who wielded the axe … and Sidney Fillery helped with the cover-up. Almost every senior officer I encountered considered the Morgan investigation a poisoned chalice and wanted nothing to do with it.[40]

He might as well have been accusing Mary Poppins. Fillery said the allegations were 'lies, lies, lies, lies – they weren't only lies, they were ludicrous lies'. Rees was equally dismissive. 'Nine years of taping, probing, sticking their noses in, putting spies into the offices,' he said.

> Not one single bit of evidence they came up with that we were involved in the murder of Daniel Morgan. Not one single fucking bit of evidence. And what do they do in the end? They get this mentally ill senior police officer to try and do their dirty work for them. And what does he try and do? He tries to use another mentally ill man to make up lies.[41]

It is testament to the unique nature of the Daniel Morgan case that after three decades of trauma, deceit and suffering, both the prime suspect and the bereaved family of his supposed victim agree on one crucial point. Whatever they might privately think of each other, they are both convinced that finding Daniel's murderer was not one of Scotland Yard's priorities. Rees put it this way: 'I don't think the Met Police ever gave a fuck about the Daniel Morgan murder, or his family, or anybody else. It has always been about protecting their own image.'

Given how strongly Alastair feels about the man he believes killed his brother, it is ironic that his view of the case is remarkably similar: 'I don't think the Metropolitan Police ever really had a true appetite to solve this crime. Institutionally, the Met stinks from beginning to end on this case.'[42]

Daniel Morgan's mother, Isobel, died in 2017. She never saw the justice she sought on behalf of her youngest son. 'It's all been so crooked and unjust and despicable,' she once said. 'We have been treated in a despicable way. I feel at times that because we have no power and no money we are supposed to forget this and let it go. But I won't. Ever, ever...'[43]

When the case against Rees and his supposed accomplices collapsed in March 2011, Scotland Yard had little choice but to address the mess. Giving a statement on the steps of the Old Bailey, Superintendent Hamish Campbell said: 'This current investigation has identified, ever more clearly, how the initial inquiry failed the family and wider public. It is quite apparent that police corruption was a debilitating factor in that investigation.' Deputy Commissioner Tim Godwin issued a public apology at City Hall:

I recognise how important it is to the family that the part played by corruption in the original investigation is acknowledged publicly. You are entitled to an apology not only for this failure but also for the repeated failure by the Met over many years following Daniel's murder to accept that corruption had played such a part in failing to bring those responsible to justice.[44]

In total, the police inquiries into Daniel's murder had cost more than £50 million of taxpayers' money. It remains the most investigated crime in British history.

In 2013, the collapse in trust in the Met triggered by this and other scandals led the Home Secretary, Theresa May, to finally take action. For the first time since 1987, she removed the Daniel Morgan case from the Yard's control. She agreed to set up an independent panel, chaired by Baroness O'Loan, the former police ombudsman in Northern Ireland, to examine 'police involvement' in the murder, the 'role played by police corruption in protecting those responsible for the murder from being brought to justice' and the 'failure to confront that corruption'.

According to Nick Timothy, May's chief of staff at the Home Office, there was friction before the panel was even established:

The Home Office was so resistant to it. In the meeting to decide whether or not there should be an inquiry, a senior civil servant involved in policing sat there saying: 'We just can't have an inquiry into this.' And Theresa said: 'Why not?' He spoke about it being lengthy and distracting but we pushed him. Eventually he said: 'No, you don't understand, if you start pulling at this piece of string we don't know where it will end with the Met.'

Chapter 11

Plebgate

In the early evening of 19 September 2012, Andrew Mitchell MP made a journey up Downing Street that would lead to his resignation from the Cabinet and provoke another crisis in relations between the Conservative Party and Scotland Yard. As he cycled up to the security gates on Whitehall, Mitchell was involved in a confrontation with the police officers on duty. The Chief Whip in David Cameron's government was anxious to arrive at a meeting on time and demanded to be allowed to cycle out through the main gate, used by ministerial cars. The disputed exchanges that took place during those forty-five seconds would reverberate through Westminster for years to come.

Mitchell has the air of a character from Tory central casting. With his clipped officer's accent and boyish looks, he would not seem out of place next to Bertie Wooster in the Drones Club. But the Conservative MP is no lightweight; Mitchell is the son of David Mitchell, who served as a minister under Margaret Thatcher, and is the fourth member of his family to become an MP. The former president of the Cambridge Union also served in the Royal Tank Regiment, and at Rugby, the £37,000-a-year public school, he was such a stern disciplinarian that he earned the nickname 'Thrasher'. Before entering Parliament, he amassed a fortune working as a director of the investment bank Lazard. Friends say that Mitchell can be immensely charming, but also suffers from a short temper, which might explain why he ran into difficulty at the entrance to Downing Street.

Mitchell had been busy that day. The Chief Whip had lunched at the Cinnamon Club, a Michelin-starred Indian restaurant in Westminster where diners can choose from Norwegian king crab with Thalassery pepper butter and clove-smoked Anjou squab pigeon, all washed down with a £228 bottle of Chassagne-Montrachet Premier Cru. Later that evening, Mitchell was due to have dinner with wealthy Tory donors at the Carlton Club, the private members' club in St James's Street founded by the Tories in 1832.

At the Downing Street gates, the MP lost his temper when asked by officers to dismount and wheel his bicycle through a smaller pedestrian entrance. Within twenty-four hours, details of the incident were leaked to *The Sun*. The resulting splash across the front page of Britain's biggest-selling daily newspaper alleged that Mitchell had called the officers 'plebs' and 'morons', and had told them to 'learn your fucking place'.

The exact words he used were disputed. But the exchange enraged many at Scotland Yard who believed it was a contemptuous outburst from an arrogant member of the establishment. Mitchell issued a statement apologising for not giving the police 'the respect they deserve', but he denied using the language attributed to him. He said it had been the 'end of a long and extremely frustrating day' but admitted that was not 'any excuse at all for what happened'. Those lunching near Mitchell at the Cinnamon Club that day were surprised at his comments. George McGregor, a former government adviser who had sat next to the minister in the restaurant, quipped: 'He didn't seem to be having a long and frustrating day to me.'[1]

The incident would trigger weeks of wall-to-wall media coverage, mushrooming into a major political scandal that caused the Conservative Party to lose yet more confidence in Scotland Yard. 'Plebgate' made the arrest of Damian Green look like a modest squabble and would precipitate tough new reforms to policing, pushed through by Home Secretary Theresa May.

Ten years after the incident, Mitchell admits that he had spoken sharply to parliamentary officials and police officers in the past – but this was par for the course in the Palace of Westminster. 'There are lots of records of members of Parliament being late for a vote in the House of Commons, turning up and bollocking the staff for not letting them through quickly enough,' he told me. 'Some of it was undoubtedly heavy-handed and some of it was justified … if you give someone a uniform, they think they're the boss.'

> I once had a meeting with Cameron, and the police around the back [of Downing Street] wouldn't let me in. So, I had to rush around the front and into the meeting with Cameron. Afterwards I was incensed. I went to the head of security at Downing Street and said: 'This is absolutely intolerable; you must discipline them. You must stop them behaving in this way.'

His complaint led to new instructions for police officers, who were told not to 'impede Cabinet ministers', and to 'facilitate' their movements. As Mitchell wryly recalls: 'They were determined to get their revenge.'[2]

The fallout became politically toxic for David Cameron, the Old Etonian who had urged people to 'call me Dave' in an attempt to be a man of the people. Mitchell's alleged use of the word 'pleb' threatened to blow a hole in the Prime Minister's efforts to persuade the public that his government was in touch with ordinary people's concerns, and not just a bunch of pompous public-school boys. Almost at once, an anonymous senior police officer was quoted in the press suggesting that the incident 'lifted the veil' on ministers' real feelings. Miranda Green, former press secretary to Paddy Ashdown, the one-time Liberal Democrat leader, said Mitchell's use of the word 'pleb' – if he did use the word – was like 'the mask slipping': 'You think, who are these people?'[3] Mitchell was forced to put out a further clarification, claiming that he had said: 'Look, I'm the Chief Whip, I work at No. 9 [Downing Street],' before muttering: 'You guys are supposed to fucking help us.' Allies of Mitchell rallied around. His friend of twenty-five years, Michael Brown MP – who had worked with the Chief Whip since the early 1990s – said the incident was 'totally and utterly out of character'. He said it was a 'thirty-second moment of madness' by someone he knew to be a 'very decent and honourable man'. 'I come from the wrong side of the tracks,' Brown said. 'I'm a secondary modern schoolboy, an eleven-plus failure and I can tell you working with Andrew Mitchell was an absolute delight and a privilege.'[4]

When I spoke to him recently, Mitchell said: 'There's only two people that know what happened. It was the injection of the word "pleb" that was the problem. Nothing else was really disputed.' But the damage had been done. The Police Federation, which represents more than 100,000 rank-and-file officers across England and Wales, backed the officer's version of events and called for Mitchell to be sacked from his government post.

Three days after the incident was first revealed, the Plebgate affair blew up even more. A 442-word police log that purported to detail the Downing Street row was leaked to the *Daily Telegraph*. The record, said to be a contemporaneous note of the incident, recorded Mitchell having used the term 'pleb' amid a flurry of expletives. The log claimed that when Mitchell was asked to dismount from his bike, he said: 'Best you learn your fucking place ... you don't run this fucking government ... you're fucking plebs.' The officer noted that members of the public looked 'visibly shocked' by Mitchell's language and the Chief Whip had been warned that if he continued to swear he would be arrested under the Public Order Act. The police record noted: 'Mr Mitchell was then silent and left saying "you haven't heard the last of this" as he cycled off.' The officer who wrote the report stressed that officers were 'extremely polite' at all times.

* * *

The Plebgate saga, which still had a long way to run, opened up deep divisions between the government and Scotland Yard's high command. In years to come this would have grave consequences for the force. But at the time the Metropolitan Police commissioner, Sir Bernard Hogan-Howe, who had recently replaced Sir Paul Stephenson, said he was 'very disappointed at the lack of respect shown towards the police'. This surprised many in Westminster as the commissioner had forged a close relationship with the Tories. It had been a meteoric rise for Hogan-Howe, who seemed an unlikely bedfellow for the Conservative Party. Hogan-Howe began his career at South Yorkshire Police and, in 1989, was involved in the infamous Hillsborough disaster, when police errors led to a lethal crush during an FA Cup semi-final between Liverpool and Nottingham Forest in which ninety-six people lost their lives and a further 766 were injured. In the weeks that followed, South Yorkshire Police blamed Liverpool fans, falsely citing drunkenness, hooliganism and late arrivals to the ground. That version of events was amplified by some news outlets, particularly *The Sun*, which reported that fans had urinated on police officers and picked the pockets of fallen victims. On the day of the disaster, Hogan-Howe had reported for duty and taken charge of some operations. Stephen Lowe, then the Archdeacon of Sheffield, criticised the police, including Hogan-Howe, for being defensive and not communicating sympathetically with families.[5] The future Met commissioner later gave misleading accounts about the evidence he provided to various inquiries following the disaster, but was cleared of any misconduct.[6]

Hogan-Howe's direct manner was perhaps needed at Scotland Yard following the anarchy of Ian Blair's time at the helm and the tumult caused by Stephenson's early departure in the wake of the phone hacking scandal. A City Hall source said: 'When Hogan-Howe took over in 2011, the senior Met Police was in chaos, people were leaving. Bernard is an alpha-male and he ruffled feathers. It wasn't all his fault. He took over a chaotic situation.'[7] Some found his assertive style verged on rudeness, however. 'Hogan-Howe was regarded as a bully in the same way [John] Stevens was,' said a senior Met officer who worked with him.[8]

Even if Plebgate had never happened, there is little doubt that Hogan-Howe inherited one of the worst situations facing any incoming commissioner in the Met's history. It is worth examining the antagonism with Andrew Mitchell in that context. David Cameron's government was elected in 2010 on a platform of swingeing cuts to public spending in an attempt to cut Britain's yawning deficit, triggered by the 2008 global financial crisis. When Hogan-Howe took charge of the Met, the Home Office was in the midst of slashing a mammoth 19 per cent from police budgets – a move that had a huge influence on the diminished Scotland Yard we see today.

This cut was one of the largest savings achieved in the public sector during the 'austerity' years. Many were surprised that the Tories should take funding from the police given both their historically close relationship and the key role that police play in one of the primary goals of any government: the security of the nation.

But should it have come as a surprise? When Cameron became leader of the Tory Party in 2005, he signalled that he was prepared to take on the police in a manner very different from his predecessors. The year after he took charge Cameron warned that the party 'cannot be tough on crime unless we are tough on police reform'. 'A Conservative Party that I lead will not flinch from the things that need to be said, and doing the things that need to be done, to raise the level of police performance so we can really fight crime in this country,' he said in a speech that would have caused Margaret Thatcher to raise her eyebrows.[9]

As the incoming Home Secretary, it was up to Theresa May to implement Cameron's combative police agenda. For Nick Timothy, her senior aide and the architect of the reforms, it was a painful experience. 'The cuts were just unbelievable. They were front loaded.' He told me that May argued against the draining of police resources. But the move was forced through by Cameron and his Chancellor, George Osborne. 'Theresa didn't want police cuts at all. She knew that they would need to be cut but she wanted to limit them and she was very upset early on because she felt completely stiffed by George.'

May's chief of staff said that neither Cameron nor Osborne thought much of the police. In Cameron's case, Timothy said the animus dated back to the 1990s when the future Prime Minister was a special adviser to Michael Howard, who was Home Secretary during the aborted Sheehy reforms. 'David was a spad at the Home

Office in the 1990s and he never had much time for the cops,' says Timothy. 'George never liked the police either because he was a metropolitan liberal.'[10]

The political appetite for change meant that Hogan-Howe had to cut police officer numbers and force through enormous reductions in back office staff, which many blame for the soaring levels of violent crime that we see in London today. Some of the commissioner's peers believe that he did not do enough to speak out against the dangers of such an approach. Bob Quick, the former assistant commissioner at the Met who was behind the arrest of Damian Green, criticised the 'silence of chief police officers' in the face of 'savage cuts'. 'They knew full well that they would result in people losing their lives, and that's exactly what happened in London,' he told me. 'They were the worst cuts to any public service.' Sir Paul Stephenson, Hogan-Howe's predecessor as commissioner, was more measured. But the underlying message is consistent. 'It is the responsibility of senior police leaders to advise governments – and that doesn't mean always agreeing with them. You have a duty to give bad news and fight tooth and nail for what you believe to be right.'[11]

Once the Conservatives came to power in 2010 Quick noticed a 'marked change in the ability and willingness of police chiefs to stand up and say "This is wrong"'. 'And we then saw a decade of carnage,' he added ruefully.[12] Another senior Met officer who worked with Hogan-Howe agreed: 'He didn't stand up for the Met,' said the source. 'It is a problem when the Home Secretary is responsible for appointing you, you must feel under some sort of obligation to do what they want.'[13]

Not everyone agrees that slashing police budgets was linked to the rise in offending; indeed, Ken Clarke, the former Home Secretary, who became Justice Secretary under Cameron, insists that it was 'essential':

> No one had ever had the nerve to cut police budgets. God knows
> how many years it was before 2010 since anybody had cut the police
> budget. The years of austerity were economically absolutely essen-
> tial and saved us from disaster. In the case of the police, there was so
> much fat in the system that I don't think it made a difference.[14]

This was the febrile political climate when police officers blocked Andrew Mitchell from cycling out of Downing Street. The row rumbled on for several weeks and Cameron faced repeated calls to sack Mitchell. When the political conference season began, it was clear that the Met's battle against the government had gained wider support. Officers from the West Midlands force stood outside the Conservative Party conference in Birmingham wearing 'PC Pleb and Proud' T-shirts. The following month, Mitchell attempted to defuse the row by offering to meet representatives from his local force in his Sutton Coldfield constituency. But the forty-minute encounter, which was designed to clear the air, only piled on more pressure. Officers who attended the meeting were furious when the Chief Whip again refused to accept the police's account of the Downing Street confrontation. Ken Mackaill, chairman of the West Mercia Police Federation, who led the delegation, brought the meeting to an abrupt end and immediately left to tell waiting journalists that Mitchell should step down. 'I think Mr Mitchell now has no option but to resign,' he said.

> He is continuing to refuse to elaborate on what happened. His po
> sition is untenable. He repeated a profound apology about what he

did say – that was a comment around officers being there to help them. But that is balanced with his denial of specific and precise speech recorded by police officers at the time. He has refused to tell us what he did say on the grounds he did not want to impugn police officers' integrity and start a 'fire fight with police'. Unfortunately, that is exactly what happened. The question of integrity remains unresolved.[15]

To call for the resignation of a Cabinet minister was a bold move on the part of the police. It would come back to haunt them. Some senior officers were immediately uneasy. Tim Brain, the former chief constable of Gloucestershire, said: 'I think where the police made mistakes is to become overly politicised themselves, to take political stances. I think it was a mistake to call for a Cabinet minister's resignation.'[16]

The government faced days of further negative media coverage, but Mitchell only realised how bad it was when MPs returned to Parliament after the conference season. 'It was clear that my authority as Chief Whip was shot,' he recalled. 'That role has got to be a figure of authority and menace and it was clear that I couldn't do it any more.'[17] Senior ministers, including Theresa May and Iain Duncan Smith, the Work and Pensions Secretary, also told Mitchell his position was untenable. Just over a week after the fractious constituency meeting with the police, the Chief Whip drove to Chequers to inform Cameron that he would quit his government post. 'Cameron had been at a European summit meeting and he hadn't slept,' Mitchell told me. 'I was driven up to Chequers, we had a natter and I resigned. He later said in his book that he never believed I called anyone a pleb, and that is true.'[18] Mitchell remains quite proud of the resistance he put up. 'Alastair Campbell used to say that the maximum time a minister can hang on for is nine days. I hung on for thirty-three.'[19]

Some leading commentators already smelt a rat. The columnist Dominic Lawson, son of the former Chancellor Nigel Lawson, wrote that the Police Federation had assassinated Mitchell and raised questions that were a portent of events to come.

> It is this body of men that has done for the Government Chief Whip, Andrew Mitchell; first by telling *The Sun* about the contretemps he had with one of their officers and then by leaking the entire log of the incident to the *Daily Telegraph*. This stood up the claim, repeatedly denied by Mitchell, that he had called one of the coppers guarding Downing Street a 'pleb', apparently for making the MP leave through a side exit rather than the main gate.
>
> I leave it to readers to decide if they would regard the log of a policeman involved in an argument with a member of the public as invariably the gospel truth. What cannot be in doubt is that such a leak was a brutally effective way of intimidating a government which is attempting to introduce dramatic reforms to police working practices.[20]

Despite the simmering tensions, the matter seemed to be at an end. Two months later, however, the row spectacularly reignited when new evidence obtained by Mitchell and handed to *Channel 4 News* completely undermined the police version of events.

The programme revealed that a constable in the elite Diplomatic Protection Group, posing as a member of the public, had falsely claimed to have witnessed the incident at the gates of Downing Street. The officer, Keith Wallis, alleged that Mitchell had used the toxic word 'pleb' on three separate occasions. The police constable had sent an email to his local MP, Tory Deputy Chief Whip John Randall, the day after the encounter, giving an account of events in Downing Street that was strikingly similar to the version published in *The Sun*. Wallis falsely claimed he had been passing Downing Street with a nephew, sightseeing, at the time of the incident recorded in the police log. He also told Randall that he was a chauffeur and did not disclose that he was, in fact, a police officer. The truth of the matter was that Wallis had not witnessed the outburst. He was off duty and at his home address in Ruislip, west London, when the incident took place. But Randall, who did not know this at the time, had been troubled by his constituent's claims and passed them to No. 10 – a move which assisted his boss's downfall.

Deceit had been layered on deceit. *Channel 4 News* also revealed Downing Street CCTV footage which showed Mitchell with the two police officers on the evening in question. The film did not appear to show any visible signs of an argument – and also appeared to dispel another key claim. According to the police log, officers claimed 'members of the public looked visibly shocked … by the language used'. But the film showed only three people walking past the gate, two of whom looked too far away to hear anything, and one who appeared to express no more than a passing interest in what was going on.

For the *coup de grâce*, *Channel 4 News* also revealed that Mitchell had secretly recorded his meeting with the Police Federation in his local constituency. 'My wife said: "You've got to tape the thing,"' Mitchell told me. 'I said: "I can't go around taping police officers," but she said: "You must tape it."'[21] It was wise counsel. The recording revealed that Mitchell had, in fact, given his own account of the exchange and, crucially, the officers twice thanked him for doing so. Moments later, the organisation's representative, Ken Mackaill, had left the meeting to tell reporters, falsely, that Mitchell had refused to do just that, and to call for his resignation.

The former Chief Whip told *Channel 4 News* he had been the victim of a police 'stitch-up'. 'There were phrases which were hung around my neck every day in the press, which were used to destroy my political career and were used to toxify the Conservative Party,' he said. 'They are completely untrue, I never said phrases like that at all, I would never call someone an effing pleb. Anyone who knows me well would know that it is absolutely not in me to use phrases like that.'[22]

Downing Street rowed in behind him. Craig Oliver, No. 10's director of communications, took the unusual step of issuing a public statement condemning Wallis's actions: 'Any allegations that a serving police officer posed as a member of the public and fabricated evidence against a Cabinet minister are exceptionally serious. It's therefore essential that the police get to the bottom of this as a matter of urgency.'

Bernard Hogan-Howe triggered widespread anger in the Conservative Party when he stood by the original account of the two officers involved in the confrontation. For many Tories, this amounted to pig-headed intransigence given that he had been confronted with prima facie evidence of his officers' misconduct. Brian Paddick, a former deputy assistant commissioner in the Met, told me that 'Plebgate' contributed to declining trust in his leadership of Scotland Yard. 'The otherwise loyal Bernard Hogan-Howe proclaimed Andrew Mitchell guilty by defending his officers, and put the Tories and the Met in direct conflict. That hardened views amongst senior Tories.'

For Nick Timothy, who had to handle much of the fallout, what the police did to Mitchell was 'totally disgusting and completely wrong'. He said:

> It felt to me like that was a more damaging episode for the cops and the Tories than the Damian [Green] one. It was so much more in your face. Trying to fit up a serving Cabinet minister? That shocked a lot of people. I think that was the moment when a lot of Tories who didn't normally have a bad word to say about the police thought 'Hang on a second, if they do that on Downing Street, to a Cabinet minister, with cameras around, and then they carry on keep trying to set him up in different ways, what on earth do they do to people when nobody is looking?!' The Damian thing was egregious but it was less in your face.[23]

Backing from the normally supportive press also drained away. The day after the Channel 4 exposé was broadcast, *The Times* ran a damning editorial noting there was 'little love to be lost between this Government and the police'. 'The thought of even lone figures within the police advancing their own political agendas through the manipulation of policing is, of course, horrifying. But this is about trust, not politics. No individual, politician or otherwise, should have to live in fear of a mendacious grudge in a uniform.'[24]

Nick Herbert, who had recently resigned as Tory police minister, called for urgent reforms to restore public trust, arguing that while 'corruption may not be endemic, neither is it an aberration'. Lord Macdonald, a former director of public prosecutions, realised the gravity of the situation, saying that if the word 'pleb' had been fabricated by officers it would be like a missile 'heading straight for the heart of the Metropolitan Police'.[25]

Scotland Yard was under attack on several fronts. Senior officers decided to launch an investigation into the debacle on Downing Street in an attempt to rebuild bridges. Operation Alice was born. The inquiry saw eight people arrested, including Wallis and five other Met Police officers, for allegedly fabricating evidence or leaking it to the media. There were further censures for the West Mercia police officers who had also misrepresented Mitchell's comments at the constituency meeting during an evidence session before the Home Affairs Select Committee. Following the *Channel 4 News* programme, they were hauled back to the Commons and forced to apologise for misleading Parliament. The committee's report on the affair condemned the three officers for giving evidence that was 'misleading, possibly deliberately'. The chairman of the committee, the Labour MP Keith Vaz, said their accounts were 'fiction'.

'We were appalled by the evidence given,' Vaz said in a news interview. 'The narrative of what we have seen could rival any great work of fiction. At every point and at every level, instead of being transparent, we have uncovered a process that obstructs the truth. If this can happen to a Cabinet minister, what hope is there for anyone else?'[26] The chief constables of Warwickshire, West Mercia and West Midlands, the three forces represented by the federation officials, also rushed out apologies.

Yet the $64 million question looming large over the mayhem was whether or not the web of lies woven around Mitchell was an organised conspiracy by police officers. When later questioned by Operation Alice, Wallis – the PC who lied about being present at the gates of Downing Street – hinted that others were involved in a plot. But the PC was adamant that he had not colluded with anyone else, and had acted alone. Wallis's version of events started to border on the absurd when he claimed that he had 'fantasised' about the incident from his living room, and 'convinced himself that he was there with his nephew and had seen the incident'.[27]

During Operation Alice, Mitchell received a tip-off from inside the Met. A senior police officer approached Mitchell's lawyers to blow the whistle on what he claimed was a conspiracy by protection officers to 'stitch up' the Cabinet minister. Mitchell decided it would be inappropriate to meet the source during the police investigation. He arranged for the officer to be debriefed by his friend David Davis, the veteran Tory MP and former shadow Home Secretary, who was no stranger to duels with Scotland Yard.

The whistleblower, a superintendent, said he was willing to provide an account of the alleged conspiracy. He said the 'genesis' of the Plebgate incident was in an earlier confrontation between Mitchell and officers at the Downing Street gates – on the night before the infamous row itself. On that occasion, Mitchell is said to have jabbed his finger at one of the gate officers, demanding that he open the gates. The whistleblower stated: 'On 18 September 2012, Mr Mitchell had also insisted on being let out through the main gate. Following this [the officer] said to the other officers: "Right, we can stitch him up."' The whistleblower then went on to state that the word 'plebs' was added to the original police log of the conversation that Mitchell had with the officer at the Downing Street gates on 19 September. The whistleblower also claimed that a senior officer went on to 'orchestrate' the writing of the bogus emails that Wallis sent to John Randall.[28]

Mitchell told me that Davis believed the superintendent to be 'completely credible'.[29] But knowing the Met all too well, the whistleblower was terrified of potential reprisals. Unfortunately for Mitchell, when the whistleblower's account was revealed in the *Sunday Times* in October 2013, the source became nervous. 'They were very nearly identified and they took fright,' Mitchell told me 'They would not give evidence. We were then asked by the police to identify them, but we didn't.'

In February 2014, eighteen months after the 'Plebgate' incident took place, Wallis pleaded guilty to misconduct in public office. He was jailed for a year. Deborah Glass, head of the Independent Police Complaints Commission, said his actions had helped turn 'a largely inaudible altercation lasting less than a minute into a national scandal'. She added that the rogue PC had caused an 'injustice' to Mitchell and 'brought shame upon the police service'.[30] Hogan-Howe personally apologised to Mitchell. Three other Met officers faced gross misconduct hearings for dishonesty and were dismissed without notice.[31] Reflecting on the extraordinary affair, Davis said: 'You can pick your own words, whether it's collusion or conspiracy, but clearly something went on which, if it wasn't planned, it was certainly co-ordinated.'[32]

The Plebgate scandal had wide-reaching ramifications for policing in Britain. By the time of Wallis's conviction in 2014 ministers had become gravely concerned about the integrity of the police. 'It was one more thing that added to the sense that the cops were out of control,' Nick Timothy told me. 'It added to the sense that this was an institution in need of really, really serious reform.'[33]

At the start of her time in the Home Office in 2010, Theresa May was forced to implement major changes because of the huge budget cuts forced on her by David Cameron and George Osborne. In the following years, tens of thousands of police officers retired or resigned early from the service without being replaced. Pensions were also slashed. Timothy says: 'We thought: "We can't salami-slice our way through these budgets because it means we will be doing the same things in the same way, but worse." And so the more efficiency-related reforms started then.' He admits that Plebgate and other scandals involving the Metropolitan Police also played a role in the government's decision making:

> More stuff emerged in relation to probity and historical injustices … Some of these things came to light from the passage of time but some stuff came to light because we invited it. On [Stephen Lawrence], on [Daniel] Morgan, we were prepared to say 'No, I'm sorry, we are not ignoring this'.[34]

After Wallis was convicted in 2014, journalists were briefed that the Home Secretary wanted to change the law to allow foreign police chiefs to become chief constables, under plans to improve leadership. May also created 'direct entry' at superintendent level, allowing 'exceptional' individuals from the military, the security services, industry, business and the other professions to join the police. She also announced a new 'integrity charter' which would force all police officers to register their second jobs, expenses, and details of any gifts and hospitality they receive, on a public website. Brian Paddick says the radical strategy was a naked bid to secure electoral success:

> There was a general anti-police narrative, a lot of it brought on themselves. Lots of them were about things from a long time before, like Hillsborough, but there were a series of bad-cop stories that were prominent in the media. I think the Tories thought it would be a vote winner to adopt an anti-police narrative, because the police had done some pretty dreadful things which were indefensible, albeit a long time before.

The police couldn't seem to catch a break. Every development throughout May's tenure as Home Secretary seemed to make their position more vulnerable. Just as the budget cuts began to be implemented, their workload increased dramatically following more statutory demands issued from Westminster. The shift was once again triggered by the media, which started to publish and broadcast stories exposing rotten corners of society that had long been ignored by the police; the rise of 'modern slavery' offences and the industrial-scale abuse of children – from Asian child-grooming gangs to Jimmy Savile. When disturbing details of these 'new' offences spilled out into the public domain, the government ordered the police to make them as much of a priority as traditional crimes such as violent offences and drug trafficking. Scotland Yard and other forces quickly became overwhelmed.

The perfect storm the police faced included the consequences of mass internet use. The digital explosion in the twenty-first century ushered in a new era in cyber and online offences, estimated to cost UK victims £10 billion a year. Soon, the police were submerged to such an extent that officers were allowed to record them differently from other types of crime, which kept them off the official crime statistics by which forces are measured. For years, in fact until 2017, the government simply didn't recognise online fraud and computer misuse offences. When the Office for National Statistics, which compiles the Crime Survey for England and Wales, finally started to do so, the change captured an astonishing 5 million more offences in the previous twelve months alone, doubling the overall crime rate overnight.

For some, this was long overdue. Savas Hadjipavlou, a former senior civil servant at the Home Office and the Ministry of Justice, believes that the Crime Survey – widely heralded in Whitehall as the best measurement of offending rates – failed for fifteen years to acknowledge that millions of additional crimes every year had been being committed. He told me that annual crime statistics since 2002 may have been 42 per cent greater than government figures had shown.[35] The police and government had agreed to ignore countless victims for the best part of twenty years, which surely contributed to the decline in public confidence.

After Plebgate, the political climate around the police became increasingly noxious. A few months after Wallis's conviction May made a remarkable speech at the annual conference of the Police Federation, warning that the legitimacy of British policing was in jeopardy as a result of the never-ending series of scandals. The Home Secretary stunned delegates as she criticised officers for displaying a 'contempt for the public' in their handling of sensitive cases, and said wrongdoing seemed to be widespread rather than the preserve of a 'few bad apples'.

> If there is anybody in this hall who doubts that our model of policing is at risk, if there is anybody who under-estimates the damage recent events and revelations have done to the relationship between the public and the police, if anybody here questions the need for the police to change, I am here to tell you that it's time to face up to reality.

Will Riches, one of two candidates to be federation chair, said afterwards the reaction of delegates was one of 'shock and bewilderment'. Ian Pointon of Kent Police publicly called May a 'bully'.[36]

The author of the speech was Nick Timothy. He still chuckles at the memory:

That might be the speech I am most proud of writing because I think it caused a lot of people to confront the truth about the cops. I really admired Theresa for going and giving it. I remember giving it to Fi [Fiona Cunningham, another senior aide to May]. She read it, looked at me and said: 'Do you fully appreciate what this speech is?'[37]

May's warning went down like a lead balloon among the policing community. Mike Bennett, a veteran Police Federation member, said that Plebgate and other police reforms had destroyed relations with the Conservative Party. 'The world has been turned upside down,' he told the BBC in 2014:

> You will not find a police officer now – certainly not amongst the rank and file – who would be willing to vote Tory. In fact, the hatred of the Tory Party is visceral. They look at the Tory Party, the reforms, they see what's been done to their pensions, the fact that they haven't had an above-inflation salary increase for some time, they see promotion opportunities have basically collapsed and the vast majority of junior officers and not so junior officers think it was never meant to be this way. We were the favoured group, always looked upon by government as the people who did their dirty work. This is the payback, and it's unfair.[38]

With the conviction of PC Wallis and the censure of several other police officers, Andrew Mitchell looked set for political redemption. Unfortunately, the former minister then resolved to sue for libel the police officer who stopped him at the Downing Street gates. It was a decision he would bitterly regret:

Had I not gone to the law I would have gone straight back in the Cabinet. I made lots of massive errors of judgement in all this. But one of the big ones was to think that I, as a senior politician, could take on the police and win. It just wasn't going to ever happen.

Mitchell embarked on a costly two-year fight through the High Court, trying to prove that the officer in question, PC Toby Rowland, had lied when accusing the MP of using the politically toxic word 'pleb'. He lost his case against *The Sun*, which had first reported the incident based on Rowland's account. He also failed in his defence to the counter libel action brought by the PC and funded by the Police Federation. Mitchell's counsel, James Price QC, told the court that a 'web of lies, deceit and indiscipline' by police officers led to a press campaign and public hostility and the version of the encounter that was leaked to the newspaper was 'wholly false'. Lawyers for Mitchell supplied statements in court from a range of people, including the musician Bob Geldof and the painter and decorator Richard Robinson, which attempted to show he was not a 'Tory toff' who would use a 'toxic and class-laden' expression like 'pleb'. But Desmond Browne QC, for PC Rowland, claimed Mitchell was a 'Jekyll and Hyde' character whose capacity for menace found its outlet in foul temper and foul language.

In his ruling Mr Justice Mitting sided with Rowland. He said the officer was 'not the sort of man who would have had the wit, imagination or inclination to invent on the spur of the moment an account of what a senior politician had said to him in temper', prompting quips that the judge had decided Rowland too was a 'pleb'.[39] Mitting also rejected the allegation that there was collusion by the officers on the gate that night. He identified a number of inconsistencies in Mitchell's evidence, while playing down a number of incongruities that Rowland had also made. In an extraordinary comment that might have fallen from the lips of Lord Denning, that staunch defender of police misconduct, Mitting said: 'Embellishment of a true account by a police officer on the defensive is, of course, not acceptable, but it is understandable if done for that purpose.'[40] Joseph Harker, a journalist on *The Guardian*, tweeted: 'Andrew Mitchell really does know what it's like to be black. Courts will always believe an officer's word over yours.'

Litigation is a blood sport, a gladiatorial contest with only one winner, and PC Rowland was victorious. The police officer told waiting journalists that he was 'delighted' that his 'innocence and integrity and reputation as a police officer' had been recognised. 'The pain myself and my family have been through is indescribable, and it is particularly saddening that all this happened because I was merely following procedures,' he said following the verdict. 'I was doing my job without fear or favour.'[41]

For Mitchell, the case was a nightmare. He is understood to have faced a final legal bill of around £2 million. He was forced to sell a ski chalet that he owned in the Alpine resort of Val d'Isère in order to pay his legal costs. 'What started as a principled bid to expose police felony went on and on and on for ever, and it rapidly turned into an attempt to get out of the nightmare because of the expense of it,' he told me. 'I wanted a jury but the [Police Federation] fought it and I was told it would cost £200,000. I had no idea that the Police Federation was so rich and they could use their wealth to drive a civilian into the ground and bankrupt them. It was simply appalling.'[42]

The case has made him change his outlook on life:

I was the most establishment figure you could find. I was educated at prep school where royals went, I was educated at Rugby, I was an officer in the Army, I was at Cambridge, I was a member of Parliament, I was in the Cabinet, I was in the City. I'm the most establishment person you could come across.

But I remember that day when I thought: 'I'm going to resign from the establishment. I'm never going to have anything to do with these dreadful people again.' Of course, I'm amongst them all the time. But mentally, I've resigned from the establishment and when I see the establishment do anything now, my knee-jerk reaction is to question it.[43]

Mitchell admits the case took a heavy toll. 'David Blunkett said to me: "When you go through these searing political resignations it takes three years to get over." And sure enough, that was true.'[44]

Chapter 12

The Long Fella

As he entered an east London police station, David McKelvey had no idea that his life was about to change for ever. It was 2007. The genial yet razor-sharp detective chief inspector (DCI) had risen through the ranks at Scotland Yard to lead the London Borough of Newham's proactive crime, drugs, robbery and motor vehicle squads. That day, McKelvey had a typically vast workload befitting a 'vocational' police officer who threw himself into the 'job' every day of his twenty-eight years at the Met. He was rushing to cover for one of the fifty police officers under his command. A criminal, a police informant codenamed 'Eastwood', had been arrested for burglary and wanted to explore what information about the underworld he could trade in return for leniency in the courts. McKelvey stepped into the breach. But as the meeting unfolded in the dimly lit interview room, the DCI became more and more alarmed as the criminal chattered away about corruption in the Metropolitan Police.[1]

The information provided by the informant centred on the east London crime syndicate led by David Hunt, a near-mythical figure in the capital's underworld, known for decades by the nickname 'The Long Fella'. A former bouncer and leading amateur boxer, Hunt had built an 'extensive criminal empire' involved in suspected drug trafficking, fraud, money laundering and 'extreme violence'. By 2007, it rivalled any gang in Britain. It seems he was helped on his way up by rogue elements inside the Metropolitan Police. 'The Hunt syndicate has evaded significant penetration from law enforcement,' noted one police intelligence report. 'The syndicate has achieved this invulnerability through a mixture of utilising corrupt police contacts and the intimidation of witnesses brave enough to give evidence against them.'

It seems McKelvey's plucky team had got on the wrong side of the Hunt network. Chief among Eastwood's many allegations was the suggestion that the DCI and two of his junior detectives, Darren Guntrip and Paul Clark, were in 'immediate danger' from a 'planned assassination'. The informant said that one of Britain's leading hitmen, known as 'The Predator', had been summoned to a boat in Spain and promised £1 million if he could kill three police officers. The informant told McKelvey that the contract killer had been keeping watch on his targets from a parked car near Stratford police station. The Predator was said to have been passed details of a Ford Mondeo driven by Clark and was 'planning to shoot him with a machinegun kept in another car nearby'.[2]

'I remember literally going cold, a moment of sheer terror. Then a sort of controlled panic sets in,' said McKelvey, who became even more concerned when he corroborated the informant's claims from four separate intelligence sources.[3]

It seemed that recent successes he and his team had had against the Hunt organised crime group might have triggered a reprisal. The squad had taken on serious cases – big drug seizures, kidnappings, murders – and were getting results way beyond the capacity of a run-of-the-mill borough outfit. 'We basically became a small cell operating against organised crime completely outside the specialist departments,' said McKelvey. 'I know from the feedback that it caused chaos among the criminal network because they didn't know what was going on. We were taking out major villains all the time and they couldn't work out who it was, and why.'[4]

The saga began in March 2006. At the time, it seemed like just another routine raid at a scrap yard in the Docklands area of east London. But the operation set off a chain of events that McKelvey now believes put him on a collision course with the Hunt group. 'It started as a small job,' he said. 'It was a search warrant for stolen metal at a scrap yard. We started searching this premises across the road which consisted of forty-two big containers. As soon as we started opening up the containers we realised very quickly, it was an Aladdin's cave of stolen goods.' His team found the spoils of eighteen lorry thefts, plus a safe containing £250,000 worth of jewellery. There were so many ill-gotten gains on the premises that it took McKelvey and his team five days to complete the search. Charles 'Chicky' Matthews Jr, a close associate of the Hunt organised crime network, and two other men were arrested. Around £1 million worth of stolen goods were seized.

By any measure, it was a notable success for the Met and McKelvey, one of the Met's brightest detectives. The Essex-born father of three commenced service in February 1982 and went on to be commended on more than sixty separate occasions. Yet success came with its own problems. By 2003, McKelvey's strong record had bred jealousy among senior officers, some of whom started to circulate false rumours about his methods. It was a foretaste of events to come. On this occasion, a review by assistant commissioner John Yates dismissed the concerns out of hand. concluding that McKelvey was 'clearly an able detective' who had 'achieved impressive results throughout his career'. In a review, Yates wrote:

His involvement at the cutting edge of crime fighting, particularly in east London and Essex, has meant that his name has been linked to both corrupt officers and corruptors of the same. In my experience this should not be seen as unusual and should not necessarily attract adverse comment. I have seen no direct evidence to suggest that this officer is corrupt and to label him so cannot be justified on the material reviewed.[5]

It would not be the last time McKelvey faced false suspicions of corruption.

The DCI might have been cleared immediately on this occasion. The next time he would not be so fortunate. As his career progressed, McKelvey appeared to make more and more enemies among the increasingly risk-averse new breed of senior leaders at Scotland Yard, who saw him as a dangerous maverick. Principally, he believes, because the upper echelons of the force had become dominated by officers from the uniformed branch of the service, who had little or no experience of investigating complex organised crime. Some even seemed afraid of his success.[6] 'Nowadays, there are no career detectives in senior roles,' said McKelvey. 'You have an entire senior rank structure who have no idea, and no comprehension, of what the role of a detective is actually about. They do not have a Scooby-doo.' He told me of one occasion where a uniformed superintendent sheepishly asked for his help with a problem. 'He called me in embarrassed one day and said: "Dave, Dave, you've got to help me out. I've got to give evidence at court." And I said: "Right … so what's the issue?" And he said: "Well, I've never actually had to give evidence in court."'[7]

The revelation astounded McKelvey. He could not believe a superintendent with nineteen years' service had never done such basic police work. 'The evidence he was due to give was no more than "I ordered some PCs onto the roof of a garage so they could get someone down". That was the evidence. And he was absolutely cacking his pants. It was embarrassing beyond belief.' McKelvey claims such problems are now endemic across the Met's leadership.[8]

The lack of investigative experience among the Yard's management team seemed to lead them to suspect McKelvey's stellar results. One senior officer said managing McKelvey was like 'trying to hang on to the tail of a mad crocodile'.[9] Some privately referred to him as 'Gene Hunt on speed'– a reference to the old-style cop in the police drama *Life on Mars* and its sequel, *Ashes to Ashes*.[10] The relationship between hard-bitten crime-fighter and impotent top brass deteriorated in October 2006 when McKelvey travelled to Scotland Yard. The detective chief inspector was on a mission to secure more resources to target the Hunt network, but he did not get his extra money. The commander was remarkably frank when delivering McKelvey the bad news: David Hunt was now believed to be so powerful that he was 'too difficult and dangerous' to take on, and 'potentially beyond the capability of the [Met]'.[11]

With no backing from senior management, the DCI became increasingly anxious. He started to receive more underworld intelligence warning that the Newham crime squad had locked horns with a fearsome organised crime gang. McKelvey became even more alarmed when the informant Eastwood suggested that he and his men were the target of the assassination plot. On learning the news, the DCI once again begged Scotland Yard for support. But an emergency meeting of senior officers – a gold group – concluded that McKelvey was over-reacting.

After the Eastwood debrief, McKelvey got his team together. 'We put locks on the doors and I sat them all down and I explained to them that we were now investigating one of the biggest crime families in the UK.'[12] Drawing on his years of experience in the CID, McKelvey told his young charges what they could expect. 'You will get potentially followed. They will undoubtedly make allegations against you. They will use corrupt officers against you. They could assault you, or even threaten to kill you. There is nothing these people will not do.'[13] As the Newham crime squad braced for impact, McKelvey decided to read through archived Met files to get a better understanding of what he was up against. It turned out that that he was far from the first officer in the Met to warn management about the Hunt network.

The crime boss was not always destined for a life of crime. David Hunt left school in 1977 aged sixteen to embark on a career as a footballer. When injury forced him to retire early from Millwall Football Club Hunt turned to boxing and became an undefeated light heavyweight while also working as a bouncer for local pubs.[14]

By 1984, police in east London had picked up on darker pursuits. Officers were raising concerns about Hunt's suspected leadership of a dangerous local gang, known as the Snipers. In a report to superiors, a DCI at Plaistow said:

This concerns a group of people operating in the East End of London, particularly in the area of Plaistow and Canning Town, whose influence on crime in London and the Home Counties has grown steadily over a period of eight to ten years. In proportion to this growth has been the development of fear that they engender in the local population until a point has now been reached where the indigenous population would rather tolerate the outrageous behaviour of these people than become involved as a witness.

The Snipers were suspected of carrying out armed robberies and running protection rackets stretching from the City of London to the Essex coast. The Hunt family, including David, was said to have founded the gang. 'Witnesses go missing, are "got at" or just forget their evidence,' the report said. 'The Snipers represent the single most serious crime threat in the Division, their sphere of influence is growing and their territory widening. The type of crime they undertake is becoming ever more serious.'[15]

In April 1986 Hunt had his first significant brush with the law. He was arrested along with his brother Christopher in the office of a new scaffolding business in Stratford, east London. Police found £5,000 worth of stolen clothing and a sawn-off 410 shotgun. David Hunt pleaded guilty to handling stolen goods and received a suspended nine-month sentence. Christopher pleaded guilty to possessing the shotgun without a permit. Police believed he had agreed to take the rap for his brother.[16]

By this stage, Hunt had teamed up with Jimmy Holmes, a former West End rent boy who introduced the East Ender to the lucrative prostitution and protection rackets of the Soho sex trade. Holmes also taught him how to hide the proceeds of crime in offshore companies. The pair would be close associates for years until a spectacular falling out led Holmes to flee the UK. In an interview with the journalist Michael Gillard, Holmes later lifted the lid on his activities with Hunt: 'We moved into serious armed robbery, drugs smuggling, pub protection rackets, porn, prostitution, and other more serious stuff which I can't mention specifically because loads of it is still on old Bill's open files.'[17]

Hunt's potent blend of ruthlessness and psychotic villainy led him to rise up the criminal underworld. In 1988, he left Canning

Town to buy a large home in Epping Forest on the outskirts of the capital. The purchase was obtained with a fraudulent mortgage. By this stage, Hunt was parleying directly with the powerful Adams family in north London. Police suspected he was involved in the distribution of their drugs.[18] One report from 1990 noted a belief that Hunt's network had penetrated Scotland Yard. 'Both Hunt and Holmes are equipped with bearcats, which can monitor any police radio transmissions, and are very surveillance conscious, as are the Adams',' it read. 'It is said that very little of what occurs in Plaistow police station remains secret from this criminal fraternity and they even target this police station with long-range listening devices.'[19] In 1993, Hunt upsized again, buying a luxurious family home in Great Hallingbury, Essex.

Hunt may have been protected by corrupt Met Police officers. But he was also capable of looking after himself. This was brought home in 1999 during a dispute with Paul Cavanagh, a fraudster, who had borrowed a Land Rover from Hunt and sold it to pay off mounting debts. This proved to be an unwise decision.

Hunt found out about the sale and summoned a terrified Cavanagh to a meeting in a car showroom in South Woodford. The crime boss had promised via intermediaries that the fraudster would come to no harm. But when Cavanagh arrived Hunt pulled out a knife. 'I thought he was going to plunge me [in the stomach] but instead he pulled the knife round my face,' Cavanagh later recalled.

I felt a scraping noise. Then it was over. I stood there stunned.

I remember him putting his hands on the tops of my shoulders. I remember looking in his eyes. He said, 'I f***ing really didn't want to hurt you, mate, I really didn't. Nothing else is going to happen to you, your punishment's over. Take him to the hospital. Get him stitched up and bring him back.'[20]

He was dumped at Whipps Cross University Hospital in Waltham Forest. He lost so much blood that doctors later told Cavanagh he almost died.

After a transfusion, a plastic surgeon stitched his face. 'I bottled up the courage to look and see what Hunt had done,' Cavanagh said. 'No words can describe what I felt like. My face was swollen. I had fifty-odd stitches in my face, inside and outside. I was marked for life. I have a reminder every time I look in the mirror.'[21]

After being discharged, Cavanagh went into hiding. But then he was arrested on suspicion of fraud. Police told Cavanagh they knew about the assault and proposed a deal – give evidence against Hunt in return for witness protection and help with the outstanding fraud charges. Cavanagh took the deal and made a statement detailing how Hunt had attacked him. The crime boss was charged and spent nine months awaiting trial on remand in the top-security Belmarsh prison in south-east London.

But Cavanagh started to doubt that the police could protect him. He then made a decision that would wreck the best chance of bringing Hunt to justice: he retracted his statement and disappeared from the witness protection programme. He later claimed that a senior associate of Hunt had paid him £25,000 in cash through two intermediaries to do so.[22] Hunt has always denied this and his lawyer issued a statement: 'My client maintains, as he has throughout, that he was not responsible for the attack on Mr Cavanagh; nor was he responsible for Mr Cavanagh's withdrawing his original statement.'[23]

Hunt was a free man. He proceeded to tighten his grip on Britain's criminal underworld. By 2002, Scotland Yard viewed him as on a par with the Adams family. Operation Tiberius, the secret Met Police report detailing corruption inside the force, warned that a network of rogue Met detectives had been helping Hunt evade justice for years.

But few in Scotland Yard knew the truth. McKelvey and his band of junior detectives in the Newham crime squad had no idea of the suspicions about Hunt's network when he launched his successful assault on organised crime in 2006. Had he known that his own force was believed to have been infiltrated by the target of his inquiries, perhaps McKelvey would have left well alone. After all, many others in the Met seemed to have given up after the aborted prosecution in 1999. Could Hunt really be 'too difficult and too dangerous' to take on?

In any event, once McKelvey reported Eastwood's threats to kill him and two of his subordinates they received no help from the Yard. Instead, they found themselves under investigation by the anti-corruption command.

The inquiry was led by DCI Ashfaq Siddique, the Muslim undercover officer allegedly caught up in the honour killing of his niece's boyfriend. Senior officers had caught Siddique lying about his whereabouts in the run-up to the murder, but he then accused the officers investigating that crime of racism. The Met backed down and paid him a sizeable out-of-court settlement, transferring Siddique to a unit of his choice. The detective had chosen the anti-corruption command, where he took up the inquiry into McKelvey with gusto.[24]

The internal investigation – codenamed Operation Kayu – inched forwards for almost two years. Its immediate effect raised doubts about the integrity of McKelvey, Darren Guntrip and Paul Clark. This threatened to derail all the prosecutions that they were involved with, including two linked to the Hunt network.

One was the trial of Charles 'Chicky' Matthews Jr, the man charged following the discovery of the 'Aladdin's cave' of stolen goods during the Docklands raid. His Old Bailey trial was about to start in October 2007 when officers from the Met's anti-corruption command handed a secret eight-page memo to the prosecutors on the case. The document listed a number of concerns about McKelvey, none of which turned out to be true.[25]

One bogus claim concerned the intelligence provided by Eastwood, which had led McKelvey to fear for his officers' safety. The memo to prosecutors alleged that McKelvey had 'manipulated' the intelligence in order to secure an earlier adjournment to the Matthews trial. There was a suggestion that the information provided by Eastwood had been 'monkeyed up' by the DCI. In actual fact, anti-corruption officers working for Siddique had debriefed Eastwood a month earlier. The informant had confirmed everything that he had originally told McKelvey. So why on earth was the anti-corruption unit suggesting to prosecution barristers that the intelligence had been fabricated?[26]

Once in receipt of the memo, prosecutors felt they could no longer rely on the integrity of McKelvey and the other investigating officers. The case was aborted at the last minute, at a cost of millions of pounds to the public purse. Matthews was released.

It was not the only trial to fall apart. Another prosecution set to begin was the case of Danny McGuinness, a local council contractor, who had been accused of using an official Newham parks police warrant card to steal high-quality cars to order. Some of the vehicles were bound for Ghana and allegedly stuffed with dirty money belonging to east London villains. Since his arrest, McGuinness had threatened to expose a nexus of Freemasons, bent police officers, criminals and council employees all said to be involved in the alleged scam. He brazenly told McKelvey's team that the case would never get to court.[27]

McGuinness's arrest had caused waves inside the Met. McKelvey was summoned to a meeting with his borough commander, who castigated the detective for failing to tell him about the operation and 'embarrassing me in front of my partners'. The case also seemed of huge concern to Newham council. In April 2007, Guntrip received an email from a senior manager in Newham council's enforcement division. Nigel Mould, a former police officer, revealed he was 'greatly concerned' by a recent phone call from a former colleague who had been responsible for the contracts before moving to work at the Home Office. 'John [Tisshaw] asked me about the case and stated that he had been contacted by the [McGuinness] defence as a witness for them. I made no comment other than to affirm that I was a prosecution witness,' Mould wrote. 'This is hugely significant and will have a direct impact on the case if the defence are indeed asking Tisshaw to act as a witness,' Mould told Guntrip. 'This simply reinforces my increasing concerns about this investigation, its potential ramifications … [are you] fully aware that Newham, the Department of the Environment and Rural Affairs, the Home Office and potentially all the London boroughs may be drawn into this?' In October 2007, the prosecution of McGuinness was abandoned, too.

The upshot of Operation Kayu was that McKelvey and his team were immediately suspended from duty, and forced to endure an agonising 529 days under investigation. The allegations against them were so thin that the DCI became more and more enraged.

At one point, McKelvey displayed his contempt for the process by wearing fancy dress for his interview with the anti-corruption command. 'They called me bent so I've come dressed as a banana,' he said on arrival.[28]

When asked about his supposed fabrication of Eastwood's 'assassination' allegation, McKelvey replied:

What possible motive could I or any of the other officers have in wanting to make this up? The suggestion is ludicrous and insulting. I have spent nearly twenty-seven years fighting serious organised crime. I do not scare easily. I have been subject to threats and been assaulted. Unarmed I have faced armed suspects without wavering. This 'threat to life' is of a completely different order. David Hunt is one of, if not *the*, most powerful criminals in the south of England. He had the motive and the means to put together the contract. He employed a well-known assassin to carry out that contract. Both know my address. How can the Yard possibly believe that no threat exists? It is ridiculous.[29]

The ill-fated operation finally collapsed in April 2009 when lawyers advised the Met that there was no chance that McKelvey, Guntrip and Clark could even be disciplined, let alone prosecuted. Six months later, an officer from outside the anti-corruption command was brought in to review the operation. He concluded that senior officers had exerted 'too much influence' on operational decisions and the 'interventions were perceived to be political and not based on the developing investigation'.

Junior officers on the inquiry felt they were not being listened to and those in charge 'put their spin on the material which was not supported elsewhere ... the briefings were overhyped and opinionated rather than having any proper basis. This overhyping manifested itself to some as close to bullying them into carrying out enquiries and actions without properly sourced material.'

On the decision to abandon the trials, the inquiry found that the briefings provided to counsel by the anti-corruption command were 'overhyped and excitable'. Had they been more realistic, the trials could have progressed. None of this was of particular comfort to McKelvey and Guntrip, who were still worried about reprisals from the Hunt organised crime group. On one occasion, McKelvey said he was approached by a van containing 'three men armed with firearms'. For his part, Guntrip said he was headbutted and kicked in an unprovoked attack outside Scotland Yard 'in broad daylight' as he walked along Victoria Street. He maintained that the attack was a 'warning' from the organised crime network, and the Met failed to investigate it.[30]

On another occasion, McKelvey's wife Joanna saw someone tailing her in a car, and later had the sense she was being followed around a supermarket. Her husband reported it to senior officers at the Met. CCTV footage of the incidents was pulled and the number plate of the car revealed it belonged to David Hunt's son. The crime boss received an official warning from Scotland Yard but no further action was taken.[31]

It was all too much for McKelvey. For twenty-eight years he had worked hard for the Metropolitan Police. But after two years of intimidation and threats, McKelvey felt betrayed by the force he loved. In 2010, he was medically retired after developing severe anxiety and depression that doctors said were linked to fears for his safety.

New life was breathed into the long-running saga a few months after McKelvey left the Met. The *Sunday Times* published an investigation into a number of organised crime groups at loggerheads over a stretch of derelict land in east London. The gangs were alleged to be squabbling over ownership of the site, about 2 miles from the London Olympic stadium. Organised criminals including the Hunt syndicate were reportedly vying for millions of pounds of taxpayer funds that were due to be paid out in compensation after the land was placed under a compulsory purchase order by the London Development Agency. The article, by investigative journalist Michael Gillard, named Hunt as a 'crime lord' who controlled a vast network involved in murder, drug trafficking and fraud.[32] It was the first time such allegations had ever been made in the media. Hunt professed to be 'crucified and heartbroken' over the damaging allegations and sued the *Sunday Times* for libel. What followed was nothing short of extraordinary.

To defend itself, the newspaper would have to face up to David Hunt across a courtroom. It quickly became apparent that the *Sunday Times* would receive no support from the Met. Rather than back the newspaper, lawyers for Scotland Yard tried to prevent it from using leaked police documents that supported the story, claiming they were too sensitive. The Met sued both the paper and Gillard personally for breach of confidence. The application was hotly contested by the *Sunday Times*, its counsel, Gavin Millar QC, telling the court: 'It's disgraceful and an infringement on a journalist's right to rely on documents in defence of his own reporting.' He accused Scotland Yard of assisting a crime boss to bring a 'corrupt claim'.[33] The judge ruled that the paper had to lose some of its key documents. But the Met was ordered to give the court a public assessment of David Hunt. They told the judge that they regarded him as the 'head of an organised crime group'.[34]

The libel trial began at the Royal Courts of Justice in May 2013.

The *Sunday Times* was forced to provide protection for the witnesses who were prepared to give evidence to defend the story. On the day the proceedings were due to begin, however, the newspaper's security detail disappeared. McKelvey and some of his former team at the Met ignored the risks, bravely appearing to give evidence after being served with witness summonses. The retired DCI told the High Court of his 'genuine belief' that he, Guntrip and Clark were the subject of the alleged contract to kill taken out by the Hunt organised crime syndicate. During his evidence, McKelvey also accused Ashfaq Siddique, the officer who led the ineffective internal inquiry, of pursuing him for 'corrupt' purposes.[35]

Hunt also gave evidence, in which he said that the *Sunday Times* article had 'crucified' him and had an effect similar to the feeling he experienced when his parents died. Hunt told the High Court that he had started out as a scaffolder and freelance scrap dealer before building a legitimate property empire. He denied a series of allegations including assault, witness intimidation and involvement in protection rackets, and said there was 'no way in the world' that he would seek to kill police officers.[36] His lawyer, Hugh Tomlinson QC, said McKelvey was 'obsessed' by the idea that his client was seeking revenge over a criminal investigation and there was no evidence of a contract to kill. McKelvey replied: 'What do you want, a man standing in front of me with a gun?'[37]

After several weeks of evidence, Mr Justice Simon sided with the *Sunday Times*. He concluded that Hunt was the 'head of an organised crime network implicated in extreme violence and fraud' and had also engaged in money laundering and witness intimidation to evade justice.[38] In a severe blow to the Met and Siddique, the judge also ruled that Operation Kayu was 'misdirected'. Given that McKelvey's team were closing in on members of his gang,

Mr Justice Simon said this 'undoubtedly assisted' Hunt to avoid prosecution.[39] Of McKelvey, Guntrip and Clark, the judge said: 'The three police officers had to live their lives understanding that a contract had been taken out to kill them, and endure a protracted anti-corruption investigation, which … resulted in them being entirely exonerated.'[40] It was a huge victory for the *Sunday Times* and for press freedom. The newspaper had taken on David Hunt in court and won – something the Met had failed to do for thirty years. It was a bittersweet victory for Michael Gillard, the *Sunday Times* reporter who had exposed the crime lord. In the aftermath of the trial, the risk to his life was deemed so great he was forced temporarily to flee the UK until the heat died down.

*   *   *

I first met David McKelvey not long after the conclusion of the *Sunday Times* libel trial. I had recently revealed the shocking findings of Operation Tiberius, a confidential report by the Met's anti-corruption command.

The story, which ran in *The Independent*, had piqued McKelvey's interest, not least since one of the syndicates named in the report was led by David Hunt. Tiberius recorded, in minute detail, how the gang had evaded justice for decades by obtaining inside information on police operations from rogue officers. McKelvey contacted me over social media. He was still worried about reprisals and wanted any information that might help to protect himself and his family.

One of the officers named in the report as having helped the Hunt syndicate had been a member of McKelvey's team when he was investigating the gang. He had thus been afforded access to information about sources, raids and police tactics. McKelvey was appalled: 'I can't believe it. This means they would have known everything.'

This revelation made him even more furious with Scotland Yard.

Tiberius shows the anti-corruption command suspected that this man was bent and working for organised crime. Yet they leave him in place and let me and my team waste years of our time and millions of pounds of public money chasing targets that they know will never be caught. It just beggars belief.[41]

By this stage, McKelvey had applied for an injury award from Scotland Yard, seeking compensation for the damage to his mental health wrought by Siddique and Operation Kayu. The Met referred this to an independent review led by Albert Patrick, a retired detective chief superintendent with a thirty-year career on Scotland Yard's elite squads.

Patrick examined all the intelligence and decision logs of Operation Kayu. His conclusions were damning. Kayu was a 'fatally flawed investigation' and Siddique's anti-corruption unit had passed 'inaccurate and misleading' information about McKelvey and Guntrip to the Crown Prosecution Service, which led to the collapse of the Matthews and McGuinness trials.[42]

Nor could Patrick understand the basis for the lengthy investigation of the innocent officers. 'The Review Team are concerned that having investigated Mr McKelvey on a number of occasions and apparently cleared him of any wrongdoing, a different section of the [anti-corruption command] later used and continue to use the original allegation as a "cause for concern" or continued evidence of his supposed corruption.'[43]

Armed with the Patrick report, McKelvey and Guntrip launched a claim against Scotland Yard for misfeasance in a public office, malicious trespass, false imprisonment and other human rights breaches. The documents they lodged at the High Court were hair-raising, outlining in excruciating detail a number of failed operations targeting the Hunt syndicate that dated back to the 1980s. At a hearing in the High Court, lawyers for the two officers claimed that their success in the job had caused them to become a 'thorn in the side' of organised crime in east London.

According to court documents, McKelvey and his team uncovered links between the Hunt network and suspected drug trafficking, armed robberies and serious violent offences, along with suspicions of witness intimidation, jury tampering and attempts to infiltrate the Old Bailey, where Britain's most sensitive criminal trials are held. McKelvey further alleged that he had 'gathered evidence of large-scale systemic police corruption and links between organised crime, police and terrorist organisations'. Most serious of all, the two officers claimed that Scotland Yard had intelligence that pointed to a police cover-up of eight gangland killings stretching back to the 1980s. 'Many of these gangland executions remain unsolved. Many have direct links to police corruption or, intelligence suggests, have been covered up by corrupt police officers.'[44]

One of the murders was that of Rocky Dawson, who was shot dead in 2006 as he put his stepdaughter, then six, and son, two, into the back of his Fiat Punto in Hornchurch, east London. He managed to crawl back into his mother's house, where he died in her arms. Contract killers Christopher Pearman and James Tomkins were later jailed for life, but McKelvey believes others were involved in the hit. Another was Nicky 'Snakehips' Gerard, a gangland enforcer who was shot dead in Canning Town, east London, in June 1982. Gerard, who was himself suspected of ten killings, was gunned down on his daughter's eleventh birthday as he got into his car near his home. His killers shot him once and chased him down the street, before clubbing him with a gun and shooting him again in the head. Armed robber Tommy Hole was arrested and charged with the murder after an identity parade, but his accuser later backed down and he walked free from the Old Bailey in 1983.[45]

McKelvey and Guntrip's claim also shed new light on Operation Kayu. According to court papers, that investigation had been based on 'flawed evidence, discredited intelligence and information which the Met knew to be false'. The two officers also branded Siddique a 'corrupt and dishonest' detective who 'manufactured and manipulated information' in an attempt to 'discredit' them.[46]

They also criticised Cressida Dick for misleading the Home Affairs Select Committee about the extent of corruption inside Scotland Yard. In July 2013 Dick, then an assistant commissioner, had appeared before the committee to answer questions about Hunt following the *Sunday Times* libel victory. She had downplayed the significance of the case, telling MPs that she was not 'aware of any infiltration' of the Met. McKelvey and Guntrip said this statement was in 'direct conflict' with the findings of Operation Tiberius, and other evidence held in the Met's files.[47]

In the defence submitted to the High Court, Scotland Yard initially tried to claim that the investigations into McKelvey and Guntrip were 'proportionate and necessary', and all the officers involved acted 'professionally and impartially'. When details of the High Court claim were reported in the media, however, Scotland Yard started to get nervous. Politicians began to ask questions. David Davis, the former shadow Home Secretary, wrote to the commissioner, Sir Bernard Hogan-Howe, to ask what action had been or was being taken to investigate Hunt. 'It seems inexplicable that no criminal action has followed against Mr Hunt after the civil courts found he was an organised gang boss involved in fraud, money laundering and extreme violence,' Davis told me.[48] 'Both that case and the documents from Operation Tiberius were founded on allegations of widespread police corruption. The public will quite properly ask why such corrosive and damaging claims have not been answered in a criminal court.'

The public scrutiny – and the ongoing damage to the Met's reputation – seemed to have an effect. Scotland Yard backed down and agreed to issue an apology to McKelvey and Guntrip. The two men also received a substantial six-figure settlement. In a letter to the detectives, Fiona Taylor, deputy assistant commissioner of the Met's anti-corruption command, said:

> The [Met] would like to apologise to the claimants and their families for any injury or damage caused to them as a result of the investigation. The [Met] regrets any distress caused and hopes that this apology will go some way to the claimants being able to put this matter behind them.
>
> The MPS sincerely hopes that the claimants will now be able to get on with their lives and their careers.

McKelvey may have been forced out of the Met, but he did not let his investigative skills go to waste. Instead, he ploughed his compensation payment into the establishment of a new business, intended to fill the void created by the Met's retreat from crime fighting. McKelvey's firm, TM Eye, now investigates and prosecutes criminals on behalf of paying private clients and has become the UK's largest private prosecutor. It has dealt with over 500 successful cases to date, and boasts a 100 per cent conviction rate.[49] McKelvey and the dozens of other Met detectives who retired to join him are a loss to the 8 million residents of London, a city which has suffered soaring levels of violent crime since 2015. Scotland Yard lost one of its best men. His treatment seems yet another catastrophic blunder by a force reeling from crisis to crisis.

In fairness, however, they did eventually get one thing right. Scotland Yard has since reviewed the risk to McKelvey and Guntrip. Both now live under armed police protection.[50]

Chapter 13

The Avalanche

Two guilty verdicts for the murder of Stephen Lawrence may have delivered a measure of relief to the dead boy's family. But if anyone in Scotland Yard hoped that the case might now quietly fade from public scrutiny, they were in for a serious disappointment. Within the ranks of the Metropolitan Police there were officers who knew exactly what lengths their superiors had gone to in their efforts to derail the pursuit of justice. Twenty years after Stephen's murder, and eighteen months after Gary Dobson and David Norris had been sent to jail, a former officer named Peter Francis could no longer remain silent.

A retired member of a secretive Met unit known as the Special Demonstration Squad (SDS), Francis had been deployed undercover on the Lawrence case in the months following Stephen's murder in 1993. He came forward in June 2013 and told his story to shocking effect, in a television interview on Channel 4's *Dispatches* programme. Calmly facing the camera, Francis claimed that he had been tasked to dig up 'dirt' that might be used to 'smear' the Lawrence family. 'I had to get any information on what was happening in the Stephen Lawrence campaign,' he said. 'They wanted the campaign to stop. It was felt it was going to turn into an elephant.'[1]

Francis claimed to have infiltrated a left-wing activist group,

Youth Against Racism in Europe, which had attached itself to the Lawrence campaign. He had come under 'huge and constant pressure' from his Met superiors to 'hunt for disinformation' that might be used to undermine those criticising the botched police investigation into the murder.[2] He further claimed that members of a police liaison team supporting the bereaved family in the days following Stephen's murder had reported the names of visitors to the Lawrence home so Francis's unit could assess the family for potential vulnerabilities.

The allegations were a new low for Doreen Lawrence, who told *Dispatches* that she was 'shocked' that 'someone was sitting somewhere calculating, infiltrating into our family' while they were still grieving for her son. 'Out of all the things I have found out over the years this certainly has topped it. Nothing can justify the whole thing about trying to discredit the family and people around us.'[3]

The claims triggered uproar. The Prime Minister, David Cameron, described the allegations as 'horrific' and vowed to 'get the full truth out'. Cameron added: 'Let's be clear, these are absolutely dreadful allegations and we can only think of the Lawrence family, who have suffered so much already from the loss of their son. To hear that, potentially, the police that were meant to be helping them were actually undermining them – that's horrific.' The Prime Minister offered the only reassurance he could: 'We have investigations under way. We must make sure those investigations get rapidly to the bottom of what's happened and we get the full truth out.'

Sir Bernard Hogan-Howe, the Met commissioner, was contrite. He declared that 'smearing the family of a murder victim would never be acceptable to me or my officers' and pledged to apologise if the allegations proved to be true. The following day, Jack Straw, the Labour Home Secretary at the time of the 1999 Macpherson inquiry, called for an independent investigation. 'I am absolutely appalled by these revelations,' he told BBC Radio 4's *Today* programme. 'They go to the heart of the issue of the integrity and the ethics of the police service, or the lack of both, in part of the Metropolitan Police at the time of Stephen Lawrence's murder in 1993 and for some years after that.'[4]

The anger and revulsion were unanimous and it was clear that only a truly independent review could be trusted to get at the truth. A few days later, Doreen Lawrence was invited to meet Theresa May, the Home Secretary. Senior Scotland Yard officers had previously tried to dissuade Lawrence from meeting May, assuring her that they had done all they could to bring her son's killers to justice. But by 2013, Doreen had become a public figure. Her years of tireless campaigning for her son had earned her widespread respect and she had influential friends. The previous year she had carried the Olympic flag during the opening ceremony for the 2012 London Games, broadcast to a global audience of billions. She had become a force the police could no longer subdue. When this modest, middle-aged mother from Deptford went to meet Theresa May, it was the Home Secretary and future Prime Minister who looked the more vulnerable.

After forty-five minutes Doreen emerged from the Home Office to tell journalists that she didn't trust the police, and that only a reprise of the Macpherson inquiry would be able to address her concerns. 'The fact that this family has had to go through another revelation, how many more are there?' she said. 'We've no idea, but I think unless we have a public inquiry that goes through the whole thing, we'll never get to the bottom of this.'

The pressure told. May swiftly referred the case to be assessed by Mark Ellison QC, who was already conducting a review of alleged police corruption in the original Lawrence inquiry. Ellison duly interviewed Peter Francis, the officer whose admissions had blown the case open. Francis told him that he had passed on rumours that relations between Doreen and Neville might have been 'less happy ... than otherwise appeared'. He told Ellison that his handler was 'pleased' to hear this and 'said it was exactly the sort of thing they were looking for'. Any crack in the Lawrence marriage might help destroy their campaign for justice.

Francis then explained why the Lawrence case had become so threatening to the Met. Within his undercover unit, he said that many of the 'black justice' campaigns were 'perceived as presenting less of a problem than the Lawrence family'. 'This was because there was often existing police information concerning the dead or injured person ... that enabled them to be presented as unreliable (such as a criminal background or other discreditable conduct).'

But there was nothing discreditable about the Lawrences. 'Together with the support they had from their solicitor Imran Khan, and from some public figures, their campaign was seen as particularly difficult for the Metropolitan Police Service (MPS) to deal with,' Francis told Ellison.[5] The idea that a black man could be innocent was something some police officers evidently struggled with.

* * *

DCI Clive Driscoll, who led the investigation that secured the convictions of Gary Dobson and David Norris a year earlier, was still trying to do what the judge had instructed him to do. He was after the rest of the murder gang, despite his superiors' lack of interest. Two days after the trial ended, Driscoll had been summoned to Scotland Yard to be told that an internal report had concluded that the Met had 'exhausted every opportunity of further convictions'. Bizarrely, the senior officers refused to give him a copy of the report.[6]

'I was left in no doubt that certain people around that table wanted the investigation shut down,' said Driscoll, who had been forced to weave around so many obstacles during his six-year inquiry that he was not surprised.

> If I'm honest, they'd wanted it buried years ago. How else do you explain my team being disrupted the way it was: moved five times, including once to a building without HOLMES (Home Office Large Major Enquiry System) computers, and briefed against in the press? Report or no report, I could not stand by and let that happen without a fight.

The veteran detective stood his ground. 'Didn't Judge Treacy just tell us to keep looking?' he told his superiors. 'Since when do police start disagreeing with judges?'[7]

His argument seemed to make an impact and a compromise was agreed. If Driscoll could produce promising leads, he could put his case to a murder review panel that might allow him to proceed. It quickly became clear that nothing of the kind was likely to happen.

A month later Driscoll received a call from his boss, Cressida Dick, who was now assistant commissioner en route to the top job. 'What's this report the murder review group is chasing me for?' she asked him. Driscoll was still after the internal report concluding that all opportunities for further convictions in the Lawrence case had been exhausted. Dick didn't know anything about it.

'That's when the penny dropped,' said Driscoll. 'If I hadn't dug in my heels, the investigation would have been closed – thanks to a report that didn't exist. So, I carried on.'[8]

Driscoll soon came up with a new lead – or rather, an old one that no one else had bothered to follow up. Shortly after Stephen Lawrence's death, a man had made a phone call to police saying that he had information about the murder. The records of this potential witness's approach had been lost until Driscoll's team found them after the 2012 trial.[9] Driscoll thought it was worth pursuing. He went to the man's terraced house in south London. When the detective explained what he was doing there so long after the murder, the man laughed and said: 'You're rushing this job, aren't you?'

After hearing what the witness had to say, Driscoll was confident there was a 'real chance' that a third person could be prosecuted. But events outside his control would once again impede his progress.

*   *   *

It started with a meeting in a north London garden. Three police officers with connections to Scotland Yard and its Special Branch undercover operations had gathered to discuss the Lawrence case, and did not want to be overheard. It was a time of acute tension for the Metropolitan Police, which in August 1998 was preparing a defence of its handling of the Lawrence investigation, for submission to the Macpherson inquiry. Months of excoriating public testimony had shaken the force. Senior officers were desperate for a persuasive riposte.

One of those present was an SDS officer designated N81, operating under the cover name of Dave Hagan. Hagan had been deployed by the Met to gather intelligence on the activities of left-wing groups. Along the way he had come across the Lawrence family and its supporters, a development that greatly interested his Scotland Yard superiors.[10]

That warm summer evening Hagan was summoned to the home of the officer who steered his undercover activities: DI Bob Lambert, a former undercover officer with a chequered past. Lambert had stolen the identity of a dead boy in 1984 in order to infiltrate environmental and animal rights groups. In 1987, he was also accused of seeking to cement his radical credentials by setting fire to a branch of Debenhams during a protest against the fur trade – an allegation he has always denied. Lambert had intimate relationships with four female targets of his operations. He fathered a child with one of them, abandoning both mother and baby when his undercover mission was over. When his activities were eventually exposed she would receive £400,000 from the Met in compensation.[11]

By 1998, Lambert was a desk man, his field-working days behind him. He had arranged the meeting in his garden so Hagan could meet one of the key figures in the team responding to the Macpherson inquiry. DI Richard Walton, an ex-Special Branch officer, was helping to draft Scotland Yard's final written submissions to the inquiry. Walton was a high-flyer. He later rose to become a commander in charge of Scotland Yard's fight against counter-terrorism, but that night he was in Lambert's garden to gather information on the Lawrence case and return to Scotland Yard to brief the then commissioner, Sir Paul Condon.[12]

The meeting would stay secret for years. When the details finally emerged in 2014, they formed the centrepiece of Mark Ellison's explosive report into the Stephen Lawrence case. The publication of that report caused irrevocable damage to the reputation of Scotland Yard and moved Sir Bernard Hogan-Howe, one of Condon's successors as commissioner, to admit it was one of his 'worst days' as a police officer.[13]

Ellison should have been provided with full access to all material on the Lawrence case still held by Scotland Yard. The QC tried to substantiate Peter Francis's claim that he was asked to find compromising information on the Lawrence family following Stephen's murder. Ellison was told, however, that 'significant tranches' of records had been 'destroyed' – an excuse that would reoccur as his review progressed. His team did unearth one meeting note from the initial murder inquiry that seemed relevant. Written by a detective inspector on 31 August 1993, the note made fleeting reference to an 'undercover officer' in the context of a meeting with the family. Why should an undercover officer have met with the Lawrences? Ellison's team never found the answer. When they quizzed the officer concerned he said he could not recall the 'meaning or context' of the reference.[14]

Documents that detailed the meeting between Hagan, Walton and Lambert, held five years later in the middle of the Macpherson inquiry, did remain in existence, however. They would prove far more damaging for Scotland Yard. A contemporaneous file note detailing the encounter, written by Lambert, said it had been a 'fascinating and valuable exchange of information on an issue that DI Walton had said continued to dominate the Commissioner's agenda on a daily basis'.[15]

According to the note, Lambert was delighted with his 'in-depth discussion' with Hagan. The undercover officer had enabled him to 'increase his understanding of the Lawrences' relationship with the various campaigning groups', which was 'of great value as he continued to prepare a draft submission to the inquiry on behalf of the Commissioner'.[16] Lambert further noted that Walton said there was 'great sensitivity around the Lawrence issue' with 'both the Home Secretary and the Prime Minister extremely concerned that the Metropolitan Police could end up with its credibility – in the eyes of London's black community – completely undermined'.[17]

Other records found by Ellison's team confirm that the fate of a murdered black youth was of much less concern to senior officers than preserving police credibility. One SDS file from 1998 noted that Hagan had a 'unique insight into the behind-the-scenes machinations of the Lawrence campaign' which had proved 'invaluable' to Walton. In 2001, Hagan was also commended for providing a 'perspective to those charged with formulating the [police] position on key strategic issues'.[18]

It is tempting to conclude that if the same effort the police put into smearing the Lawrence family had gone into hunting down Stephen's killers, there would have been no further scandal. Ellison was understandably troubled by the meeting between Hagan, Lambert and Walton. His concerns increased exponentially when his team found another report submitted by Hagan himself. Dated July 1998, the undercover officer took aim at Stephen's bereaved parents, reporting that the couple had quietly separated, as we saw in Chapter 8, and only continued to appear together as a 'front for the campaign'.

'Doreen and Neville Lawrence split up during the first stage of the Inquiry (although this is not public knowledge),' Hagan wrote. 'Neville remains the more politicised of the two although Doreen has recently been vocal in her calls for the Commissioner to resign.'

The dissection continued: 'Neville feels a measure of "ownership" of the Inquiry and resents others who seek to make capital of it, particularly when they call for public disorder. He is not a good public speaker, but will attend meetings and speak if invited.'

Hagan also offered an analysis of the couple's different strategies. 'Doreen ... wished to wind the campaign up at this point and simply await the findings of the inquiry. Neville is more open to continuing but only until the inquiry releases its findings.'[19]

Years later, when Ellison questioned Walton about the propriety of spying on the Lawrence family, the Yard commander was unapologetic. 'This is the dilemma of all undercover information,' Walton said. 'We talk about it now as collateral intrusion ... which is something that we are aware of now, perhaps, more than we were then.'

'This is a highly, highly intrusive tactic,' he continued.

> You cannot avoid it. You cannot avoid those odd kinds of coincidences. If you are putting somebody in the field against a certain target ... then don't be surprised that they are going to be covering in awkward places and times and exchanges with ordinary members of the public, and that is collateral intrusion.[20]

When Ellison's team first interviewed Walton, the Yard commander 'largely signed up to the accuracy' of the contemporaneous SDS documents. Walton admitted that his role on the Stephen Lawrence 'review team' had prompted his meeting with Hagan, who had 'coverage' on the 'periphery of the Lawrence family'.[21] Yet when Ellison notified him that he might be criticised in the forthcoming report, Walton wanted to change his story.[22]

He now claimed that the outdoor meeting had occurred as part of his new role focusing on community relations for the racial and violent crime task force (CO24), headed by Deputy Assistant Commissioner John Grieve. In a remarkable about-turn, Walton insisted the meeting had nothing to do with the Macpherson inquiry. Hagan had got it all wrong, he argued. Unfortunately, it seems Walton failed to agree his new story with others. Grieve told Ellison that

Walton was, in fact, working on the Lawrence review team and 'was not in any way in my chain of command at the time'.[23] Scotland Yard's inept handling of successive Lawrence-related inquiries was getting sorrier and messier.

Ellison's report ultimately found Walton's responses 'less than straightforward', 'unconvincing' and 'somewhat troubling'. The QC concluded that his original version – that the meeting had been about the Lawrence family – was the most likely. Ellison found it 'difficult to comprehend' how such a senior officer's memory could have been 'refreshed' quite so dramatically.[24]

The QC was also alarmed by reports he was receiving from Hagan. The undercover officer told the independent review that senior Scotland Yard officers were now 'incredibly hostile' towards him, and he felt 'under attack, threatened and lonely, having done nothing wrong'. Walton, who was now his line manager in the counter-terrorism command, was apparently 'denying' that the garden meeting had ever taken place.[25]

Ellison also questioned Sir Paul Condon, who Walton was supposedly briefing personally. Condon replied that he wasn't 'aware' of Hagan's work, nor would he 'seek to justify it'. 'It feels as if there is a transition from legitimate concern and monitoring of public order issues into either a casual or sort of prurient gossip around the family and/or revelling in that knowledge of the family,' Condon continued, adding: 'There can be no justification for anything which is a sort of "them and us" tactical advantage over the Lawrences in any way. That was never part of my agenda and it should not have been a part of anyone's agenda.'

Condon's deputy at the time was Sir John Stevens, who described the undercover activities against the Lawrences more bluntly:

I would have been appalled at that, to be frank. The thought that someone was inserted into the family … one, it is totally unacceptable in the circumstances and, secondly, if they were then giving information of that sort into the process and to supervisors, that should have been stopped straight away.[26]

Ellison's report on the Hagan–Walton meeting was disastrous for the Met. He described Hagan as a 'spy in the Lawrence family camp'. The parents of a murdered youth had somehow come to be seen not as victims determined to get at the truth, but as the 'primary party in opposition' to Scotland Yard.

'The mere presence of an undercover officer in the wider Lawrence family camp in such circumstances is highly questionable,' Ellison concluded. The meeting to discuss the family's relationship with supporters and how all this might help the police defend itself to the public inquiry amounted to 'completely improper use of the knowledge [Scotland Yard] had gained by the deployment of this officer [Hagan]. Such a meeting was wholly inappropriate.'

Ellison went on:

Given the contested issues at the public inquiry as to the honesty, integrity and openness of the Met, and the disputes as to the true causes of the seriously flawed investigation of Stephen Lawrence's murder, the objective impression created by any public revelation of the fact of such a meeting could only have been dire for the Metropolitan Police Service.[27]

The QC added that Sir William Macpherson would have 'deplored such conduct' during his original inquiry and the Met should have told him what was going on. As it turned out, Hagan's snooping was far from the murkiest of police activities that were hidden from the judge.*

*   *   *

In 2007, Clive Driscoll's team of detectives was searching for paperwork on the Stephen Lawrence case when they made yet another startling discovery. It was relatively early in the new investigation that would conclude five years later with the convictions of David Norris and Gary Dobson.

Driscoll's officers were sifting through old files on the eighth floor of New Scotland Yard. They were in an office once used by John Grieve, the deputy assistant commissioner who had distanced himself from Walton's erratic memories.[28] The detectives came across a red file that the Met's anti-corruption command had put together following a request from Grieve, who had led a previous, unsuccessful inquiry into the case in 2000.[29] Not the least depressing feature of the entire Lawrence affair is the amount of police investigating that supposedly went on, to no publicly discernible effect.

The newly discovered file contained damaging intelligence that the Met had secretly put together on John Davidson, one of the detectives involved in the original investigation. It was an unexpected discovery as Scotland Yard holds its internal corruption intelligence

---

*   Following the publication of the Ellison report, the police mounted an investigation, led by Mick Creedon, then chief constable of Derbyshire Police. His inquiry found that undercover police officers secretly gathered intelligence over two decades on eighteen families fighting to get justice from the police. The intelligence covering high-profile campaigns was collected between the mid-1980s and 2005 and affected grieving families whose relatives had been murdered or had died in police custody. However, Creedon's report said that the information or 'mentions' reported by undercover officers on these justice campaigns were as a result of information and knowledge that was obtained from conversations often in public meetings or with members of the target group. 'There is no evidence of covert operations targeted against any of the respective families or Justice Campaigns.' Creedon also said that Hagan was never 'directly or indirectly asked or tasked by anyone at any level in the [Met] to do anything in relation to the Stephen Lawrence family or campaign'.

tightly and officers involved in routine investigative police work – such as Driscoll's murder inquiry – cannot normally access it. The information was never disclosed to the Macpherson inquiry.

The intelligence file now in the hands of Driscoll's team included claims that Davidson had a corrupt relationship with criminal informants. One file said he was 'intrinsically corrupt' and the 'weight of intelligence … levelled against him is damning'.[30] The most alarming revelation in the file was that Davidson was 'known to associate' with some of the prime suspects for the murder of Daniel Morgan.

Driscoll knew the Met was then reinvestigating the Morgan murder and immediately realised that the file was 'very relevant' to that inquiry, named Operation Abelard. He handed them the Davidson file, telling them: 'It's talking about the very people that you are talking about'.[31]

Years later, Mark Ellison ran into difficulties in his Lawrence inquiry, and sought Driscoll's help. At the time, Ellison was looking into claims made by *Panorama* about detective-turned-supergrass Neil Putnam, notably that Davidson had a corrupt relationship with Clifford Norris, the gangster father of one of Stephen's murderers.

As so many times previously, Scotland Yard was unhelpful, telling Ellison that no relevant records about Davidson could be found. The QC went to Driscoll, who bravely agreed to help. 'It was outlandish to assume they'd withhold anything from him,' he later said.[32]

Driscoll knew exactly what had happened to the missing Davidson files – he had given them to the Abelard team, 'so I went and got them'.[33] This was clearly in the interests of justice and public understanding, but it would cause no end of grief for the Met. Ellison realised immediately that the files had not been given to

Macpherson, despite featuring a key officer whose actions were examined by the public inquiry. As a result, he went back to examine the exchanges between the Metropolitan force and the judge between 1998 and 1999 in microscopic detail.

Putnam had blown the whistle on Davidson's allegedly criminal activities right in the middle of the Macpherson inquiry, when the Met was desperate to persuade the judge that Scotland Yard was innocent of all charges. Sir John Stevens wrote to the judge privately in a bid to defuse the supergrass's bombshell. Stevens acknowledged that 'recent information' had 'implicated ex-DS John Davidson'. He stressed, however, that Davidson was not under 'active investigation' and 'the intelligence does not necessarily indicate corrupt or suspect behaviour and much of it is background information'.[34]

Given that the Met had uncovered mountains of intelligence against Davidson and a supergrass was prepared to give evidence against him in court, this was, to put it politely, a deeply misleading characterisation of the intelligence files. At the time, Macpherson was sufficiently perturbed by Stevens's explanation to fire off an immediate reply. 'Naturally we are most concerned to know whether any contact, however remote, may have existed between Mr Davidson and, in particular, Clifford Norris,' wrote the judge. 'You will appreciate that any wrongdoing would go to Mr Davidson's credit ... much may turn upon this retired officer as the inquiry proceeds.'[35] From Stevens and the rest of the Yard there followed a deafening silence.

Once Ellison started digging deeper into the exchanges over Putnam and Davidson, it emerged that Stevens had not consulted the Met's lawyers about Putnam, nor about the Yard's own intelligence on the case, before sending his letter to Macpherson.

By the time Ellison conducted his review in 2014, Judge

Macpherson was almost ninety and privately admitting that his memory was not what it once was.[36] Ellison's team turned instead to Anesta Weekes QC, counsel to the original inquiry in 1998. Weekes confirmed that no one on Macpherson's team knew the details of Davidson's allegedly corrupt activity before or after he worked on the Stephen Lawrence murder investigation.[37] Weekes told Ellison that this would have been of 'great significance to the issue of DS Davidson's (and potentially other officers') motives'.[38]

Ellison tried to establish why the Yard had been so unforthcoming about Putnam and Davidson. He first turned for answers to Roy Clark, then deputy assistant commissioner in day-to-day charge of the anti-corruption command. Clark denied that the Met was hiding anything about Putnam and insisted there was no cover-up. He also implied that the intelligence on Davidson had been made available to the inquiry, which Ellison knew was not the case.

Stevens's answer was even more impenetrable, smacking less of candour and more of 'if I'm going down, I'm taking everyone with me'. When Ellison asked him what he knew of the intelligence held by the Met's anti-corruption command, Stevens replied, barely coherently:

Well, in terms of intelligence, obviously, the briefings that I had, but, on the Commissioner's floor, where the Commissioner is, right at the other end was a unit that had been set up I think by Paul Condon and Sir Brian Hayes [Stevens's predecessor as deputy commissioner] dealing totally – and headed by Matt Baggott [the future chief constable of Northern Ireland] … with Sara Thornton [the future chief constable of Thames Valley Police and future chair of the National Police Chiefs Council] … That unit from my knowledge had been set up a lot earlier and was there to actually service what Macpherson wanted for his Inquiry. That unit was very much linked into Dennis O'Connor [the future chief constable of Surrey and Her Majesty's chief inspector of constabulary], because he had specific responsibility. Ian Johnston [the future chief constable of British Transport Police] was in the mix as well. So all of that was dealt with down at that end of the corridor to my knowledge.[39]

In short, it seemed to be everyone's fault except Stevens's.

Ellison asked the former deputy commissioner who he thought was actually in charge of assessing the intelligence and deciding what should be revealed to the inquiry. Stevens passed the buck to Thornton. But when she was questioned, Thornton said she had 'no recollection of having anything to do with any intelligence held by CIB3 [the anti-corruption command], or even knowing that CIB3 held corruption intelligence on witnesses due to give evidence to the Inquiry'.

Next up was Bob Quick, who had led the Met's Lawrence review team. Questioned by Ellison on the matter of responsibility for the Davidson intelligence, Quick passed the buck back to Stevens and Clark: '[Intelligence] would have gone through the DPS [anti-corruption] chain of command, so it would have gone to the Deputy Commissioner (via Roy Clark) and back down into the Inquiry from the Deputy Commissioner's office.'[40]

Luckily for Ellison, John Yates, the anti-corruption commander whose team debriefed Putnam in 1998, had a very clear memory of who was told what. He told the QC: 'It was actually me that brought Davidson to the attention of the Deputy Commissioner.' The buck was back with Stevens. Yates, who later became the third most senior officer in Britain (although not without difficulties, as we have seen), claimed he told both Stevens and Clark that Davidson was 'about to become a target'. He added: 'Macpherson is sitting, you need to be aware of this.' However much his superiors tried to wriggle away from any knowledge of Davidson's activities, Yates was sure of the chain of command. 'It would have been Roy Clark, John Stevens – not necessarily in order – so the sort of circle, you know, the briefing upwards was pretty clear.'[41]

Ellison was far from happy with the shambolic responses he had received to straightforward questions. His report wasted no words. The Macpherson inquiry had not been shown incriminating allegations against one of the policemen who played a key role in the Lawrence case. 'This amounted to a significant failure,' the QC concluded. It was another black mark for the Met.

Roy Clark featured in another part of the Ellison review. The long-retired head of the Met's anti-corruption command was interviewed shortly before the report was published and was stunned by what the lawyers told him. Scotland Yard had apparently been unable to find any of the intelligence generated from Operation Othona, the painstaking, four-year covert investigation into criminality inside Scotland Yard he had led in the 1990s.

Othona found widespread evidence that organised crime groups had recruited corrupt officers inside the Met to sabotage police operations against them.[42] The inquiry, which cost more than £14 million,[43] covered the years from 1994 to 1998. Among the policemen it named as being suspected of corrupt activities was John Davidson.

Ellison asked to see the Othona files to investigate possible links with Stephen's murder, and to establish what was known about police corruption at the time of the Macpherson inquiry. But Scotland Yard told him that they were nowhere to found. When this message was relayed to Clark, who had seen the documents at a meeting at Scotland Yard in 2004, he was appalled and angry.

I'd be shocked if it doesn't exist … there would be no good reason to get rid of it. It was gold dust stuff … I am on record as saying that the failure of the police service is lack of long-term consistency. [Othona] was there not to be closed down, to roll on … How you can go to those lengths and spend all that money and it is not there, I am just amazed.[44]

A rare surviving document from the Othona file summarises its damaging findings and may provide an explanation why it was not shared with Ellison. The internal investigation had found a 'structured network of traitors' operating at 'all levels within the Police Service'. The document's summary ended with a punch to the gut: 'Paranoia about what might be revealed if corruption was investigated with vigour, resourcefulness and cunning was running high in some very powerful and influential circles.'[45]

Regrettably for the Met, the explanation it advanced for the apparent disappearance of the bulk of the Othona files made things even worse. Ellison and his team were told there had been a 'mass shredding' in 2003 – a year before Clark claims to have seen the files intact. Denied yet another avenue of enquiry, Ellison complained that it had not been possible to carry out a 'fairly fundamental task' of his review.

Yet all was not quite lost. Clive Driscoll, seemingly one of the few policemen in Scotland Yard willing to hang on to evidence instead of destroying it, was continuing to amass scraps of intelligence about police corruption. The disturbing contents of the files that his team uncovered by chance spelt yet more misery for Scotland Yard.

One report concerned a previously undisclosed alleged relationship between two officers connected to the Lawrence case: former

Met commander Ray Adams and ex-detective sergeant David Coles.[46] Both officers' activities had been examined closely by the Macpherson inquiry. Coles was the officer who had inexplicably driven Duwayne Brooks to Eltham, yards from where the murder took place, just before the first Lawrence trial, terrifying him, perhaps intentionally – an allegation that had been hotly denied. During the Macpherson inquiry, it emerged that Coles had been observed exchanging packages with Clifford Norris. Coles denied any corruption and Macpherson eventually cleared him of any impropriety in regard to the Lawrence case.[47]

The judge also looked at Adams's involvement in the case. The Met's second youngest-ever commander had repeatedly been investigated for corruption amid claims of links to organised criminals in south London. It had been Adams, in the days following Stephen Lawrence's death, who had written to the teenager's parents questioning their decision to seek legal representation and arguing that there should be 'no conflict of interest or purpose' between them and Scotland Yard. Adams, too, had been exonerated by Macpherson.[48]

In 2014, however, as Ellison retraced the earlier inquiry, the intelligence provided by Driscoll cast the two officers in a different light. One file revealed that Operation Russell, a previous anti-corruption inquiry into Adams, had concluded he behaved in a 'reprehensible' fashion and was guilty of 'highly questionable and unprofessional conduct'. Another report claimed that Adams intervened to protect Coles during a disciplinary process after another senior officer had recommended the detective be 'removed from duties that utilise aspects of police work of a delicate and confidential nature'.

The alleged link between Coles and Adams troubled Ellison because Adams had told Macpherson: 'As far as I can recall I have not encountered the officer.'[49] Were there to be any 'clear evidence' that the former commander was lying, Ellison concluded, then his entire testimony to Macpherson 'may need to be re-evaluated'.[50]

Other details regarding the Met's hostile treatment of Duwayne Brooks were also handed to Ellison. Senior police officers had secretly recorded a meeting with him in May 2000 which Ellison did not believe was 'necessary or justified in the circumstances'. The Met's undercover SDS unit had also targeted Duwayne in 1999 and 2000, during the period he was suing the Scotland Yard for substantial damages. The files showed that undercover officers had reported back on the strategy that Duwayne planned to deploy against the Met,[51] and confirmed that Scotland Yard knew the sex crime allegations against him were bogus at the time.[52] Long before the case was dropped, intelligence passed to Ellison shows that the undercover officers who spied on Duwayne were reporting back potential problems in the case against him, yet the case was allowed to continue.[53]

When the Ellison report was published in the House of Commons in March 2014, its findings were devastating. The QC concluded that Judge Macpherson had been misled and roundly condemned the deployment of an undercover spy in the Lawrence family camp.

On the issue of corruption tainting the original Lawrence murder investigation, Ellison said Macpherson 'might have been driven to the conclusion that there must have been more to John Davidson's failure to develop information and evidence than simply an inappropriate manner and unfortunate unconscious racism'. He said the 'suggestion' that Davidson was a 'corrupt officer' with a 'corrupt relationship' with Clifford Norris had 'persisted' and was now 'more supported than it was on the material that was made available' to Macpherson.

'DS Davidson was in a position, if so minded, to act corruptly in the "light-touch" manner we have identified,' said Ellison. 'He had access to significant information and the opportunity to subtly affect the investigation, and this would plainly have been of value to those under suspicion.'[54]

Ellison's findings were ruinous in three specific areas. The Met had deployed an undercover spy against the Lawrences; it had shredded key files; and it had downplayed evidence of corruption in the ranks. Any one of these would have been damaging enough; all three emerging at once was disastrous. The Lawrence affair had snowballed for years. By 2014 it had become an avalanche, crashing with unstoppable force throughout Scotland Yard.

Politicians of all stripes were unanimous in their condemnation. Labour's Jack Straw, who as Home Secretary had commissioned the Macpherson inquiry, said he had never been more shocked in thirty-five years of frontline politics. Straw was sufficiently angry to reveal that he had been the 'final court of appeal for police discipline cases' and had had a 'window on the actuality of police corruption'. There were 'staggeringly corrupt police officers around at that stage' and 'corruption' was 'endemic in parts of their CIDs'.[55] In retrospect, it seems a shame he did not tell the public this at the time.

Theresa May, the contemporary Home Secretary, described the Ellison report as 'profoundly shocking'. The future Tory Prime Minister went on:

The Macpherson inquiry couldn't look at everything because information wasn't given to it ... Here was a family who suffered twice. The first time it was absolutely devastating to hear that your son has been brutally murdered, as Stephen was. But then to find that the very group of people who you should be able to trust, haven't done the job that you expected them to do. And you wonder why it is that they haven't done that job. There was a concern in some quarters that police officers felt they were above the law.[56]

A few days later, Sir Bernard Hogan-Howe was summoned to the Home Affairs Select Committee. During a fractious appearance, the then commissioner was forced to admit that the 'mass shredding' of the Othona files might have allowed rogue officers to evade justice. MPs variously described the situation as 'terrible', 'shocking' and an 'out-and-out disgrace'. They ridiculed reports, purportedly put out by Scotland Yard sources, that the shredding was an innocent attempt to comply with data protection laws.[57]

Nicola Blackwood MP questioned Hogan-Howe over a discredited internal review of the Stephen Lawrence case, published by Scotland Yard under his watch in 2012, which failed to mention the destruction of the Operation Othona files.[58] David Hurley, the detective superintendent who led that review, had told Ellison that he had no control over the editorial content that was turned over to unspecified 'senior officers' in the final analysis.

Hogan-Howe apologised. The committee chairman, Keith Vaz, commented that the commissioner appeared to be in a state of shock and expressed concern that Britain's most senior policeman did not have a grip on his institution.[59]

In 2014, after a formal complaint by Neville Lawrence, the Independent Office for Police Conduct (IOPC) launched an investigation into Stevens and Clark for failing to inform Macpherson of suspected police corruption in the original Lawrence investigation. The IOPC and the National Crime Agency (NCA) were also asked to look into police corruption in the Lawrence case, at the direction

of Theresa May. Justice may not always be blind, but in the Lawrence case it is always disturbingly slow. In 2019, five years later,
the IOPC announced that its inquiry – Operation Probitas – had
concluded there was 'no indication of corruption on the part of
Davidson relating to the original Stephen Lawrence murder investigation'. The IOPC stressed that the investigation had reviewed
and tested all of the available evidence including the lines of inquiry identified by the Ellison review. The watchdog reached that
view notwithstanding the mountains of police corruption intelligence against Davidson exposed in the Ellison report, laid before
Parliament. Yet the policing establishment would doubtless stress
that intelligence isn't evidence, and intelligence can sometimes be
wrong. Perhaps the whole affair was simply a storm in a teacup. We
will never know for sure. It must be emphasised that Davidson has
never been charged with any crimes and has always insisted he is
the victim of false allegations and smears.

At the time of writing, it seems the NCA has more concerns
about Neil Putnam, the former friend of Davidson who turned
supergrass and caused his ex-detective and the wider Metropolitan
Police Service no end of trouble. Putnam is currently under investigation for perjury and has been interviewed by the NCA, raising
questions about his allegations regarding Davidson.

Duwayne Brooks had several meetings with the NCA team
and was not impressed: 'I never had any confidence in them.' He
said the NCA team had spent nearly two years going through old
police files in their corruption investigation, which Brooks said was
always going to fail. 'It was pointless,' he said. 'You are not going
to find a smoking gun or someone saying in writing they have been
corrupt.'[60]

*   *   *

Sir William Macpherson died in February 2021 aged ninety-four. Although he never publicly professed any recollection of key moments in his inquiry, he told me not long before he passed away that that he was troubled by elements of the unfolding drama. He said he had become 'concerned' over recent years that 'things were not handed over', adding: 'I asked for all the information they [the Met] had, and thought and believed they had given all the information at the time. I expected to be told everything.'

Years later, the sense of crisis generated by the Ellison report and other recent scandals is still palpable. 'I think if something like [Ellison] had happened in our first year, with very little context, we would have found it unbelievable,' Nick Timothy recalled. 'In truth, our expectations [of the Met] had fallen so low. The culture of the organisation was so problematic in our lives that, do you know what, it didn't even feel that surprising. As appalling as it was, it was just yet another thing.'

Timothy went on:

I am not a conspiracy theorist but the [scandals] show that if enough people invest in the importance of an organisation, and feel a sufficient debt of loyalty to one another, then actually it is possible to keep things covered up, and tell lies in a systematic way, and get away with it for fucking decades. I mean, isn't that extraordinary?

Timothy believes that the Ellison report, combined with other controversies, has created a sense of 'the inevitability and necessity of change'.[61]

One immediate change was Clive Driscoll's job status. Rather than address Ellison's criticisms, the Met turned on the detective who had helped gather evidence for the inquiry. 'You would think that the Met would have redoubled their efforts to nail Stephen's other killers,' said Driscoll. 'But they didn't. Instead, they got rid of me.'[62]

A source close to the case told me that Cressida Dick, then Driscoll's boss, was among the senior officers infuriated by the detective's perceived betrayal, but although Driscoll had been told that Dick was 'put out', she had never confronted him directly. In any event, Driscoll's 32-year policing career was over. Despite his abrupt departure, the veteran detective still offered to be on permanent standby on the Lawrence case, in case the Met ever needed help. He is still waiting for the phone to ring.[63]

Chapter 14

'Friendship of Convenience'

Jonathan Rees left the Old Bailey in March 2011 elated. The last attempt to prosecute someone for the murder of Daniel Morgan had failed. But although Rees was now a free man, the aborted trial caused him plenty of new problems. Since his initial arrest in 2008, the UK's strict contempt of court laws forbidding publication of material that might prejudice a future trial had effectively barred the media from revealing any of Rees's illegal activities on behalf of the *News of the World*. In March 2011, the phone hacking scandal had exploded, and Britain was about to be shocked by the newspaper's treatment of murdered teenager Milly Dowler and her family. There were a number of journalists itching to expose Rees's hacking adventures. As soon as his murder trial collapsed, the media was unmuzzled. A stream of stories followed which alleged bribery, corruption, hacking and burglary at Southern Investigations, stretching back decades.

Leading the charge was *The Guardian*, led by Alan Rusbridger, regarded by many of his paper's readers as a courageous and mercurial editor. He saw himself as an heir to the fearless reporting traditions pioneered by the late Sir Harold Evans at the *Sunday Times*, which frequently trampled over nervous lawyers en route to momentous scoops. Like Evans before him, Rusbridger was more supportive of his investigative journalists than any other editor of his generation, and he had no qualms at all in taking on a rival newspaper proprietor. *The Guardian* went to war with Rupert Murdoch, and rapidly expanded hostilities against the Metropolitan Police and the Conservative-led government. If you judge an editor by his or her list of enemies, Rusbridger was in a class of his own. He would later admit that the summer of 2011 had produced the most 'intense weeks of my life', encompassing the resignations of the Met's commissioner, Sir Paul Stephenson, and assistant commissioner John Yates, the arrests of Andy Coulson and Rebekah Brooks, the closure of their newspaper, the *News of the World*, and Murdoch's eventual appearance in front of a UK government select committee, where the abrasive Australian tycoon told MPs it was 'the most humble day' of his life.[1]

When I spoke to him, Jonathan Rees made no effort to conceal his rage at *The Guardian* and Alan Rusbridger. But he once let slip that Rusbridger had hired another private investigator – someone Rees claimed to know – to sweep his home for listening devices at the height of the phone hacking scandal. 'He's very paranoid, he thinks he's under surveillance the whole time. He pays someone once a month, or once every couple of months, to have his house debugged.' He added a few more personal details. Shocked, I alerted contacts at *The Guardian* to warn Rusbridger of the breach.

However, on that occasion, and indeed at all our other meetings, Rees was always surprisingly relaxed about the Metropolitan Police. He was forever embroiled in one scandal or another but he never seemed terribly worried that the police would catch up with him, or he might go to jail. Rees never picked up a phone worrying that it might be bugged. He would gabble away undeterred by any threat of the call being intercepted by police. Even if he said something indiscreet, what was anyone going to do? He was more worried about his reputation and media coverage of his activities. Rees had an uncanny knack for sidestepping the criminal justice system. He appeared to believe instinctively that neither the police nor the Crown Prosecution Service would ever dare put him on trial in open court. He simply knew too much. Any action that might be taken against him could end up embarrassing powerful people.

One of the few developments that rattled him was the appointment of Lord Justice Leveson, a retired judge, to lead a public inquiry into newspaper ethics, criminal behaviour, and the relationship between the press, police and politicians. Rees's activities for Southern Investigations on behalf of the *News of the World* fell squarely into the Leveson inquiry's terms of reference and these were matters that were now out of the hands of Rees's chums at Scotland Yard. There would be live hearings, streamed on the internet for anyone to watch. Would this be Rees's day of reckoning, at last?

* * *

In April 2006, then commissioner Sir Ian Blair's senior management team held a confidential meeting at their offices at New Scotland Yard. It was the meeting that launched Abelard 2, the fifth police investigation into the murder of Daniel Morgan. There was no public announcement, and the last person to find out about it should have been the investigation's prime suspect – Jonathan Rees. Yet within forty-eight hours of the secret meeting, Rees not only knew about it but was discussing it with his mates on the phone.[2] What he didn't know – and very probably didn't care – was that officers from Scotland Yard's intercept unit were already listening to his calls. His conversations featured in a contemporaneous intelligence report, created by a detective inspector in the Met's anti-corruption command.

'Rees is aware a member of the Commissioner's inner sanctum is reporting back to [a very senior former Met officer] with regard to actions taken by the Commissioner and proposed policy decisions,' the report read. Why did it matter that someone was leaking secret police strategies to a former police chief? The report's answer: 'Rees has had this confirmed [by] Marunchak from the *News of the World*.'[3] The intelligence harvested from the mouth of Rees, even allowing for the concerns around its veracity, was potential dynamite and would cause repercussions for years to come. The prime suspect for one of Britain's most notorious unsolved murders is in touch with a *News of the World* editor who in turn is allegedly in touch with a former senior Scotland Yard officer. The ex-cop supposedly receives an inside tip which somehow reaches the ears of the suspect. The conduit between the two – Alex Marunchak – is up to his ears in the illicit goings-on at his soon-to-be disgraced tabloid. With friends like that, why should Rees be worried? Armed with inside knowledge helpfully provided by a former policeman – if his version of events is to be believed – Rees was in a position to destroy evidence, intimidate potential witnesses and generally screw up Abelard 2 before it got anywhere near him.

Thanks to the intercepted phone call, the Met's anti-corruption command was now at least aware that Blair's management team – which regularly discussed matters of national security – had been compromised. Yet the commissioner was never told of the breach. Years later, when I asked Rees about the contents of the intelligence report detailing the phone intercepts, he ducked and dived over several pints of lager before confirming it: 'They obviously picked me up talking on the intercepts.' When I asked if one of his sources was Marunchak, he replied: 'Yeah … I can remember discussing it with Alex.'[4]

As with many of Rees's claims, his allegations were never backed up by evidence. The former senior officer strongly denies ever leaking highly sensitive information to Marunchak and says Rees's claims are 'utter nonsense'. Others are not so sure. Sir Ian Blair, Lord Blair of Boughton since 2010, is understood to have his suspicions about the identity of the leaker in his team.[5] He was forced out of his post in 2008 following years of bitter internal fighting at the top of Scotland Yard. Former Home Secretary David Blunkett said that the intelligence report on intercepts 'confirms the suspicions and feelings that we had'. 'Ian Blair was being done over big time,' he said.[6]

Whatever the credibility of Rees's claims, there was no explaining the failure to alert Blair to the breach of his team's security. No one I have spoken to can believe that the commissioner was never briefed about the suggestions of a potentially ruinous leak. When the intelligence report on intercepts was passed to me during the Leveson inquiry in 2012, I asked Detective Chief Superintendent Alaric Bonthron, then the head of the Met's anti-corruption command, whether he thought Blair should have been warned about the intercept discoveries. 'I can't account for what structures were in place at that time and who did what. The DPS [anti-corruption command] is a very different beast now. None of that command team are left at all in the organisation.'

The intercept report was also leaked to Blair at the start of the Leveson inquiry. When he discovered that his own anti-corruption officers had intelligence to suggest his senior team had been compromised six years earlier – yet told him nothing about it – he was shocked. He took up the matter with his former subordinate Deputy Assistant Commissioner Sue Akers, who at the time was leading the myriad criminal investigations into police and newspaper corruption.

Blair also handed the document to Scotland Yard lawyers working on the Leveson inquiry. They assured him it would be passed to Leveson's team to be evaluated and considered for the judge's final report. Yet when Blair was called to the witness box at the Royal Courts of Justice, nobody bothered to ask him anything about it.

I was covering the Leveson inquiry for the London *Evening Standard* at the time and, aware of the significance of the intercept report, began making enquiries behind the scenes to find out why it hadn't been mentioned. The point of contact for journalists with the public inquiry was John Toker, a senior civil servant on secondment from the Cabinet Office, who had previously dealt with press enquiries relating to Britain's security services. This was an interesting background for a press officer nominally deputed to handle questions about journalistic misconduct. Was there some kind of security threat we didn't know about? Why put a friend of the spooks in charge of talking to newspaper hacks? The Leveson inquiry might cause significant national embarrassment, but would it harm national security? In my experience, the British establishment often treats the threat of embarrassment as seriously as it worries about the threat to security. Toker, however, was adamant that the Leveson inquiry 'did not receive this document'.

Bob Quick, Scotland Yard's former head of counter-terrorism operations, is a friend of Ian Blair. He was startled to learn that the intercept report had not been presented to the inquiry. 'The contents of this intelligence report, if true, are disturbing,' he told me. 'When it was discovered, it was swiftly and properly handed over to the Met prior to the Leveson hearings and I am surprised its content was not examined during the inquiry.'[7]

These were serious allegations involving a former police officer and a senior journalist, yet the inquiry into police relations with the press didn't seem interested. Ian Hurst, the former Army intelligence officer who had been hacked by associates of Rees at Marunchak's behest, was amused to hear about the disappearing intercept report. 'I did tell you this would happen,' he told me. 'They don't want it all to come out. They see it as too destabilising.' I asked him who 'they' were and he said 'the establishment'. I asked who that meant and Hurst laughed grimly, adding: 'Who the fuck knows?'[8]

To nobody's great surprise, Lord Justice Leveson ended up publicly clearing the Met of wrongdoing, somehow deciding that the force had conducted itself with 'integrity' at all times. He was able to reach this dismally inaccurate conclusion by declining to hear evidence from a number of witnesses who knew a great deal about alleged corruption inside Scotland Yard.

One of them was Derek Haslam, the former police officer who had gone undercover at Southern Investigations for nine years and had been stunned when Scotland Yard took no action on any of the intelligence he procured. In the wake of the phone hacking scandal, Haslam concluded this was down to improper ties between senior Met officers and Murdoch's media empire. When he approached the Leveson inquiry ready to discuss what he knew, he was given a polite but firm brush-off.[9]

Peter Tickner, the former head of internal audit at the Met and the Treasury, also submitted a witness statement to the Leveson inquiry detailing how senior police officers used the media to discredit rivals and promote their own careers. Days before he was due to give evidence Tickner was told by a member of the inquiry team not to bother. Leveson had blocked his testimony after objections by the Metropolitan Police. At the time, Tory MP Rob Wilson said it was a 'matter of great concern' and accused the Leveson inquiry of focusing on the press while 'going soft on wrongdoing by others'.[10]

Leveson's actions were at least nominally based on the terms upon which his inquiry had been established. Once the parallel criminal investigations and prosecutions had concluded, he was supposed to launch a second stage of the inquiry, intended to delve more deeply into the relationship between journalists and the police. However, given that evidence as compelling as the Scotland Yard intercept report had been shelved for phase one of the inquiry, it is impossible to conclude anything other than that Leveson did not want to look too closely, and that the second stage of his inquiry was certain never to take place.

It was clear to me that the inquiry knew of the existence of the intercept report. A very senior source inside the Met told me that officers had offered details of the alleged relationship between Rees, Marunchak and the former senior officer. 'They said they didn't want it,' whispered the source.[11] A formal statement in response to my request for an explanation about what had happened to the report not only confirmed this, but also raised serious questions about what Toker had told me. The Met said: 'We are extremely disappointed that matters brought to the attention of the Leveson Inquiry have been placed in the public domain against the instruction of Lord Justice Leveson. We will be raising this with the Inquiry and we will not be commenting on any such leaks.'

Why would an independent inquiry shy away from such an explosive topic, which was indisputably central to its terms of reference? The surveillance of Rees had touched on just about everything the

Leveson inquiry was supposed to be considering: alleged links to a former senior Met officer; suggestions of foul play in the investigation of one of London's most notorious unsolved murders; a corrupt *News of the World* hack; and a dirty tricks campaign against a Met commissioner. Ian Hurst pointed out that during the period when Leveson might have been able to examine the intercept report, the judge had instead decided to take 'evidence from regional police press officers rather than dealing with issues of real substance'.

But why shelve the intercept report? Over lunch with John Toker, who had since retired, I showed him the Met's statement and briefed him on what my source had told me. He blanched and glanced frantically around the room as he tried to come up with a plausible response.

Toker then variously claimed that the report definitely hadn't been passed to the inquiry (it had), there had been a horrible mistake (yes, but perhaps not in the way he meant) or maybe it had been missed – or concealed – by someone on the inquiry team. Finally, another thought occurred to him and he looked at me triumphantly: 'Maybe [Leveson] thought this was better dealt with in part two.' It was then that I knew it would never happen.

An approach to Robert Jay, the inquiry's QC, who had since been promoted to judge, confirmed my suspicions – and added a new layer of intrigue. Jay said that Scotland Yard did not provide him with a copy of the Rees intercept report until April 2012 – six weeks too late to have been discussed publicly with Ian Blair in the hearings. He acknowledged, however, that he had been 'informed of the existence of the document, its nature and the details of the intelligence' two months earlier, and weeks before Blair took the stand.[12]

The inquiry's counsel had known of the document's allegations in plenty of time to raise them with witnesses. So why didn't he mention them? Jay explained that the Met's lawyers had claimed 'public interest immunity' (PII) over the intercept report.[13] Many a defence lawyer might shudder at the mention of 'public interest immunity', a harmless-sounding legal principle that is ostensibly intended to prevent sensitive material from being referred to in open court. It often figures in cases involving the Official Secrets Act, where disclosure of certain evidence can be deemed harmful to the public interest. It can also be used to protect the identities of police informants.

Yet its critics often describe PII as a 'gagging order', used by the state to serve its own interests. They have long invited debate over how the 'public interest' should be defined, with repeated complaints that the restrictions have been abused to suppress embarrassing evidence.[14] It is scarcely surprising that the Met turned to PII to conceal allegations of corruption at the top of the force. But any PII application has to be approved by a judge. On what possible grounds did Leveson agree to exclude this particular document? The intercept report wasn't new – the conversations it referred to occurred in 2006, five years before Leveson's public hearings began. The court cases arising from the Abelard 2 investigation had all ended. The method by which the intelligence was obtained – the interception of the phone call – might have qualified as sensitive, but it was scarcely a secret to its target, Jonathan Rees, who had already boasted to me that he knew all about it. The sorry truth is that the Leveson inquiry had allowed itself to be gagged for no good reason by the police force it was supposed to be investigating.

* * *

At the top of Tower 42, a £300 million skyscraper at the heart of the City of London, two embattled British institutions were circling the wagons in a quest to keep the wolves at bay. In the middle of the Leveson inquiry, senior Met Police officers and lawyers from Scotland Yard and News International (NI), the UK division of the Murdoch media empire, assembled in a boardroom to plot a joint response to an unprecedented scandal. Outrageous behaviour by Rupert Murdoch's tabloid newspapers was being exposed on an almost weekly basis. For years, Scotland Yard had been aware of rampant media criminality, and done nothing about it. From the Prime Minister downwards, politicians from both major political parties had been so shocked by the public backlash to the phone hacking revelations that neither the police nor the hacks could expect any further favours.

Now the scandal had forced the Met to open a new investigation. There was a snag, of course. The UK's laws protect material gathered for the purposes of journalism. If the police want to seize servers or files from a newspaper group they must first convince a judge that the evidence is relevant to a criminal investigation. Then the rules of 'journalistic privilege' no longer apply.

Under normal circumstances, law enforcement and media organisations do not make cosy partners. But Murdoch's News Corp was now openly co-operating with Scotland Yard. On 25 March 2011, Scotland Yard and NI signed a legal agreement mandating the company to 'voluntarily co-operate in, produce, disclose and make available' all documents 'relevant' to the investigation. They included the computers and phone records of named journalists, including Rebekah Brooks and Andy Coulson, stretching back to 1997.[15] Under the agreement, the company also agreed to disclose 'all documents in respect of editorial policy in dealing with sources, source-related issues, e.g., handling, recruitment, payment, etc.'.

The agreement was signed by Deputy Assistant Commissioner Sue Akers on behalf of the Met. Akers told senior officers that the Met was constrained by privilege issues and had little choice but to negotiate with one of the main targets of its investigation. She described it as a 'friendship of convenience rather than a marriage made in heaven'.[16] The relationship would certainly prove convenient for Rupert Murdoch.

In July 2011, in the wake of the Milly Dowler scandal, NI closed the *News of the World*, then the biggest-selling newspaper in the UK. In what seemed like a frantic attempt to construct a new image of robust corporate governance, the company announced a new 'management and standards committee' (MSC) headed by Lord Grabiner QC and reporting directly to the US parent company's board of directors in New York.

By October, the Met had identified over 300 million office emails and more than 16,000 boxes of NI material relevant to their inquiries. On 6 October 2011, a meeting between senior Met officers and company executives discussed the ongoing investigation. Akers was present for the Met, while Will Lewis, the former editor of the *Daily Telegraph*, represented the MSC.

Minutes of the meeting noted that all parties decided the 'best option' for the Met was to continue being fed evidence by the company, although they accepted it created the 'perception of a close relationship between the MPS and NI'.[17]

In a legal opinion for the Met that month, Kennedy Talbot QC recognised that the force would be obtaining material that went way beyond anything they might have obtained using normal legal channels, including 'material provided in confidence from lawful sources'. It sounded as though NI was determined to come clean and even to overlook legal protections to which it might have been entitled. But could the disgraced company really be trusted?

In January 2010 – a few months after Rebekah Brooks had become CEO – Murdoch's UK news arm launched a new policy 'to eliminate in a consistent manner across NI (subject to compliance with legal and regulatory requirements as to retention) emails that could be unhelpful in the context of future litigation in which an NI company is a defendant'.[18] At first, it was proposed that all emails dating from before December 2007, the year Coulson left the *News of the World*, should be permanently deleted; but Brooks subsequently moved the cut-off point to 1 January 2010, allowing another two years' worth of emails to be deleted. 'How come we haven't done the email deletion policy discussed and approved six months ago?' she later demanded in an internal email. The change of deletion date was queried by a colleague who pointed out that 'the revised date is likely to be misconstrued if circulated externally'. Brooks replied: 'Yes to 2010. Clean sweep.'[19]

What did this mean in practical terms? In her own trial, Brooks would tell the jury that old emails stored on company servers had to be got rid of because they were slowing computers down or causing them to freeze. The company 'wanted to design a completely new system and come bang up to date'. Brooks insisted that the policy had been carried out 'in conjunction with lawyers and they were absolutely aware of what needed to be kept (for the police investigation)'. Whatever the reasoning behind the deletions, the effect was dramatic: more than 10 million emails were lost for ever, including all but a few thousand sent before 2008, when according to the prosecuting barrister, Andrew Edis, the *News of the World* was functioning as a 'thoroughly criminal enterprise'.[20]

Brooks's rearguard actions did little to slow the public pressure building on Murdoch and his company's senior executives. Brooks had her offices, home and car regularly swept for bugs. Meanwhile, senior Scotland Yard officers, company lawyers and officials from the CPS continued to trawl through the company's paperwork from the boardroom in Tower 42.

In November 2011, another meeting took place. Will Lewis asked the Met over and over again about 'corporate vulnerability' and the potential for 'corporate charges'. DCS Gordon Briggs told him that prosecutors were 'nervous about the MSC being asked to provide the evidence [as] you are employed by people who may become subject to charges'. Lewis replied that NI's new management standards committee had been 'structured' in a way to prevent any conflict and promised the company was not engaged in 'tactical disclosure'. According to the minutes, Lewis said the MSC reported to Joel Klein – a former White House lawyer who was now executive vice-president of News Corp in the US.

In April 2012, Sue Akers asked Lord Grabiner for minutes of NI board meetings to determine 'any potential indictment around corporate liability'. By this point, the phone hacking scandal was crashing through Murdoch's defences and threatening to drag him into the case in person. On 18 May Akers again wrote to Grabiner to confirm there was an 'active investigation into the corporate liability of News International in relation to phone hacking and illegal payments to public officials'.[21]

This development caused pandemonium in Murdoch's New York HQ. A News Corp analysis of the effects of a broad corporate charge warned that the consequences could 'kill the corporation and 46,000 jobs would be in jeopardy'.[22] Executives were worried about the conglomerate's ability to operate in the US if the serious corporate charges envisaged by Akers were brought against the company in London. NI's London lawyers pleaded with the Met and the CPS not to prosecute the company as it would not be in the 'public interest' to put thousands of jobs at risk. Gerson Zweifach, the American group general counsel of News Corp, flew to London to join emergency talks in Tower 42. He told the police: 'Crappy governance is not a crime. The downstream effects of a prosecution would be apocalyptic. The US authorities' reaction would put the whole business at risk, as licences would be at risk.'[23]

The UK's prosecutorial guidelines appear to contain no legal provision for dropping a corporate prosecution simply because a company under suspicion happens to be a major employer. There were precedents, however. As Prime Minister, Tony Blair had ordered the cessation of a three-year Serious Fraud Office investigation into the British defence giant BAE Systems in 2006 as it would affect 'thousands of British jobs'. Citing the 'public interest', Blair said the company should not be prosecuted for paying bribes worth hundreds of millions of pounds to the Saudi royal family in order to secure the multi-billion-pound al-Yamamah arms contract. When members of the Saudi government had found out that Britain's Serious Fraud Office was probing their personal Swiss bank accounts, they threatened to cut off intelligence and other co-operation with Britain.

Shortly after News Corp was warned it was under corporate investigation, US executives ordered the company to scale back its co-operation with the Met. A month later, Murdoch announced he was splitting the empire he'd spent six decades building into one of the most powerful companies in the world. The 82-year-old tycoon hived off his highly profitable television and film assets – among them 21st Century Fox and Fox News – into a separate entity, leaving his lesser media assets lumped together in what was widely perceived as an attempt to prevent his diseased British arm from infecting his American stock. Lawyers for News Corp continued to plead with Scotland Yard not to prosecute the company, citing a recent case involving Southwark Council in south London, which avoided corporate manslaughter charges by providing full co-operation with an investigation into a fire that ripped through a dilapidated tower block, killing six people.[24]

The diminishing co-operation with NI appeared to be unnerving the Met. Previously unpublished minutes of meetings in Tower 42 between senior police officers and the company's lawyers show that Scotland Yard then came up with a remarkably benevolent assurance.

At a meeting on 1 June 2012, Grabiner said he was 'mystified' by the way the investigation was heading as he thought there had been a 'presumption' there would be no corporate charges if the company co-operated. Akers replied that she had 'never said that police would not look at corporate liability, and would always go where the evidence took us'. The Met's deputy assistant commissioner then suggested the opposite. Akers said that the MSC should continue to provide 'voluntary co-operation' but assured its lawyers that Scotland Yard was 'not looking … to try and get information re Rupert Murdoch'.[25] Very nice of them, all things considered.

It is also clear from the minutes that the CPS could have charged News Corp with corporate offences – but chose not to do so. They reveal that the legal advice from UK prosecutors was that corporate liability 'does lie at editor level' and that both Rebekah Brooks and Andy Coulson had recently been cautioned for additional corporate offences.[26] In one meeting, Akers told News Corp lawyers that the 'editors' were the 'controlling mind' and 'we think corporate liability offences are made out'. But the corporate charges never materialised, even when Coulson, the former *News of the World* editor, was convicted of phone hacking. During his trial, he was forced to admit that he had listened to recordings of hacked voice-mails – the messages left by former Home Secretary David Blunkett for his girlfriend, Kimberly Quinn.

If an editor's criminality amounted to corporate liability, as the Met was hinting, then NI was dead in the water. With Coulson behind bars, it almost didn't matter that a jury later found Brooks not guilty of all the charges she faced. The jury decided that she had no knowledge of her staff hacking phones or paying public officials. It further cleared her of conspiracy to pervert the course of justice.[27]

A former senior Met officer reviewed the minutes of the Tower 42 meetings. His view on the lack of police interest in Rupert Murdoch, and the failure to press corporate charges against News Corp, is stark: 'That is unhelpful for the Met. It looks like they are colluding to keep the corporate entity out of the charges. It doesn't read well.'

Scotland Yard's assurances about Murdoch take on further significance when you consider what happened a year later. Mutinous staff on *The Sun* subjected their ultimate boss to a classic tabloid 'gotcha' tactic – by secretly recording him without his knowledge. Murdoch had flown into London to try and quell a rebellion from previously loyal journalists on his favourite tabloid. The hacks were furious that the company had begun sharing with Scotland Yard the confidential emails and details of payments they had made to their sources. This was all part of the deal News Corp initially struck with the Met to avoid the dreaded corporate charge and protect Murdoch's legacy.

Around twenty reporters and executives on *The Sun* were prosecuted for payments to public officials, using an obscure offence that the Met and the CPS had press-ganged into use for the purpose: conspiracy to commit misconduct in public office. The investigation into phone hacking had spawned Operation Elveden, a separate inquiry into inappropriate media payments to police officers in return for inside information. Despite blowing £15 million of public money on one of the largest criminal investigations in British history,[28] police failed to convict a single journalist (although dozens of their confidential sources were convicted, much to the disgust of the rest of Fleet Street, which concluded that News Corp had breached a sacred tenet of journalistic endeavour: never betray your sources). Many considered the charges in Operation Elveden to be unfair as the journalists had operated within an industry culture that had existed for decades.

The witch-hunt collapsed after the Court of Appeal ruled that for journalists to be convicted for paying public officials it had to be proved that the stories they subsequently published had somehow harmed the public interest. The opposite was generally the case. Many of the payments to sources had helped expose failings in state agencies, to the public's benefit. The police could find no example of the public interest being harmed. The *Press Gazette*, Fleet Street's trade paper, called it 'a shameful episode in the history of this country's criminal justice system'.[29] A senior *Sun* executive who was charged before later being cleared suffered from mental ill-health and his marriage almost collapsed. 'We all felt like we had entered a parallel universe,' he told me.

What we were doing had been company policy since we joined News International. We were taught how to do it by people who already worked there. And everyone knew about it. Scotland Yard seemed to know about it for years and didn't think it was a problem. Everything we exposed was in the public interest. And then suddenly everyone pretends this was actually really bad and your life gets turned upside down.[30]

John Kay, the veteran chief reporter of *The Sun*, was broken by NI's decision to hand the Met evidence of payments to one of his sources, Bettina Jordan-Barber, a Ministry of Defence official. A gregarious and generous man, Kay became a virtual recluse and died in a care home aged seventy-seven.[*] When his death was announced in May 2021, Kelvin MacKenzie, Kay's former editor at *The Sun* and long-time confidant of Rupert Murdoch, spoke out about the horrors of Operation Elveden. 'John was among twenty-two staff that Murdoch threw under the bus to save his own skin when threatened with a corporate charge which would have forced him out of his own company', MacKenzie told the *Press Gazette*.

In my years of running *The Sun* Murdoch never asked where John's fantastic tales came from; he was only interested that we had them so we could sell more papers, make more money and stuff the opposition. All 22 were cleared, but what broke John was one of his best contacts over the years ended up being jailed. The trial took its toll on John. He spent his last years in a nursing home in Hertford. As guilt money Murdoch paid £25,000 towards the care costs.[31]

Lucy Panton, the former crime editor of the *News of the World*, was put through two trials and nineteen months on police bail. She said

---

[*] One aspect of Kay's life cannot be excluded. In 1977 he had a mental breakdown and killed his wife Harue, before trying to take his own life. He pleaded guilty to manslaughter on grounds of diminished responsibility and was sent by a judge for treatment at a psychiatric hospital before being taken back by *The Sun*.

she had been 'completely hung out to dry' by a company which she had loyally served for a decade. 'When my daughter Lily was born she was very ill and on a life support machine. I was made to work by her bedside after her second and third operations. The loyalty I had shown to the company meant nothing.'[32] But Panton, who is married to a police officer, was even more furious at the betrayal of her sources:

> Six police officers got questioned and arrested for giving me what investigators alleged was unauthorised information. These were matters of public interest and in some cases given out at briefings. They were never paid for stories and none of them were charged.
>
> It's been horrible knowing that people who were just doing their jobs, as I thought I was doing my job, have suffered as a result of News International handing my sources over. Your sources are the one thing you are supposed to protect as a journalist and I was unable to do that.

She said she regards the public officials she spoke to who were prosecuted as 'whistleblowers who were turned over by News International'.[33]

At the height of Operation Elveden, when Murdoch agreed to meet his disgruntled journalists in person and was secretly recorded, he acknowledged that the culture of paying police officers for stories 'existed at every newspaper in Fleet Street'. In one clip later broadcast by *Channel 4 News*, Murdoch was asked by a journalist: 'I'm pretty confident that the working practices that I've seen here are ones that I've inherited, rather than instigated. Would you recognise that all this predates many of our involvement here?'

Murdoch replied: 'We're talking about payments for news tips from cops. That's been going on a hundred years, absolutely. You didn't instigate it.' At another point on the tape, *The Sun*'s agony aunt, Deidre Sanders, read extracts of a letter on behalf of a relative of a *Sun* journalist. The emotional letter describes how journalists and their families felt 'betrayed', 'abandoned' and 'isolated'.

Murdoch's management team had played a crucial role in getting their own staff locked up, but he tried to undo some of the damage. 'I will do everything in my power to give you total support, even if you're convicted and get six months or whatever,' he said.

> You're all innocent until proven guilty. What you're asking is: what happens if some of you are proven guilty? What afterwards? I'm not allowed to promise you – I will promise you continued health support – but your jobs. I've got to be careful what comes out – but frankly, I won't say it, but just trust me.

During the meeting, Murdoch also appeared to regret the extent of his company's co-operation with the police. One of the journalists questioned the volume of documents handed over. 'Because – it was a mistake, I think,' he said. 'But, in that atmosphere, at that time, we said: "Look, we are an open book, we will show you everything." And the lawyers just got rich going through millions of emails.'[34]

Over at Tower 42, the police officers surveying those documents were feeling the effects of Murdoch's regret. As the flow of material to Scotland Yard dried up, DCS Gordon Briggs complained to News Corp: 'The role of the police is simply to search for the truth and the higher up the organisation our investigation goes, the more you appear to withdraw co-operation.'[35]

* * *

By the time the phone hacking trials concluded in December 2015, they had laid waste to the public image of both Rupert Murdoch and Scotland Yard. But it could have been a lot worse. In total, nine people were eventually convicted of phone hacking. The most notable scalp was Andy Coulson. Various other news desk executives and reporters from the now-defunct Sunday tabloid were also convicted, along with Glenn Mulcaire, the prolific hacker.[36] But Rebekah Brooks had been cleared, and Murdoch was able to swiftly reappoint her as chief executive of his UK news division, now rebranded as News UK. The empire had also escaped corporate charges, despite mounds of evidence the CPS might have chosen to use.[37] Best of all, the Leveson inquiry had shied away from probing the darkest aspects of the scandal, involving the company's links to corrupt police officers and its relationship with Jonathan Rees, the prime suspect for one of Britain's most notorious unsolved murders.

After *Panorama* broadcast the details of Rees's involvement in computer hacking to millions of viewers in March 2011, the Met was obliged to at least go through the motions of pretending it cared. Operation Kalmyk, which examined the hacking of Ian Hurst, the former Army intelligence officer, was launched soon after the programme aired. Hurst, it will be remembered, had worked in Northern Ireland recruiting double agents inside Republican groups. Alex Marunchak at the *News of the World* had hired Rees to try and find one of the British Army's most valuable Irish agents. As ever with cases involving Rees, Operation Kalmyk posed more questions than it ever managed to answer.

The inquiry was evidently intended to take the heat out of the situation. Things were getting uncomfortable at the Met, what with the phone hacking scandal, trouble in the commissioner's office, politicians becoming increasingly hostile, the establishment of the

Leveson inquiry, and all manner of complaints about journalists paying off police officers. The last thing Scotland Yard needed was for the Daniel Morgan murder to be thrown into the mix.

Luckily the Met had plenty of ways of spinning out the investigation long enough for the crisis to pass. It would take another eighteen months to arrest the suspects identified by *Panorama* – Rees, Marunchak and Philip Campbell Smith. They were finally picked up in October 2012.

It hadn't helped that the Met began by investigating its suspects for the wrong crime. All three were questioned for offences under the Computer Misuse Act, which any police officer with two brain cells to rub together should have known was a daft idea. At the time, the relevant legislation was drafted in such a way that any prosecution had to be brought within six months of the original offence. Hurst's computer was hacked in 2006 – six years earlier, so the Computer Misuse Act could scarcely apply. Hurst pointed this out to officers on Operation Kalmyk at the start. 'Right at the outset I had worked out that the Computer Misuse Act was not going to fly as it was time-barred,' he told me. 'The Met kept telling me "Don't worry about it, you are wrong". Platitudes were flowing freely.'[38]

As the victim, Hurst had done his own research and argued to the police that they should consider offences under data protection legislation. Why did he think that the Met was spending hundreds of thousands of pounds investigating a case it appeared to be simultaneously trying to hobble? 'Everything got delayed while the police investigated. Contempt of court laws mean the media can't expose what's going on until the suspects are convicted or cleared. Without Kalmyk, the scandal would have been brought to the attention of the public on a much quicker timescale.'

In short, Hurst's opinion was that

Kalmyk's intention was to degrade the scandal. It is what the civil service and the police always do when things are getting a bit frisky. Announce a review or an investigation. Claim nothing more can be said on the matter until it has concluded. When the bland findings are finally published, everyone has forgotten what the trouble was all about.[39]

Sure enough, several years went by before the Met finally announced in September 2015 that no further action could be taken against any of the suspects. Those contempt of court laws had served their purpose – the case had been quietly strung out without further media intervention. When the Met's decision was announced, Marunchak said he was 'relieved for my family who have been through an awful lot while this witch-hunt has been going on'. He added: 'It's a monumental waste of money. I imagine Scotland Yard has got better things to spend money on than that.'

Unfortunately for Murdoch and Scotland Yard, Hurst had weapons of his own. The retired intelligence officer had quickly realised he would get no satisfaction waiting for Operation Kalmyk. So he decided to mount his own investigation. His operational HQ was his modest semi-detached home in Bolton, Greater Manchester. In his intel heyday he had recruited agents inside the IRA, pressuring, threatening and cajoling Republican sympathisers who had suffered centuries of discrimination to switch allegiances and work on behalf of a British state they despised. After that, taking on Murdoch's men (and woman) would prove to be remarkably straightforward.

By the time Scotland Yard announced that no one would face

charges as a result of Operation Kalmyk, Hurst was long beyond caring. The former spook had amassed so much evidence of his own that he was preparing to sue all of those involved for substantial damages. 'There was no great desire for a prosecution on my part,' Hurst told me. 'I knew Kalmyk was a political exercise and it was blindingly obvious that it wasn't going to work. The authorities left a vacuum that I was only too happy to fill.'[40]

Hurst joined hundreds of hacking victims in suing the Murdoch empire. Thus far, the global media group has quietly paid out more than half a billion pounds to settle hacking cases, thereby preventing public airings of potentially damning evidence. Nathan Sparks, who is a member of the campaign group Hacked Off and represents many victims, said the 'apparent willingness' of News UK to settle cases 'at seemingly any price indicates a desperation to avoid having these claims heard in open court – which would expose multiple allegations of corporate wrongdoing and criminality to the public gaze'.[41]

This is the first time that the inside story of Hurst's battle against Murdoch has been told. It features a surprise witness: one of the people Hurst recruited to assist him in his 'David and Goliaths' battle against the Met and Murdoch was none other than Jonathan Rees. Why on earth would the man who arranged for the hacking of Hurst's computer decide to help the victim of that hacking? Not only might Rees have to admit his own role in the crime, he would risk taking a giant bite of the NI hand that had fed him for more than twenty-five years.

Hurst gently reeled Rees in over a period of twelve months. 'I played on the fact that he was fucked,' Hurst told me. 'I cold-called him one day and made clear I had incontrovertible evidence of what he had done to me.' The former spook then set out to convince Rees that, like Hurst, he was also a victim of NI, and was being hung out to dry. 'I told him I thought he was a proxy,' said Hurst. 'I said I felt Marunchak was the directing mind of the operation. I told Rees it would better if he worked with me, rather than against me.'

He eventually persuaded Rees to make a statement supporting his claim against News UK. In return, Hurst promised the private eye he would persuade the Murdoch empire to accept 'vicarious liability' for the computer hacking. In practice that meant the company would be formally obliged to accept responsibility for the 'rogue' behaviour of its employee, Marunchak, and its agents, Rees and Smith.

It helped Hurst's cause that Rees was angry that Murdoch's people were no longer defending him or paying his legal bills. Finally he agreed to co-operate. Over a series of three meetings at Hurst's solicitor's office in London, Rees agreed to sign a witness statement detailing twenty-five years of activities on behalf of the *News of the World*. Hurst refused to tell me what the statement said, as it formed part of his confidential legal proceedings against NI. It was only recently that another source agreed to brief me on what Rees said. It was immediately clear that the document would trigger fear and panic at the highest levels of the Murdoch group – and the Met.

Rees said that he started working for Marunchak and the *News of the World* in 1989, two years after he became prime suspect for the murder of Daniel Morgan. 'It was a great opportunity for a small private investigators' firm such as ours as it gave us the opportunity to be a firm with a relatively unlimited budget,' he said. Rees also claimed that in his efforts to get exclusive stories, Marunchak 'linked' him up with 'policemen, some of whom have been convicted of corruption'. He further alleged that Marunchak and his billionaire proprietor had a close personal relationship:

> Alex Marunchak was a heavyweight journalist at the *News of the World*. It was my impression, from what I saw and heard during my work for the newspaper, and from what Alex told me, that he was a favourite of Rupert Murdoch. My impression was that Mr Murdoch loved Alex and protected him.
>
> Alex was promoted to being the editor of the Irish edition of the *News of the World* in, I believe, 2002. He did a brilliant job and managed to triple the circulation. Mr Murdoch was delighted. He conducted a 'state' flying visit to Ireland and personally congratulated Alex, calling him 'the greatest man'. I remember it clearly since Alex was gloating afterwards that they both kept the then Taoiseach of Ireland waiting while they had a celebratory drink together.
>
> Mr Murdoch, I understand from my work for the *News of the World* and my conversations with Alex, was very involved in the day-to-day running of the newspapers. I believe he kept on top of what they were publishing. Piers Morgan and the other editors at the time knew that Murdoch would go to Alex to get his opinion on those stories, which was extremely unusual. My impression was that Mr Murdoch adored Alex and his contacts. Alex got him in contact with all these politicians and the police, which was something I believe he valued and enjoyed. Alex, in return, had a direct line to Mr Murdoch and was one of the only journalists that could call him directly.[42]

According to Rees, Marunchak was enmeshed in a bitter internal rivalry with Rebekah Brooks, who was also a Murdoch favourite. She would later far outstrip Marunchak by becoming the editor of the *News of the World*'s much more important UK edition, moving after that to *The Sun*, and then becoming the CEO of News International. Marunchak was apparently left fuming, and according to Rees, retaliated by hiring the private eye to place his rival under surveillance. 'I was told by Alex … that it was because the *News of the World* were worried that she was leaking information to someone at another paper.'[43]

The idea that a senior Murdoch editor hired a private eye to spy on the activities of his own boss is frankly bizarre.

Rees went on to make a number of serious allegations of corruption and potentially improper behaviour involving NI executives and very senior Metropolitan Police officers, which have never been placed into the public domain. He also confirmed for the record that he had been part of the *News of the World* operation to illegally access Hurst's computer. He said the hacking was commissioned by Marunchak and executed by Smith, a computer expert.[44]

The signed witness statement represented yet another existential threat to both Scotland Yard and the Murdoch media empire. News UK must wish it had never clapped eyes on Jonathan Rees. That said, Rees is, of course, a convicted criminal, and suspected of murder. Why should anyone believe a word he says?

Nonetheless, his statement was political and reputational nitro-glycerine. News UK needed to settle with Hurst before any of Rees's allegations emerged in open court. It also needed to be sure that no loose ends remained. In October 2017, the company agreed to apologise to Hurst and is understood to have paid around £80,000 in damages to the former Army intelligence officer. The company accepted that Smith had hacked Hurst on behalf of Rees, and that his private emails had been sent to Marunchak in Ireland.

News UK further agreed that Rees had commissioned Smith to infiltrate Hurst's computer and monitor information and correspondence. Lawyers for News Group said the company offered its 'sincerest and unreserved apologies' to Hurst and his family. Crucially, the company also accepted 'vicarious liability' on behalf of all of those involved – this is understood to be the only time the Murdoch empire has ever agreed to do so in relation to any of the hundreds of hacking cases that have come before the courts. The reason they did so is that Hurst is understood to have privately offered the company a solution to a problem they did not know how to solve: how to keep Rees from saying anything else. By now, the relationship between the private investigator and his most valuable client had completely broken down. Rees had become toxic and the company was fearful of triggering yet more corporate governance questions by providing him with any kind of financial support.

Hurst is understood to have offered News UK a deal. During the private communications over his settlement, the former spy offered to act as a conduit between the company and Rees. 'Hurst offered to facilitate a payment to Rees, as long as the company accepted vicarious liability,' said a source familiar with the negotiations.[45] The company agreed and is understood to have increased Hurst's settlement figure so that he could secretly pass on thousands of pounds to Rees, in return for his future silence. The man still suspected by many of a role in the murder of Daniel Morgan had received a final pay-off – courtesy of Rupert Murdoch.

Chapter 15

The Fantasist

On 14 November 2014, Scotland Yard electrified the nation when it announced that it was investigating a series of murders during child sex abuse parties involving ministers, spy chiefs and prominent military figures. A former public sector worker who police gave the pseudonym 'Nick' had come forward to allege that he was sexually abused as a child by a 'VIP paedophile ring'. His attackers had included the late Prime Minister Sir Ted Heath, former Home Secretary Lord Brittan, D-Day hero Lord Bramall and Tory MP Harvey Proctor.

Nick was interviewed by the BBC on the same day and his claims led the news bulletins, watched by millions. Although he did not publicly name his alleged attackers on television, Nick said they were 'very powerful people' who 'controlled my life for the next nine years'. 'You didn't question what they wanted, you did as they asked without question, and the punishments were very severe.'[1]

Nick claimed that between the ages of seven and sixteen he had been collected on numerous occasions from his schools in Wiltshire, Oxfordshire and Surrey and driven to London. There he and other boys had been tortured by a circle of abusers also including the ex-head of MI6 Maurice Oldfield, the former director general of MI5 Sir Michael Hanley, Labour peer Lord Janner, BBC television entertainer Jimmy Savile and his own stepfather. Nick also claimed that he witnessed three child murders, including one boy who was strangled and stabbed to death by Proctor right in front of him. The Tory MP had allegedly hacked the boy with a penknife for forty minutes before handing the weapon to Nick. Most of the offences were committed in the Carlton Club, or Dolphin Square near Westminster. Once the abuse was over, Nick said that he would be returned home by car to his mother.[2]

Before any Metropolitan Police officer had tested Nick's account or gathered any corroborating evidence, Detective Superintendent Kenny McDonald held a press conference to announce that his officers believed the wild allegations to be 'credible and true'. So began Operation Midland, one of the most ill-fated inquiries in the Met's long history. Once again, Scotland Yard would be left embarrassed and exposed. Once again, the ensuing scandal would hasten the departure of a Metropolitan Police commissioner and severely damage the force's relationship with politicians and the public.

Nick was interviewed by Scotland Yard detectives on three separate occasions. The allegations were some of the most fantastical ever to reach the ears of a British police officer. The former nurse who rose to become a manager in the NHS claimed that he was flown as a child to Paris in a private plane and sexually abused in France by members of the Saudi royal family. Nick also claimed that he was abused at the village of Imber – a derelict settlement on Salisbury Plain used by the Army for training. Nick alleged that he was manhandled there by Hanley and Oldfield, who 'tipped' spiders over him, subjected him to electric shocks and used him as a human dart board.[3]

Scotland Yard had proved a lot more gullible than Wiltshire Police. Officers at one of Britain's most rural police forces had dismissed Nick's outlandish claims when he approached them two years before. They were able to do so because, unlike their counterparts at the Met, Wiltshire had tested the strength of the allegations by actually doing some police work. Officers had interviewed Nick's mother. She had said that her son had never presented with any sign of sexual abuse and, together with a lack of any other corroborating evidence, the inquiry was shelved in May 2013. One Wiltshire policeman had noted it was 'all a bit odd'.[4]

By contrast, when Nick approached Scotland Yard his treatment bordered on reverence. Operation Midland was swiftly set up and the Met seemed happy to ignore the many inconsistencies between Nick's account to the Wiltshire force and his later statements to Scotland Yard. They also delayed interviewing Nick's mother for six months, declined to ask him for his computers and mobile phone, ignored medical records that showed no injuries consistent with his allegations, and failed for eighteen months to ask Nick to undergo a full medical examination – despite his claims of severe physical abuse.[5]

Despite gaping holes in the investigation, Kenny McDonald called his press conference and told the national media: 'Nick has been spoken to by officers from the murder command. They and I believe what Nick is saying to be credible and true and as such with those allegations we will investigate them.' The basic detective's ABC rule of 'Assume nothing, Believe no one, Check everything' had been thrown out of the window. After the briefing McDonald was confronted by DCI Clive Driscoll, who was about to retire. He was so concerned at what he had just heard that he struggled to sugar-coat his words to the senior police chief. 'What were you thinking?' said an aghast Driscoll. 'You've just driven a coach and horses through the Magna Carta and the rule of law!'[6]

McDonald's decision was all the more ridiculous as his boss, Deputy Assistant Commissioner Steve Rodhouse – who sanctioned the statement – had already written a note saying: 'A full investigation was required to establish the credibility of Nick as a witness.'[7] So why was he now being described as 'credible and true'? Assistant Commissioner Cressida Dick, who was in overall charge of the operation in 2014, heard the press conference on the radio. She would later claim to have realised instantly that the words should not have been spoken. Scotland Yard failed to correct the error for over a year. Investigative journalists began picking holes in Nick's story – yet still the Met ploughed on.

Could the credulity sweeping through the Met have anything to do with the case of Jimmy Savile? The TV star had recently been exposed as a serial sex offender and paedophile. Soon after his death in 2012, it emerged that police up and down the country had fielded hundreds of complaints against Savile, but no action had been taken. A subsequent inquiry concluded that his decades of abuse could have been stopped fifty years earlier. Information on high-profile suspects such as Savile was marked 'restricted' or 'secret' and effectively hidden in police databases to which only a handful of officers had access. Failure to join the dots meant that the opportunity to prosecute Savile was missed, according to a report by HM Inspectorate of Constabulary.[8]

Rodhouse had also led a bungled investigation into Savile when he was at Surrey Police. The force had been accused of failing to examine the allegations properly and being 'too soft' with the television star. When Nick presented himself to Scotland Yard, the force seemed terrified of being blamed yet again for 'covering up' VIP child abuse, and basic policing rules were ignored.

Two months after Nick's claims were made public, one of his alleged abusers died. Lord Brittan had been Home Secretary under Margaret Thatcher. but had passed away with a cloud hanging over his head. This, too, was down to rank incompetence at the Yard. Brittan had been questioned by the Met the previous summer regarding a separate rape allegation made by a Labour activist with severe mental health problems. By the time of his death the force had privately concluded that the former Home Secretary should be exonerated. For reasons known only to the Yard, this did not happen, in direct contravention to the advice given by the senior investigating officer, DCI Paul Settle. He would later be drummed out of the force for arguing that the investigation should follow the evidence. After he had retired Settle said that 'facts had been ignored' and branded the Met 'institutionally incompetent'.[9]

Operation Midland then decided to search the homes of the other men accused by Nick. This would prove to be one of the most controversial aspects of the whole affair. In order to obtain search warrants, Scotland Yard had to satisfy district judge Howard Riddle that were 'reasonable grounds' for believing that an offence had been committed. The application authorised by Rodhouse and submitted by Operation Midland said: 'The victim in this matter has been interviewed at length by experienced officers from the child abuse investigation team. His account has remained consistent and he is felt to be a witness who is telling the truth.'[10]

This was despite the fact that Nick's account to Scotland Yard was demonstrably inconsistent with what he had told Wiltshire Police. The names of his abusers, the locations of the abuse and his injuries were all different. The statement that Nick's mother made to the Wiltshire force did not support her son's allegations.

No witnesses had emerged despite extensive media coverage. Nor was there any evidence to support Nick's wild claims of ritualistic killings at the top of Britain's security establishment.[11]

Judge Riddle was severely misled. But Operation Midland had their warrants. Officers searched five properties: Lord Bramall's home in Surrey, Lady Brittan's flat in Westminster and her country home in north Yorkshire, and Harvey Proctor's home in Grantham, Lincolnshire, and his office on the nearby Belvoir Estate. Bramall, who had had a long and distinguished military career, was ninety-one and his wife Avril was terminally ill when twenty-two police officers spent ten hours trampling around their home. They found nothing. Four months later, the distressed Lady Bramall died aged ninety-three.

Nothing of note was found in the homes of Lord Brittan and Harvey Proctor either. On one level, it almost didn't seem to matter to the suspects as their reputations had already been destroyed. Days before the raids, Operation Midland had briefed Nick. He immediately leaked the suspects' identities and details of the searches to the media. The ensuing coverage was devastating. Proctor lost both his grace-and favour home and his job.

Operation Midland limped on. Police interviewed Lord Bramall at Aldershot police station in Hampshire. For a man in his ninety-second year who had given so much for his country, it was a degrading ordeal. When confronted with the allegations, Bramall told Midland that he was 'absolutely astonished, amazed and bemused'. 'I deny absolutely any of these things ... but I find it quite incredible that someone of my career, standing and integrity should have been capable of any of these things, including things like torture, which are unbelievable.'[12]

Operation Midland could have avoided traumatising elderly war heroes and esteemed former ministers of state by simply speaking to Nick's mother. Unfortunately, the police didn't get round to conducting an interview with her until a month after Bramall was interviewed, and long after the very public raids had taken place. Of course, she immediately contradicted much that her son had said. But by this stage it was far too late to save anyone's reputation.

Proctor was interviewed in August 2015 when police asked him whether he had ever threatened to castrate Nick with a penknife before being stopped by Sir Edward Heath. It proved to be the final straw. The very next day Proctor marched into St Ermin's Hotel in Westminster and held a press conference that exposed the absurdity of his predicament. 'My situation has transformed from Kafkaesque bewilderment to black farce incredulity,' he said. 'I'm completely innocent of all these allegations. I'm a homosexual. I'm not a murderer or a paedophile. Nick should be stripped of his anonymity and prosecuted for wasting police time and money.'[13]

Conservative MPs, already fuming over the arrest of Damian Green and the 'Plebgate' affair, started to realise that Operation Midland was a slow-motion car crash. In total, twenty-seven police officers spent fourteen months chasing Nick's allegations – at a cost of more than £2 million to the taxpayer. The Met finally exhausted all its leads. The force bowed to public pressure and called a halt to the inquiry in March 2016. Its press office issued a 1,200-word statement admitting that the force had been wrong to describe the unsupported claims as 'credible and true'. But the Yard also claimed there was no evidence Nick's stepfather had 'knowingly misled' officers – a statement it would come to regret.

The hapless Rodhouse added insult to injury by briefing the media that the inquiry had been triggered by three complainants – not just Nick on his own. The senior officer failed to mention, however, that the other two alleged victims had been immediately dismissed as

'prolific liars' by the Met. The misleading briefing wrongly suggested that Nick's claims had been supported by others.[14]

By now the establishment had completely lost patience with
the Yard. Veteran Conservative MP Nicholas Soames, grandson
of Winston Churchill, said that 'no slimy PR spin from the Met
will ever disguise its repulsively dishonourable treatment of Lords
Bramall and Brittan and Harvey Proctor'.[15] General Sir Mike
Jackson, another former head of the British Army, described Sir
Bernard Hogan-Howe, the Met commissioner, who had mounted
a very public defence of the investigation, as that 'wretched man'.[16]

The level of vitriol directed at the Met forced Hogan-Howe into
action. He decided to order an independent review of the case led
by a retired judge. Sir Richard Henry Quixano Henriques was
painting benches in his garden on the Fylde coast in Lancashire
when he took a call from Lord Thomas, the Lord Chief Justice.
Henriques, who had witnessed some of the most unsettling trials
of recent years, was a perfect choice to lead the review. He realised
within hours of receiving the Operation Midland documents that
a terrible mistake had been made. 'I had a mountain of papers –
thousands and thousands of papers – but you learn over the years
where to locate the relevant page of a brief,' he told me.

It seemed to me as certain as night follows day that if Nick was being
treated as he alleged then it was impossible for him to be picked up
from homes in Oxfordshire and Surrey and Wiltshire, driven to central London, seriously abused and then driven home to his mother.
So the first thing I looked for was the interview of Nick's mother.

Fortunately she was a woman of high standing. When I read her
statement that said she never saw any soiled clothing, he'd never

been absent, he'd never been missing. It all led on from there. It was solved within a few hours of me receiving the papers.[17]

In November 2016, the judge's findings were published. They savaged the Metropolitan Police for giving credence to Nick's bizarre allegations. The judge identified an astonishing forty-three separate blunders by police officers and said the reputation of the suspects had been 'shattered by the word of a single, uncorroborated complainant'. 'The principal cause of the many failures in this investigation was poor judgement and a failure to accurately evaluate known facts and to react to them.' Most damagingly of all, Henriques concluded that officers had used false evidence to obtain search warrants to raid the homes of Bramall, Proctor and Brittan. He said that several officers may have perverted the course of justice.[18]

The backlash was considerable – not least from some of the Met's officers who had tried to warn management they were barking up the wrong tree. DCI Paul Settle, whose career had been destroyed when he tried to question the thin case against Lord Brittan, said: 'We have seen the level of incompetence which permeated right to the very top, and we have to ask: are these people fit to lead what was the greatest force in the world?'[19] For Henriques, the most glaring unanswered question was a simple one: 'It just beggared belief that so many police officers had got the thing so wrong – how is it possible that the investigators came to believe Nick?'[20]

The deficiencies of Operation Midland expose a noxious culture inside Scotland Yard that we have seen elsewhere in these pages: a system that penalises success and celebrates failure. Fewer and fewer police officers knew how to solve crimes. Institutionalised incompetence had been added to institutional racism and widespread corruption. But how and why had the Met sabotaged its best officers, leading to disastrous outcomes over and over again?

* * *

DCS Tony Nash looked despairingly at the junior officers standing in front of the then borough commander of Newham. They were trying to close a case without making an arrest. Nash, a veteran of the Met's once-prized detective branch, suspected a series of burglaries committed in the area were the work of James Williams, a criminal who was well-known to the police.

Across the borough, Jewish residents were being targeted on Friday nights, the Sabbath day of rest. Met officers who attended one scene had discovered a cigarette lighter in the front garden and traced the DNA back to Williams. But he denied involvement, saying that his lighter must have been stolen. The investigating officers had lost heart. The case was too difficult to solve and they wanted to persuade Nash that they should be allowed to close it.

Nash, who had solved dozens of murders during his time as a detective, was beginning to lose patience. The officers repeated the same ridiculous story about the lighter. 'That's not an investigation,' snapped Nash. 'What about ANPR [automatic number plate recognition technology], what about Section 18 searches [of a suspect's property]? How do you think Williams is getting rid of the goods? He lives in Bournemouth. It's full of antique shops. You need to get down there and check out the pawn shops. Take a half-mile radius from his house and start from there.'[21]

Nash's team grudgingly set off for Bournemouth. They traced Williams's car driving up to Stoke Newington on the night of the burglary, recovered the stolen goods from a pawnbroker near his home, and even secured CCTV footage which showed him handing over the silver. In April 2013, Williams was jailed for six years. But it was a case that nearly got away. 'At every stage, the [officers] couldn't get over the fact that he had given them an excuse for why the lighter was at the window,' said a source familiar with the case. 'They thought that was the investigation, asking him a few questions.'

Before he became a borough commander, Nash had fought hard to become a plain-clothes CID detective, an elite band of investigators who once solved the most complex and serious crimes. Today, they are a dying breed. Like many former detectives, Nash laments this. 'I look back to when I joined,' he told me.

> I had eight really experienced detectives who mentored me. So you were getting really good on-the-job training. Now, it's armchair detectives. A lot of people coming through the process are not getting that exposure to proactive work, and they shy away from it. We have programmed some very good people to become investigators but they have become almost sedentary. They are very fond of picking up the phone and it's all become very reactive.[22]

It is widely believed that Sir Paul Condon's 1996 decision to reappraise the Met's world-famous training school at Hendon, north London, is central to the decline in standards. Condon pushed through measures which allowed officers who in some cases had never investigated a single crime to become detective inspectors, who would then be put in charge of murder and rape investigations.

Roy Ramm joined the Met in 1970 and rose to become commander of specialist operations, leading the Flying Squad and

other units responsible for tackling serious and organised crime. He
told me:

> The demise of the detective training schools was a tragedy. It was
> appalling, just appalling. Detectives learnt their skills from some of
> the most successful specialists in the police service. They heard from
> judges, scientists and pathologists. They were centres of excellence. I
> can remember what I was taught about crime, about the definitions
> of offences, to such a degree that I can remember them now. I met
> plenty of young barristers who knew less about the offences I was
> prosecuting than I did.[23]

David McKelvey, recalling his eight-year battle to become a detective, says very few achieved it and he had to work hard to stick out.
'There wasn't a day went by when I didn't nick someone,' he told me.

> At 6 a.m. you would come on duty and be thrown out on the street
> and by breakfast at 9 a.m. you were expected to have done bus lanes,
> parking offences and red lights. You had to sit there over your break-
> fast and write up your evidence. It was done properly and methodi-
> cally, and checked by sergeants. You weren't sitting there typing away
> at crime sheets all day. After breakfast, you were expected to go and
> arrest criminals. Your focus was on actually catching them in the act,
> or with the [stolen] property. You learned how to give evidence. When
> you had crown court cases and you were facing barristers who had
> trained for years in how to pull you to pieces, you were able to give that
> evidence with confidence in front of a jury. And people got convicted.

One of the key skills detectives have to develop is the simple art of communication. Clive Driscoll, who solved the Stephen Lawrence murder, said:

> Give me a suspect or a witness and I could normally make them talk. There was no trick to it. I just like to chat to people, see what they know; I don't try and be clever or threatening. I might buy them a cup of tea or a bun, or tell them a joke – whatever it takes to put them at ease. Too many people hate the idea of Old Bill. I tried to make it as hard as possible to hate this particular one.[24]

McKelvey was finally selected for CID training in 1990. 'You didn't understand the significance of it until you went to detective training school at Hendon. You were expected to learn the law back to front so you could quote it verbatim. It was very, very intensive learning.'

The idea of an elite within Scotland Yard was not universally popular, however. According to McKelvey detectives 'did rub [the] uniform [branch] up the wrong way. You were seen as a very special person. But you *were* special. You felt special. You had done an awful lot to get where you got, and you felt you had earned that respect.'[25]

The prevailing culture of the Met then may have been rougher, but it encouraged detectives to take on personal responsibility. Ramm remembers that the 1980s were 'part of a criminal justice system that demanded that police officers took ownership of cases from complaint to conviction', adding: 'There was great pride in the quality of work and significant risk of embarrassment and in-force censure of poor case preparation.'[26]

Detectives were also expected to know their patch and be capable of targeting the most dangerous criminals in London. 'The Krays were violent psychopaths,' said McKelvey.

There were the Richardsons ... But there was an effort to take them out. When they got too big for their boots we would put a team on them. We knew who they were. That is something that doesn't happen now. If you were to ask a PC now, or a DC on division, who are the biggest criminals in London, they wouldn't have a clue. Even as PCs, we knew who the major villains were.[27]

According to McKelvey, senior officers in today's Met – almost all of whom have graduated from the uniform branch – are terrified of running criminal informants. 'As a young PC, you were encouraged to have your own informants,' he said.

At Stoke Newington I had eight, ten informants. Every time you arrested someone your aim was to turn them into an informant. Now, you don't have individuals who run informants, you don't have detectives who run informants, you have source units. And they are not very good. Organised crime has worked out how to corrupt the source units anyway. This has decimated the Met's intelligence capabilities.[28]

This is bad enough, but the refusal to promote detectives into senior roles is almost unfathomable. The best investigators in Scotland Yard are largely forced to languish at the rank of detective constable or detective sergeant, each working on dozens of serious cases. The result is that the officers best suited to preventing and detecting crime do not progress to strategic leadership roles. Imagine an NHS that refused to promote surgeons beyond foundation level, with complex open-heart procedures being overseen by administrators.

What makes the situation inside the Met so tragic is that most detectives are, according to McKelvey, vocational police officers who wanted to make a difference. They didn't base success on 'Billy Smith has done well, he's become a sergeant; Billy Smith has done well, he's become an inspector'. You based it on 'Billy Smith has done well, he's just nicked someone for two kilos of heroin'. You looked at the quality of work people were doing, not whether they had been promoted.

I passed a sergeant's exam in 1990 but I didn't actually seek promotion until 1998 because I didn't want to go back to uniform to be a sergeant. I wanted to be a detective. There was a PC at Stoke Newington that was a complete and utter buffoon. He was so useless people just used to feel sorry for him. He went on to be a commander![29]

Like Tony Nash, former commander Roy Ramm is one of the few detectives to rise to a senior level in the Met. He too is appalled at the quality of senior officers at Scotland Yard. 'They are professional police managers who have risen through the ranks without trace, without ever standing in the witness box and giving evidence. This breed of political senior officers has done immense damage to policing.'

Bob Quick, a former detective, rose higher than either Ramm or Nash. In 2008, as the Met's assistant commissioner in charge of specialist operations and counter-terrorism, he was effectively the third most senior officer in Britain. He also served as national lead for workforce development for the Association of Chief Police Officers, so he has a unique insight into the collapse of the detective class. 'In the 2000s, there was a failure really – despite the best efforts of many people, including myself – to underline the importance of the detective role. There was a strong push from government to dumb down the training.'[30]

'There was a homogenisation of police training and police

careers; they were all seen as level pegging,' Quick told me. 'It was a bit like saying if you are ground crew for British Airways there's no reason why you can't be a pilot. So we will train you to be a pilot.' Quick was against the reforms but he was powerless to stop them and remains frustrated.

'Commercially no business would operate like that,' he told me.

Someone once said to me: 'The trouble with you, Bob, is that you are thinking rationally about this.' But the police don't operate in a rational, commercial market like a business. They operate in a political market, which is completely irrational. And that was absolutely the point. Common sense just went out the window because we were slavishly pursuing an agenda of equality. These old methods were seen as counter-productive. Putting barriers in to stop people becoming whatever it was they wanted to do was seen as counter-productive. Elitist obstacles to preventing one and all becoming a detective were removed. Actually, there was a cost to that because the detective side was really dumbed down, and we lost so much of the expertise.[31]

Nash agrees. 'There has been a lack of investment and a one-size-fits-all approach that meant [the training] got dumbed down,' he told me. 'I take my hat off to all police officers. But we have eroded something that we did not have to erode. It's become painting by numbers. Become detectives by numbers. We've gone to the lowest common denominator rather than aspiring to perfection.'[32]

* * *

The incompetence of Scotland Yard was brought home during the Hatton Garden jewel heist over the Easter bank holiday in 2015, one of the most infamous crimes of recent years. A gang of pensioners mounted a daring raid on London's famous jewellery district, disabling several alarms, abseiling down a lift shaft and drilling into a vault containing seventy safety deposit boxes. The career thieves made off with cash and jewellery worth an estimated £14 million. It was one of the biggest burglaries in British history. The gang got away and managed to stay on the run for several months.

Embarrassingly, Scotland Yard had ignored an alarm call from the Hatton Garden Safe Deposit Company when the burglars were still in mid-heist. Insiders claimed that the force had been 'degrading' alarm calls for years, with officers rarely dispatched to a scene unless suspects had been seen by a witness. The decision looked particularly foolish given that Hatton Garden, a street in Holborn, central London, is the centre of the UK diamond trade and well known as an 'incubator and facilitator for organised crime'.[33] The aftermath led to a phone call from Prime Minister David Cameron to Sir Bernard Hogan-Howe which is said to have left the Met commissioner 'very rattled'.[34] The Flying Squad was deployed and technical equipment from the counter-terrorism command was eventually used to track down the brazen gang.

In recent times, it seems as though only the threat of public ridicule will jolt the Met into launching an investigation. Roy Ramm told me: 'In 1839, Sir Richard Maine – one of the first Met commissioners – said: "The primary object of an efficient police is the prevention of crime: the next that of detection and punishment of offenders if crime is committed." These days detection doesn't seem that important to many chief officers.'

Across England and Wales there is an estimated shortfall of 5,000 detectives. The Met alone is officially down by 700, although sources tell me the figure is far higher. 'People are leaving in their droves,' said one senior Met source. 'At one stage there were ninety qualified experienced detectives leaving the service every month.' Sadiq Khan, mayor of London since 2016, with political oversight of the Metropolitan Police, told me there has been a 'massive reduction' in detective numbers that has 'only recently started to be rectified'. He said that the Met is hoping to bolster its ranks of detectives by use of a direct entry programme, which attracts professionals into the police from other industries.[35] In 2017, Scotland Yard also announced that new recruits to the Met could become detectives without having to spend two years as a uniformed bobby on the beat. After just six months, trainees would be asked to solve burglaries, assaults and muggings. Following a year's training, they can now work on rape cases – and after two years they can apply to join the murder squad or even the counter-terrorism command.[36]

The new rules are treated with disdain by former Met detectives who went through the previously rigorous training regime. 'Scotland Yard has direct entry superintendents from Waitrose!' says David McKelvey. 'How can they possibly review how somebody handled an informant? Or how someone responded to someone threatening to kill you, or your children? There is no one with any experience to know how to deal with anything.' Tony Nash says it is vital that trainee detectives have experienced at least two years on the beat. Ramm says such an initiation teaches rookie police officers how to wield 'power'. 'It's an important thing,' he told me.

You have the power to arrest people and detain them. You need to get used to speaking with people. When I joined I had worked in a bank and had had the occasional chat through the banking counter. But had I engaged with someone who had just lost a loved one through a sudden death or a car crash? No, I hadn't. So, you need to understand how to engage with people. You need to have a degree of maturity before you can become a detective.[37]

Nash, the former borough commander of Newham, said he tried to resist the dilution of detective training before he retired in 2017. When he found himself on promotion panels being asked to sign off new detectives who had presented 'theory storyboards' on what it might be like to arrest someone, rather than actually doing it, he became uncomfortable.

I said: 'No, there are loads of people who are wanted on warrant in this borough. Go and get some evidence that you need to get a search warrant, and go and nick someone.' I don't want the theory; I want them to put it into practice. I want to make people do the job.

Nash said this went down very badly with senior officers in charge of the training.

I had them phoning me up saying: 'Oh, they are allowed to do theory storyboards.' I said: 'Hang on a minute, there are God knows how many people who are wanted, and most of them you can probably knock on their door at five in the morning and find them.' I had a big row with them and it got quite political. The development programme is not fit for purpose.[38]

For Ramm, if the Metropolitan Police want to build successful cases it is crucial that the dying art of detection is preserved.

Officers once learned how to take statements from a witness that, if not watertight, were at least of sufficient quality to support a prosecution. In the last few years, I have seen quite a few police state-ments. In general, they have been desperately poor, full of hearsay, opinion and irrelevance and weak on evidence. Little wonder that the CPS do not progress cases to trial. They think they are going to lose and they are right.[39]

This leads back to the lamentable Operation Midland. None of the people I interviewed could understand how on earth it had ever got off the ground. 'Accept nothing, Believe no one, Check everything, first rule of detective training school,' said McKelvey. 'Why the fuck did they believe Steve Rodhouse, who ran the job? If you'd gone back to the 1980s and 1990s he would have been sacked. How the hell did he ever get in that role?!'[40]

* * *

When Sir Richard Henriques delivered his withering report into Operation Midland in November 2016 it was a disaster for the Met. Henriques concluded that Metropolitan Police officers had broken the law and failed to follow basic procedures. Once the case was handed to the Northumbria force to investigate, however, it metas-tasised. Northumbria Police were asked to examine the background of the Met's star complainant. They didn't much like what they found. Officers discovered more than 350 indecent images of chil-dren on three laptop computers, a USB stick and an iPad, including files named 'Man and two boys twelve years of age', 'Little boy and man' and 'Thirteen-year-old with ten-year-old'.

The anonymity the police had granted to 'Nick' as an alleged victim of sexual abuse fell away as his fantasies were exposed. He was revealed to be Carl Beech, a former nurse who worked as an inspector for the Care Quality Commission, a medical regulator.

In January 2018 Beech fled to Sweden as his twisted lies began to unravel, paying £17,000 for a property in the remote northern region of Överkalix. He used several aliases and changed his appearance, travelling on overnight trains and using gift cards bought with cash to pay for tickets in order to avoid leaving a financial footprint.

Beech was finally arrested in Sweden in October 2018 on a European arrest warrant and was returned to the UK to face prosecution for paedophile offences. During the trial, it emerged that Beech had tried to frame his teenage son when police caught him downloading indecent images. The jury was also told that he viewed child pornography of the 'gravest kind' during the period he was being interviewed by Met detectives over his VIP abuse claims. Consultant clinical psychologist Roy Shuttleworth told the court that Beech 'gained sexual gratification from the stories he was telling … in my professional opinion, I think he got a thrill out of it'.

Beech was convicted of voyeurism and making and possessing indecent images of young boys. Prosecutors described him as a 'committed and manipulative paedophile'. Months later, he was charged with perverting the course of justice and Scotland Yard's embarrassment was complete. Prosecutors concluded he had invented the lurid claims that so entranced the Met. The Northumbria Police inquiry found that Beech had picked his targets by browsing the internet on a computer and smartphones that Scotland Yard detectives had agreed not to examine. He had also tried to boost his credibility by creating a false email account, using it to pose as 'Fred', a bogus third party who repeated the same allegations to gullible detectives.

Prosecutor Tony Badenoch QC said that Beech's claims were once described by the Met as 'credible and true'. They had proved to be quite the opposite. The prosecutor added that the basic detective work performed by Northumbria Police had rendered Beech's story 'totally unfounded, hopelessly compromised and irredeemably contradicted by other testimony'.

Beech was convicted of twelve counts of perverting the course of justice and one count of fraud in July 2019. The impact on his victims was judged to be so grave he was handed an eighteen-year jail sentence. In a powerful statement, the 95-year-old Lord Bramall – a former head of the British Army – recalled the impact the 'monstrous' allegations had on him and his legacy: 'In service of my Queen and country I have done all that has been required of me,' he said.

I have suffered both physically and emotionally as a result and did so without regret or complaint. I thought I could be hurt no more. I can honestly say, however, I was never as badly wounded in all my time in the military as I have been by the allegations made by 'Nick' that formed the basis of Operation Midland. I had seen my home searched by the [Metropolitan Police]; been accused of heinous sexual acts against children; been linked to people who were accused of murdering children; had my family approached by members of the press in search of information for the ongoing media frenzy; watched my children lose their mother and worry about the impact of these allegations on their father; and seen my wife pass not knowing that I had been cleared of all wrongdoing.[41]

Harvey Proctor, the retired Conservative MP, summed it up more succinctly: 'It was a truly disgraceful chapter in the history of British policing'.

The ensuing furore led the Conservatives to withdraw the offer of a new contract to Commissioner Hogan-Howe, something that Nick Timothy is ambivalent about. 'What happened with Operation Midland had all the hallmarks of an organisation that had lost any kind of confidence, to trust its own instincts, to hold the line,' Theresa May's former chief of staff told me. 'After the Jimmy Savile scandal, it was an over-reaction and an over-calibration that reflects an organisation that had been badly beaten up, that basically didn't have trust in its own integrity.

'I actually think Bernard was a good cop,' he added. 'Scotland Yard is an absolute viper's nest so it's so difficult for any incumbent and everyone is out to get your job.'

Chapter 16

Dick's Downfall

The walk home planned by Sarah Everard was exceptionally normal. It was the type of journey taken by millions of young women across Britain every single week, which is partly why the events that followed were so shocking.

Everard, a 33-year-old marketing executive, had finished a bottle of wine at her friend's house in Clapham, a wealthy area of south London, before leaving to walk home. It was the middle of lockdown in March 2021 when she pulled her green rain jacket around her shoulders, placed a white beanie hat on her head and headed out into the cool, spring evening. She crossed Clapham Common and was last seen on CCTV heading towards her Brixton Hill home at around 9.30 p.m.

Wayne Couzens, a Met Police firearms officer, had just finished a twelve-hour shift guarding the US embassy in Battersea. He was cruising the streets of London in a rented Vauxhall Crossland, searching for prey.

Witnesses saw the police officer stop his car by Sarah. Couzens used his police warrant card and handcuffs to 'arrest' her on the pretext of a breach of coronavirus regulations. The police officer used the draconian new laws as a ploy to force her into his rental car before raping and strangling her to death in a sickening five-hour ordeal.

The despicable crime, committed by a serving Metropolitan Police officer, would appal the nation. And Scotland Yard's cack-handed response to the crisis triggered a chain of events that would lead to the abrupt removal of yet another commissioner.

Couzens's crime was meticulously planned. He hired the car and plastic sheeting in the days before the attack. Once he had captured Sarah, the PC drove her 80 miles to Dover where he transferred the terrified victim from the rented vehicle to his family car. Couzens then raped Sarah in a rural area not far from the home in nearby Deal that he shared with his wife and two young children. Finally, he used his police belt to strangle her before burning the body in woodland. In the days afterwards Couzens travelled around Kent buying materials, including petrol, to help dispose of the body. He returned to the scene three times, including one brazen trip with his wife and children.

For such a horrific murder to have been committed by a police officer sparked soul-searching across Britain. Women across the country took to social media to discuss their own experiences of walking the streets, and the lengths they went to to feel safe.

Scotland Yard faced initial criticism in the days following the murder when police broke up a vigil on Clapham Common to commemorate Sarah. Several officers were pictured bundling women to the ground, causing outrage across the political spectrum. A parliamentary inquiry and the courts later found that the Met had breached the 'fundamental rights' of the protestors.

The embarrassment deepened when it emerged that Couzens, an armed officer tasked with protecting politicians, dignitaries and VIPs, should never have passed the Met's supposedly tough vetting procedures. An investigation later found he regularly cavorted with prostitutes, took dangerous body-building steroids, and earned the nickname 'The Rapist' at his previous force, Kent Police, for reasons that have never been explained.

Just three days before raping and murdering Sarah, Couzens had allegedly flashed two female members of staff at a McDonald's restaurant. Tragically, despite CCTV cameras identifying his car, he was not arrested for the alleged offence until it was too late. At the time of writing, an investigation is also ongoing into claims that Kent Police could have stopped Couzens years ago, but they failed to properly investigate an allegation of indecent exposure when he was seen driving naked from the waist down. The Independent Office of Police Conduct (IOPC), the police watchdog, said twelve gross misconduct or misconduct notices have so far been served on police officers from several forces relating to the Couzens case.

Confidence in the Met among women plummeted. Cressida Dick had been lauded as the first female commissioner in the Met's 188-year history when she was appointed in 2017. But when Couzens was sentenced, new information came to light which revealed a shocking picture of misogyny inside the force she led. Over the previous eleven years, more than 750 officers and staff had faced sexual misconduct allegations – including sexual harassment, sexual assault, rape and using a position of power for sexual gain. Just eighty-three were sacked.[1]

Only 1.6 per cent of rapes in England and Wales reported to police result in a charge. At least eighty women in the UK were killed by men in the seven months between Sarah's murder and Couzens's sentencing. Parm Sandhu, a former chief superintendent in the Met, revealed that Scotland Yard was 'very sexist and misogynistic' and warned that female police officers fear reporting male colleagues as they worry they will be abandoned if they need help on duty:

> What happens is that male police officers will then close ranks and the fear that most women police officers have got is that when you are calling for help, you press that emergency button on your radio, they're not going to turn up and you're going to get kicked in in the street. So you have got to be very careful which battles you can fight and which ones you can actually win.

Sandhu added that women officers who are married to male police officers 'won't report domestic violence either because of the same sort of issues'.[2]

When police officers had examined Couzens's phone they discovered that he had been part of a group on WhatsApp with officers from three different forces, including the Met. The chat group was found to have swapped alleged misogynistic and racist messages. The police officers from the other forces were suspended and removed from their workplace while the matter was investigated but the two Met officers were allowed to stay on duty, prompting widespread criticism. Sue Fish, a former chief constable of Nottinghamshire, said: 'That beggars belief. It sends the most appalling message. That clearly demonstrates the Met does not get it ... does not get the seriousness.'[3]

One troubling aspect of the Couzens case, never previously revealed, is the distinct possibility that Sarah was not his first victim. Experienced murder detectives have told me they are alarmed at some of the evidence to emerge during his trial. 'You don't suddenly, aged forty-seven, pick a girl off the streets, kidnap her, take her, rape her and murder her, cut her body up and dump it in a fridge,' said

Albert Patrick, a former detective chief superintendent in charge of the Met's CID. 'And then to go back with his missus and kids to the woods where he dumped the body? He's just not somebody who has done that as a one-off. There is a strong possibility Couzens has done it before. I wouldn't put it past him.'[4]

David McKelvey, a former detective chief inspector who investigated dozens of murders, agreed. He told me:

Everything was pre-planned. Couzens hired the vehicle, he prepared, he pre-planned to dispose of the body. He went to extreme lengths to dispose of the body. It stinks of someone who has done it before. He had historically used sex workers. It's too detailed. It's too sophisticated for a first-time offence. You don't suddenly go out and commit such a horrific murder. Couzens has all the hallmarks of a serial killer.[5]

Patrick has investigated several serial killers including Colin Ireland and Robert Napper. He told me that he hoped the Met is reviewing missing-persons cases in a bid to find out if Couzens has offended before.

I would like to think the Met would have looked back over cases over the last ten years. He seemed to be preying on young girls; how many young girls have we got missing in London and Kent? What offences have taken place in south-east England, where has Couzens been historically? Was he on annual leave, off sick, working up in the Midlands? You do a timeline of where he was and then look at the offences across the country and ask, could he have done it?

I would be looking for girls who have been reported missing with no real reason why, bodies never found.[6]

McKelvey is less hopeful that Scotland Yard is making much effort in that regard. 'They all just want it to go away now,' he told me. 'If it turned out that Couzens was involved over a period of time it would be catastrophic for the Met. They would have missed a horrific serial killer in their midst and let down victims and families.'[7]

Patrick said that the lack of resources available to Scotland Yard today meant that the only way to answer the question would be for Couzens to 'admit it'. 'The way to deal with him is let him get locked away, let him settle down into his new harsh reality inside four walls, and then go and visit him. That would be the sensible way to do it.'

The Met's 'tin-eared response' to the murder of Sarah Everard had serious ramifications. Priti Patel, the Home Secretary at the time of the murder, had been appalled and disgusted at the handling of the case ever since it became obvious that PC Wayne Couzens was the perpetrator. Patel, who was in contact with Sarah's parents over Zoom in the days following her disappearance, found Cressida Dick and her deputy, Sir Stephen House, to be 'very defensive' when she made enquiries on their behalf.[8] 'Priti told Cressida to cut the crap,' said a senior Home Office source.

> She said this case is important and is of national significance. We have lost count of the number of conversations she had with Cressida and Steve House. They are not interested. It is institutional. They are very defensive. Policing is very defensive, but the Met are absolutely the worst.

Patel and other politicians were further infuriated following the sentencing of Couzens when the Met appeared to distance itself from the rogue PC by describing him as a 'former police officer'. Scotland Yard also triggered ridicule by issuing guidance to any women concerned about being arrested by a single officer, advising them to flag down a bus to beg for assistance. How the Met expected a bus driver to have the power to override a police officer making an arrest remains an open question. Louise Haigh, the shadow Northern Ireland Secretary, who used to volunteer as a Met special constable, was outraged: 'The constant refusal to describe the officer in question as a serving officer when he used his position of power to kidnap and murder Sarah is sickening,' she said.

> This kind of response – a lone bad apple that the institution instantly distances itself from and refuses to accept responsibility for – is typical. It's the kind of wilful blindness that leads to every type of scandal from abuse in care to CSE [child sexual exploitation] to MPs' expenses and phone hacking. But if we're to stop this happening again, culture needs to change. That's much harder and requires leadership, at every level.[9]

In October 2021, Patel announced an independent inquiry into the Sarah Everard case. It had yet to report at the time of writing, but the Home Secretary already believes it could be another catastrophe along the lines of Macpherson, Ellison or Daniel Morgan. 'I don't think the Met has got their head around this yet in terms of what the Everard case actually means,' said the Home Office source. 'The Met is like a horrible onion. You start peeling back [the layers] and you cry more and more.'[10]

* * *

The misogyny scandal triggered by the Sarah Everard murder came at a difficult time for Dick. She had already been damaged by the fallout of the Stephen Port murder case. Port, a serial killer, drugged, raped and killed four men in Barking, east London, between June 2014 and September 2015. He sexually assaulted more than a dozen others. An inquest jury in December 2021 ruled that Met Police officers had failed to carry out basic checks which could have prevented three of the victims' deaths. The finding came in the same week that Deniz Jaffer and Jamie Lewis, two police constables, were jailed for thirty-three months after sharing pictures of two murdered sisters, Nicole Smallman and Bibaa Henry, whose bodies they were supposed to be guarding.

Some wondered how Dick had managed to survive the personal criticism contained in a long-awaited independent panel report into the Daniel Morgan murder. Initially supposed to take one year, the panel finally reported in June 2021 – eight years after it was first commissioned by the then Prime Minister, Theresa May. The reason for the delay? Dick and other senior officers had repeatedly blocked the panel's access to Met records with no 'reasonable explanation', causing significant further distress to the Morgan family.[11]

Beyond the extraordinary behaviour of the commissioner, the panel's wider findings were devastating. It concluded that the Met did not suffer from a 'rotten apple' model of corruption but instead had 'systemic failings, including a 'corrupt culture'. Its report said:

The family of Daniel Morgan suffered grievously as a consequence of the failure to bring his murderer(s) to justice, the misinformation which was put into the public domain, and the denial of failings in investigation, including failures to acknowledge professional incompetence, individuals' venal behaviour, and managerial and organisational failings. Unwarranted assurances were given to the family, and the Metropolitan Police placed the reputation of the organisation above the need for accountability and transparency. The lack of candour and the repeated failure to take a fresh, thorough and critical look at past failings are all symptoms of institutional corruption, which prioritises institutional reputation over public accountability.[12]

Such was the endemic dishonesty uncovered inside the Met, the panel recommended the creation of a 'statutory duty of candour', to be owed by all law enforcement agencies to 'those whom they serve'.[13]

The family of Daniel Morgan, who had suffered for so long, finally achieved some measure of justice. 'We find in the report an accurate reflection of our lived experience: the complicity and worse of the British state in all its guises in the police corruption and criminality that has wracked our lives,' they said in a statement following the report's publication.

No family should have to go through what we have had to suffer over these decades. No family should have to find as we did that our confidence was betrayed by those to whom we should be able to turn for help. No family should be cut adrift in the way we were left to fend for ourselves in the face of the most serious criminality that can be imagined. No family should have to bear the immense and indescribable cost we have paid in terms of our health, emotional, physical and otherwise. Above all, no family should be left to find, as we do, that we are no longer able to place our trust in the police, the state or any other form of authority in this country.

Scotland Yard's response to the independent report was to deny its central findings. But Dick then became embroiled in yet another furore. This time, it involved her political master in Downing Street.

* * *

The biggest scandals are often slow burners, starting life as a whiff of smoke and smouldering for months before crackling into flame.

Just as Watergate began with an unremarkable story in the *Washington Post* two years before Richard Nixon, the US President, was eventually impeached, 'Partygate' seemed to pose little threat to Prime Minister Boris Johnson when a report of drinks events within Downing Street during lockdown first appeared in November 2021.

The stories made a mockery of the draconian rules that Johnson had imposed on the public to combat the spread of coronavirus. Millions of people had been ordered not to see family members for many months during the worst of the pandemic. Hospital patients were prevented from having visits from loved ones – even if they were dying. Couples were forced to cancel weddings, and families had to limit the number of funeral attendees in order to minimise Covid transmission.

Despite the reports in national newspapers, Scotland Yard showed little interest in partying politicians. But this caused significant public disquiet as the force led by Dick had treated ordinary people very differently. During the lockdowns, the Met had operated dedicated Covid patrols with vans of officers on standby across London to break up illicit gatherings. Those further down the socio-economic ladder had been pursued relentlessly. Lorraine Kent, a persistent beggar, was ordered to pay almost £2,500 for just sitting outside a south London Tesco Extra during the third national lockdown.[14]

With no action taken by the Yard, the No. 10 press operation was able to dismiss early Partygate questions from the media. The controversy appeared to be fizzling out until a video emerged of staff joking that the illicit Christmas parties might be explained away as 'business meetings'.

More revelations started to appear on a near-daily basis, including events in the Department for Education and at the Conservative Party's campaign headquarters, where London mayoral candidate Shaun Bailey was pictured partying with activists. Weeks later, leaked emails revealed that up to 100 people had been invited to a Downing Street garden party on 20 May 2020 by Martin Reynolds, Johnson's principal private secretary, who told guests to 'bring your own booze'. The Met still showed no interest, despite issuing a £100 fine to Nuradeem Mohammed, from Hayes, west London, for simply standing in the street talking with other people. The sanction had occurred on the same day as the Downing Street 'bring your own booze' party.[15]

The disclosures kept coming, but the Met kept looking away. The press revealed that two leaving parties were held in Downing Street on the eve of Prince Philip's socially distanced funeral, Johnson had a birthday party in the Cabinet room on 19 June 2020, and he and his wife held a further gathering in their Downing Street flat to celebrate the departure of hated aide Dominic Cummings, with ABBA music including 'The Winner Takes It All' being blasted out.

Johnson's response to reports of parties inside his house had been typically farcical for a Prime Minister so socially distanced from the truth. He initially said he was unaware of them happening. Then, when it emerged he had attended a drinks party in his garden, Johnson said he believed it was a work event and no one had told him it was 'against the rules' he himself had imposed on the British public. On allegations that Johnson had had a birthday party in the Cabinet room, Downing Street sources tried to spin the story as an unwitting Prime Minister being 'ambushed by a cake'.

Police officers had interrupted a Downing Street Christmas party when revellers accidentally set off an alarm but failed to shut it down.[16] The parties had occurred in places where dozens of police officers were permanently stationed, which may explain why Scotland Yard was reluctant to get dragged into an investigation. They left Sue Gray, the veteran Whitehall mandarin whose previous probe had ended the career of Damian Green, to establish what had happened.

But the Met's decision was untenable given the police action taken elsewhere. On the same evening as one 'cheese and wine' party held in Downing Street, three women with no links to Westminster attended a different event and fell foul of the law. Ebru Sen, twenty-six, Ami Goto, twenty-three, and Emilia Petruta-Cristea, twenty-four, were arrested at a party by Met Police officers and each ended up with criminal convictions and a £1,100 fine.[17]

The British public was furious. In the 100 days between November 2021 and February 2022, Johnson suffered a vast fourteen-point swing in the polls away from the ruling Conservatives towards the Labour Party. As he received yet another Partygate pasting during Prime Minister's Questions, protestors gathered in Parliament Square to sing 'Bye Bye Boris' to the tune of the Bay City Rollers' 'Bye Bye Baby'.

The anger was spilling over onto the Met. A waspish campaign group, Led by Donkeys, drove a lorry with a massive screen up to the front door of Scotland Yard and broadcast a video directly addressing Cressida Dick. In the five-minute clip, a voiceover sounding remarkably like Ted Hastings, the ethical police chief in the hit

BBC police corruption show *Line of Duty*, asked: 'Who exactly does the Met Police work for, ma'am? Our citizens, or Boris Johnson?

'Last week, senior officers who work in this building issued a statement declaring they would not be investigating the unlawful Christmas party held in Downing Street last year,' boomed Hastings.

The statement claimed a criminal inquiry is not possible because there is, quote, 'an absence of evidence'. Correct me if I'm wrong here, ma'am, but the whole purpose of a police inquiry is to gather evidence, but because your officers are unwilling to get off their backsides and find it, my team are bringing that evidence direct to Scotland Yard.

The clip has been viewed almost 250,000 times on YouTube.

Another campaign group also issued formal legal proceedings against the Met over its failure to investigate the parties. Jolyon Maugham, director of the Good Law Project, said: 'You can have the rule of law, or you can defer to the powerful. But you can't have both. It shames the Met, and ultimately all of us, that Cressida Dick refuses to investigate.'

The pressure finally had an effect. Two months after the Partygate revelations began, Scotland Yard announced Operation Hillman, a criminal investigation into eight of seventeen alleged parties that took place between May 2020 to April 2021. But the news emerged just as Gray was about to publish her report into the affair, which many had expected to trigger Johnson's removal as Prime Minister. Dozens of Tory MPs had submitted letters calling for a confidence vote in Johnson, which would trigger a leadership election. Just as the threshold of fifty-four letters was in sight, the Met appeared to force Gray to shelve her report in order not to prejudice the criminal inquiry, prompting allegations of a 'stitch-up' between the Yard and No. 10.

Even senior police chiefs were surprised at the Met's response. One told *The Times* that the Yard 'couldn't have handled it worse'.[18] Sir Peter Fahy, a former chief constable of Greater Manchester police, said: 'It feels to me that she [Dick] strangely allowed Boris to get off the hook.' Lord Macdonald, a former director of public prosecutions, said that the Met's request seemed disproportionate because its investigation was 'purely into lockdown breaches' that would result only in fixed-penalty notices rather than a trial in front of a jury.

Andrew Neil, the former *Sunday Times* editor and veteran broadcaster, said the Prime Minister was 'very close to being toppled' and warned that Johnson had been 'saved by Knacker of the Yard'.[19] David Blunkett, the former Home Secretary, accused the Met of a 'shoddy fix' and 'losing the plot'.[20] 'Whatever sympathies I've had for Dick and her colleagues is rapidly seeping away,' he said.

> Sadly, at a time when so many of our great institutions and organisations are being eroded by constant attack, it gives me no pleasure to say so, but unless the Met starts to show the logic, rational and clear leadership expected of them, heads, as in the political arena, must surely roll.*

* * *

In February 2022, London mayor Sadiq Khan lost patience with Dick. His confidence in her snapped when a scandal emerged at

---

* Johnson, who was badly damaged by Partygate, eventually resigned six months later following a series of other scandals.

Charing Cross police station, one of the most centrally located and important in the Met. Officers had shared racist, sexist, misogynistic and Islamophobic messages discussing the rape of women and the use of African children as dog food. The messages emerged during an investigation by the IOPC, launched after one of the policemen had sex with a vulnerable woman inside the police station. Yet another case involving the serial mistreatment of women – coming hot on the heels of the Sarah Everard murder – was too much for the mayor. Khan was horrified to read some of the detail. One officer had written to a female colleague: 'I would happily rape you … chloroform you … if I was single.' Another said: 'Getting a woman into bed is like spreading butter, it can be done with a bit of effort using a credit card, but it's quicker and easier just to use a knife.' A colleague said over WhatsApp:

> You ever slapped your missus? It makes them love you more. Seriously, since I did that she won't leave me alone. Now I know why these daft c**** are getting murdered by their spastic boyfriends. Knock a bird about and she will love you. They are biologically programmed to like that shit.[21]

Officers expected to serve without prejudice had descended into a swamp of bigotry, committing affronts to common decency for which the term 'gross misconduct' is hardly sufficient. The IOPC called on the Met to overhaul its culture, warning that the incidents were not isolated or the behaviour of a 'few bad apples'. Yet Scotland Yard still retains the power to decide officer sanctions. The behaviour uncovered at Charing Cross police station did not seem to concern the Met's disciplinarians. Two of the officers involved were later promoted while another nine were left to continue serving.

The scandal prompted renewed outrage among women across the country. It also moved a Met Police constable known only as 'Andrea' to break ranks. She told *The Times* how her inspector summoned her into a room, lunged at her, grabbed her breasts and forced his hands into her pants. It was not the first misogyny that Andrea had witnessed during her twenty years at the Met. She had once been paired with an officer who liked to park near secondary schools to ogle teenage girls' breasts. Some of her colleagues constantly watched pornography on their phones. A PC convicted for masturbating on a train was allowed to keep his job. Male officers would return from scenes of domestic violence saying the victim was crazy. This time, however, Andrea's patience snapped. She decided to lodge a complaint against her 'handsy' superior. It was a decision that would end her policing career. The inspector told investigators that Andrea had given him oral sex in his car, and labelled her a stalker who was attempting to destroy his career and marriage. She was threatened with a charge of perverting the course of justice. One year into the investigation, Andrea attempted suicide. She eventually ended up dismissed for discreditable conduct. The inspector kept his job.[22]

The misogyny scandal seemed to jolt the Met into action. Another officer, David Carrick, was charged with twenty-three sexual assaults, including an astonishing thirteen rapes. At the time of writing, he had yet to stand trial. But many were starting to wonder whether Dick had the strength or courage to take on the Met's toxic culture. Sources close to Sadiq Khan worried that she was over-compensating for being the first female woman to lead the Met since its inception in 1829.[23] Some started to question whether the admiration and respect Dick felt for the people she worked with had warped her judgement. She seemed to be tolerating deeply offensive attitudes and conduct in order to safeguard Scotland Yard's overall reputation and maintain morale among the workforce.

Dick's problems crystallised following the Charing Cross scandal when Khan ordered his commissioner to come up with a plan to respond. Dick wrote to Khan saying that she fully shared the 'depth of your concern', adding: 'I recognise that this is very serious and urgent action is required. We still, sadly, see far too many examples of bullying and abuse of trust, of disrespect and lack of compassion.' But she refused to sack the officers embroiled in the Charing Cross scandal, claiming that she could not intervene in an independent misconduct process. One of the Met's official Twitter accounts then criticised Khan by claiming he did not understand the disciplinary system.

Khan made clear, publicly and in private, that he was not satisfied with Dick's plan to address cultural issues in the wake of the Charing Cross report. The commissioner felt she had no option but to call time on the job she loved.

After he withdrew his support for Dick, Khan said the Charing Cross scandal – and the Met's response to it – had left him feeling 'disgusted and extremely angry'. 'We have a longstanding tradition in this country of policing by consent,' he added. 'At the heart of this approach is the recognition that, for policing to be effective, public approval, respect and confidence in the service is paramount. When this trust is eroded, our model of policing, and therefore public safety, is put at risk.'[24]

Khan said he was 'deeply concerned by how public trust and confidence in London's police service has been shattered so badly' and said he now believed there were 'deep cultural issues within the

Met'. 'I concluded that the only way we were going to start seeing the level of change urgently required was with new leadership right at the top of the Met.'[25]

Dick's underlings were incandescent. Ken Marsh, chairman of the Metropolitan Police Federation, said the commissioner had been treated unfairly. 'She was much loved across the rank and file of the Metropolitan Police Service. We feel the way she has been treated is wholly unfair and we did believe that she was the person who could take us through this and bring us out the other side.'[26]

Priti Patel said the challenges facing the new commissioner were 'stark and could not be more sobering'. In a statement, the Home Secretary added that Dick's replacement must demonstrate 'strong and decisive' leadership to 'restore public confidence' and rid the force of sexism, racism and institutional corruption.[27]

Dick's enforced resignation was an ignominious end for the trailblazing officer, whose long career in the Met straddles much of these pages. She had joined as a beat bobby in 1983 and her fierce determination saw her rise through the ranks of a force riddled with endemic misogyny. No one can deny it was a remarkable feat. Dick also played a leading role in – and survived – some of the most notorious recent cases including the murder of Stephen Lawrence, the controversial arrest of Damian Green, the phone hacking scandal, Operation Midland and, of course, the death of innocent Jean Charles de Menezes.

To achieve such success, one suspects that Dick had to work harder than almost anyone to find her place in the Met's macho culture. Following the turbulent tenure of the irascible Hogan-Howe, the commissioner had seemed to go out of her way to praise her officers. She defended the Met robustly when it was criticised.

Although Dick won favour with the rank and file, it also meant there was no attempt to take a meaningful look at the culture, standards, supervision and behaviour at the heart of some of the Met's problems. It almost seemed as though Dick feared what would be found underneath the stone if she turned it over.

Chapter 17

Future Threats

Shoppers in Salisbury city centre were startled to see an elder- ly man and a young woman staggering around, apparently hallucinating.

The stricken pair were foaming at the mouth and making pecu- liar noises. They seemed to be gasping for breath before they finally collapsed unconscious on a park bench. No one present – not the anxious shoppers nor the police and ambulance crew that attended the scene – knew they were in the presence of Sergei Skripal, the MI6 double agent who had defected from Russia to the UK. Skripal and his daughter Yulia had just fallen victim to the first chemical weapons attack in Europe since the end of the Second World War.

The retired spy and his daughter survived. But their attempt- ed assassination in March 2018 led to uproar across the Western world. Prime Ministers and Presidents lined up to condemn Russia, which has made no secret of its policy to eliminate perceived trai- tors. Hundreds of counter-terrorism officers from Scotland Yard were deployed to Salisbury. Police seized more than 5,000 hours of CCTV footage, examined more than 1,350 exhibits and took state- ments from 500 witnesses. The painstaking six-month investigation by the Met's SO15 unit was an extraordinary success. The attackers were identified as Anatoly Chepiga and Alexander Mishkin, who had travelled to the UK under false names. Chepiga was a decorated colonel with the GRU, the Russian military intelligence service. The agency had employed Skripal when MI6 recruited him in the 1990s. Detectives from SO15 uncovered evidence showing the assassins visiting Salisbury and spraying novichok, a lethal nerve agent, on the door handle of Skripal's home. Later the same day, they flew to Moscow.

It was a dazzling result for Scotland Yard – and Theresa May's government. Suspicion had fallen immediately on Russian President Vladimir Putin's administration. But in the immediate aftermath it was unclear how the UK and a fractured West could respond to an enemy armed with thousands of nuclear warheads. The evidence gathered by the Yard gave May enough to argue that twenty-three Russian 'diplomats' should be expelled from the London embassy. The detective work, in collaboration with MI5, also persuaded more than twenty other allies – including the United States – to expel over 100 more. In a sombre statement to the House of Commons, May welcomed the 'largest collective expulsion of Russian intelligence officers in history'.[1] Scotland Yard was riding high. The inquiry had been an example of the Metropolitan Police at its best.

Details of the operation never previously disclosed also highlight the courage that most officers display on our behalf. It seems the risk to police investigating the chemical weapons attack did not emerge solely from novichok. Some officers working on the Skripal inquiry reported break-ins at their homes. Pets were decapitated and faeces smeared across walls. An assessment by the UK government is understood to have concluded that the antics were some form of Russian-backed retaliation for a job well done.[2]

Despite the grave errors and the corruption that has plagued the Met for many years, it should never be forgotten that many, many officers perform miracles each and every day. The counter-terrorism command stands out, in particular. In 2001, the 9/11 attacks on New York and Washington led the UK into two controversial wars in Iraq and Afghanistan. Some of the UK's 2.5 million Muslims were furious at the conflicts that raged for years on Islamic soil. As a result, Britain faced a considerable threat from home-grown terrorists who were radicalised by a warped version of the Koran promulgated by Al-Qaeda and other preachers of hate. Baroness Manningham-Buller, the head of MI5 between 2002 and 2007, has admitted the conflicts 'radicalised … a whole generation of young people … who saw our involvement in Iraq and Afghanistan as being an attack on Islam'. 'We were pretty well swamped – that's possibly an exaggeration – but we were very overburdened with intelligence on a broad scale that was pretty well more than we could cope with.'[3]

Given the scale of the threat, it is a wonder that the number of successful terror attacks since 2001 can almost be counted on the fingers of both hands. But the response has taken a heavy toll, sucking the Met's finest officers away from units dealing with other crimes.

'Policing has become more complex,' said Tony Nash, the former borough commander of Newham.

The threat from global terrorism has meant there has been significant growth in the investigative capacity of the counter-terrorism command. We had really, really good units doing work that people want to write books about, and make films about. But as soon as anyone is shown as having any degree of investigative talent they get snapped up.[4]

As the Met's counter-terrorist units have rushed to snuff out the threat from Islamist terrorism – and in more recent times, a new and emerging menace from the far right – other divisions of the Yard have been allowed to wither. Such as those dealing with the drugs trade, the lifeblood of organised crime.

The latest statistics on the so-called war on drugs are depressing. Drug-related deaths have hit a record in the UK. A surge in cocaine purity has continued for eight years and the UK has the highest usage in Europe among young people. The government's own Serious Violence Strategy, published in April 2018, identifies 'drugs and profit' as a main driver in the recent surge in 'county lines' gangs, and the dramatic increase in stabbings nationwide. Knife crime offences have risen from 23,665 in 2013/14 to 39,818 in 2017/18. In the same period, the number of hospital admissions for knife wounds is up by almost a third, and in 2018 the number of homicides by knife, 285, was at its highest level since the end of the Second World War.

Yet drugs are not listed as one of the National Crime Agency's (NCA) six key threats, a surprising omission given the trade is the biggest illegal enterprise in the world and powers much of organised crime. 'It is not just about seizing powder off the streets,' says a former senior manager who worked in the NCA. 'Drugs in our world is a collective term for murder, manslaughter and many other crimes. It is a whole ambit of criminality, health and social issues.'[5]

Emerging threats also pose new headaches for Scotland Yard and the rest of the policing establishment. Sir Richard Henriques, the retired judge who was first called to the Bar in 1967 and who reviewed the disastrous Operation Midland, knows this better than most. Henriques believes that the threat and complexity of crime has increased substantially over the last fifty years. 'The rewards accrued by organised criminals have grown over time,' he says. 'The Krays and the Richardsons had to commit very daring robberies of jewellers' shops and other secure premises. That was how organised gangs raised their funding. Now it's drugs and online fraud, cyber and people trafficking. It's much more sophisticated.'[6]

It is easy to understand why criminals decided to eschew the risky trade of armed robberies in favour of online fraud. While most crimes are reported to local police forces, for many years victims of fraud were told to log their cases with Action Fraud, an online and telephone service outsourced to a private American company. In 2019, an undercover investigation by *The Times* exposed failings in Action Fraud. The report found as few as one in fifty fraud reports led to a suspect being caught and only one in 200 police officers were dedicated to investigating fraud – even though fraud and cybercrime account for half of all crime in the UK. The undercover reporter found that Action Fraud trained call handlers to mislead victims into thinking their cases would be investigated when most were never looked at.

A lord justice of appeal, one of Britain's most senior judges, told me he is extremely concerned about the growing phenomenon. He believes the failure to tackle economic crime is fuelling 'chaos, confusion and anarchy'. The judge is particularly scathing about the police's attitude to victims of fraud. He recalled a personal experience when called at home by a man impersonating an officer from Holborn police station. 'They said they had apprehended two people using my credit card, and they'd like a few details from me.' The judge knew it was a scam so tried to report the crime to real police officers at Holborn police station. 'I told them that there are some people impersonating you. And they said: "Well, it's nothing to do with us! Nothing to do with us!"'

The judge believes policy makers do not prioritise economic crime. He quoted Dr Samuel Johnson, the eighteenth-century poet and playwright, in an attempt to emphasise its terrible consequences: 'Whoever commits a fraud is guilty not only of a particular injury to him who he deceives, but also the diminution of that confidence which constitutes not only the ease but the very existence of society.'

'The real danger of economic crime is that it undermines the very existence of society,' the judge told me.

The former FBI director J. Edgar Hoover famously said: 'I don't even know what the truth is anymore.' But this is what economic crime is all about. It's about telling lies, it's not telling the truth.

The whole motive for actions is whether you believe things. You will do something if you believe it to be a true thing. You won't do something if you believe it to be a lie, a dishonest thing. I'm afraid when you get to the stage when you don't really know what to believe, or who to believe, it's chaos, confusion and, in the end, anarchy. There is no order left. The whole of society becomes both fraudsters, and victims of fraud. People are just defrauding one another. Until the whole system breaks down. The economy, law and order really does depend on the eradication of economic crime, of deception. Obviously violent crime towards the person is very serious. But economic crime is more insidious in its effects over a wider area of society.

Something has got to be done. It just can't go along like this. These economic criminals are enemies of the people, which should mean something to readers of the *Daily Mail*. Not just of their victims, they are enemies of the people as a whole. And if we let this go on, they will destroy our whole society.[7]

Lynne Owens, the long-serving director general of the NCA who stepped down in October 2021, openly admitted to me that law enforcement is overwhelmed by 'new' threats from cybercrime, modern slavery, organised immigration crime and the dark web – which all have to be dealt with alongside the more traditional work fighting drug traffickers and gun runners. She told me that terrorism is rightly treated very seriously by policy makers but, in reality, the threat pales into insignificance compared to organised crime.

In 2013, the NCA estimated that organised crime cost the British public £24 billion every year. Owens, who rejoined the Met as deputy commissioner in September 2022, told me the figure was probably an under-estimate and the phenomenon has grown since then. She pointed out that the annual funding of around £377 million handed to the NCA is far less than the billions available to counter-terrorism, despite the former being a greater national security threat.

'If you look at the resourcing … it's massively disproportionate,' said Owens.

This isn't an argument that counter-terrorism should be less well resourced, but I am saying that … we have got to recognise that [the fight against organised crime] needs investment if we are going to protect the public.

Terrorist events are awful and they play out very publicly, but many more deaths each year are attributed to serious and organised crime than all the other national security threats combined, including terrorism, national disasters and state threats.[8]

It seems odd, therefore, that successive UK governments have not made organised crime more of a priority. In 2014, the Office for National Statistics started adding profits accrued from the drugs and sex trades to their assessment of the nation's gross domestic product. Once the calculations were amended, the UK's economy grew by up to £65 billion – almost 5 per cent – leading it to overtake France as the fifth largest in the world.

A lot of people are making a lot of money. Keith Bristow, Owens's predecessor as head of the NCA, said in 2015 that billions of pounds of criminal assets are laundered in London every day by a network of lawyers, accountants, financial managers and estate agents. Roberto Saviano, the author of *Gomorrah*, a bestselling investigation into the Neapolitan mafia, once said that the flow of dirty money into London makes the UK the 'most corrupt place on earth'. When I put Saviano's allegation to Owens she grimaced before replying that there are 'other cities in the world that are probably more corrupt' than London.[9] Of course, this is undeniable.

* * *

Yet when David Cameron's father is revealed to be hiding money using the same dodgy Panamanian law firm as the crime boss David Hunt, we can probably agree that something has gone wrong.* Can anything be done to turn the tide?

Curtis 'Cocky' Warren was a Liverpool-born drug trafficker whose tentacles once stretched from the cocaine cartels of Colombia to the heroin godfathers of Turkey, the cannabis growers of Morocco to the ecstasy manufacturers of the Netherlands and eastern Europe. A Customs officer once admitted that Warren could 'single-handedly affect the supply and price of coke on the streets

---

* In 2016, the Panama Papers, 11.5 million documents leaked from the offshore agent Mossack Fonseca, showed that Ian Cameron, David Cameron's father, ran an offshore fund that avoided ever having to pay tax in Britain by hiring a small army of Bahamas residents – including a part-time bishop – to sign its paperwork. An offshore company connected to David Hunt, EMM Limited, used to own an industrial property in east London at which Hunt ran an iron and steel business. Mossack Fonseca acted for Hunt's company even after the crime boss was exposed at the *Sunday Times* libel trial detailed in Chapter 12.

of Britain'.[10] He has been described as the 'richest and most successful British criminal who has ever been caught'.[11]

But UK law enforcement did not catch him. Quite the reverse. Customs officers caught Warren seemingly red-handed importing several shipments of cocaine from Venezuela to the UK in 1993. When the trial collapsed, the crime lord rose from the dock and marched up to a room on the third floor of Newcastle crown court, reportedly taunting a small huddle of shell-shocked Customs officers: 'I'm off to spend my £87 million from the first shipment and you can't fucking touch me.'[12]

Yet British law enforcement had all the information they needed to convict Warren. They just couldn't use it. Police and Customs had bugged 14,000 phone calls made by Warren where he had admitted extensive criminality. But for reasons that almost no one appears to understand, the UK is one of the few jurisdictions that bans intercepted communications as evidence in criminal trials. They can only be used as 'intelligence' to help inform police investigations. Other countries are bemused at the UK's stance, not least because cross-border communications have become more essential as crime grows ever more sophisticated and international. Lord Macdonald, the former director of public prosecutions (DPP), says the policy is the sort of 'anomaly that makes the public think we are in Alice in Wonderland', adding: 'We need to get a grip on this.'[13]

Macdonald was Britain's leading prosecutor during the foiled airline bomb plot in 2006, when three British Muslim terrorists tried to blow up aeroplanes with liquid explosives hidden in bottles. Abdulla Ahmed Ali, Assad Sarwar and Tanvir Hussain almost escaped justice when intercepted emails they had exchanged with their handlers in Pakistan were ruled inadmissible as evidence. The first trial ended with a jury failing to agree a verdict. For the second trial, however, prosecutors had obtained a court order in California formally requiring Yahoo! to hand over the emails they had already intercepted. The communications revealed Ali, Sarwar and Hussain recruiting activists, acquiring bomb making chemicals and engaging in a dummy run to test airport security. At the end of the second trial, they were convicted and jailed for more than thirty years each.[14]

Macdonald has repeatedly called for intercept material to be included as evidence in British courts, believing that it would be highly effective in helping to convict terrorists and serious organised criminals. 'The best evidence against a man is the talk coming out of his own mouth,' said the former DPP.

> People, whether they are traders in the City or Taliban in the Swat Valley, have to talk to do business. They all use phones. And, as Yahoo! helpfully reminded us in the airline trial, they use the internet, too. It's time for these rules of evidence to encounter the modern world.[15]

Such material could, of course, be used to target many organised criminals, including those who feature in these pages. Arming Scotland Yard and other law enforcement agencies with this new weapon would also lessen the reliance on supergrasses with chequered pasts, and whose evidence has often disintegrated during trials.

There is a view that the use of such evidence might compromise the intelligence sources and methods of the security services. The former commander of the Flying Squad Roy Ramm is not convinced. 'It's a load of bollocks,' he told me.

> If you turn the clock back, there possibly was an argument that villains didn't know we could tap phones. But that ain't the reality

today. You only need to watch the telly for fifteen minutes on any night of the week to know that police and security services can intercept telephone conversations. It is a critical piece of evidence that we should be putting into cases. It is all very well for the security services to come up with all sorts of bizarre reasons why we shouldn't, but it doesn't wash with me.[16]

Curtis Warren, the international drug trafficker who enjoyed a charmed existence in the UK, was eventually brought to book. After his acquittal Warren moved his operations to the Netherlands, where telephone taps can be used as evidence. Every word spoken into Warren's phone could now be used against him. It worked. In 1997, he was prosecuted for importing 317 kilograms of cocaine into the Netherlands from Venezuela, and for the possession of MDMA, more than 1 tonne of cannabis, guns, three hand grenades and 940 canisters of CS gas. During the trial, Warren tried and failed to argue that phone evidence was inadmissible. 'The setting up of this operation came from UK telephone taps,' said Judge Holtrop.

The argument that they could not be presented in a Dutch court has been rejected. Curtis Warren was for a long time the head of a criminal organisation, involved in large-scale importations of ecstasy, cocaine and hashish. He is the leader of an international criminal group involved in exportation to other countries and importation here, and is a dealer in firearms. There is no doubt that he is the leader.[17]

Holtrop jailed Warren for twelve years without any chance of parole.[*] Apart from new laws of evidence, there seems little doubt that

---

[*] The sentence would be extended after Warren killed a fellow inmate in a prison yard fight.

Scotland Yard and the rest of the UK policing establishment needs a colossal rise in resources. According to Sir Paul Stephenson, 'the current funding does not reflect the scale and breadth of the challenges [the Met] has to deal with'. One of the 'very, very sad consequences' of recent budget cuts was the mass retreat of bobbies from the beat. The Met's neighbourhood policing model, brought in under Sir John Stevens's commissionership during the high-spending New Labour years, saw one sergeant, two constables and two police community support officers dedicated to every ward in London. For Stephenson that was the 'jewel in the crown' of Scotland Yard and 'made a huge difference'. 'Moving away from that fundamental commitment, having that intelligence from the ground up, getting to know the community, getting their confidence, seems to be missing,' Stephenson told me. 'I think it has been a retrograde step.'[18]

Police officers perform vital duties on behalf of the public, for which a starting salary of £30,000 a year for constables seems low. During a speech in 2014, Sir Hugh Orde, the president of the Association of Chief Police Officers, appeared to compare Britain to some developing countries where illegal payments to law enforcers are engrained in society. 'There are certain ranks in the service who are vulnerable in terms of their income and expenditure, which means we should be worried,' he said.

One thing around learning from corruption and integrity is that if you underpay police officers – for example, there are some forces around the world where officers are hardly paid at all – the consequence is corruption.

I am not saying that is the case here at all, but it is something we should be mindful of. Some officers are under some financial pressure and they don't dump those worries when they come to work.[19]

Sadiq Khan told me that he fears that the reduced budgets since 2010 have also fuelled corruption. 'When you have massive cuts, you have even less time for checks and balances,' he said. 'I know some of the high-profile cases you are looking at are institutional failings. It is a big concern because we have had £1 billion going out and that means less time, effort and resources for scrutiny. It is a challenge.'[20]

*   *   *

The chronic lack of funding available to the Met and other police forces was an issue that came up time and time again during the research for this book. Law enforcement bodies in the UK have never been less able to perform their statutory functions and protect the public. Nick Timothy is frustrated at the scale of the cuts that Theresa May was forced to implement by Downing Street and the Treasury from 2010 onwards. He is greatly concerned about the impact on the security of Britain's borders, but was never able to persuade the Cameron government that they should spend more on customs checks and tackling major drug traffickers. HM Customs and Excise has been abolished and rolled into the National Crime Agency, which has far less funding overall. The Border Agency has withdrawn customs checks at minor ports and airports. Today, you could sail a yacht loaded with cocaine into Fleetwood or Little-hampton and nobody would take any notice.

'I feel like the state has basically said "Too many people come in and out of the country, we can't do anything about border-related crime",' says Timothy.

> Unless it happens to be part of a very significant operation, I think they have basically decided 'Sorry, we can't do this, it's too difficult'.

The border is completely porous and the answer from officials, if they are being honest, is 'It's too difficult', or 'We would be able to do something, but with a budget that is ten times bigger'. But at spending reviews, nobody ever says 'Which budgets need to be ten times bigger or ten times smaller?'. They just say 'This is the status quo, should it go up by 3 per cent or 1 per cent?'.[21]

How, then, might policing budgets be hiked just as the public finances look set to absorb the largest estimated plunge in economic output for 300 years, caused by the coronavirus pandemic of 2020–21? Are there any savings that could be made? What about Scotland Yard's 'extraordinary rank structure' – identified almost thirty years ago by then Home Secretary Ken Clarke? Clarke was worried that many in the police were not out on the streets fighting crime and was critical of the fact that many ranks were little more than pen pushers 'whose main job was to hold the person below them to account for their performance', and whose 'main obligation was to account for their own performance to the people above them, without doing very much else'.[22]

For Clive Driscoll, it is the lower ranks who should be protected, as they do all the work. 'The job is still done by police constables and sergeants, detective constables and detective sergeants,' he said. 'That is who do the job. So at least have the decency to protect them, and allow them to investigate to the best of their ability.'[23]

Sir Richard Henriques, the retired High Court judge whose withering review torpedoed Operation Midland, also believes there are 'far too many' ranks in the Met:

There are five ranks above chief superintendent. In Midland they were all involved. The commissioner, the deputy commissioner, and an assistant commissioner were all receiving reports. There was a deputy assistant commissioner who was very heavily involved, a commander, a chief superintendent, a chief inspector, an inspector, a sergeant and some twenty constables.[24]

Abolishing layers in the Met's top brass would certainly save money. Chief inspectors are paid up to £60,000 a year, superintendents up to £72,000, commanders can get up to £110,000, deputy assistant commissioners take home up to £153,000 and the four assistant commissioners are on around £200,000. Imagine if their salaries were reallocated to more and better-paid constables and sergeants.

One serendipitous consequence of such a move might also be a much-needed boost in police accountability. Henriques says he was infuriated by the rank structure during his review of Operation Midland. Officers at varying levels were all involved in a court application that misled a judge, with disastrous consequences (see Chapter 15). 'In Midland, whilst it was the deputy assistant commissioner who gave authority for the search warrants, it was drafted by an inspector and signed by a chief inspector,' Henriques told me.

The deputy assistant commissioner then played absolutely no part in the process. When the ball looks like it's going to rest with him, he is able to say: 'Well, I had absolutely nothing to do with it. They should have disclosed that, and they shouldn't have done that, but it's nothing to do with me.' It was very difficult to attribute responsibility for the fact that a district judge was misled to any one particular officer.[25]

According to Henriques, Scotland Yard's inter-rank blame game was also a factor in the Jean Charles de Menezes case. In 2007, the Met as a corporate entity was successfully prosecuted over the tragic death of the Brazilian electrician on health and safety grounds. But no individual officer faced censure for the disastrous operation. 'You can't convict a police force of manslaughter and you can't convict a police force of perverting the course of justice,' said Henriques. 'Cressida Dick was grilled in the witness box during the de Menezes prosecution but she was exonerated by the jury, so no other police officer could be prosecuted as they could point to her and say she was in charge.'[26]

The situation inside Scotland Yard is so grave that some are now starting to voice thoughts that were once unthinkable. For Henriques, the Met is perhaps unmanageable now. 'One possibility for consideration is the refinement of the Met, which may be too large to be governable,' he told me. 'It could be broken up into four, with a completely separate force for non-detection duties.'[27]

Yet there are also those who believe that a few modest adjustments would make a world of difference to the Yard, forcing it to return to an era when police officers spent more time managing risk than monitoring stats. But any reforms will be contentious. They would doubtless be resisted by the 'professional police managers'[28] who, according to former Met commander Roy Ramm, currently control Britain's most famous force, and who have 'risen without trace'.[29]

Conclusion

Sir Craig Mackey, the deputy commissioner of the Metropolitan Police, was being driven out of the Palace of Westminster after a ministerial meeting in March 2017 when he heard an 'abnormally loud bang'. The police chief glanced out of the window of his car to see a man wielding a butcher's knife march past him and into the parliamentary grounds. Mackey later recalled that the man 'had one of those looks where, if they get you in that look, they would be after you', adding that he 'was clearly a threat'.[1]

One of Mackey's junior officers, PC Keith Palmer, then confronted the man. The deputy commissioner said his first instinct was to get out and help the unarmed constable defend Parliament. But Mackey and the two civilian members of staff in the car were worried that they had no protective equipment with them. So they locked the doors and drove away.

PC Palmer was repeatedly stabbed by Khalid Masood, an Islamist terrorist, in the attack. Tobias Ellwood, a Foreign Office minister, heard screams and saw people fleeing. Unlike Mackey, the former soldier ran towards the scene, where he would later try to resuscitate the dying policeman. Masood was shot dead by an armed ministerial bodyguard who happened to be loitering near the Carriage Gates in Westminster.

The rage directed at Mackey by the police rank and file was visceral. Hundreds of junior police officers flooded online petitions with angry comments, calling for the deputy commissioner to be sacked and stripped of his knighthood. Many claimed they would be disciplined if they failed to assist a fellow officer under attack. *The Sun* ran a photograph of Mackey under the headline 'Commander Coward'. Mocked-up images of him being presented with a white feather were also circulated online.

In the aftermath of the 2017 Westminster terror attack, every single police source was unanimous. Police officers run towards danger, not away. Police officers always have each other's back. Police officers do not watch another officer being stabbed to death from inside a locked car.

In a *Guardian* column published just after the inquest, Gaby Hinsliff wrote:

> Like First World War soldiers forced to go over the top while their generals sat back safely at headquarters, what apparently most enrages those officers now condemning Mackey is a sense that their own leaders wouldn't do what is asked of them every day, and that perhaps speaks to a more deep-rooted sense of betrayal going back years. It's horribly unfair to call Craig Mackey a coward, particularly from the safety of civilian armchairs. He made what was in all probability the rational decision. But it does not, somehow, look like the decision of a leader.[2]

This view was not shared by Mackey's colleagues on the management board at Scotland Yard, however. Cressida Dick, the Met commissioner, emphasised that the coroner at Masood's inquest found that Mackey had acted properly. The coroner said that the deputy commissioner had acted 'sensibly' and could have done nothing to save Palmer. Mark Lucraft QC said that the officer had already been stabbed before Mackey had realised what was happening. 'What Sir Craig did was sensible and proper, intending to protect others in the car with him. None of them had any way of protecting themselves from the risk of attack,' he said. 'Even if he had got out of the car, it is clear he wouldn't have reached PC Palmer before Masood had inflicted the fatal wounds.'

Following the inquest Dick said that criticism of her deputy was 'confused, unpleasant, personalised and ignorant' and was 'simply not supported by the evidence'. Neil Basu, Britain's top counter-terrorism police officer, added that the backlash had been 'abhorrent'.[3]

The civil war that erupted after the incident neatly sums up the malaise at the heart of Scotland Yard. As we have seen, the once-powerful force has been brought to its knees by soaring crime rates and open warfare with the electorally dominant Conservative Party. The Met's close ties with the press have been shattered, leading to increased scrutiny of corruption and incompetence in murder cases such as Stephen Lawrence and Daniel Morgan, where the police's search for the truth was so limp they seemed deliberately designed to fail. Over the last thirty years Scotland Yard has been exposed for telling so many lies that it sometimes seems as if the aim is to swamp the public in mendacity.

Does the fish rot from the head? Scotland Yard's management is now being openly questioned by those who once led it. Former assistant commissioner Bob Quick, a one-time boss of Cressida Dick, believes that the Met is in a 'bad way'. 'People of my generation, the people who left in the late 2000s when the police were just about still intact, look on at what has happened over the last decade in horror.'

Quick is critical of the silence of chief police officers in the face of savage budget cuts. 'They knew full well that they would result in people losing their lives, and that's exactly what happened in London,' he says. But the moment that really angered him was when the Met's leadership team failed to speak out over Theresa May's controversial attempt to reduce stop-and-search checks. In 2014, the Home Secretary introduced stricter rules which meant police had to prove they had reasonable grounds before carrying out a search. Searches plummeted and violent crime rocketed. The policy was reversed in 2019.

The one that really caught my eye was the silence of people like Cressida [Dick] when Theresa May began to campaign to reduce stop-and-search. She was completely and utterly complicit, certainly on the public face of it, to try and stop it used as a routine tactic. Now, that strikes at the core professional *raison d'être* of policing because any police officer knows that this is a very powerful tool to stop street crime.

The fact the police in about 2015 just withdrew in large numbers, in London in particular, with the apparent support of the commissioner, I just thought: what on earth is going on? And it was so predictable. All the people of my generation were saying 'This is going to end in tears'.

The fact that the police could ever sign up to that was indicative of something that had gone very wrong in the relationship between police and politics. The police have to stand apart and have to be able to speak up and voice their professional advice publicly, about how to keep the streets safe and how to deal with crime. That doesn't seem to happen much any more. These police chiefs have been very silent.[4]

Roy Ramm, the former commander in charge of the Flying Squad, puts it more succinctly: 'Cressida is unique in lots of ways but she's not the first Dick we've had as a commissioner.'

Are these fair criticisms? Sir Paul Stephenson did the job and has the scars on his back to prove it. 'The commissioner of the Met is known as one of, if not *the*, most difficult public sector job in the United Kingdom, and one of the most difficult policing jobs in the world,' he told me. Tim Brain, former chief constable of Gloucestershire, is also sympathetic. 'It's very difficult for senior officers who are closest to national politicians to strike the right balance,' he said.

> It's easy if you are chief constable of Gloucestershire to provide some distance. You are not cheek by jowl with these people. But in order to get some of these top jobs you have to be on message. It doesn't mean you are in cahoots, it doesn't mean you are political allies, it doesn't mean you are a member of their political party, or anything like that. But you have to be speaking, and to a degree thinking, the same kind of thoughts as the politicians who are likely to appoint you.[5]

It seems clear that progress in the Metropolitan Police is dependent on a degree of malleability, an ability to bend to the whim of whoever occupies the Home Office and Downing Street. Even if the policies are disastrous for the police. Some say that is how Cressida Dick got the top job. In 2017, her main rival was Mark Rowley, then in Quick's old job as the assistant commissioner in charge of counter-terrorism. One source involved in the commissioner's appointment told me that the then Home Secretary, Amber Rudd, actually preferred Rowley. But she was concerned that he had 'challenged'

Theresa May, her predecessor, now Prime Minister, too often. Rudd is said to have plumped for Dick in order to please her boss.[6]

Yet if the highest ranks of Scotland Yard are now filled with yes-men and -women, it doesn't seem to be getting them very far. Nick Timothy, May's chief of staff in both the Home Office and later Downing Street, worked with Dick. But even he admits that she was 'best of a bad bunch' and told me:

> The senior ranks of the police are aloof, arrogant and dismissive of accountability. Rather than thinking 'How are we going to cut crime today?', they are thinking 'Have we arrested the right ratio of people based on the diversity of our community?' and 'Which community organisations are being brought into the tent?', rather than doing what [they] are paid for.[7]

Timothy believes that the 'purpose' of the police is to 'cut crime'. 'That is literally their purpose, and they deny it,' he said. 'I don't think you could look at any single chief constable and say "If I wanted to get really tough on crime in a big urban area like London, I would want that person,"' he said. 'Not one of them.'[8]

Jackie Malton, meanwhile, Cressida Dick's mentor, is defensive of her protégée:

> I think she's had the hardest tenure of any other commissioner in history. Everything has been thrown at her, with Brexit, the protests, austerity. She is highly intelligent and politically astute. She is the most articulate commissioner I have ever come across. I would never criticise her for one minute because the police are just political foot-balls with the current government, and have been for some time. She

has the Metropolitan Police running through her veins. She cares so much. She was a quality commissioner, I think she was brilliant.[9]

In July 2022, Mark Rowley, who had lost out in the race for commissioner five years earlier, was appointed as Dick's replacement. He immediately pledged to implement urgent reforms. 'Our mission is to lead the renewal of policing by consent, which has been so heavily dented in recent years as trust and confidence have fallen,' he said. Rowley added that the vast majority of Met staff were dedicated, but he vowed to be 'ruthless in removing those who are corrupting our integrity'.[10]

One simple reform Rowley might consider is to ditch the extraordinary defensiveness. From Stephen Lawrence to Operation Midland, the Met tries to defend the indefensible, arguing against a reality that seems all too clear to others. Blatant lies and cover-ups are counter-productive and sap public confidence in a vital institution. Like many police officers I spoke to in the course of writing this book, former detective chief inspector Clive Driscoll is genuinely upset about the travails of an organisation he still holds in high regard. 'The Met breaks my heart at the moment,' he said. 'It is in a bubble. It doesn't tend to listen to anybody outside. It knows best until it goes horribly pear-shaped, then [it has] to apologise.' Driscoll says that 'people that would normally be 100 per cent behind the police' are worried, yet senior officers 'can't understand why'. 'Someone needs to save the Metropolitan Police Service from itself. Never mind the people that want to attack it. They need to save it from itself.'[11]

Sometimes the defensiveness can cause terrible miscarriages of justice. Sometimes it just makes Met chiefs look foolish. During an interview with the *Radio Times* in 2019, the normally cool-headed Dick was asked about the BBC drama *Line of Duty*, a series depicting widespread corruption, and *Bodyguard*, which featured a sexual relationship between a fictional Home Secretary and her close protection officer. Both were written by the acclaimed screenwriter Jed Mercurio. Dick, so often a consummate media operator, admitted to being 'absolutely outraged by the level of casual and extreme corruption' portrayed in *Line of Duty*. The commissioner added that *Bodyguard* drove everyone at the Met 'absolutely up the wall', adding that 'the moment when the Home Secretary made a pass at the protection officer was just beyond me, I'm afraid'.[12]

Her criticism prompted a pithy tweet from Mercurio: 'My inspiration for creating Line of Duty was @metpoliceuk shooting an innocent man and their dishonesty in the aftermath. So thanks to Cressida Dick for reminding me of our connection.' Mercurio added that *Bodyguard* was based on the story of a Met close protection officer who was dismissed for conducting an affair with the wife of Alan Johnson when he was Home Secretary.

One senior politician who has had political oversight of Scotland Yard admits that the force suffers from a 'God complex'. 'There is a feeling that they think they can't be questioned, they don't like being challenged'.[13] Clive Driscoll cannot understand why his former employer is so intent on dividing the world into groupings of close friends and implacable enemies. 'I have never understood the "anti-police" thing,' he said. 'If people want to criticise the police they should be able to. People have died for that right in this country. We are not a police state and the police aren't above criticism.'[14]

Many are starting to wonder if more detectives with investigative experience should be encouraged to move up the ranks. Shaun Sawyer, a former Met commander who is now chief constable of

Devon and Cornwall, is one of the very few current police leaders to have been a detective. He told me: 'The public expect us to be investigators, and that discipline is currently very thin.'[15] Tony Nash, the former Met borough commander, said:

A lot of the decision makers have not had an investigative background, a CID background. A lot of them have been almost political figures rather than police figures. They are very ambitious, very good public speakers, but not necessarily investigators, and therefore they don't really understand what it actually entails. They could explain it, they can tell you what needs to happen, but they've never actually done it.[16]

Sir Richard Henriques, the retired High Court judge, is equally scathing. 'Some senior officers seem better suited to the world of education, rather than the world of policing.' He said the 'driving force in many police officers' seems to be 'obtaining promotion rather than solving crime'. 'There are some very, very dedicated detectives who would rather be working on their outstanding cases rather than studying for their inspector's exam,' he told me. 'Many detective sergeants have struck me as very high-quality officers who work exceptionally hard and are not apparently interested in promotion. They [are] interested in detective work.' Henriques said the calibre of detective sergeants when measured against 'some very senior police officers' is 'impressive', but this is not reflected in the value placed in them by the organisation. 'The differential in salary between some very senior police officers and detectives who do exceptionally fine work is wholly disproportionate,' he added.[17]

Some may argue the CID has been weakened for good reason. Much of the corruption in the Met outlined in this book radiated from London's detective branch. Efforts to tackle internal criminality, sanctioned by successive commissioners including Sir Robert Mark and Sir Paul Condon, set out to weaken the Yard's elite CID class. But has the pendulum swung too far the other way? 'There were some bad apples but the detectives all got tarred with the same brush,' said Ramm. 'In an organisation the size of the Met there are always going to be some wrong-uns. But what you do as a good manager is you deal with the wrong-uns, you don't throw the baby out with the bathwater.'[18]

Former detective chief inspector David McKelvey believes the issue of corruption has historically been misunderstood by senior officers. 'Some people got greedy. Some got blackmailed. Some got too close to informants and weren't clever enough to work out what was going on [but] it was nowhere near as bad as it was portrayed at the time.

'Informant handling is an extremely difficult area,' said McKelvey, warming to his theme.

> You need robust supervision. You should be able to go to a pub and drink with a villain. But if he turns around and says 'Can you find out A, B, C and D' you should say 'Fuck off and don't ever talk to me like that again'. Or potentially nick him. That's not murky, but all that's gone.

McKelvey said the number of informants now is 'horrifically low'. 'The whole fantastic system of intelligence gathering, and the art of handling, has been completely lost,' he added.[19] Ramm agrees. 'I don't think it is valued today in the same way that it was,' he said. 'I don't see any evidence of police officers having proper local knowledge to tackle even basic crimes.'[20]

Nash believes the government should establish a new 'national detective agency' to retrain an elite band of investigators and drive up standards. 'They need to professionalise it more, he said. 'There need to be formal qualifications. At the moment it is too generic, it should be specific. I don't think the National Crime Agency has got it.'[21]

In his original nine principles of policing, Sir Robert Peel, the founder of the Met, wrote: 'The police are the public and the public are the police.' The power of the police depends on openness, honesty and public consent. Recent commissioners seem to have forgotten these sacred words. For some, the most important change would be for Met chiefs to shelve the ruinous notion that the Yard's reputation takes primacy over all else. Ignore political intrigue. Ignore the media mêlées that blow up from time to time. Instead empower police officers to follow the evidence, without fear or favour. Clive Driscoll now lectures young recruits and is troubled by some of the complaints he hears.

A lot of them say 'Oh, I wouldn't like to do that in case someone says I'm a racist', or this, that and the other. And I say: 'Well, look, if you are honourable and you are following an investigation, who gives a toss what they called you, because at the end of the day that will shine through, that you followed your investigation.'

For Driscoll, the solution is straightforward. 'If you are honest and honourable and do your job, then people will support you.'[22]

Afterword

Sir Mark Rowley did not shirk the challenges facing Scotland Yard when he started work as commissioner in September 2022. The Metropolitan Police was still reeling from the murder of Sarah Everard by PC Wayne Couzens and the Charing Cross police station scandal, in which several groups of officers were found to have exchanged racist, sexist and homophobic messages on social media, leading to the departure of Dame Cressida Dick as commissioner.

Scotland Yard had also faced the ignominy of being placed into special measures by HM Inspectorate of Constabulary (HMIC). In early media appearances as Met commissioner, Rowley sought to make it clear that he understood how low the force had fallen, promising to restore trust and 'root out racists and misogynists'.

Rowley, a maths graduate from Cambridge University, had returned to the Met after four years in the private sector, having lost out to Dick in the race to be commissioner in 2017. In an interview with the flagship BBC Radio 4 *Today* programme in September 2022, Rowley said he wanted to be able to show the public that key progress had been made in his first 100 days. 'We need to be ruthless at rooting out those who are corrupting the integrity of the organisation – the racists and the misogynists,' he said. 'My mission is about more trust, less crime and high standards.'[1] Rowley also acknowledged that rescuing the Met would mean harnessing the 'constructive anger' of its critics and outlined his ambitions to increase levels of 'visible policing'.[2]

Yet the challenges facing Rowley and his beleaguered officers swiftly became apparent.

At the time of writing, Just Stop Oil (JSO), a determined band of eco-activists, have brought chaos to the streets of London over the past twelve months. By blocking and supergluing themselves to key roads across the teeming UK capital, the protesters hope to put pressure on the government to halt all licences for the exploration, development and production of new oil, gas and coal projects.

The activists have repeatedly shut down the M25 and other major roads. Some of their controversial disruptions have blocked fire engines and ambulances responding to emergencies.[3] The Scotland Yard response to Just Stop Oil has come in for severe criticism. Rowley told his officers that they had to wait until the protests met a legal threshold of causing 'major disruption' before they could be shut down. As a result, police officers have been filmed on smartphones standing around watching as protesters block the roads, causing serious frustration among motorists. The lack of police action has led to many cases where members of the public have taken matters into their own hands, dragging the protesters off the road to allow traffic to flow freely.

One incident in October 2022 saw JSO activists block the Mall near Buckingham Palace to object to new fracking licences proposed by then Prime Minister Liz Truss. They managed to shut down the road for around two hours before police officers finally intervened.

During the delay, Charlotte Lynch, a journalist from LBC Radio who was covering the protest, reported hearing one police officer offering to buy coffee for the activists.* Her report led Nick Ferrari, the host of LBC's popular breakfast programme and a respected commentator on policing, to lose his rag. 'These are cops that couldn't nick themselves shaving, they're so hopeless,' he told millions of listeners.

> Why are they in the job? Utterly incompetent. Two weeks ago, one woman sent a couple of offensive messages on Twitter, she was arrested in front of her five children and taken down to a police station for eight hours. Here we have twenty-five herberts who closed down a part of London, people can't go and do their job, possibly go to hospital, make appointments, see loved ones, whatever it might be, and the police say, 'Can we get you a cup of coffee?'[4]

Scotland Yard's light-touch approach to the JSO demonstrations has been questioned by many policing experts. David McKelvey, one of the Met's leading former detectives, told me that there are already several obvious criminal offences on the statute book that could easily be used against the protesters, including the Highways Act 1980, which states that a person cannot 'wilfully obstruct the free passage along a highway' and a police officer 'may arrest without warrant any person whom he sees committing an offence against this section'.[5]

'The JSO protests are yet more evidence of the collapse in standards inside the Met,' McKelvey told me.

---

* Charlotte Lynch was later arrested by Hertfordshire Police officers for covering another JSO protest on the M25. She was detained for five hours before being released without charge. The incident sparked national concern and led to an intervention from the Prime Minister, whose spokesperson told reporters: 'It's vital journalists are able to do their job freely without restriction.' The government later brought in a new amendment to the Public Order Bill offering special protections for journalists covering protests.

There are very few people inside the force who know what criminal offences can apply to specific situations. The recent disruption across London could have been nipped in the bud if more Met Police officers were competent and actually knew what they are supposed to be doing. But with all the problems in recent years, too many are now scared of their own shadows.[6]

Additionally, in July 2023, the unsolved case of Daniel Morgan, the private investigator murdered in 1987 amid alleged links to police corruption, once again reared its ugly head. Mark Rowley announced that the force had reached a £2 million settlement with Morgan's family, admitting liability for a 'cycle of corruption and incompetence' that mired the investigations into his killing. The payout is one of the largest in British policing history. In a statement, Rowley said:

I unequivocally and unreservedly apologise for the failure of the Metropolitan Police Service to bring those responsible for the murder of Daniel Morgan to justice. From the earliest stages, his family have been repeatedly and inexcusably let down by the Metropolitan Police … Daniel Morgan's family were given empty promises and false hope as successive investigations failed and the Metropolitan Police prioritised its reputation at the expense of transparency and effectiveness.

Since the publication of the *Broken Yard* hardback edition in October 2022, however, the problems for Scotland Yard have only deepened.

* * *

PC David Carrick joined the Metropolitan Police in 2001. Yet even before his job application was accepted, there had been warning signs of what he would become. Carrick had been reported to the force over an alleged burglary at his ex-girlfriend's home. After this, the same partner reported him for alleged abusive and aggressive phone calls. No action was taken. Instead, he passed the Met's vetting system and joined the force as a response officer in Merton, south-west London. Shortly after joining the Met, it was alleged that Carrick had harassed and assaulted another ex-girlfriend, but senior officers did nothing.

The power afforded to Carrick as a police officer seemed to have a notable effect. Over the next twenty years, he embarked on a horrific sex-crime spree, committing eighty-five serious offences, including forty-eight rapes alongside sexual assaults, false imprisonments and occasions of coercive and controlling behaviour. As ever, the Met ignored multiple chances to catch Carrick, who in 2009 was promoted to the parliamentary and diplomatic protection command, an elite firearms unit that guards embassies, Downing Street and the Houses of Parliament. He was finally arrested in 2021 after multiple female victims were moved to come forward by the case of Sarah Everard, the young woman who was raped and murdered by Wayne Couzens, another Met Police officer. As detectives investigated the allegations against Carrick for the first time, they became 'staggered' at the extent of his crimes.

The constable had often lured his unsuspecting victims by flashing his warrant card and reassuring them that they were safe because he was a police officer. Carrick's first known rape took place in 2003. He invited a twenty-year-old woman to his flat on the pretext of attending a housewarming party. She arrived to find an empty flat. The victim was held for hours against her will; her ordeal included having a gun put to her head. It was nearly twenty years before the victim felt she had the courage to go to the police.

Another Carrick victim was a female police officer. During the later trial, she recalled attending Carrick's flat and consenting to sex. However, the policeman then anally raped her. She reported the rape in 2021, saying she was ashamed of not having done so sooner.

According to prosecutors, any woman who crossed Carrick's path was a target, including girlfriends, long-term partners, schoolfriends and total strangers. He met some victims on dating apps such as Tinder and others at social events. Carrick imprisoned some of his victims in a small downstairs cupboard at his home in Stevenage, Hertfordshire. After he carried out the violent rapes and submitted his victims to degrading acts, Carrick warned the women it would be useless to report him to the authorities as no one would believe them. Police-issue handcuffs were used to restrain some of his victims. He even sent a photo of his police gun to another, warning her: 'Remember I'm the boss.'

Carrick's abusive nature did not go undetected at the Met – colleagues nicknamed him 'Bastard Dave'. After his trial, Carrick's former schoolfriend told *The Guardian* that he fell out with Carrick because he took advantage of the power his position gave him and 'treated women like crap'. He said:

When we were younger I thought he was a cool lad. A lot of people liked him. He was one of those lads who was good at everything – I think he had good grades and he was very much a sports person. He was very popular with the women, he was a good-looking lad, he was a fit lad.

The pair lost touch after school but reconnected in 2008.

Quite quickly, I saw things I didn't like. He drank a lot and he was out of control. He could be quite nasty. He would use his being in the police and he would use his power to get his way. He would start arguments and then say he's in the police and throw his weight around a little bit too much. So I used to say to him: 'Look, Dave, you can't be doing that, you're a police officer.'[7]

In February 2023, Carrick was jailed for thirty-two years. Mrs Justice Cheema-Grubb, the judge who ordered Carrick to appear in person for sentencing, was disgusted with him and did not hold back. 'You behaved as if you were untouchable,' she said. 'You were bold and at times relentless, trusting that no victim would overcome her shame and fear to report you. For nearly two decades you were proved right.'[8] She said Carrick had taken 'monstrous advantage' of his position as a police officer, which gave him 'exceptional powers to coerce and control', with which he had caused 'irretrievable devastation'. Of the victims, Cheema-Grubb said: 'These women are not weak or ineffectual. They were victims of your criminal mindset. The malign influence of men like you in positions of power stands in the way of a revolution of women's dignity.'[9]

Cheema-Grubb identified Carrick's position as a police officer as an exacerbating factor: 'This violent sexual offending against women commenced almost immediately after you became a police constable, and you referred to your job when offending.'[10]

The sentencing hearing heard emotional victim testimony. One woman described him as 'evil'. Others said he had destroyed their lives. One victim said that Carrick was a sex addict and alcoholic, telling the court how he started drinking early in the morning after returning home from night shifts guarding Westminster VIPs. She said his house was full of pornography and that his sexual tastes became ever-more twisted and brutal. 'Sex became really violent,' she said. 'He wanted me to be the same as a prostitute but I didn't want to do this kind of stuff … I didn't accept it and that's when the fights started.'

She claimed that if she refused his advances, Carrick would become violent, often throwing her out of his bed and strangling her. On one occasion, she said that he tried to force her to drink his urine. 'We had a really bad fight because he wanted me to do that,' she said. Beginning to sob, she added: 'One time he made me do it. We were having a shower together. You say no and he forces you. He forces you. You want to get away from that situation but you can't. It's awful.'[11]

The survivors had a powerful effect on the judge. Addressing Carrick at his sentencing, Cheema-Grubb said:

> There is powerful and compelling evidence of irretrievable devasta-
> tion in the lives of those you abused. Denial, anger, hatred, betrayal,
> shame, self-blame and fear of being labelled a victim are common
> emotions. You have shaped their lives, deprived them of the ability
> to trust men and form relationships. Some have damaged mental
> health and suffer loneliness. They continue to question their own
> judgement. They don't trust the police.

The national horror at Carrick's behaviour came hot on the heels of the depravity exhibited by PC Wayne Couzens, the murderer of Sarah Everard. The revelations prompted another wave of senior officer soul-searching, hand-wringing and pledges to reform the broken force.

After Carrick was jailed, Suella Braverman, the Home Secretary, said his crimes were a 'scar on our police', adding: 'There is no place in our police for such heinous and predatory behaviour.'[12]

Sir Mark Rowley, the Met commissioner, described Carrick as 'evil' and recognised the terrible further damage inflicted on Britain's largest police force. 'He exploited his position as a police officer in the most disgusting way,' said Rowley.

We weren't rigorous enough in our approach and as a result we missed opportunities to identify the warning signs over decades. I and tens of thousands of officers and staff in the Met are horrified by this man's crimes and recognise this will shake Londoners' trust too. We have let down women across London but we are more determined than ever to put it right.[13]

Since Carrick's sentencing, another five women have come forward with further allegations, and police are now investigating an alleged sex attack when he was thirteen.[14] Scotland Yard is now reviewing 1,000 domestic and sexual abuse claims involving around 800 of the Met's 45,000 officers and staff.

After the trial, Carrick's friend told *The Guardian* he was disturbed that he was free to perpetrate almost two decades of abuse. 'I just don't know how the police missed all this,' he said. 'I used to say to David: "How did you become a police officer, and how did you get to where you are, and still act the way you're doing?" And he would just smile.'[15]

* * *

Just one month after Carrick's sentencing, Scotland Yard's reputation was sullied further by yet another cataclysmic disaster.

Twenty-four years after a damning report by Sir William

Macpherson changed the public perception of the Met for ever, another review commissioned as a result of the Sarah Everard murder concluded that the force was institutionally racist, sexist and homophobic. The author, Dame Louise Casey, confirmed many of the findings of this book, uncovering an organisation with a rotten culture, festering with delusion, denial and hubris. She also said that the Met should accept the findings of the Daniel Morgan independent panel two years earlier, which had concluded that Scotland Yard was institutionally corrupt.[16]

Dragging the institution deeper into the mire, Casey said that the Met had discrimination 'baked' into it, found it to be failing women and children, said it was unable to police itself and concluded that public confidence in the force had been destroyed.

The review found that the 'de-prioritisation and de-specialisation' of public protection – in areas like child protection, rape and serious sexual offences – had 'put women and children at greater risk than necessary'. Casey, a straight-talking civil servant, said that officers investigating rape and serious sexual offences had to deal with 'over-stuffed, dilapidated or broken' fridges and freezers containing evidence, ensuring lengthy waits for results.[17] She spoke with one trainee police officer in Brixton, south London, who was handling thirty-one live rape cases. Casey was even told that the rape detection rate was so low that 'you may as well say it is legal'.[18]

Successive governments had asked the Whitehall veteran to examine tricky problems in the field of social affairs. She advised Tony Blair on homelessness, established a 'troubled families' unit for David Cameron and worked on the difficult issue of integration for Theresa May. But in an interview with *The Times* after her report was published, Casey admitted that the Met was by far the hardest job of all. 'The level of delusion in this building, I don't know what happens when they come through the front door and they get into the lift,' she said. 'It's like they're drunk on House Met, they can't see anything outside. And these are potentially good people.'[19] Casey said that Scotland Yard police officers have a 'sort of God-given belief that everything they do is right'.

'Out here in the world of reality, as opposed to the seventh floor with the House Met being drunk daily on how fantastic everything is, all of these people were just left to the side,' she told *The Times*. 'If it wasn't horrific it would be an Armando Iannucci comedy. But it's just not funny.'

In her report on the Met, one of its most damning assessments in its near-200-year history, Casey identified widespread bullying across the force. For instance, one Sikh officer had his beard trimmed because another officer thought it was funny. In another example, an officer's turban was hidden in a shoebox. In an instance of what can be described only as childish cruelty, a Muslim officer found bacon had been put in his boots. He was 'horrified' but chose not to tell anyone in case he was punished by his fellow officers. Some female officers reported being forced to eat whole cheesecakes until they threw up.[20] One officer quoted in the report told Casey: 'I am scared of the police. I don't trust my own organisation.'[21]

Casey was shocked at the 'anything goes' approach to misconduct, concluding that the 'system as a whole does not hold or deliver real consequences where failures persist'.[22]

In one of the few glimmers of hope, Casey said she was pleased with the new management team of Sir Mark Rowley and his deputy, Dame Lynne Owens. 'They're light years away in terms of leadership, their instincts around how to talk to their people, their ability,' she told *The Times* after her report was published. Casey said it was her confidence in the two top officers that led her to pull back from calling for the Met to be broken up – a recommendation made earlier on these pages by Sir Richard Henriques, the retired judge who reviewed the disastrous Operation Midland.

Yet even this silver lining evaporated as Scotland Yard's toxic culture of denial came into sharp contact with reality. Casey was disappointed to see Rowley reject the finding of 'institutional racism' as soon as her report was released. Rowley called the term 'institutional' political and ambiguous, but Casey rejects this argument. She believes that it amounts to a shirking of responsibility and told *The Times* that it is 'crucial to acknowledge [the findings of her report] to signal the change that is needed'.

Casey voiced concerns that Rowley had committed a potentially fatal error in his short tenure as commissioner. 'He potentially has missed his moment and I worry for him and I worry for that,' she said. Questions about Rowley's ability to confront the Met and enforce the change that is needed are starting to mount. Political aides to Suella Braverman have been known to proactively call journalists covering Scotland Yard, assuring them that the commissioner has the Home Secretary's full support. Like the football managers famously given the dreaded public vote of confidence by club chairmen before getting the sack, this is never a particularly positive sign.

When he was appointed, Rowley was depicted by the government as a new broom, coming into the broken force to sweep up the mess left by his predecessor, Cressida Dick. But that analysis fails to take account of the fact that the commissioner worked as the third-most senior Metropolitan Police officer from 2011 until he left in 2018. For seven years, Rowley worked in the hugely influential role known as ACSO – assistant commissioner for specialist operations. As we have seen, this period played host to some of the Met's most damaging episodes, including unprecedented uplifts in violent crime, continuing cover-ups regarding the murders of Stephen Lawrence and Daniel Morgan, the disastrous Operation Midland and an effective doubling of the crime rate once fraud and computer misuse offences were included in the official figures from the Office for National Statistics.

For some Met insiders, it is simply not credible to position Rowley as a reformer willing to take on the toxic culture inside the force. 'How on earth can Mark Rowley be labelled as a white knight? The man who is going to come into the Met and sort everything out?' said David McKelvey. 'As ACSO he was basically Britain's leading investigator when all this horror unfolded. He was in that role for seven years. Seven years! What did he do in that time? Nothing. All the old problems inside the Yard were left to fester.'

* * *

Former detective sergeant Bernadette Murray is still scarred by her experience with Mark Rowley. A former officer in the Met's elite Flying Squad, the famous branch of the Serious and Organised Crime Command charged with investigating armed robberies, Murray worked on some of Britain's most dangerous and high-profile cases during the 1990s and 2000s. Graduating from the Met's detective training school in Hendon at a time when the institution demanded high standards, Murray combines Machiavellian charm with a forensic eye and, unlike many of her colleagues, a total dedication to the prevention and detection of crime.

In 2010, Murray was transferred to the borough of Haringey in north London to deal with the fallout from the murder of 'Baby P', a Metropolitan Police case that had prompted yet another national outcry.

In August 2007, Peter Connelly, who was known to the public as 'Baby P', died at the hands of his mother Tracey Connelly, her boyfriend Steven Barker and Barker's brother Jason Owen. He suffered more than fifty injuries, which included a snapped spine and eight broken ribs, despite being on the at-risk register and receiving sixty visits from social workers, police and health professionals over the final eight months of his life.

A series of reviews identified missed opportunities for officials to save the toddler's life had they reacted properly to warning signs. Three of Connelly's children, including Peter, were on Haringey's child protection register because of fears they were being neglected. Connelly's lover Steven Barker was jailed in 2009 for a minimum of thirty-two years for torturing the seventeen-month-old to death and, in a separate case, raping a two-year-old girl, while his brother, Jason Owen, received a six-year jail sentence for allowing the toddler to die. Connelly, who covered up the abuse of her son, was jailed in 2009 for a minimum of five years after admitting causing or allowing Peter's death.

The disturbing case shocked the nation, leading to searching questions in Parliament and the sacking of Sharon Shoesmith, head of Haringey Children's Social Care Services. At Scotland Yard, one of the responses was the establishment of a proactive team headed by Murray, whose aim was to prevent the abuse and harm of vulnerable children through intensive risk assessment.

Whenever a child dies in such appalling circumstances, later reviews often conclude that police and other state agencies such as social services held more than enough information to have acted sooner.

The most famous case was the death of Victoria Climbié, an eight-year-old girl who was born in the Ivory Coast before moving to London. She was tortured and murdered by her great-aunt and her great-aunt's boyfriend in 2000. The troubling circumstances of her death led to a public inquiry and produced major changes in child protection policies in the United Kingdom. Lord Laming, who chaired the inquiry, found that the Met, the social services departments of four local authorities, the National Health Service, the National Society for the Prevention of Cruelty to Children (NSPCC) and several local churches all had contact with Victoria and had all noticed indications that she was being abused. However, all failed to properly investigate the case and little action was taken. The failures were described as 'blinding incompetence' by the judge in the trial following Victoria's death.

Seven years later, the same failings had led to the death of Baby P. When Murray was transferred to Haringey to get to the bottom of what went wrong, her keen investigator's eye quickly identified that very few police officers understood the bewildering array of separate databases that held potentially crucial intelligence on vulnerable children. Not only that but, according to Murray, almost nobody seemed particularly interested in correcting this damaging state of affairs. When the dedicated detective, who was one of very few to have access to all the databases, started pointing out the internal failings, she claims she was given short shrift by more senior officers who did not seem to care. 'Child protection officers refused to work together in the collation of identified risk and refused to enter police intelligence on to the police intelligence system, despite being ordered to do so,' Murray told me. 'Therefore, information was not shared with other police services across the country and Europe. The senior management team also prevented pertinent life-saving information, meticulously documented by frontline officers, from being uploaded on to the national police database.'[23]

Murray claims her protestations were starting to annoy the top brass and she was warned that she would lose her job if she continued to speak out. The senior management team totally misread their colleague. The warning only made her more determined to expose the truth. Murray prepared a sixty-page dossier for the Met's anti-corruption command. The document contained multiple incidents where she believed that officers had allegedly failed or refused to investigate crimes of child abuse and serious sexual assaults. She told me:

> Children had died, serious case reviews were misled, crime reports were altered, victims' dates of birth and names were intentionally removed or changed, suspects' details were collated in the wrong area so they were lost or hidden, which tainted the data and hid the truth. This corrupted search results for the police across the UK and Europe.[24]

Murray was particularly concerned with the bizarre decision by senior officers to restrict wider police access to troubling information regarding a two-year-old girl in Tottenham. In January 2012, the infant had been found on the kerb several hundred yards from her home by a member of the public, who had alerted the police. The case eventually landed on Murray's desk. She claims she undertook a series of painstaking searches through the many databases that other colleagues did not understand nor seem interested in understanding. Following her enquiries, Murray became very concerned about the safety of the toddler. However, other officers refused to record or investigate the case for potential neglect and child-trafficking offences. Astonishingly, Murray claims that senior officers then decided to restrict access or 'lock' the CRIS (crime reporting information system) report detailing the lack of police action – a move that would prevent others later being able to show that they failed to act.[25] CRIS is a system used to record all allegations of crime and the important details of any criminal investigation. It is mandatory for all Met Police officers to record allegations of crime that they receive on the CRIS, which is then used to inform Home Office crime statistics. If a CRIS entry is restricted or locked, the record can be viewed only by officers above the rank of detective chief inspector. Murray says a CRIS entry is locked only on 'very rare occasions', usually to prevent internal leaks from sensitive police investigations, for example, inquiries into VIPs or allegations of police corruption. Murray told me it was 'unheard of' to lock a CRIS in relation to alleged abuse of a two-year-old girl.

In total, Murray reported over sixty cases of concern, only to find out that she and her frontline colleagues had been locked out of the relevant CRIS reports to prevent wider access. She believes this was a systematic attempt to cover up the Met's failure to protect vulnerable children.[26]

Murray claims that the matter was raised all the way up to the then commissioner, Sir Bernard Hogan-Howe. In June 2012, Hogan-Howe emailed Murray directly and said: 'You raise some very serious issues. I will ask ACSO Mark Rowley to look into this matter urgently.'

Two months later, Murray received a letter from the future Met commissioner. Rowley said he had concluded that child protection officers were 'complying with MPS policies' and were 'working professionally to safeguard children'.

'I do not accept that locking a CRIS is a dangerous practice,' he went on. 'The caveat is of course that a CRIS should only be locked in appropriate circumstances and that checks and balances are in place through robust supervision, when such action becomes necessary. I'm satisfied that officers have acted appropriately.'[27]

To this day, Murray remains furious at Rowley's decision. 'His letter in 2012 authorised the "locking up" of details of police investigations to hide police failures,' she told me.

> The consequence of corrupting police criminal investigation reports is that since at least 2012 the Met may have misled all Serious Case Reviews, coroners' courts, criminal courts, MOPAC [Mayor's Office for Police and Crime], the Independent Office for Police Conduct and Her Majesty's Inspectorate of Constabulary [HMIC]. Investigators and frontline police officers must have been prevented from establishing the facts in cases of domestic violence, rape and murder. Analysts are preparing reports based on tainted data. The HMIC cannot inspect an investigation that is hidden and therefore no longer exists. The detectives cannot arrest a suspect who has never existed according to their own information and intelligence systems.[28]

Despite Rowley's decision, Murray would not stay quiet. She continued to raise internal failings of the safeguarding system across the Met. Murray claims she was repeatedly told to 'shut up', was spat at and was transferred around the force a further seven times. She finally retired in February 2017 after thirty-two years in the force, thirty of which were spent as an elite detective.

Despite the Met's apparent attempt to bury dark secrets, the question of exactly what safeguarding data was available to HMIC, the police watchdog, still remained of concern. In 2021, it published a damning report about the Met, which found 'fundamental and widespread deficiencies in the way the force understood and dealt with the needs of and risks to children'. HMIC concluded that 'children were being adversely affected'.[29]

Despite the damning findings, Murray said the watchdog had no idea of the gravity of the threat to children. 'You cannot inspect what you cannot see,' she told me.

Murray attributes many of the failings to the current commissioner. She told me:

In 2012, Mark Rowley should have asked for a full investigation into the allegations I had documented. I provided facts and details of corrupt senior police officers, violent dangerous suspects and innocent child victims of crime. Rowley had the opportunity to establish the facts and put an end to the corruption. He had a choice, and he chose to shut me down. The HMIC report supported everything I had uncovered. Imagine my disgust when I realised that this man was to be re-employed as commissioner, charged with tackling the same sort of failings he had previously covered up. I fear for the future of Scotland Yard and for Londoners under his leadership.[30]

Acknowledgements

Broken *Yard* would not have been possible without my agent, Martin Redfern. I had tried and failed to write a book about the Metropolitan Police for years, and it did not take shape until Martin sat me down and brought order to my cluttered thoughts.

A book of this nature would never get into print without a courageous publisher. I am very grateful to Olivia Beattie and her team at Biteback.

The events of this book span several decades. Some occurred before I was born; the murders of Daniel Morgan and Stephen Lawrence happened when I was still at primary school. As a result, several fine journalists have already examined these cases and I was grateful to draw upon their work, in addition to my own enquiries.

Recommended further reading includes *Untouchables* and *Legacy* by Michael Gillard, *Hack Attack* by Nick Davies, which details the phone hacking scandal, and *Who Killed Daniel Morgan?*, a definitive take on the terrible murder, co-authored by Alastair Morgan, brother of the victim. The tireless pursuit of justice displayed by Alastair and other grieving relatives such as Doreen and Neville Lawrence has been humbling to report on.

Other heroes detailed in these pages have also produced their own versions of events. Clive Driscoll, the detective whose team caught the killers of Stephen Lawrence, has written *In Pursuit of the Truth*, a wonderful book about the case. And Duwayne Brooks, the surviving victim of the racist attack on Stephen, has also written movingly of his experiences in *Steve and Me*.

Broken Yard has also benefited from the skilled reporting of superb crime correspondents including Sean O'Neill and Fiona Hamilton of *The Times*, Vikram Dodd of *The Guardian*, Mark Daly of the BBC, and Stephen Wright and Richard Pendlebury of the *Daily Mail*.

I have also learnt so much from amazing journalists throughout my newspaper career. They are too numerous to mention, but special thanks must go to James Mellor, Jonathan Wynne-Jones, Andrew Alderson, Ian Gallagher, Dennis Rice, Daniel Boffey, Amy Iggulden, Dan Gledhill, Charles Hymas, Nick Hellen, Dipesh Gadher, Jonathan Ungoed-Thomas, Mark Hookham, Jonathan Leake, Tony Allen-Mills, Tim Rayment and James Gillespie.

Broken Yard would not have been possible without its sources. A few brave souls have stuck their heads above the parapet and been prepared to be honest about the problems facing the Metropolitan Police. They include Frank Matthews, Bob Quick, Brian Paddick, Ian Hurst, Peter Tickner and David McKelvey. It is a shame that many who contributed to this book cannot be heralded, but that is the nature of the beast.

Finally, a huge thanks to my late parents, who imbued me with an unquenchable thirst for curiosity; to my sister Alice, for her lifelong support; and to my partner Caroline, a constant source of inspiration and delight.

No book belongs to the author. The stories and ideas are the results of collective endeavour and generosity. Needless to say, however, any remaining errors are all mine.

About the Author

Tom Harper is a multi-award-winning investigative journalist. His honours include Scoop of the Year and Young Journalist of the Year at the British Press Awards. Tom has also been nominated as Specialist Journalist of the Year, News Reporter of the Year and Crime and Legal Affairs Journalist of the Year at the British Journalism Awards. He has held senior roles at a number of national newspapers, including *The Independent* and the *Sunday Times*.

Notes

Introduction

1. Crime in England and Wales: year ending March 2020, Office for National Statistics
2. Year ending March 2020
3. Crime in England and Wales: year ending March 2020, Office for National Statistics
4. Ibid.
5. *The Sun*, 16 October 2017
6. Confidential documents seen by author
7. *The Sun*, 15 July 2021
8. *The Times*, 14 July 2021
9. John Sutherland, *Blue: Keeping the Peace and Falling to Pieces* (Weidenfeld & Nicolson, 2017)
10. *Evening Standard*, 20 February 2019
11. *The Times*, 1 October 2018
12. BBC Radio 4, *The Tories and the Police: The End of the Affair* (2014)
13. Ron Evans, *On Her Majesty's Service* (John Blake, 2008)
14. Ibid.
15. *Washington Post*, 7 March 1981
16. Ibid.
17. *The Observer*, 2 April 1994
18. Graeme McLagan, *Bent Coppers: The Inside Story of Scotland Yard's Battle against Police Corruption* (Weidenfeld & Nicolson, 2003)
19. *The Guardian*, 19 August 2018
20. McLagan, *Bent Coppers*
21. 'Cleaning Up the Yard', *World in Action*, ITV, 2 August 1982
22. Ibid.
23. Ibid.
24. Peter Walsh, *Drug War: The Secret History* (Milo, 2018)
25. Ibid.
26. Andrew Jennings, Paul Lashmar and Vyv Simson, *Scotland Yard's Cocaine Connection* (Jonathan Cape, 1990)
27. Walsh, *Drug War*
28. Jennings et al., *Scotland Yard's Cocaine Connection*
29. Ibid.
30. Ibid.
31. Andrew Jennings/YouTube, 19 May 2009, https://www.youtu.be/i7EoydCfziE (accessed 30 June 2022)

Chapter 1: The Snowball

1. Macpherson report
2. Clive Driscoll, *In Pursuit of the Truth: My Life Cracking the Met's Most Notorious Cases* (Ebury Press, 2015)
3. Duwayne Brooks, *Steve and Me: My Friendship with Stephen Lawrence and the Search for Justice* (Abacus, 2003)
4. Macpherson report
5. Driscoll, *In Pursuit of the Truth*
6. Macpherson report

7. Driscoll, *In Pursuit of the Truth*
8. Author interview
9. Author interview
10. *The Independent*, 21 July 1993
11. Ibid.
12. BBC Radio 4, *The Tories and the Police: The End of the Affair* (2014)
13. Ron Evans, *On Her Majesty's Service* (John Blake, 2008)
14. BBC Radio 4, *The Tories and the Police: The End of the Affair* (2014)
15. BBC One, *Stephen: The Murder That Changed a Nation* (17–19 April 2018)
16. BBC One, *Panorama*, 'Stephen Lawrence: Time for Justice' (3 January 2012)
17. *The Independent*, 4 January 2012
18. Ibid.
19. Driscoll, *In Pursuit of the Truth*
20. Macpherson report
21. BBC One, *Stephen: The Murder That Changed a Nation* (17–19 April 2018)
22. *The Independent*, 25 March 1998
23. Driscoll, *In Pursuit of the Truth*
24. Macpherson report
25. Brooks, *Steve and Me*
26. Macpherson report
27. BBC One, *Stephen: The Murder That Changed a Nation* (17–19 April 2018)
28. Ibid.
29. *gal-dem*, 15 August 2018, https://gal-dem.com/treasured-moment-doreen-lawrence-nelson-mandela/ (accessed 30 June 2022)
30. *The Guardian*, 7 May 1993
31. Macpherson report
32. Ibid.
33. Brooks, *Steve and Me*
34. Evans, *On Her Majesty's Service*
35. Ibid.
36. Macpherson report
37. BBC One, *Stephen: The Murder That Changed a Nation* (17–19 April 2018)
38. Macpherson report
39. *The Independent*, 16 June 1998
40. BBC One, *Stephen: The Murder That Changed a Nation* (17–19 April 2018)
41. Police document seen by author
42. Witness statement of Duwayne Brooks, Ellison report
43. Macpherson report
44. Michael Gillard, *Untouchables: Dirty Cops, Bent Justice and Racism in Scotland Yard* (Bloomsbury, 2012)
45. Macpherson report
46. Brooks, *Steve and Me*
47. Macpherson report
48. Author interview
49. Neil Woods and J. S. Rafaeli, *Drug Wars: The Terrifying Inside Story of Britain's Drug Trade* (Ebury Press, 2018)
50. *The Times*, 12 February 1997
51. *The Independent*, 12 February 1997
52. Macpherson report
53. BBC One, *Stephen: The Murder That Changed a Nation* (17–19 April 2018)
54. Ibid.
55. Ibid.
56. *Daily Mail*, 14 February 1997
57. BBC One, *Stephen: The Murder That Changed a Nation* (17–19 April 2018)
58. Ibid.
59. Norman Dennis, George Erdos and Ahmed al-Shahi, *Racist Murder and Pressure Group Politics* (Institute for the Study of Civil Society, 2000)
60. Driscoll, *In Pursuit of the Truth*
61. Ibid.
62. *The Independent*, 25 March 1998
63. Macpherson report
64. Ibid.
65. Ellison report

66. Macpherson report, 9.7–9.22
67. Ibid.
68. Ibid.
69. Ibid.
70. Ibid.
71. Ibid., p. 230
72. Gillard, *Untouchables*
73. Ibid.
74. Macpherson report
75. Graeme McLagan, *Bent Coppers: The Inside Story of Scotland Yard's Battle against Police Corruption* (Weidenfeld & Nicolson, 2003)
76. Gillard, *Untouchables*
77. Ibid.
78. Macpherson report
79. Ibid.
80. BBC News, 5 May 2004
81. Macpherson report
82. Brooks, *Steve and Me*
83. Ibid.

Chapter 2: Infiltration

1. Operation Tiberius report
2. Ibid.
3. *Daily Mirror*, 17 November 2017
4. UnsolvedMurders, http://www.unsolved-murders.co.uk/murder-content.php?key=2794&termRef=Michael%20per%20cent20Olymbius (accessed 1 July 2022)
5. Operation Tiberius report
6. Ibid.
7. Ibid.
8. Author interviews with confidential sources
9. Ellison report, p. 103
10. Ibid., p. 105
11. Ibid., p. 105
12. Ibid., p. 105
13. Graeme McLagan, *Bent Coppers: The Inside Story of Scotland Yard's Battle against Police Corruption* (Weidenfeld & Nicolson, 2003)
14. Ellison report, p. 106
15. Ibid.
16. Ibid., p. 107
17. Ibid., p. 107
18. Ibid., p. 108
19. Ibid., p. 107
20. BBC One, *Panorama*, 'Cops, Criminals, Corruption: The Inside Story' (29 February 2016)
21. *Daily Mirror*, 17 November 2017
22. *Daily Mail*, 25 February 2019
23. Operation Tiberius report
24. Ibid.
25. 'Tackling Drugs Together', UK Government White Paper, 10 May 1995. HMCE would later be folded into the Serious Organised Crime Agency, and then the National Crime Agency, with disastrous results.
26. *Financial Times*, 3 July 2010
27. Author interview
28. Peter Walsh, *Drug War: The Secret History* (Milo, 2018)
29. Ibid.
30. Peter Tickner Associates, www.petertickner.co.uk (accessed 1 July 2022)
31. Author interview
32. Author interview
33. Author interview
34. *Esquire*, September 1995
35. Ibid.
36. Author interview
37. Author interview

38. Author interview
39. Author interview
40. Author interview
41. BBC One, *Panorama*, 'Cops, Criminals, Corruption: The Inside Story' (29 February 2016)
42. Author interview with confidential source
43. Ellison report
44. BBC One, *Panorama*, 'Cops, Criminals, Corruption: The Inside Story' (29 February 2016)
45. Ibid.
46. Author interview
47. Court papers reviewed by author
48. Court papers reviewed by author
49. Court papers reviewed by author
50. Neil Woods and J. S. Rafaeli, *Drug Wars: The Terrifying Inside Story of Britain's Drug Trade* (Ebury Press, 2018)
51. Report by the United Nations Office on Drugs and Crime, 18 October 1999
52. *Sunday Times*, 17 April 1994
53. Ibid.
54. *The Independent*, 9 October 1997
55. Walsh, *Drug War*
56. Author interview
57. Author interview
58. Author interview
59. Author interview
60. Author interview
61. Author interview
62. Author interview
63. Author interview
64. Operation Tiberius report
65. Ibid.
66. Ibid.
67. Peacock Gym, www.peacockgym.com
68. Ibid.
69. Ibid.
70. Operation Tiberius report
71. Ibid.
72. Ibid.
73. BBC News, 16 October 2004
74. Author interview with confidential source

Chapter 3: Axe in the Head

1. Daniel Morgan independent panel report, vol. 1, p. 422
2. Nick Davies, *Hack Attack: How the Truth Caught Up with Rupert Murdoch* (Chatto & Windus, 2014)
3. Confidential documents seen by author
4. Author interview
5. Channel 4, *Murder in the Car Park* (15 June 2020)
6. Ibid.
7. Ibid.
8. Ibid.
9. Ibid.
10. Alistair Morgan and Peter Jukes, *Who Killed Daniel Morgan?* (Blink, 2018)
11. Ibid.
12. *Daily Mail*, 29 March 2014
13. Ibid.
14. Channel 4, *Murder in the Car Park* (15 June 2020)
15. Morgan and Jukes, *Who Killed Daniel Morgan?*
16. Michael Gillard, *Untouchables: Dirty Cops, Bent Justice and Racism in Scotland Yard* (Bloomsbury, 2012)
17. Morgan and Jukes, *Who Killed Daniel Morgan?*
18. Channel 4, *Murder in the Car Park* (15 June 2020)
19. Daniel Morgan independent panel report
20. Channel 4, *Murder in the Car Park* (15 June 2020)
21. Ibid.
22. Morgan and Jukes, *Who Killed Daniel Morgan?*

23. Ibid.
24. Ibid.; Daniel Morgan independent panel report
25. Morgan and Jukes, *Who Killed Daniel Morgan?*
26. Gillard, *Untouchables*
27. Channel 4, *Murder in the Car Park* (15 June 2020)
28. Ibid.
29. Daniel Morgan independent panel report, vol. 1, p. 204
30. Graeme McLagan, *Bent Coppers: The Inside Story of Scotland Yard's Battle against Police Corruption* (Weidenfeld & Nicolson, 2003)
31. Gillard, *Untouchables*
32. Morgan and Jukes, *Who Killed Daniel Morgan?*
33. Police document seen by author; Daniel Morgan independent panel report, p. 542
34. Gillard, *Untouchables*
35. Morgan and Jukes, *Who Killed Daniel Morgan?*
36. Gillard, *Untouchables*
37. Ibid.
38. Morgan and Jukes, *Who Killed Daniel Morgan?*; Daniel Morgan independent panel report, pp. 311–15
39. Daniel Morgan independent panel report
40. Ibid.
41. Ibid.
42. Morgan and Jukes, *Who Killed Daniel Morgan?*
43. Ibid.
44. Ibid.
45. Author interview
46. Author interview with confidential source; documents seen by author
47. Confidential documents seen by author
48. Adams was also involved in the Stephen Lawrence case and was questioned at the Macpherson inquiry; see other chapters
49. Author interview with confidential source. See also Morgan and Jukes, *Who Killed Daniel Morgan?*
50. Morgan and Jukes, *Who Killed Daniel Morgan?*
51. Ibid.
52. Operation Russell report
53. Confidential documents seen by author
54. Morgan and Jukes, *Who Killed Daniel Morgan?*
55. Ibid.
56. Daniel Morgan independent panel report
57. Channel 4, *Murder in the Car Park* (15 June 2020)
58. *The Independent*, 5 April 2014
59. Ibid.
60. McLagan, *Bent Coppers*
61. Confidential documents seen by author
62. Confidential documents seen by author
63. Gillard, *Untouchables*
64. Davies, *Hack Attack*
65. Author interview
66. Confidential briefing seen by author
67. Confidential briefing seen by author
68. Author interview
69. Author interview
70. Morgan and Jukes, *Who Killed Daniel Morgan?*
71. John Stevens, *Not For The Faint-Hearted: My Life Fighting Crime* (Weidenfeld & Nicolson, 2005)
72. Author interview

Chapter 4: Above the Law?

1. Witness statement of Martin Smith
2. Ibid.
3. Witness statement to public inquiry
4. Witness statement to public inquiry
5. Witness statement of Ashfaq Siddique
6. Witness statement to public inquiry
7. Witness statement to public inquiry

8. Witness statement to public inquiry
9. Witness statement to public inquiry
10. Witness statement of Martin Smith
11. Author interview with confidential source
12. Police documents seen by author
13. Police documents seen by author
14. Witness statement of former DS Gary Staples
15. Police documents seen by author
16. Witness statement of Gary Staples
17. *Sunday Times*, 11 September 2016
18. Ibid.
19. Ibid.
20. Ibid.
21. Author interview with confidential source
22. Author interview
23. *Daily Mail*, 9 February 2010
24. Ibid.
25. Ibid.
26. Ibid.
27. Ibid.
28. Ibid.
29. *Daily Mail*, 10 November 2018
30. *The Times*, 24 October 2020
31. *Daily Mail*, 11 August 2017
32. Witness statement of Steve Hobbs
33. Witness statement of Gary Staples
34. Stephen Kamlish submission to public inquiry
35. Interview with confidential source
36. Witness statement of Steve Hobbs
37. Ibid.
38. Ibid.
39. Thames Valley Police review of the case
40. Witness statement of Steve Hobbs
41. Thames Valley Police review of the case
42. Witness statement of Ashfaq Siddique
43. Witness statement of Martin Smith
44. Letter from Mohammed Siddique to Khalid Ahmed, seen by author

Chapter 5: Sabotage

1. Confidential police documents seen by author
2. Confidential police documents seen by author
3. Alistair Morgan and Peter Jukes, *Who Killed Daniel Morgan?* (Blink, 2018)
4. Confidential police documents seen by author; Daniel Morgan independent panel report, p. 509
5. Daniel Morgan independent panel report, p. 1085
6. Jacqui Hames witness statement to Leveson inquiry
7. Confidential police documents seen by author; the claim that Marunchak was involved in the surveillance of Cook is also supported by the findings of the Daniel Morgan independent panel review
8. Michael Gillard, *Untouchables: Dirty Cops, Bent Justice and Racism in Scotland Yard* (Bloomsbury, 2012)
9. Daniel Morgan independent panel report, p. 509
10. Morgan and Jukes, *Who Killed Daniel Morgan?*; Daniel Morgan independent panel report, p. 504
11. Morgan and Jukes, *Who Killed Daniel Morgan?*; Daniel Morgan independent panel report, p. 525
12. Daniel Morgan independent panel report, p. 528
13. Morgan and Jukes, *Who Killed Daniel Morgan?*; Daniel Morgan independent panel report, vol. 2, p. 540
14. *The Independent*, 17 September 2012
15. Author interview
16. Confidential briefing seen by author
17. Channel 4, *Murder in the Car Park* (15 June 2020); Daniel Morgan inquest
18. Channel 4, *Murder in the Car Park* (15 June 2020)
19. Ibid.
20. Ibid.
21. Ibid.

22. Morgan and Jukes, *Who Killed Daniel Morgan?*; Met police submission to Leveson inquiry https://webarchive.nationalarchives.gov.uk/ukgwa/20140122145147/http://www.levesoninquiry.org.uk/wp-content/uploads/2012/03/Exhibit-MPS-56-Lord-Stevens-meetings-with-the-Media.pdf (accessed 4 July 2022)
23. Daniel Morgan independent panel report, p. 512
24. Nick Davies, *Hack Attack: How the Truth Caught Up with Rupert Murdoch* (Chatto & Windus, 2014)
25. Daniel Morgan independent panel report, p. 1077
26. Morgan and Jukes, *Who Killed Daniel Morgan?*
27. Leveson inquiry
28. Confidential documents seen by author
29. Author interview
30. Morgan and Jukes, *Who Killed Daniel Morgan?*
31. Graeme McLagan, *Bent Coppers: The Inside Story of Scotland Yard's Battle against Police Corruption* (Weidenfeld & Nicolson, 2003)
32. Ibid.
33. Gillard, *Untouchables*
34. *Daily Mail*, 29 March 2014
35. Morgan and Jukes, *Who Killed Daniel Morgan?*
36. Ibid.
37. Ibid.
38. Ibid.
39. Ibid.
40. Confidential documents seen by author; interview with author
41. Confidential briefing seen by author
42. Confidential documents seen by author
43. Confidential documents seen by author
44. Confidential documents seen by author
45. Letter from Jonathan Rees to Sid Fillery, 23 June 2002
46. Author interview
47. *The Independent*, 1 October 2012
48. Daniel Morgan independent panel report, p. 140
49. Confidential documents seen by author
50. Author interview
51. Author interview
52. Author interview
53. Author interview
54. Confidential documents seen by author
55. Confidential documents seen by author
56. Confidential documents seen by author
57. Leveson inquiry
58. Letter from Neil Basu to Ian Hurst
59. BBC One, *Panorama*, 'Tabloid Hacks Exposed' (14 March 2011)
60. Morgan and Jukes, *Who Killed Daniel Morgan?*
61. Ibid.
62. Ibid.
63. McLagan, *Bent Coppers*
64. Author interview with confidential source
65. Gillard, *Untouchables*
66. Author interview with confidential source
67. Gillard, *Untouchables*
68. Ibid.
69. Daniel Morgan independent panel report, vol. 1, pp. 436–7
70. Author interview
71. Author interview
72. Confidential documents seen by author
73. Confidential documents seen by author
74. Confidential documents seen by author
75. Confidential documents seen by author

Chapter 6: The Electrician

1. Sir Richard Henriques, *From Crime to Crime* (Hodder & Stoughton, 2020)
2. *Daily Mail*, 1 November 2007

3. Interview with confidential source
4. 'Stockwell One', IPCC, 2007, http://policeauthority.org/metropolitan/downloads/scrutinites/stockwell/ipcc-one.pdf (accessed 4 July 2022)
5. *Daily Mail*, 1 November 2007
6. *Sunday Times*, 24 July 2005; 'Stockwell One'
7. *Sunday Times*, 4 November 2007
8. Author interview with confidential source
9. 'Stockwell Two', IPCC, 2007, http://policeauthority.org/metropolitan/downloads/scrutinites/stockwell/ipcc-two.pdf (accessed 4 July 2022)
10. Ibid.
11. Ibid.
12. *Sunday Times*, 24 July 2005
13. Author interview
14. *Sunday Times*, 15 January 2006
15. *Daily Mail*, 13 December 2008
16. ITN, 8 May 2006
17. Author interview
18. Author interview
19. ITN, 8 May 2006
20. *Daily Mail*, 8 May 2006
21. Ibid.
22. Ibid.
23. Author interview
24. Author interview
25. *Daily Mail*, 18 July 2006
26. Press Association, 26 October 2007
27. Ibid.
28. Henriques, *From Crime to Crime*
29. Ibid.
30. *Daily Mail*, 1 November 2007
31. Ibid.
32. Ibid.
33. 'Stockwell Two'
34. Ibid.
35. Ibid.
36. Ibid.
37. *Daily Mail*, 13 December 2008
38. Ibid.
39. *Daily Mail*, 7 October 2008
40. Ibid.
41. *The Times*, 13 December 2008
42. *The Guardian*, 12 December 2008
43. *Daily Mail*, 13 December 2008
44. *The Guardian*, 13 March 2006
45. *Sunday Times*, 3 February 2008
46. BBC News, 5 February 2008
47. *The Guardian*, 22 February 2008
48. *The Guardian*, 21 March 2009
49. Author interview
50. Ron Evans, *On Her Majesty's Service* (John Blake, 2008)
51. Author interview
52. Author interview
53. BBC News, 2 November 2004
54. Author interview
55. Evans, *On Her Majesty's Service*
56. Author interview
57. *Daily Mail*, 23 September 2008
58. Author interview
59. Author interview
60. Leveson inquiry
61. Ibid.

62. Ibid.
63. *Mail on Sunday*, 19 July 2008
64. Author interview
65. Author interview
66. Witness statement of Peter Tickner to Leveson inquiry
67. Author interview
68. Author interview
69. *The Guardian*, 2 October 2008

Chapter 7: Damage Limitation

1. RISC emails seen by author
2. BBC News, 14 June 2006
3. Confidential police document seen by author
4. Operation Limonium report
5. Court documents seen by author
6. Police documents seen by author
7. Documents seen by author
8. Documents seen by author
9. Documents seen by author
10. Court documents seen by author
11. Documents seen by author
12. *The Guardian*, 27 February 2012
13. Documents seen by author
14. Submission of John McDonald to Home Affairs Select Committee, https://publications.parliament.uk/pa/cm201213/cmselect/cmhaff/correspondence/John-McDonald-submission.pdf (accessed 5 July 2022)
15. Ibid.
16. Documents seen by author
17. Documents seen by author
18. Documents seen by author
19. Documents seen by author
20. Documents seen by author
21. Speechly Bircham submission to Home Affairs Select Committee
22. Documents seen by author
23. Documents seen by author
24. Documents seen by author
25. Documents seen by author
26. Documents seen by author
27. Documents seen by author
28. Documents seen by author
29. Documents seen by author
30. *Sunday Times*, 27 May 2018
31. Documents seen by the author
32. Documents seen by author
33. Documents seen by author
34. Documents seen by author
35. Documents seen by author
36. Documents seen by author
37. Documents seen by author
38. Documents seen by author
39. Documents seen by author
40. Documents seen by author
41. Documents seen by author
42. Documents seen by author
43. Agreed statement
44. Submission of John McDonald to Home Affairs Select Committee
45. Ibid.

Chapter 8: The Supergrass

1. Author interview with Clive Driscoll
2. Author interview with Clive Driscoll
3. BBC One, *Stephen: The Murder That Changed a Nation* (17–19 April 2018)

4. Clive Driscoll, *In Pursuit of the Truth: My Life Cracking the Met's Most Notorious Cases* (Ebury Press, 2015)
5. Ibid.
6. Ibid.
7. Ibid.
8. Ibid.
9. Ibid.
10. Ibid.
11. Graeme McLagan, *Bent Coppers: The Inside Story of Scotland Yard's Battle against Police Corruption* (Weidenfeld & Nicolson, 2003)
12. Ellison report
13. Ibid.
14. Author interview
15. BBC One, *Panorama*, 'The Boys Who Killed Stephen Lawrence' (26 July 2006)
16. *Daily Mail*, 27 July 2006
17. *The Guardian*, 27 July 2006
18. Ibid.
19. Ellison report
20. Michael Gillard, *Untouchables: Dirty Cops, Bent Justice and Racism in Scotland Yard* (Bloomsbury, 2012)
21. Ellison report
22. Ibid.
23. Macpherson report
24. *The Independent*, 6 March 2012
25. Ibid.
26. Author interview with confidential source
27. Ellison report
28. Author interview
29. *Daily Mirror*, 28 November 1995
30. McLagan, *Bent Coppers*
31. Ellison report
32. *Evening Standard*, 23 March 1998
33. Ellison report
34. Ibid., vol. 1, p. 145
35. Ibid.
36. Ibid.
37. *The Independent*, 6 March 2012
38. 'The Boys Who Killed Stephen Lawrence'
39. Author interview
40. Driscoll, *In Pursuit of the Truth*
41. Ibid.
42. Ibid.
43. Ibid.
44. Ibid.
45. Ibid.
46. Author interview with Duwayne Brooks
47. *The Guardian*, 22 March 2000
48. Duwayne Brooks, *Steve and Me: My Friendship with Stephen Lawrence and the Search for Justice* (Abacus, 2003)
49. Ibid.
50. Ibid.
51. Ellison report
52. Brooks, *Steve and Me*
53. Ibid.
54. Ibid.
55. Ellison report
56. Brooks, *Steve and Me*
57. Ellison report, vol. 1, pp. 280–96
58. *The Guardian*, 22 March 2000; Ellison report, vol. 1, pp. 280–96
59. Ellison report
60. Driscoll, *In Pursuit of the Truth*
61. Ibid.
62. Ibid.
63. Author interview

64. Driscoll, *In Pursuit of the Truth*
65. Ibid.
66. Ibid.
67. BBC One, *Stephen: The Murder That Changed a Nation* (17–19 April 2018)
68. Ibid.
69. Ibid.
70. Driscoll, *In Pursuit of the Truth*
71. Ibid.
72. Ibid.
73. Ibid.

Chapter 9: Tory Wars
1. Witness statement of Bob Quick to Leveson inquiry
2. Ibid.
3. Ibid.; author interview with confidential sources
4. Witness statement of Bob Quick to Leveson inquiry
5. Ibid.
6. Author interviews with confidential sources
7. Witness statement of Bob Quick to Leveson inquiry
8. Ibid.
9. *The Guardian*, 3 February 2009
10. Ibid.
11. *The Guardian*, 27 November 2008
12. Author interview with confidential source
13. *The Guardian*, 16 April 2009
14. Witness statement of Bob Quick to Leveson inquiry
15. Ibid.
16. Leveson inquiry
17. Witness statement of Bob Quick to Leveson inquiry
18. Ibid.
19. Author interview with confidential source
20. Witness statement of Bob Quick to Leveson inquiry
21. Ibid.
22. *The Guardian*, 22 December 2008
23. Author interview with confidential source
24. BBC News, 17 April 2009
25. Author interview
26. Author interview
27. *The Times*, 1 November 2017
28. Witness statement of Bob Quick to Leveson inquiry
29. Author interview with confidential source
30. Author interview with confidential source
31. *Today*, BBC Radio 4, 1 December 2017

Chapter 10: Cover-Up
1. Alistair Morgan and Peter Jukes, *Who Killed Daniel Morgan?* (Blink, 2018)
2. Ibid.
3. Nick Davies, *Hack Attack: How the Truth Caught Up with Rupert Murdoch* (Chatto & Windus, 2014)
4. Ibid.
5. Ibid.; Leveson inquiry
6. Leveson inquiry
7. *Private Eye*, 11 July 2014
8. Leveson inquiry
9. *Private Eye*, 11 July 2014; Brooks later accepted this in cross-examination during her own trial at the Old Bailey
10. *Private Eye*, 11 July 2014
11. *The Guardian*, 8 July 2009
12. Davies, *Hack Attack*
13. Ibid.
14. Leveson inquiry
15. Author interview
16. Author interview

17. *Private Eye*, 11 July 2014
18. Ibid.
19. Damian McBride, *Power Trip* (Biteback, 2013). McBride said Brooks's power knew no constraints. 'While everything was framed in terms of requests and favours and preferences, the operative verb was always "must", with the perennial implied threat that if such requests weren't heeded, a prolonged shit-bagging would follow. What mattered most was ensuring that the ultimate winner was herself, and by extension News International, in terms of continually strengthening that influence.'
20. *Daily Mail*, 18 July 2011
21. Author interview
22. *The Times*, 18 July 2011
23. Author interview
24. Author interview
25. *The Guardian*, 13 July 2011
26. Author interview
27. Author interview
28. Confidential police documents seen by author
29. Mr Justice Maddison judgment
30. Morgan and Jukes, *Who Killed Daniel Morgan?*
31. Jonathan Rees QC, Note on Disclosure, September 2010
32. Author interview
33. Morgan and Jukes, *Who Killed Daniel Morgan?*
34. Author interview
35. Confidential documents seen by author
36. Daniel Morgan independent panel report
37. Channel 4, *Murder in the Car Park* (15 June 2020)
38. *Sunday Express*, 16 May 2021
39. Channel 4, *Murder in the Car Park* (15 June 2020)
40. Ibid.
41. Ibid.
42. Ibid.
43. Ibid.
44. Daniel Morgan independent panel report, vol. 3, p. 1056

Chapter 11: Plebgate

1. *The Sun*, 25 September 2012
2. Author interview
3. *The Times*, 23 September 2012
4. BBC News, 24 September 2012
5. *The Guardian*, 15 December 2016
6. Ibid.
7. Author interview
8. Author interview
9. *The Guardian*, 16 January 2006
10. Author interview
11. Author interview
12. Author interview
13. Author interview
14. Author interview
15. *The Guardian*, 12 October 2012
16. BBC Radio 4, *The Tories and the Police: The End of the Affair*, 12 August 2014
17. Author interview
18. Author interview
19. Author interview
20. *The Independent*, 23 October 2012
21. Author interview
22. *Channel 4 News*, 18 December 2012
23. Author interview
24. *The Times*, 20 December 2012
25. *Sunday Times*, 13 October 2013
26. *Channel 4 News*, 3 November 2013

27. Operation Alice
28. *Sunday Times*, 13 October 2013
29. Author interview
30. BBC News, 6 February 2014
31. Operation Alice
32. BBC News, 6 February 2014
33. Author interview
34. Author interview
35. Author interview
36. *The Guardian*, 21 May 2014
37. Author interview
38. BBC Radio 4, *The Tories and the Police: The End of the Affair*, 12 August 2014
39. *The Spectator*, 11 December 2014
40. Plebgate libel judgment
41. *The Sun*, 5 April 2016
42. Author interview
43. Author interview
44. Author interview

Chapter 12: The Long Fella

1. Court documents seen by author
2. Court documents seen by author
3. Author interview
4. Author interview
5. Confidential police documents seen by author
6. Author interview
7. Author interview
8. Author interview
9. Interview with confidential source
10. Author interview with confidential source
11. Court documents seen by author
12. Author interview
13. Author interview
14. Michael Gillard, *Legacy: Gangsters, Corruption and the London Olympics* (Bloomsbury, 2019)
15. Operation Soldier Three
16. Ibid.
17. Gillard, *Legacy*
18. Operation Soldier Three
19. Ibid.
20. *Sunday Times*, 14 June 2015
21. Ibid.
22. Ibid.
23. Ibid.
24. Patrick report
25. Ibid.
26. Ibid.
27. Court documents seen by author
28. Author interview
29. Author interview
30. Court documents seen by author
31. Gillard, *Legacy*
32. *Sunday Times*, 23 May 2010
33. Gillard, *Legacy*
34. Ibid.
35. Court documents seen by author
36. *The Guardian*, 1 May 2013
37. *The Times*, 11 May 2013
38. Mr Justice Simon judgment, July 2013
39. Ibid.
40. Ibid.

41. Author interview
42. Patrick report
43. Ibid.
44. Court documents seen by author
45. *Daily Mirror*, 9 November 2015
46. Court documents seen by author
47. Court documents seen by author
48. Author interview
49. David McKelvey, LinkedIn
50. Author interview with confidential source

Chapter 13: The Avalanche

1. Channel 4, *Dispatches*, 'The Police's Dirty Secret' (24 June 2013)
2. *The Guardian*, 24 June 2013
3. Channel 4, *Dispatches*, 'The Police's Dirty Secret' (24 June 2013)
4. *Today*, BBC Radio 4, 25 June 2013
5. Ellison report
6. Clive Driscoll, *In Pursuit of the Truth: My Life Cracking the Met's Most Notorious Cases* (Ebury Press, 2015)
7. Ibid.
8. Ibid.
9. Ibid.
10. Ellison report
11. *The Guardian*, 4 December 2017
12. Ellison report
13. ITV News, 6 March 2014
14. Ellison report
15. Ibid.
16. Ibid.
17. Ibid.
18. Ibid.
19. Ibid.
20. Ibid.
21. Ibid.
22. Ibid.
23. Ibid.
24. Ibid.
25. Ibid.
26. Ibid.
27. Ibid.
28. Author interview with Clive Driscoll
29. Author interview with Clive Driscoll
30. Ellison report
31. Author interview with Clive Driscoll
32. Driscoll, *In Pursuit of the Truth*
33. Author interview with Clive Driscoll
34. Ellison report
35. Ibid.
36. Author interview
37. Ellison report
38. Ibid.
39. Ibid.
40. Ibid.
41. Ibid.
42. Ibid.
43. Interview with Peter Tickner
44. Ellison report
45. Ibid.
46. Ibid.
47. Macpherson report
48. Ibid.
49. Ellison report

50. Ibid.
51. Ibid.
52. Ibid.
53. Ibid.
54. Ibid.
55. BBC One, *Stephen: The Murder That Changed a Nation* (17–19 April 2018)
56. Ibid.
57. *The Independent*, 26 March 2014
58. Ellison report
59. *The Independent*, 26 March 2014
60. *The Guardian*, 2 July 2019
61. Author interview
62. Driscoll, *In Pursuit of the Truth*
63. Ibid.

Chapter 14: 'Friendship of Convenience'

1. Alan Rusbridger, *Breaking News: The Remaking of Journalism and Why It Matters Now* (Canongate, 2018)
2. Author interview with confidential source
3. Confidential police document seen by author
4. Author interview
5. Author interview with confidential source
6. Author interview
7. Author interview
8. Author interview
9. Confidential email seen by author
10. *Mail on Sunday*, 30 June 2013
11. Author interview with confidential source
12. Statement to author
13. Statement to author
14. See the Scott inquiry into the arms-to-Iraq scandal
15. Confidential documents seen by author
16. Confidential documents seen by author
17. Confidential documents seen by author
18. *Private Eye*, 11 July 2014
19. Ibid.
20. Ibid.
21. Confidential documents seen by author
22. Confidential documents seen by author
23. Confidential documents seen by author
24. Confidential documents seen by author
25. Confidential documents seen by author
26. Confidential documents seen by author
27. *Private Eye*, 11 July 2014
28. *Press Gazette*, 30 March 2016
29. *Press Gazette*, 27 October 2016
30. Author interview with confidential source
31. *Press Gazette*, 10 May 2021
32. *Press Gazette*, 15 June 2015
33. Ibid.
34. *The Guardian*, 4 July 2013
35. Confidential documents seen by author
36. BBC News, 11 December 2015
37. Confidential documents seen by author
38. Author interview
39. Author interview
40. Author interview
41. BBC News, 4 May 2019
42. Witness statement of Jonathan Rees
43. Ibid.
44. Ibid.
45. Author interview with confidential source

Chapter 15: The Fantasist
1. BBC News, 14 November 2014
2. Sir Richard Henriques, *From Crime to Crime* (Hodder & Stoughton, 2020)
3. Henriques report; *Daily Mail*, 14 May 2019
4. *The Guardian*, 4 October 2019
5. Henriques report
6. Interview with confidential source
7. Henriques, *From Crime to Crime*
8. *Mistakes Were Made*, HMIC report, 12 March 2013
9. *Daily Mail*, 4 August 2019
10. Henriques report
11. Ibid.
12. Ibid.
13. *The Guardian*, 26 August 2015
14. Henriques, *From Crime to Crime*
15. *Daily Telegraph*, 3 February 2016
16. *Daily Mail*, 5 February 2016
17. Author interview
18. Henriques report
19. *Daily Mail*, 4 October 2019
20. Author interview
21. Interview with a confidential source
22. Author interview
23. Author interview
24. Clive Driscoll, *In Pursuit of the Truth: My Life Cracking the Met's Most Notorious Cases* (Ebury Press, 2015)
25. Author interview
26. Author interview
27. Author interview
28. Author interview
29. Author interview
30. Author interview
31. Author interview
32. Author interview
33. Paul Lashmar and Dick Hobbs, 'Diamonds, Gold and Crime Displacement: Hatton Garden, and the Evolution of Organised Crime in the UK', *Trends in Organized Crime*, 2018
34. Wensley Clarkson, *Sexy Beasts: The Inside Story of the Hatton Garden Heist* (Quercus, 2016)
35. Author interview
36. *Daily Mail*, 1 June 2017
37. Author interview
38. Author interview
39. Author interview
40. Author interview
41. *The Guardian*, 26 July 2019

Chapter 16: Dick's Downfall
1. *The i*, 30 September 2021
2. BBC, 30 September 2021
3. *The Guardian*, 1 October 2021
4. Author interview
5. Author interview
6. Author interview
7. Author interview
8. Author interview with confidential source
9. Twitter post, 1 October 2021
10. Author interview with confidential source
11. Daniel Morgan independent panel report
12. Ibid.
13. Ibid.
14. *Evening Standard*, 27 January 2022
15. Ibid.
16. *Daily Mail*, 24 February 2022

17. *Evening Standard*, 27 January 2022
18. *The Times*, 31 January 2022
19. *Daily Telegraph*, 19 March 2022
20. *Sunday Times*, 30 January 2022
21. *The Times*, 5 February 2022
22. Ibid.
23. Interview with a confidential source
24. *The Guardian*, 13 February 2022
25. Ibid.
26. Ibid.
27. *The Times*, 12 February 2022

Chapter 17: Future Threats
1. *The Guardian*, 27 March 2018
2. Author interview with confidential sources
3. *The Independent*, 21 July 2010
4. Author interview
5. Tortoise, 13 April 2019
6. Author interview
7. Author interview
8. Author interview
9. Author interview
10. Tony Barnes, Richard Elias and Peter Walsh, *Cocky: The Rise and Fall of Curtis Warren, Britain's Biggest Drug Baron* (Milo, 2000)
11. *Daily Mail*, 25 November 2011
12. Barnes et al., *Cocky*
13. *The Times*, 11 December 2009
14. *New York Times*, 14 September 2009
15. *The Times*, 9 September 2009
16. Author interview
17. Barnes et al., *Cocky*
18. Author interview
19. *Daily Mail*, 12 January 2014
20. Author interview
21. Author interview
22. Author interview
23. Author interview
24. Author interview
25. Author interview
26. Author interview
27. Author interview
28. Author interview
29. Author interview

Conclusion
1. *Sunday Times*, 14 October 2018
2. *The Guardian*, 12 October 2018
3. *Sunday Times*, 14 October 2018
4. Author interview
5. BBC Radio 4, *The Tories and the Police: The End of the Affair*, 12 August 2014
6. Author interview with confidential source
7. Author interview
8. Author interview
9. Author interview
10. *The Guardian*, 8 July 2022
11. Author interview
12. *Radio Times*, 24 September 2019
13. Author interview with confidential source
14. Author interview
15. Author interview
16. Author interview

17. Author interview
18. Author interview
19. Author interview
20. Author interview
21. Author interview
22. Author interview

Afterword

1 *Daily Mail*, 27 September 2022
2 Ibid.
3 *Daily Mail*, 12 October 2022
4 LBC, 11 October 2022, https://www.lbc.co.uk/radio/presenters/nick-ferrari/how-utterly-pathetic-nick-ferrari-slams-policing/ (accessed 19 June 2023)
5 Highways Act 1980, https://www.legislation.gov.uk/ukpga/1980/66/part/IX/crossheading/obstruction-of-highways-and-streets/enacted?view=plain#:~:text=(1)If%20a%20person%2C,an%20offence%20against%20this%20section (accessed 19 June 2023)
6 Author interview
7 *The Guardian*, 16 January 2023
8 *The Guardian*, 7 February 2023
9 Ibid.
10 Ibid.
11 *The Guardian*, 16 January 2023
12 Home Office, 'Angiolini Inquiry to investigate David Carrick', 7 February 2023, https://www.gov.uk/government/news/angiolini-inquiry-to-investigate-david-carrick (accessed 19 June 2023)
13 Ibid.
14 *Daily Mail*, 9 April 2023
15 *The Guardian*, 16 January 2023
16 Casey report
17 Ibid.
18 Ibid.
19 *The Times*, 24 March 2023
20 BBC News, 21 March 2023
21 Casey report
22 Ibid.
23 Author interview
24 Author interview
25 Author interview
26 Author interview
27 Letter from Mark Rowley to Bernadette Murray
28 Author interview
29 HMICFRS, 'Metropolitan Police Service – National child protection inspection assessment of progress', 1 September 2021, https://www.justiceinspectorates.gov.uk/hmicfrs/publication-html/metropolitan-police-service-national-child-protection-inspection-assessment-of-progress/ (accessed 19 June 2023)
30 Author interview